About Pearson

Pearson is the world's learning company, with presence across 70 countries worldwide. Our unique insights and world-class expertise comes from a long history of working closely with renowned teachers, authors and thought leaders, as a result of which, we have emerged as the preferred choice for millions of teachers and learners across the world.

We believe learning opens up opportunities, creates fulfilling careers and hence better lives. We hence collaborate with the best of minds to deliver you class-leading products, spread across the Higher Education and Test Preparation spectrum.

Superior learning experience and improved outcomes are at the heart of everything we do. This product is the result of one such effort.

Your feedback plays a critical role in the evolution of our products and you can contact us – reachus@pearson.com. We look forward to it.

Understanding Natural Language Processing

Machine Learning and Deep Learning Perspectives

T V Geetha

Pearson

Senior Manager—Product: Neha Goomer
Senior Editor—Production: C. Purushothaman

ISBN 978-81-198-9600-4

First Impression, 2025
Third Impression, 2025
Fourth Impression, 2026

Published by Pearson India Education Services Pvt. Ltd, CIN: U72200TN2005PTC057128.

Head Office: 1st Floor, Berger Tower, Plot No. C-001A/2, Sector 16B, Noida – 201 301, Uttar Pradesh, India. Registered Office : 6th Floor, Tower A, Unit A and B International Tech Park, Capita Land Chennai, 200 Feet Radial Road, Zamin Pallavaram, Old Pallavaram Chennai – 600117, Tamil Nadu, India
Website: in.pearson.com; Email: companysecretary.india@pearson.com

Compositor: MAP Systems, Bengaluru
Printer: Rajkamal Electric Press, Kundli, Haryana-131 028.

Table of Contents

Preface

Understanding Natural Language Processing – *Machine Learning and Deep Learning Perspectives* discusses the need, history, core tasks, challenges, applications, and future trends of natural language processing (NLP) and hence helps learners in understanding the magic of NLP from both learning and research perspectives.

An abstract conceptual view of core natural language processing tasks and applications is explained in the context of both how machine learning and deep learning can be applied using appropriate use cases that run throughout the chapters. A basic introduction to machine learning and machine learning approaches have also been discussed.

The book elaborates linguistic modules of NLP including POS tagging, Syntactic Processing, semantic analysis, and discourse analysis. It also introduces both sparse and dense word vectors as well as word embedding starting from basics. The book starts with language models and goes on to discuss neural language models and its role in NLP.

The focus of this book is to make readers think of applications in terms of natural language processing so that they can plug in natural language processing components into real time applications.

In addition, many exercises and activities are included to enable the reader understand concepts and apply them to build meaningful applications using the latest techniques.

ORGANIZATION OF THE BOOK

The book follows a structured and modular design, to facilitate the instructor in the teaching of the course and the students in the reading of the book.

Chapter 1 Introduction

This chapter discusses the need, history, core tasks, challenges, applications and future trends associated with natural language processing.

Chapter 2 Approaches to Natural Language Processing

This chapter outlines the analysis aspects of NLP tasks and applications and looks at NLP from a machine learning perspective, discusses the need, the fundamentals and how machine learning and deep learning how these methods are used for NLP.

Chapter 3 Text Classification

This chapter gives an introduction to the classification problem and outlines supervised learning and classification. The chapter explains three classification methods namely naïve Bayes, perceptron and Logistic Regression for text classification. The evaluation of text classification is then discussed in detail.

Chapter 4 Language Modelling

This chapter outlines the basics of probabilistic language models and the use n-gram language models including smoothing techniques for NLP.

Chapter 5 Words, Morphology and Semantics

This chapter covers basics of NLP including morphology and types of morphology and morphological processing for NLP. Stemming and lemmatization including Porter's stemmer is discussed. Morphological analysis and generation using finite state methods is discussed. Lexical Semantics, some perspectives of word meaning, thematic rules and an important lexical resource -WordNet are explained.

Chapter 6 Representation of Text – Basic Vector Models

This chapter explains representation of text using basic vector models, distributional semantics, count based distributional vector models and short dense vectors using dimensionality reduction and class based clustering. Measuring of similarity between vectors is also discussed.

Chapter 7 Neural Language Models

This chapter discusses some limitations of n-Gram model and gives an introduction to neural language models. Then feedforward neural language models using CNN is outlined followed by RNN language models.

Chapter 8 Vector Models – Word Embedding

This chapter provides a review of distributed representation and then goes on to discuss word embedding and Word2Vec the set of methodologies CBOW and Skip Gram Model used to learn word embedding. FastText and GloVe word embedding is also discussed along with some applications of word embedding.

Chapter 9 Transformers and Pre-trained Models

This chapter discusses the issues associated with RNN language models. Then the concept of attention is outlined. Then one the most important and current model – Transformer architecture is discussed in detail. Then we go on to outline pre-trained language models and large language models. Further Generative Pre-trained Transformer (GPT)is discussed. Some pre-trained language models including Bidirectional Encoder Representations from Transformers (BERT), T5 and BART Models and Embedding from Language Models (ELMO) are described.

Chapter 10 Sequence Labelling and Part of Speech tagging

This chapter first explains Parts of Speech and Parts-of-Speech (POS) Tagging. Then POS tagging is described as a sequence labelling task and modelling approaches to sequence labelling including Hidden Markov Model (HMM), Maximum Entropy Markov Model (MEMM) and Condition Random Field Model (CRF) for POS Tagging are discussed. Finally a deep learning approach for sequence labelling using Named Entity Recognition (NER) as an example is outlined.

Chapter 11 Syntactic Processing – Constituent Structure

This chapter is concerned with syntax and parsing and first outlines constituent parsing and context-free grammar (CFG) including the syntactic ambiguity aspect. Probabilistic CFG , CKY parsing algorithm, Earley's parsing and dependency parsing and finally machine learning and neural network approaches to parsing are also discussed.

Chapter 12 Semantic Processing

This chapter again examines the basics of semantics in the context of representing meaning and then explains semantic processing, compositional semantics, neural semantic parsing, semantic role labelling and list some resources associated with thematic roles.

Chapter 13 Discourse, Dialogue and ChatGPT

This chapter explains the basics of discourse including cohesion and coherence, Rhetoric Structure Theory (RST), pragmatics and dialogue systems. Chatbots including concepts, architecture and applications of ChatGPT are explained.

Chapter 14 Applications of Natural Language Processing

This chapter considers some important and common applications of NLP. These include machine translation, information extraction, question answering, summarization, sentiment analysis and generative AI based NLP Applications.

Chapter 15 Ethical Aspects of Natural Language Processing

This chapter discusses the basics of ethical aspects of NLP including bias and fairness. The chapter outlines methods to detect and mitigate bias including data and model bias. The chapter includes a section on handling bias in word embedding, Large Language Models and Generative AI. Some case studies and challenges and future directions are also presented.

PEDAGOGICAL FEATURES

The following are the pedagogical features of this book:

In-Between Chapter Aids

- **Visualization –** "A picture is worth a thousand words" is a famous quote. This book supports the concepts with figures and tables to facilitate visualization.

- **Bulleted text –** The book follows a bulleted approach of writing the text in contrast to the long paragraphs. The bulleted text approach is easier to read, understand and grasp.

End-of-chapter Aids

- **Summary-** a summary listing all the important concepts covered is provided at the end of each chapter
- **Exercises**
  - o **Suggested Activities –** some examples, tables to be filled in, implementation have been included to enable the learner to concretize the concepts learnt in the chapter.
    - In addition, **case studies** with appropriate links to datasets have been given in most of the chapters to help the students to design and implement realistic NLP tasks and applications.
  - o **Multiple Choice Questions –** Multiple choice questions have been provided to make sure that the students have understood the nuances associated with the concepts

o   **Match the Following –** This exercise allows the learner to understand and match definitions and concepts discussed in the chapter

o   **Short Questions –** This set of questions cover all aspects of the chapter and enable the learner to solidify the learning and answer examination questions

End-of-book Aids

• A list of references (books as well as links) have been provided

TARGET AUDIENCE

Several chapters have been included that cover the syllabi of different universities in India. The book also aims to help both researchers and personnel from all types of industries to help understand NLP and develop applications in this state-of-the-art topic that is permeating all walks of life. The book is well suited for the following target audience:

• *Undergraduate and Postgraduate Engineering students*—BE (CSE), BTech (IT), BE (AI and Machine Learning), BE (AI and Data Science), and BE with allied specializations. ME (CSE), MTech (IT) and ME with allied specializations

• *Undergraduate Science students* pursuing BSc in Computer Science and allied specializations.

• *Postgraduate Science students* pursuing MSc (Computer Science), MSc (IT) and allied specializations

• *Non-science students* pursuing MCA, BCA

• *Research and Industry personal interested in* Natural Language Processing, its applications and generative AI applications like ChatGPT

• *Any learner* interested in Natural Language Processing

Acknowledgements

First of all, I would like to thank my colleagues, friends, research scholars, project faculty and students who have worked with me in this fascinating area of NLP and thus inspired me to write this book. I wish to thank my family including my husband, sons, daughter-in-law and granddaughter for their patience in bearing with me during the writing of the book. I wish to thank by students for their help in doing the figures as per my instructions. I thank my publisher Pearson Education, their editorial team; and panel of reviewers for their contributions valuable towards content enrichment.

Dr T V Geetha
Retired Senior Professor,
Department of Computer Science and Engineering,
College of Engineering, Guindy
Anna University, Chennai

Pearson would like to thank following experts who have reviewed the manuscript and provided their valuable inputs and suggestions:

- **Devi Priya R,** Professor, Department of Computer Science and Engineering, KPR Institute of Engineering and Technology, Coimbatore, Tamil Nadu

- **Himadri Nath Saha,** Head, Department of Computer Science, Surendranath Evening College, University of Calcutta, West Bengal

- **Pan Singh Dhoni,** Independent Author & Researcher

- **S Kanaga Suba Raja,** Professor & Head, Department of Computer Science and Engineering, SRM Institute of Science and Technology Tiruchirappalli, Tamil Nadu

- **S Shankar**, Professor and Head, Department of Computer Science and Engineering, Hindusthan College of Engineering and Technology, Coimbatore, Tamil Nadu

- **Shreedhara K S,** Professor, Department of Computer Science and Engineering, University B.D.T College of Engineering, Davangere, Karnataka

- **Srinath S**, Associate Professor and Head, Department of Computer Science and Engineering, Sri Jayachamarajendra College of Engineering, JSS Science and Technology University, Mysuru, Karnataka

About the Author

T V Geetha is a retired senior professor of Computer Science and Engineering with over 40 years of teaching experience in the areas of artificial intelligence, natural language processing, machine learning, deep learning and information retrieval. She has been instrumental in the formulation and updating of NLP syllabus in many universities. In addition, the Department of Information technology, Government of India requested her group to offer a specialized programme - M.E. CSE (with Specialization in Knowledge Engineering and Computational Linguistics (NLP)). The highlights included the framing of regulations. Syllabus and curriculum with state-of–the-art topics in Knowledge Engineering and NLP including Statistical NLP, Indian Language Processing, Applications of NLP, etc. Her research interests include semantic, personalized and deep web search, semi-supervised learning for Indian language processing, application of Indian philosophy to knowledge representation and reasoning, machine learning for adaptive learning and application of machine learning and deep learning to biological literature mining and drug discovery. Her focused research in NLP included morphological processing, named entity recognition, relation extraction, summarization, semantic processing, lyric mining, natural language-based search which resulted in an innovative semi–supervised methodology for NLP specially for Indian language processing. She has co-authored a book titled "Machine Learning- Concepts, Techniques and Applications". She is a recipient of the Young Women Scientist Award from the government of Tamilnadu and Women of Excellence Award from the Rotaract Club of Chennai. For her pioneering work in NLP she was awarded the BSR Faculty Fellowship for Superannuated Faculty from the University Grants Commission, Government of India for 2020-2023. Currently she is the Distinguished Research Professor, at Sri Sivasubramanian Nadar College, Chennai and Curriculum Advisor at Rajalakshmi Engineering College, Chennai.

For interacting with the author, or for suggestions and comments on this book, please send your e-mails to tv_g@hotmail.com

Course Structure

This book has been written keeping in mind readers familiar and as well as not-so familiar with the area of Natural Language Processing. The book gives three flows for different requirements of learners- namely "Natural Language Processing and Machine Learning", "Natural Language Processing with Deep Learning" and "Basics of Natural Language Processing with Concepts of ChatGPT"

Flow I – Course on "Natural Language Processing and Machine Learning"

This flow **emphasizes the statistical and machine learning approaches to NLP.** This flow of the book gives a basic introduction to NLP and rule-based and machine learning approaches to NLP. It gives a basic view of text classification and introduces different representations of text including vector models. Then it goes on to introduce all aspects of NLP including words, morphology and semantics, part of speech tagging, syntactic processing, semantic processing, discourse, dialogue using machine learning and language modelling. Finally, the flow discusses applications of NLP and some basic concepts of ethical aspects of NLP.

Chapter 1   –   Introduction
Chapter 2   –   Approaches to Natural Language Processing (2.1–2.6, 2.10)
Chapter 3   –   Text Classification
Chapter 4   –   Language Modelling
Chapter 5   –   Words, Morphology and Semantics
Chapter 6   –   Representation of Text - Basic Vector Models
Chapter 10   –   Sequence Labelling and Part of Speech Tagging (10.1–10.8)
Chapter 11   –   Syntactic Processing – Constituent Structure (11.1–11.7)
Chapter 12   –   Semantic Processing (12.1–12.4, 12.6–12.7)
Chapter 13   –   Discourse, Dialogue and ChatGPT (13.1–13.5)
Chapter 14   –   Applications of Natural Language Processing (14.1-14.2.2, 14.3, 14.4.1-14.6)
Chapter 15   –   Ethical Aspects of Natural Language Processing (15.1–15.5, 15.8)

Flow II – Course on "Natural Language Processing with Deep Learning"

This flow **emphasizes deep learning approaches to NLP** though some machine learning approaches are also covered. This flow of the book gives a basic introduction to NLP and deep learning approaches to NLP. It introduces neural language models, word embedding and the latest trends of transformer and pre-trained models. The flow introduces all aspects of NLP including words, morphology and semantics, part of speech tagging, syntactic processing, semantic processing, discourse, dialogue and ChatGPT using basic machine learning and deep learning approaches. Finally, the flow discusses applications of NLP and concepts of ethical aspects of NLP including when using deep learning models.

Chapter 1   –   Introduction
Chapter 2   –   Approaches to Natural Language Processing (2.1–2.3, 2.7–2.10)
Chapter 5   –   Words, Morphology and Semantics
Chapter 7   –   Neural Language Models
Chapter 8   –   Vector Models – Word Embedding
Chapter 9   –   Transformers and Pre-trained Models
Chapter 10   –   Sequence Labelling and Part of Speech Tagging (10.1–10.5)
Chapter 11   –   Syntactic Processing – Constituent Structure
Chapter 12   –   Semantic Processing (12.1–12.5)
Chapter 13   –   Discourse, Dialogue and ChatGPT (13.1, 13.6–13.7)
Chapter 14   –   Applications of Natural Language Processing (14.1–14.2, 14.4, 14.7)
Chapter 15   –   Ethical Aspects of Natural Language Processing

Flow III – Course on "Basics of Natural Language Processing with Concepts of ChatGPT"

This flow is meant for learners who want to **understand basic aspects of NLP and the details of components needed to understand the architecture of ChatGPT**. This flow of the book gives a basic list of different NLP components and deep learning approaches to NLP. It outlines word embedding and the latest trends of transformer and pre-trained models including large language models. The flow introduces the basics of discourse, dialogue and details of ChatGPT architecture. Finally, the flow discusses applications of NLP and concepts of ethical aspects of NLP including when using deep learning models.

Chapter 1   –   Introduction
Chapter 2   –   Approaches to Natural Language Processing (2.1–2.3, 2.7–2.10)
Chapter 8   –   Vector Models – Word Embedding
Chapter 9   –   Transformers and Pre-trained Models
Chapter 13   –   Discourse, Dialogue and ChatGPT (13.1, 13.6–13.7)
Chapter 14   –   Applications of Natural Language Processing
Chapter 15   –   Ethical Aspects of Natural Language Processing

Introduction

1.1 Introduction

Natural Language Processing or in short NLP strives to build machines that understand text data that is in the form of human language and derive meaning from this text in a smart and useful way. Natural language processing has been in existence for over 50 years.

Table 1.1 shows that NLP is associated with many areas including computational linguistics, computer science, artificial intelligence, cognitive science, etc. Natural Language Processing is a branch of Artificial Intelligence that helps computers understand, interpret and manipulate human language. Natural Language Processing involves to some extent, aspects of cognitive and social science such as handling language and describing models of language used in culture and society. It is concerned with linguistics or the scientific study of language. Natural Language Processing combines rule–based modeling of human language along with statistical, machine learning, and deep learning models in order to process natural language.

Artificial Intelligence –	**Cognitive Science and Social Science –**	**Linguistics** is the scientific study of language
Natural language processing (NLP) refers to the branch of computer science—and more specifically, the branch of artificial intelligence or AI—concerned with giving computers the ability to understand text in much the same way human beings can.	Figuring out how brain works - includes handling language and describing models of language used in culture and society	**Computational Linguistics –** computer based rule-based modeling of human language—with statistical, machine learning, and deep learning models. - 'understand' its full meaning, complete with the speaker or writer's intent and sentiment.

Machine Learning	**Automatic Speech Recognition**	**Natural Language Processing**
Machine learning techniques such as statistical techniques, neural networks, and deep learning form the core most Natural language processing systems today	Dealing with spoken words is called "Speech Recognition" and the output of such a system is the input to an NLP system	Applying computational tools to the study of language and the engineering aspect involves finding effective techniques doing what people do with language

Table 1.1: Natural Language Processing and Related Areas

The task of Natural Language Processing is to make machines understand human language, not in a shallow manner through string processing or keyword matching but enable the identification of the structure and meaning of words, sentences, texts and conversations. NLP is characterized as a difficult problem in computer science since human language is is complex, ambiguous, flexible, and subtle. To understand human language, we need to understand not only the words, but the concepts and how these are linked together to create meaning. Good solutions need linguistics and machine learning knowledge.

The dream of Natural Language Processing is to design computer systems that can for example, process our email in a useful manner, translate languages accurately, help us to manage, summarize, and aggregate information and in case speech processing is involved use speech based user interface and finally systems that talk and listen to us. Speech recognition deals with spoken words and the output of an automatic speech recognition system is the input to a Natural Language Processing system. However, in this book we will be discussing only textual data and will not talk about speech processing.

Natural language processing can be viewed as a system that automates language analysis and generation. Analysis involves taking natural language as input and building a representation of the language while generation takes a representation as input and produces natural language as output. Natural language needs to possess higher-order cognitive skills and deal with inherently discrete as well as diversity of languages.

Before we go further let us understand in detail two aspects of Natural Language Processing namely natural language analysis and natural language generation. Natural language analysis or understanding takes natural language text, analyses the text and produces a computer understandable representation of the same. This representation can be directly used for many tasks and applications associated with Natural Language Processing. On the other hand, natural language generation takes either natural language text or some representation of natural language text Natural language generation is a part of tasks like dialogue systems, chatbots and machine translation. Most of the chapters in this book deals with natural language analysis but the chapters on discourse analysis and machine translation does deal to a certain extent with natural language generation.

1.2 Need for Natural Language Processing

Human language in itself is interesting and challenging and Natural Language Processing offers insights into language and provides computer scientists an opportunity to handle challenging problems, build large scale systems and develop applications that can be used in the real world often for commercial problems.

One of the main reasons for the increased interest in Natural Language Processing is the explosion of machine-readable natural language text specifically in the web era where the amount of text available is doubling every year in the form of web pages, emails, SMSs, tweets, docs, pdfs, newspapers, medical records, financial filings. This large amount of textual content provides an opportunity and an increasing necessity to extract meaning. Another important reason for the need for Natural Language Processing is the proliferation of conversational agents as a means of human-computer communication. Another aspect is the role of computers in human interactions through social media, again providing Natural Language Processing an opportunity to be in the social context loop. Natural Language Processing helps the management and exploitation of all the information present in this text.

Natural Language Processing viewed from a real word perspective involves both processing large amounts of text from the web and corpora and converting that information into knowledge with applications such as text classification, information retrieval and extraction, question answering and enabling natural human-computer interaction with applications such as dialogue and conversational agents, machine translation.

Natural Language Processing applications goes from tackling simple tasks such as identifying spam, categorizing documents such as news stories, finding and comparing product information and assessing sentiment towards products, politicians, books, movies, etc. NLP is a very important current area of investigation as it is necessary for many useful applications. These applications include information retrieval, extraction, and filtering, intelligent web searching, automatic text summarization, pseudo-understanding and generation of natural language and multilingual systems including machine translation. Some of the benefits of Natural Language Processing include improved accuracy and efficiency of documentation, ability to automatically make a readable summary of a larger, more complex original text, useful for personal assistants such as Alexa, by enabling it to understand spoken word, enables an organization to use chatbots for customer support and advanced insights from analytics that were previously unreachable due to data volume.

1.3 History of Natural Language Processing

Now let us outline the history of Natural Language Processing. Work in Natural Language Processing began as early as the 1950s with focus on machine translation. Work in Natural language processing can be envisaged as three eras – the rule-based era extending from 1950s-1970s, the empirical and machine learning era extending from 1980s-1990s and finally the deep learning is extending from 2000s up to the present (Table 1.2).

1.3.1 Rule Based Approaches with Human Crafted Rules (1950s–1970s)

In this era Natural Language Processing largely used handcrafted rules developed by linguists with the aim to make systems that behaved comparably to humans on given linguistic tasks using models based on human reasoning such as analogy, logic, etc.

A limited version of a rule based automatic translation system from Russian to English was first demonstrated in the year 1954. Noam Chomsky found grammatically correct sentence such as "Colourless green ideas sleep furiously" was classified as improbable to the same extent as grammatically incorrect sentence as "Furiously sleep ideas green colourless". In order to tackle this aspect Chomsky created a style of grammar that revolutionized previous linguistic ideas, the **Phase-Structure Grammar** which changed the sentence structure into a format that is usable by computers.

After several years with a considerable amount of money spent on research, it was found that machine translation was more expensive than manual human translation and in 1966 U.S. National Research Council (NRC) and Automatic Language Processing Advisory Committee initiated the **first stoppage of Natural Language Processing and machine translation research** by halting funding and hence research in these areas was considered a dead end by most.

In 1964, **ELIZA**, a comment and response process, was built by Weizenbaum to replicate the conversation between a psychologist and a patient, using reflection techniques that is by simply permuting or echoing the user input which however provided a surprisingly human-like interaction. In 1971, **SHRDLU** developed by Terry Winograd at MIT worked with "blocks" in a restricted vocabulary framework that used natural language to query and manipulate objects inside a very simple virtual micro-world consisting of several color blocks and pyramids. In the late 1960s and early 1970s research focus shifted to explaining syntactic anomalies and providing semantic representations including **case grammar** (Fillmore, 1968), **semantic networks** (Collins et al., 1969), **augmented transition networks** (Woods, 1970), and **conceptual dependency** theory (Schank, 1972). During the 1970s, the need for structuring real-world data into a computer-understandable format was felt and hence the so-called conceptual ontologies were built.

1.3.2 Empirical and Machine Learning Approaches with Engineered Features (1980s–1990s)

In this era, with lexical and corpus-based phases focus shifted to empiricism, probabilistic and machine learning using engineered features obtained statistically. In addition, the evaluation process also became more rigorous.

During the 1980s, one of the famous expert systems built to mimic medical human experts was **MYCIN** which was used to diagnose blood infections.

1950–1970s	**Rule Based Approaches with Human Crafted Rules** • NLP was largely rules-based, using handcrafted rules developed by linguists to determine how computers would process language.	1950s	• Interest in Translation • Phrase Structure Grammar by Chomsky
		1960s	• ELIZA • Stoppage in Al and NLP Research
	• Goals: systems that behaved comparably to humans on given linguistic tasks • Models often build on models of human reasoning, e.g., reasoning by analogy, logic, etc.	1970s	• SHRDLU • Case Grammars • Semantic networks • Conceptual Dependency Theory • Ontologies
1980–1990s	**Empirical and Machine Learning Approaches with Engineered Features** • Lexical and corpus phase • Evaluation process becoming more rigorous • Focusing on empiricism and probabilistic models • Machine Learning for NLP	1980s	• Expert systems – MYCIN Language Modelling
		1990s	• Statistical Models for Translation • Machine Learning for NLP tasks

2000–2020s	**Deep Learning Approaches with no or limited features** • Tasks use deep learning • Pretraining	2000	• Neural Language Modelling • Word Embedding
		2010	• Word2Vec • Rise of LSTMs and CNNs • Attention and Transformers • Google Translate • Pretrained Language Models
		2020	• GPT3 • Large Language Models • Ethical NLP

Table 1.2: History of Natural Language Processing

The ever-useful **n–gram language model** based on statistical methods and useful for tracking sequences of data was first developed in the 1980s. This fundamental concept of language model enhanced with machine learning and deep learning aspects still continues to be applicable to this today.

In the 1980s and 1990s, research on natural language processing shifted to statistical models capable of making soft, probabilistic decisions. These years saw renewed interest in machine translation with IBM developing several versions of successful, complicated **statistical machine translation models**. Machine learning techniques based on statistical models such as Bayesian models and maximum entropy came into the picture. Machine learning techniques used appropriately annotated corpora to train systems based on various morphological, syntactic or semantic criteria and build systems that tackled tasks such as parsing, word sense disambiguation, question answering and summarization.

1.3.3 Deep Learning Approaches with No or Limited Features (2000s–2020s)

In 2003, Bengio et al. proposed the first neural language model consisting of a one-hidden layer feed-forward neural network and in 2006, Geoffrey Hinton, Simon Osindero, and Yee-Whye Teh extended it by developing algorithm to train a network with three hidden layers and thus, began the era of deep learning. Besides new algorithms and architectures, sufficient computing resources and a constantly growing volume of digital data that could be used to train large neural networks propelled the use of deep learning for Natural Language Processing. Around this time the concept of **word embedding**, a real–valued word feature vector which used distributed representations of words in a vector space relying on word usage, so that words with similar meanings have a similar representation was developed.

In 2013, Mikolov et al. introduced the most popular with an efficient improvement of the training procedure of the word embedding model called **Word2Vec**. This was the time when neural network models such as recurrent neural networks, convolutional neural networks, and recursive neural networks started to get adopted in NLP. In 2015, Bahdanau et al. introduced the principle of **attention**, which is one of the core innovations in neural machine translation and the key idea that enabled these models to outperform classic sentence-based MT systems. **Transformer**, a neural network architecture using the self-attention mechanism was introduced in 2017 by researchers at Google AI to process ordered sequences of text more effectively for tasks like translation and summarization. The latest major innovation in the world of Natural Language Processing is large **pretrained models**. Pre-trained language model embeddings can be used as features in a target model and have shown to enable efficient learning with significantly less data. The main advantage of these pre-trained language models for Natural Language Processing is their ability to learn word representations from large unannotated text corpora, which is particularly beneficial for low-resource languages where labelled data is scarce. These models showed great improvements in a broad range of NLP tasks, including question answering, textual entailment, sentiment analysis, semantic role labelling, coreference resolution, and named-entity extraction.

1.4 Levels of Linguistic Knowledge

Language consists of many levels of structure. Just like humans fluently integrate all of these in producing and understanding language, natural language systems need to do the same. All Natural Language Processing tasks operate by exploiting underlying regularities inherent in human languages. Let us first outline the different levels of linguistic knowledge.

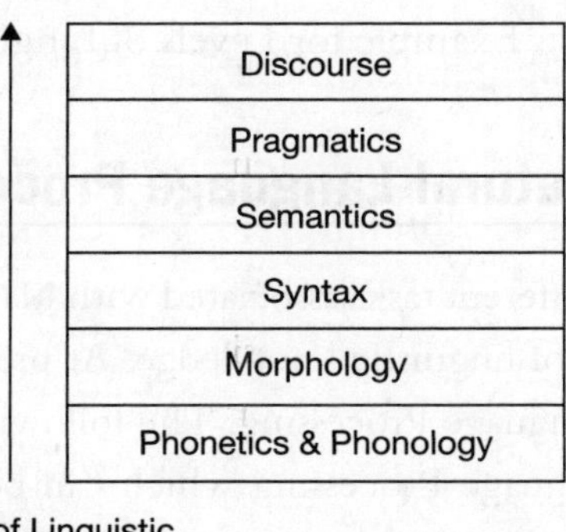

Figure 1.1: Levels of Linguistic Knowledge

Figure 1.1 shows us the different levels of linguistic knowledge. Of these six levels, phonetics and phonology are the study of the sounds of language and is the concern of speech processing which we will not be dealing with in this book. The next level is morphology which is the study of meaningful components of words that is the way words are built from smaller meaning bearing units. Syntax is concerned with the structural relationships among words that is how the words are put together to form correct sentences and what structural role each word has. Semantics is concerned with the meaning of words (lexical semantics) and of how these word meanings are combined into the meaning of sentences (compositional semantics). Pragmatics is the study of use of language to achieve goals that is concerned with how sentences are used in different situations and how this use affects the interpretation of the sentence. Finally, discourse is the study of conventions of dialogue and how the immediately preceding sentence affects the interpretation of the next sentence during a dialogue. An example of a simple sentence and associated levels of linguistic knowledge is shown below (Figure 1.2).

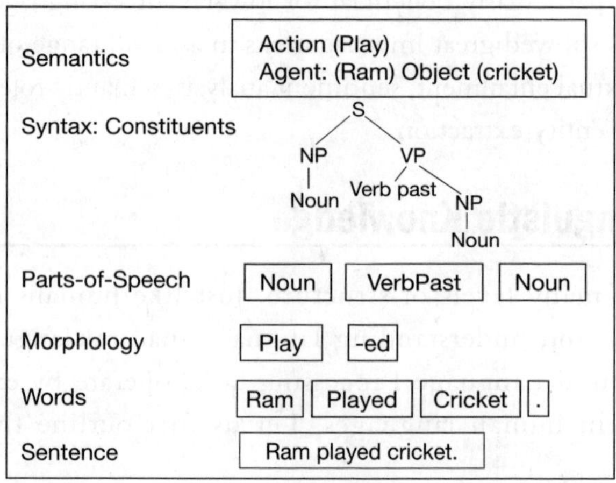

Figure 1.2: Example for Levels of Linguistic Knowledge

1.5 Core Tasks of Natural Language Processing

Now let us understand the different tasks associated with Natural Language Processing required to tackle the different levels of linguistic knowledge. At present, we are dealing with only the analysis aspect of Natural Language Processing. The following are some of the important tasks associated with Natural Language Processing which can be categorized as word component based, syntax based, semantic based and context based (Figure 1.3).

Tokenization is the process of breaking up text into text units such as words, sentences or phrases.

Stemming work by cutting off the end or the beginning of the word, considering a list of common prefixes and suffixes that can be found in an inflected word. This indiscriminate cutting may not always result in producing actual root words.

Lemmatization, on the other hand, takes into consideration the morphological analysis of the word where lemma is the base or root form of all its inflectional forms. Therefore, regular dictionaries are lists of lemmas, not stems.

Morphological analysis is essentially the splitting or breaking down of a word into its component parts to determine the root of a word, identify affixes, and to understand the function of a word in a sentence.

Part-of-speech tagging, or POS tagging involves identifying the part-of-speech category such as verb, adjective, noun, pronoun, conjunction, preposition, etc., of a word in the context of a sentence. POS tagging is useful for identifying relationships between words and, therefore, understanding the meaning of sentences.

Chunking, also called shallow parsing, is the process of grouping words or extracting phrases from text, which means analysing a sentence to identify the constituents (Noun Groups, Verbs, verb groups, etc.)

Syntax analysis is the process of identifying the structural relationships between the words in a sentence. A syntax tree is a tree structure that depicts the various syntactic categories of a sentence and aids in the comprehension of the syntax of a sentence.

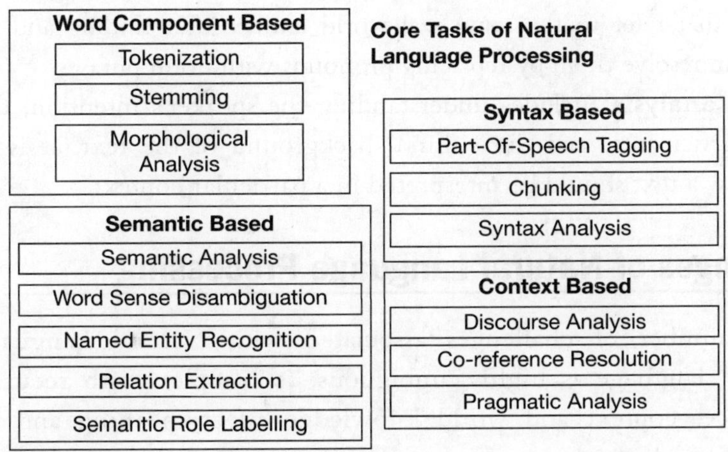

Figure 1.3: Core Tasks of Natural Language Processing

Semantic analysis, in the context of Natural Language Processing, is in general the process of understanding the meaning of text. Understanding the meaning of a word is the task of word sense disambiguation. Identifying entities and their categories that is named entity recognition is also important for semantic analysis. Another important task involved in semantic analysis is relationship extraction between these entities.

Word-sense disambiguation is the task of identifying the correct sense of a word based upon the context of its occurrence in a text. For example, in the sentences, "The dog barked at the mailman", and "Tree bark is sometimes used as a medicine", the word bark has two different meanings.

Named-entity recognition involves entity extraction, identification and categorization. It involves extracting names of locations, people and things from the text and placing them under certain categories such as person, company, time, location, etc.

Relationship extraction is the task of extracting semantic relationships between entities from a text. Extracted fall into a number of semantic categories (e.g., married to, employed by, lives in).

Semantic role labelling is the process of attaching abstract roles such as buyer seller, etc., that arguments of a predicate can take in the event such as bought, sold, purchase.

Discourse analysis is the study of the ways in which units of language are used to construct meaning above the level of the sentence. It can be used to examine texts at all levels, from individual sentences to whole books.

Co-reference resolution is the task of finding all linguistic expressions (called mentions) in a given text that refer to the same real-world entity. After finding and grouping these mentions, we can resolve them by replacing pronouns with noun phrases.

Pragmatic analysis includes understanding the speaker's intention, the relationship between the participants, and the cultural background of the text. It is the process of determining how a text should be interpreted in a particular context.

1.6 Challenges of Natural Language Processing

There are a number of challenges associated with Natural Language Processing because natural language is highly ambiguous, is complex with recursive structures and co-reference, context and world knowledge affect meaning and interpretation, involves reasoning about the world and is generally part of a social system associated with conversation and speech act (such as persuasion, advice) rules and intent. However, often simple features used appropriately can often carry out many of the functions of Natural Language Processing. Let us discuss in detail a few of the factors that make Natural Language Processing hard.

1.6.1 Ambiguity

Ambiguity can in general be defined as the capability of being understood in more than one way. This is because language is often subtle and exploits context to convey meaning and often involves reasoning about the world. In this sense natural language is very ambiguous across all levels of linguistic knowledge as follows (Figure 1.4):

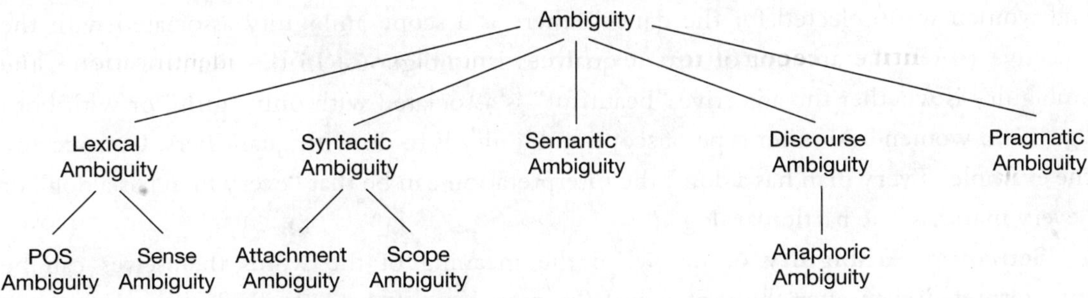

Figure 1.4: Different Types of Ambiguity

Lexical Ambiguity is the ambiguity of a single word. It is class of ambiguity caused by a word having multiple meanings under different part of speech categories especially when the word is part of sentence or phrase. Tackling lexical ambiguity is about choosing which sense of a particular word under a particular POS category.

For example, let us take the sentence "I play cricket". Here, the words *"play"* and *"cricket"* would mean multiple things as follows:

Play = present tense of the verb play (playing a game) or present tense of the verb play (playing an instrument) OR a noun play (drama), etc. According to WordNet, the word "play" is defined under 17 different senses in NOUN category and under 32 different senses in VERB category.

Cricket = a noun cricket (game) or a noun cricket (bird). According to WordNet, the word "saw" is defined under 2 different senses in NOUN category and under 1 different sense in VERB category.

Syntactic Ambiguity is a kind of structural ambiguity which occurs when a sentence can be parsed in different ways. Syntactic ambiguity can be divided into two types, namely, attachment ambiguity and scope ambiguity. A sentence has **attachment ambiguity** if a constituent fits more than one position in a parse tree. The often used example for English prepositional phrase (PP) attachment ambiguity is the sentence "The man saw the girl with the telescope", where it is ambiguous whether the prepositional phrase "with the telescope" is attached with the noun "girl" that is meaning "the man saw the girl who had the telescope", or whether the phrase is attached to the verb "saw" that is meaning "the man saw the girl using the telescope". This ambiguity arises since the semantics indicates that "the telescope" can be used for seeing. This ambiguity is not true for all languages such morphologically rich languages like Tamil which have case ending forming part of a word and the attachment is evident.

Scope Ambiguity involves operators and quantifiers. In the example "beautiful girls and women were selected for the dance", there is a scope ambiguity associated with the adjective that is the amount of text it qualifies is ambiguous. In the example above, the ambiguity is whether the adjective "beautiful" is associated with only "girls" or with both "girls and women". Another type of scope ambiguity is to do with quantifiers. Considering the example "Every man has a dog", the interpretation can be that "every man has a dog" or "every man has one particular dog".

Semantic Ambiguity occurs when the meaning of the words themselves can be misinterpreted even after the syntax and the meanings of the individual words have been resolved. For example, the sentence "The bus hit the post while it was moving" has semantic ambiguity because the interpretations can be "The bus, while moving, hit the post" and "The bus hit the post while the post was moving". The first interpretation is the correct "the bus was moving" since "post cannot move" and it is the model of the world that helps us to distinguish what is logical (or possible) from what is not. Providing this model of the world to the system is not an easy task. Another example of semantic ambiguity is "Kishan drove his car, and so did Ram" where the possible interpretations can be "Kishan drove his car and Ram also drove Kishan's car" and "Kishan drove his car and Ram also drove his own car" (the actual meaning).

Discourse Ambiguity: Discourse level processing needs a shared world knowledge, and the interpretation is carried out using this shared context. Anaphoric ambiguity comes under the discourse level. **Anaphoric Ambiguity** arises due to the use of anaphoric entities which refer to the entities that have been previously introduced into the discourse. For example, "The dog ran down the road. It was very long. It soon got tired". Here, the anaphoric reference of "it" in two situations causes ambiguity where the first "it" refers to the road because roads are associated with adjective long and the second "it" to the dog since dog is associated with adjective tired. Another example is "Seetha invited Geetha for a picnic, but she told her she was not well", here the "she" refers to Seetha and "her" refers to Geetha.

Pragmatic Ambiguity refers to a situation where the context of a phrase gives it multiple interpretations and involves conversational implicature, a process in which the speaker implies, and a listener infers. The problem involves complex processing of user intention, sentiment, belief world, modals, etc. Some examples of pragmatic ambiguity are, "Can you pass the book?", does not expect you to answer yes but for you to actually pass the book, and another example "Do you know the time?", does not expect that you tell the time but implicitly means that the person is expressing anger that you missed the due time.

1.6.2 Richness

Another factor that makes Natural Language Processing hard is the complexity associated with language. There are many ways to express the same meaning or in other words, there is a many-to many mapping between the symbolic language text and the final semantic meaning. Moreover, the scale of what is to be understood is immeasurable since there is a large amount of text available, and we need to tackle large number of different phenomena. In addition, language is not static and grows and changes continuously. Moreover, phenomena, such as social acts like persuasion, advice, etc., implicit aspects such as sarcasm, humor, etc., are other issues to be handled.

1.6.3 Variation and Expressivity

There are many ways to express the same meaning or in other words, there is a many-to many mapping between the symbolic language text and the final semantic meaning. In addition is the diversity across languages, dialects, genres, styles, etc. In addition, language is not static and grows and changes continuously and moreover there is need to tackle natural language from the perspective of modern ways of communication especially social media.

1.6.4 Sparsity Problem

Despite the large amount of text being available, a surprising sparsity problem exists. If we study the frequencies of different words in any large corpus, we can discover that the Zipf's law holds which states that $f \times r \approx k$ where f is the frequency of a word, r is its rank and k is a constant. The implication of this law is that there will be a large number of infrequent words even in a very large corpus. This fact holds across different levels of linguistic structures. Therefore, one of the main challenges of Natural Language Processing is to be able to estimate probabilities and learn about entities we have rarely or never encountered.

1.6.5 Difficulty in Engineering Natural Language Processing Systems

There is difficulty in engineering NLP systems because of the huge amount of data resources such as grammar, dictionary, large documents required for machine learning and deep learning and the computational complexity of analyzing a sentence.

1.7 Applications of Natural Language Processing

Different Natural Language Processing applications may require different kinds of representations at different levels which often poses a challenge to building Natural Language Processing applications. By utilizing Natural Language Processing, knowledge can be organized and structured to perform tasks such as text categorization, sentiment analysis, application to information retrieval and web search, question answering. Automatic summarization, information extraction, machine translation, and conversional agents (Figure 1.5). We will be discussing some of these applications in detail in succeeding chapters. Now let us study some of these applications.

Text classification assigns pre-defined labels either one label or multiple labels to text. This automatic process enables documents to be classified at lower cost, with greater consistency and accuracy. These class labels can result in documents being associated with controlled vocabulary terms which can serve as a form of metadata.

Sentiment analysis or opinion mining identifies the emotional tone behind text. Sentiment analysis can be used to discover the performance of business brand from social media, and identify areas that need to improve from customer service review notes Analyzed text can vary from emails, blog posts, support tickets, web chats, social media channels, forums and comments. Sentiment analysis is an application of text classification and can be used to identify the feeling, opinion, or belief of a statement in terms of binary classes such as positive or negative or multiple classes ranging from very negative, to neutral, to very positive.

Information retrieval or web search finds relationships between the information need expressed as queries by the user and documents in a repository or the web. The focus of information retrieval is on the user information need where information is about a subject or topic, semantics is frequently loose and natural language text which is not always well structured and could be semantically ambiguous needs to be handled. Web searching exploits all evidence such as web structure, meta-data, user context information and needs to identify different types of queries and represent the web document either automatically or semi automatically.

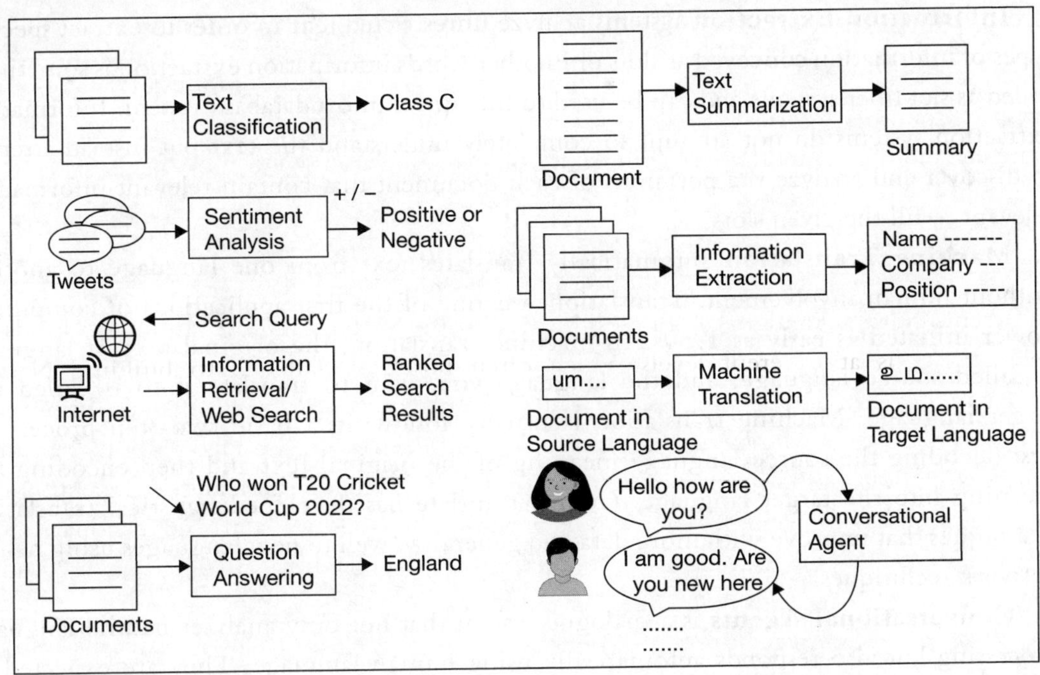

Figure 1.5: Applications of Natural Language Processing

Question answering directly provides an answer to information needs posed as questions. There are a variety of questions such as simple factual questions where a short phrase is expected from single documents, general questions such as "What do we know about country X?" which involves retrieving multiple documents, locating portions of answers and then combining them to form a single response. Complex questions additionally require judgements and deep knowledge of the user's context. IBM Watson considered a successful question answering system competed and won Jeopardy a TV quiz program. Watson analysed each question to determine exactly what was being asked, analysed the available content to extract precise answers, and quickly computed its level of confidence in the answer based on supporting and refuting information found.

Text Summarization is the process of distilling important information from a source to produce an abridged version and involves the following selection of one or more salient or non-redundant information, aggregation from different parts of source or from different linguistic descriptions and finally generalization of specific information with more general abstract information. Summarization is a condensation of single or multiple documents and can be extractive or synthetic and aggregative or representative.

Information Extraction systems analyze unrestricted_text in order to extract specific types of information conveyed as slots or in other words information extraction is sometimes called as slot filler systems and can be used to fill entries into a database system. Information extraction systems do not attempt to completely understand the text but instead attempt to discover and analyze the portaions of each document that contain relevant information relevant to fill the given slots.

Machine Translation automatically translates text from one language to another without human involvement. Translation was one of the first applications of computing power initiated as early as 1950s. In machine translation, the original text or language is called source language, and the language you want to translate it to is called the target language. Machine translation is usually following a basic two-step process by first decoding the source language meaning of the original text and then encoding the meaning into the target language. Google translate has developed statistical translation techniques that improve with more data and generalize well to new languages using neural network techniques.

Conversational Agents is a dialogue system that not only analyses natural language processing but also responds automatically using human language. They are expected to understand human emotions, answer basic questions, respond to commands, and interact through natural language conversations. These agents are often used to automate customer support and marketing campaigns. A chatbot is a type of conversational agent that is designed to simulate human users, often over the internet.

1.8 Future Trends in Natural Language Processing

In this section we look at some of the future trends in Natural Language Processing (NLP), from the viewpoint of approaches as well as application domains. Natural Language Processing is still a complex task despite recent advances. Building smarter systems that are more dynamic and mature in their functional and operational capabilities so that industry can make use of Natural Language Processing for real time applications that are of commercial value. Natural Language Processing Models should be sensitive to a wide range of phenomena and constraints in human language and ideally work across languages, modalities, genres, styles.

1.8.1 Learning Approaches

Some of the learning approaches that will be extensively used for Natural Language processing are as follows:

Mix of Supervised and Unsupervised Machine Learning Techniques – Improving Performance of NLP Tasks: Combining supervised approaches which necessitates a significant quantity of labelled data and several iterations for obtaining a good prediction model and unsupervised approaches which recognize patterns from input unlabelled data and draw conclusions on unseen data is found to improve the performance of the learning models.

Transfer Learning – for Tasks with Limited Training Data: Transfer Learning is a machine learning approach where a model trained for one job task is repurposed for a related task by fine-tuning already trained models. In general, models are unable to generalize their learning and developing and training for a task from scratch is costly and time-consuming and moreover requires large quantity of data often labelled data. However, with transfer learning NLP tasks can be accomplished faster with less labelled data. NLP tasks often share encoders that have a homogeneous network structure, enabling transfer learning Using pre-trained word embeddings. a type of transfer learning method, knowledge (word embeddings) learnt from a large-scale corpus via a language model is transferred to downstream tasks directly, by initializing corresponding network layers of downstream task models. Such methods are important to those tasks with limited training data. Transfer learning, which was first used for computer vision, is being used for NLP tasks such as sentiment analysis and named entity recognition.

Transformers – Learning General and Effective Pre-trained Models: One major difficulty faced by many natural language tasks is the limited amount of training data. Current research is investigating the learning of general and effective pre-trained representations for language understanding, where words and text are represented as vectors such as ELMo (Embeddings from Language Models) and BERT (Bidirectional Encoder Representations from Transformers). While ELMo leverages the sequence encoder from the language model, BERT uses a transformer-based encoder and a masked word approach to train a very large bidirectional representation from large amount of text. These models have been trained on massive quantities of data and can enhance the performance of a wide range of NLP issues dramatically. Use of new network structures, lightweight approaches, as well as incorporating world knowledge and common-sense knowledge to learn general pre-trained representations for language understanding will drive future research.

Reinforcement Learning – Improving Performance of Evolving NLP Tasks: Currently NLP models, mostly supervised learning-based ones find it hard to deal with situations outside of training boundaries and need to be retrained when new situations are encountered. Reinforcement learning enables NLP models to learn behavior that maximizes the possibility of a positive outcome through feedback from the environment and enables the continuous improvement of the performance of NLP models through sequences of reward-based training iterations. Such learning models thus improve NLP-based applications such as question answering, machine translation, summarization, etc.

Multi-task Learning – Improving NLP Tasks Using Common Knowledge across Tasks: Multi-task Learning is another paradigm that can use different task supervisions to improve a target task, by learning common knowledge from all involved tasks. A multi-task learning framework (McCan, 2018) which treated all involved ten NLP tasks as question-answering tasks and trained a unified model with fine-tuning.

Use of Knowledge and Common Sense for NLP: The extensive development of human-computer interaction applications such as chat, QA, and dialogue systems, the use of knowledge and common sense in natural language understanding has gained importance.

Wikipedia and knowledge graphs (such as Freebase and Satori) are two types of commonly used knowledge bases. Commonsense knowledge refers to those facts that all humans are expected to know but is however not present in text corpora. Many HCI tasks, such as QA and dialogue, need common sense to reason and generate responses. Hence, building of large-scale commonsense knowledgebases and their use for various NLP tasks has also become important.

1.8.2 The Rise of Low-code Tools and Low-resource NLP Tasks

Another trend is the emergence of low-code or no-code tools in the NLP area. For some NLP tasks, such as rare language translation, chatbot and customer service systems in specific domains and in multi-turn tasks, labeled data is hard to acquire and the data sparseness problem becomes serious. These are called low-resource NLP tasks. To enrich the training data, many data augmentation methods can be used such as introducing domain knowledge (dictionaries and rules) or leverage active learning to maximize the gain of labeling data. Semi-supervised and unsupervised methods can use unlabeled data. Labeled data from other tasks and other languages can also be used with multi-task learning and transfer learning.

Between the growing set of applications and the democratization of the technology, it will be exciting to see what is ahead for NLP as it becomes more accessible. But one thing is for certain: NLP is poised for even greater growth in 2021.

1.8.3 Multi-Lingual and Multi-Modal NLP

Majority of NLP advancements have been concentrated on English. In general, Natural Language Processing Models should be sensitive to a wide range of phenomena and constraints in human language and should work across languages, modalities, genres, styles. For Natural Language Processing to make an impact on social and commercial aspects globally, multi-lingual processing becomes very important and issues regarding multi-lingual models such as how to align models with language family needs to be tackled. Increasingly pre-trained multilingual models are being released that perform as well as or better than monolingual models. Recent improvements in language-agnostic sentence embeddings, zero-shot learning, and the availability of multilingual embeddings, show a growing trend in the development of multilingual NLP models.

Given an image and natural language question, Visual QA (VQA) aims to generate the answer to the input question and depends on the deep understanding and sufficient interaction between the input question and image. As a typical Multi-modal task, visual QA (VQA) is a future trending task for both NLP and computer vision research.

1.8.4 Futuristic Applications

Integrating natural language processing technologies with help desk software, for example, might automate time-consuming and laborious operations like labelling and routing customer support issues, freeing employees to focus on higher-value work. With advances in natural language processing (NLP) and rising customer service demand, we can expect to see significant progress toward the next generation of chatbots, which will be able to self-improve, hold more complex conversations, and possibly learn how to complete new tasks without prior training.

There is a growing interest in virtual assistants in devices and applications as they improve accessibility and provide information on demand. However, they deliver accurate information only if the virtual assistants understand the query without misinterpretation. N ovel virtual assistants and chatbots are expected to mitigate processing errors and work continuously, unlike human virtual assistants. Additionally, NLP-powered virtual assistants find applications in providing information to factory workers, assisting academic research, and more.

NLP is increasingly becoming a critical tool for detecting and preventing the spread of fake news and disinformation, saving time and effort. Cyberbullying detection is another method NLP is being utilized to make a good influence. On social media, classifiers are being developed to detect the usage of abusive and derogatory language, as well as hate speech.

Sentiment analysis, also known as opinion mining, will continue to play a significant role, allowing businesses to monitor social media and gain real-time insights into how customers feel about their brand or products. Using natural language processing (NLP) tools to assess brand sentiment can assist businesses in identifying areas for improvement, detecting negative comments on the fly (and responding proactively), and gaining a competitive advantage. Analysis of the impact of marketing efforts and evaluating how consumers react to events such as a new product introduction are two more intriguing use cases for sentiment analysis in social media monitoring.

Some domain-specific applications are now being researched. These include computational social science defined as "The science that investigates social phenomena through the medium of computing and algorithmic data processing." [adapted from CSSSA] and Computational journalism defined as the application of computation to the activities of journalism such as information gathering, organization, sensemaking, communication and dissemination of news information, while upholding values of journalism such as accuracy and verifiability. Other areas include healthcare text information processing and legal text processing.

Summary

- Introduced the basic aspects of natural language processing.
- Explained the areas that are connected to natural language processing.
- Explored the need for natural language processing.
- Outlined the history of natural language processing.
- Listed the different levels of linguistic knowledge.
- Explained the different core tasks associated with natural language processing.
- Explored the different challenges faced in processing natural language.
- Discussed the various applications of natural language processing.
- Explored the future trends associated with natural language processing.

Exercises

Suggested Activities

1. Fill the following table to list applications of Natural Language Processing:

NLP Process	Application	Description	Commercial System (if any)
Text Classification			
Morphological Analysis			
Natural Language Generation			
Discourse Analysis			

2. Give another example (not in text) illustrating different levels of linguistic knowledge.

Self-Assessment: Multiple Choice Questions

Give answers with justification for correct and wrong choices:

1. _____________ strives to build machines that understand text data and Derive meaning from this text in a smart and useful way.
    i. Computational Linguistics
    ii. Natural Language Processing
    iii. Cognitive Science
2. Natural language generation
    i. takes natural language representation and generates natural language text.
    ii. understanding takes natural language text and produces a computer understandable representation.
    iii. produces a representation that can be directly used for many tasks and applications.
3. Reason for renewed interest in Natural Language Processing
    i. Speech processing is available.
    ii. Understanding natural language is difficult.
    iii. Explosion of machine-readable natural language text.
4. "Colourless green ideas sleep furiously" is a famous example given by
    i. *Woods*
    ii. Chomsky
    iii. Fillmore

5. The system developed by Terry Winograd that worked with "blocks" in a restricted vocabulary framework that used natural language to query and manipulate objects is named as
    i. *SHRDLU*
    ii. ELIZA
    iii. MYCIN

6. One of the famous expert systems built to mimic medical human experts was
    i. *SHRDLU*
    ii. ELIZA
    iii. MYCIN

7. One of the training procedures of the word embedding model is called
    i. *WordEmbed*
    ii. WordTrain
    iii. Word2Vec

8. The process of grouping words or extracting phrases from text is called
    i. *Shallow Parsing*
    ii. Morphological Analysis
    iii. Parsing

9. The process of identifying the correct sense of a word based upon the context of its occurrence in a text is called
    i. *Semantic Sense Analysis*
    ii. Word Sense Disambiguation
    iii. Lexical Disambiguation

10. The process of finding all mentions in a given text that relate to the same real-world entity is called
    i. *Named-Entity Recognition*
    ii. Discourse Analysis
    iii. Co-reference Resolution

11. "Every man loves a girl" is an example of
    i. *Scope ambiguity*
    ii. *Semantic ambiguity*
    iii. *Attachment ambiguity*
    iv. Morphological Analysis
    v. Parsing

12. The process of identifying the emotional tone behind text is called
    i. *Emotion analysis*
    ii. Sentiment analysis
    iii. Pragmatic analysis

Self-Assessment: Match the Columns

No		Match	
1.	Linguistics	**A**	first stoppage of Natural Language Processing and machine translation
2.	NLP is difficult since	**B**	refers to a situation where interpretation involves conversational implicature, a process in which the speaker implies, and a listener infers
3.	Phase-Structure Grammar	**C**	human language is complex, ambiguous, flexible, and subtle
4.	In 1966, U.S. National Research Council (NRC) initiated the	**D**	analyze unrestricted_text in order to extract specific_types of information conveyed as slots
5.	**Stemming**	**E**	neural network architecture using the self-attention mechanism
6.	IBM	**F**	is the scientific study of language
7.	Transformer	**G**	may not always result in producing actual root words
8.	Semantic Role labelling	**H**	attaching abstract roles as arguments of a predicate can take in events
9.	Pragmatic ambiguity	**I**	statistical machine translation models
10.	Information Extraction	**J**	Noam Chomsky

Self-Assessment: Sequencing

Order	Please Arrange in Descending Order (Timeline from Earliest to Latest)
1.	IBM developing several versions of successful, complicated statistical machine translation models
2.	Mikolov et al. introduced the most popular with an efficient improvement of the training procedure of the word embedding model
3.	Rule based automatic translation system from Russian to English
4.	Bidirectional Encoder Representations from Transformers (BERT) is a machine learning technique for natural language processing (NLP) pre-training developed by Google

Order	Please Arrange in Descending Order (Timeline from Earliest to Latest)
5.	n–gram language model based on statistics methods and useful for tracking sequences of data
6.	ELIZA, a comment and response process was designed to replicate the conversation between a psychologist and a patient
7.	Developing algorithm to train a network with three hidden layers
8.	Transformer, a neural network architecture using the self–attention mechanism
9.	Providing semantic representations such as case grammar
10.	Neural language model consisting of a one–hidden layer feed–forward neural network

Short Questions

1. What is the salient difference between natural language processing, machine learning and computational linguistics?
2. What is natural language processing? Discuss.
3. What is the need for natural language processing in the current context?
4. Give a brief overview of rule-based approaches, statistical based machine learning approaches and deep learning approaches to natural language processing, from the historical perspective.
5. List and describe the various levels of linguistic knowledge.
6. What is the difference between classification and clustering?
7. Compare and contrast the following:
     i. Stemming and lemmatization
    ii. Part-of-speech tagging and named–entity recognition
   iii. Chunking and syntax analysis
    iv. Word sense disambiguation and semantic role labelling
     v. Discourse analysis and pragmatic analysis
8. Discuss the two types of lexical ambiguity with illustrative examples.
9. Differentiate between scope ambiguity and attachment ambiguity with illustrative examples.
10. What is meant by "Sparsity Problem" in the context of natural language processing?
11. Why is web search considered an application of natural language processing?
12. Why is transfer learning important for natural language processing?

Approaches to Natural Language Processing

2.1 Introduction

There are basically three approaches to Natural Language Processing or NLP as was discussed in the section of history of NLP in Chapter 1. Today many of the approaches to natural language processing are founded on deep learning, where massive amounts of labeled data are used to discover relevant correlations and patterns in data. Earlier models used rule-based machine learning algorithms based on knowledge of words and phrases in the text and the associated output required. However, deep learning is a more intuitive approach where algorithms learn by identifying patterns from a large number of examples.

Looked at from a different perspective any learning problem and here specifically NLP tasks can be viewed as consisting of three components namely data, knowledge and applications. The difference between the three approaches discussed below depends on the role of human crafting of the three components.

Rule-based Approaches: The oldest approaches to NLP are rule-based approaches based on pattern matching and parsing where were hand-coded, rules-based systems were employed. These methods perform NLP tasks using deterministic approaches with fixed hard boundaries. These methods however could not scale to handle the large number of exceptions or tackle the vast amounts of text data. Hence these approaches have low precision and high recall in that they perform well for a limited number of specific use cases and cannot be generalized to other domains or genres of text. However, these approaches such as regular expressions and context free grammar are still used mainly to understand the characteristics of text or to find patterns. From the viewpoint of these approaches data, knowledge and algorithms used are all hand coded to suit a specific task and hence cannot perform well for other similar or different cases.

Machine Learning Approaches: These approaches are more robust, probabilistic based with soft boundaries where the relevant statistics or probabilities are learned from data. These approaches include probabilistic modeling, likelihood maximization, and linear classifiers. They are characterized by training using large amounts of labelled data, feature engineering, training a model on parameters, followed by fitting on test data and then finally applying model to test data. These approaches require annotated data, paradigm tables and dictionaries as well as knowledge in the form of feature engineering all encoded with a large amount of linguistic knowledge. However, the machine learning algorithms that use this data and knowledge are basically language (human language) independent and can solve non–trivial problems efficiently using the language specific encoded linguistic knowledge.

Deep Learning Approaches: These neural network–based approaches bring about a paradigm shift from symbolic to neural computation. These methods learn important features directly from very large corpora thus avoiding feature engineering. Here streams of raw unlabeled data represented as vectors are fed into the neural networks for learning. There are a large number of deep learning frameworks including recurrent neural networks and convolutional neural networks that are used for NLP. These approaches require only annotated data and knowledge is in the form of representation learning and feature engineering is generally unsupervised and is largely language independent. all encoded with a large amount of linguistic knowledge. Similar to machine learning approaches, the algorithms are largely language (human language) independent. The neural networks of deep learning provide a convenient method to express tasks, carry out representation learning and automate feature engineering.

In this chapter as well as throughout the book we will be discussing only machine learning and deep learning approaches to NLP. Before going forward let us understand NLP core analysis and well as applications from the machine learning and deep learning perspectives.

2.2 NLP Analysis and Applications

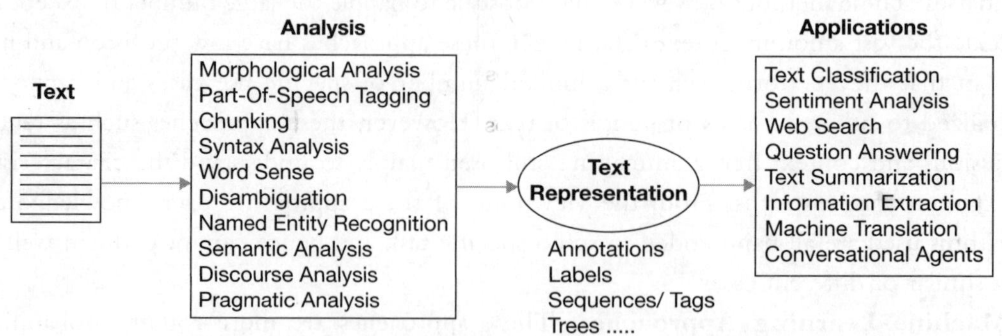

Figure 2.1: Natural Language Analysis and Applications

NLP consists of analyzing and building representations for text to tackle NLP tasks which are hard because language is ambiguous and needs to utilize appropriate data, knowledge and linguistics. Figure 2.1 shows one way to understand the flow of a typical NLP system. Let us first discuss the link between the input (text), the analysis carried out on text beginning from word-oriented analysis such as morphological analysis, etc., syntax-oriented analysis such as part-of speech tagging, chunking, parsing, etc., semantic based analysis such as named entity recognition, word sense disambiguation, semantic analysis, etc. and context based analysis such as discourse analysis and pragmatic analysis. The output of this analysis is represented as annotations, labels, sequences of words or tags, trees, etc. These representations are then used in applications such as text classification, sentiment analysis, web search, question answering, information extraction, summarization, machine translation, conversational agents, etc. Now let us understand the units of interest and the kind of features associated with NLP (Figure 2.2). The units of interest associated with NLP are basic explicit lexical units such as phonemes, words, phrases, sentences, paragraphs and documents and document collections. Words are associated with word frequencies, collocations, word sense and word sequence that where words appear in a certain order. Implicit or hidden units include word senses, named types, document categories, lexical syntactic units such as part of speech tags, syntactic relationships between words, semantic relationships and sentence meaning.

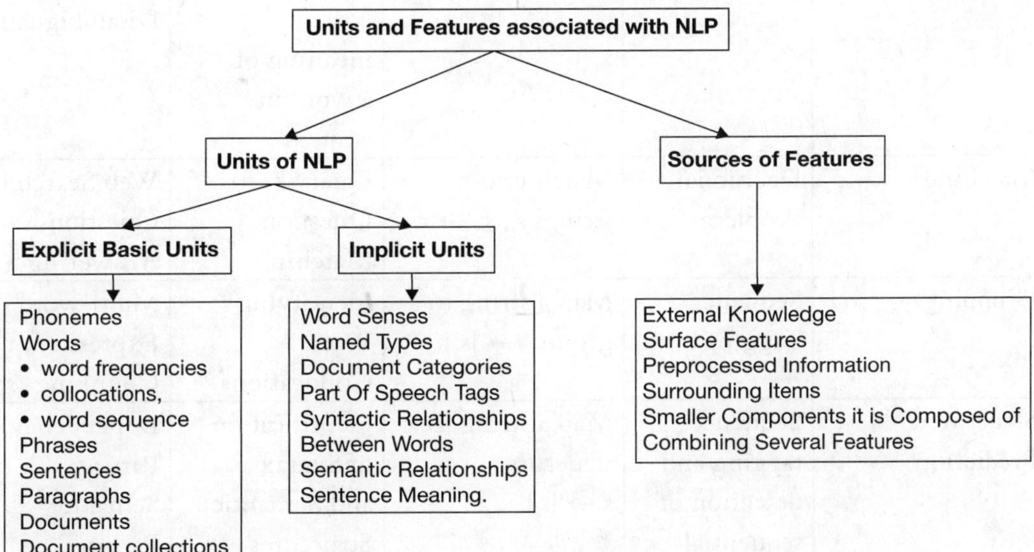

Figure 2.2: Units and Sources of Features of NLP

The next issue to be discussed is the desirable characteristics of NLP methods. These methods need to be sensitive to a wide range of phenomena and constraints associated with human language and also be general enough to handle different languages, genres, styles and modalities.

Type of Machine Learning Task	Structural Complexity of Task	Input to Output Mapping Model	Type of NLP Task	NLP Core Components & NLP Applications
Classification	Decisional Problems	Assign a label to a string $s \rightarrow c$	Text Classification	Document Classification, Sentiment Analysis
Tagging	Sequence Tagging	Assign a tag to a string $s \rightarrow t$	Identification of Appropriate Tags of Word components	Morphological Analysis,
			Identification of Appropriate Tags of a Word in a sequence	POS Tagging, Named Entity Recognition
			Identifying correct meaning of a word in context	Word Sense Disambiguation
Matching	Decisional Problems	Match two strings $s_1, s_2 \rightarrow r$	Query / Question Matching	Web Search, Question Answering
Grouping	Sequence Tagging	Map a string to a group $s \rightarrow [s_g]$	Identifying Word Collocations	Multi-word Expression, Chunking
Structured Prediction	Sequence tagging and detection of sequential structures	Map a string to a structure $s \rightarrow [s_s]$	Identification of Syntax and Semantic Structures	Dependency Parsing, Semantic Parsing
	Hierarchical structures		Identification of Hierarchical Structures	Clause Detection Syntactic Parsing

Type of Machine Learning Task	Structural Complexity of Task	Input to Output Mapping Model	Type of NLP Task	NLP Core Components & NLP Applications
Identification of Components & Linking	Sequence tagging and detection of sequential structures	Map a string to another identified string $s_1 \rightarrow s_2$	Identifying referents of a Word	Coreference Resolution
Complex Structure Prediction	Sequence tagging and detection of sequential structures	Map a string to a structure $s \rightarrow [s_s]$	Identification of Complex structures	Semantic Relation Extraction Information Extraction, Event Detection
Complex Structure Prediction Generation	Sequence tagging and detection of sequential structures and generation	Map a string to a structure to another string $s \rightarrow [s_s] \rightarrow s_2$	Identification of structure of text and Natural Language Generation	Summarization, Machine Translation
Sequential Decision Process	Sequence tagging and detection of sequential structures and generation	Map a string to a structure to another string $s \rightarrow [s_s] \rightarrow s_2$	Analysis, Sequential Decision Process and Natural Language Generation	Conversational Agent

s, s_1, s_2 – string, sequence of strings (text) c- label, $\rightarrow$ t – tag or set of tags, $\rightarrow$ r – non-negative real value, $[s_g]$ – grouping of strings, $[s_s]$ – simple / hierarchical/ complex structure of strings

Table 2.1: Understanding Tasks Associated with NLP from a Learning Perspective

Moreover, these methods need to be computationally efficient at the time of implementation and at run time. They need to be consistent and accurate when judged against human annotations or task-oriented performance.

2.3 NLP Viewed from the Learning Perspective

The purpose of the table (Table 2.1) is to explain the various NLP tasks from a learning perspective. The first three columns of Table 1 show the type of learning tasks, the structural complexity of the tasks, and the understanding of the associated models from the input output mapping viewpoint while the last two columns show the mapping of the learning tasks to NLP tasks and the related NLP core components such as morphological analysis, POS tagging, syntax analysis, etc. and NLP applications such as text classification, text summarization, machine translation, etc.

The learning tasks include classification, tagging, matching, grouping, structured prediction, identification of components and linking, complex structure prediction, complex structure prediction and generation and sequential decision process. We will explain these tasks as well as the models using associated NLP tasks. The second column indicates the type of structure associated as output with the learning tasks — basically whether they need a single decision, a sequence needs to be tagged, a sequential or hierarchical structure needs to be the output representation. Classification is the simplest task to understand, where given a string or text s, we need to obtain a class c— either the topic of the text or document (**text classification**) or the sentiment associated with the text (**sentiment analysis**). The next group of NLP tasks is associated with tagging task. In this category comes **morphological analysis** where the word s is segmented into sequential components and each component is tagged as t. Analyzing a sequence of words s, the appropriate tags t are assigned as in **POS tagging, named entity recognition and word sense disambiguation**. In matching, two strings s_1, s_2 are matched to obtain a real value r which is then used by **search engines** and **question answering** systems. In grouping, string of words s are grouped $[s_g]$ as in **multi-word expression** and **chunking**. The next category is the identification of components in a string s_1 to map and link another string s_2 (**coreference resolution**) or to complex structures $[s_s]$ as in **dependency parsing, semantic relation extraction, information extraction** and **event detection**. In some cases, these structures are hierarchical as in **clause detection** and **syntactic parsing**. In addition to mapping to complex structure, natural language text needs to be generated as in **text summarization and machine translation**. Finally, we look at a task that requires analysis, sequential decision process and natural language generation as in **conversational agents.** The units and features shown in Figure 2.2 are used in different ways for the learning process. We also need to understand that a NLP task can be modelled in different ways, for example POS tagging can be modelled either as a classification problem or as a sequence labelling problem.

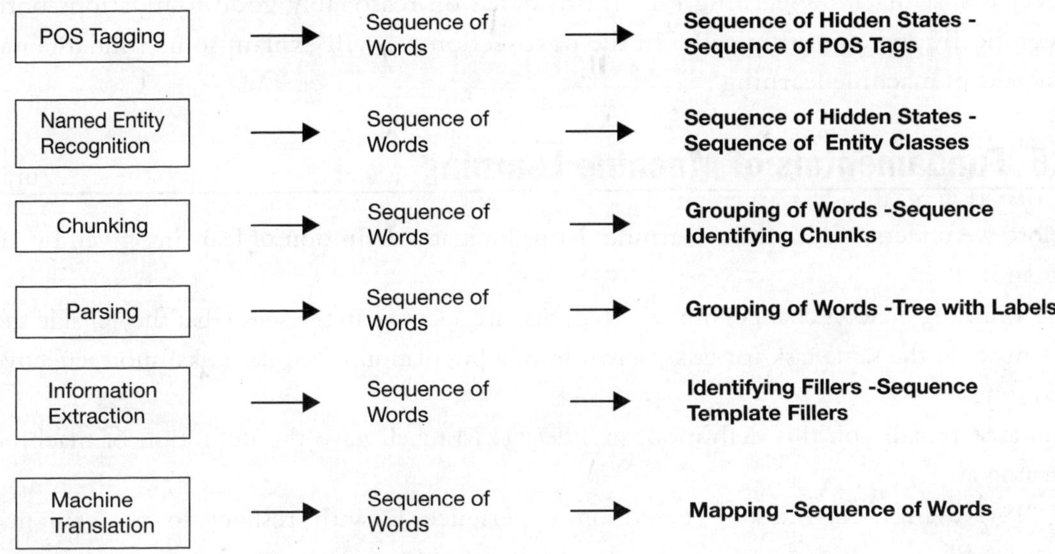

Figure 2.3: Sequence Handling Tasks of NLP

The most interesting and challenging problem associated with NLP is the sequence handling problem and many of the NLP tasks can be described as sequence labelling tasks where a sequence is produced as output is decided by the sequence of input features or words as shown in Figure 2.3.

2.4 Need for Machine Learning for NLP

The earlier approaches to NLP used ruled based approaches and these rules were too rigid to characterize the use of language by humans since humans used language in a flexible manner in order to meet their communication needs. As already discussed in Chapter 1, a large amount of human language text has become accessible both due to the proliferation of web-based data and due to digitization of other documents. NLP becomes necessary to handle this information overload and make sense of this data. Traditional knowledge engineering methods are not able to manage this deluge of data. In addition, NLP requires large amounts of knowledge of different types. Moreover, language behavior is preferential in nature and therefore there is need to acquire both quantitative and qualitative knowledge. It is in this scenario that machine learning makes knowledge acquisition and inferencing feasible either in an automatic or semi-automatic manner. Machine learning methods model language using statistical methods and hence are able to handle the flexibility associated with the human use of language. Another important aspect is that machine learning for NLP is based on reasonably good foundations both theoretically and algorithmically. In the next section we will explain some fundamental concepts of machine learning.

2.5 Fundamentals of Machine Learning

Before we understand machine learning, let us look at a definition of learning given by H. Simon in 1983.

"Learning denotes changes in the system that are adaptive in the sense that they enable the system to do the same task (or tasks drawn from a population of similar tasks) more effective next time".

Based broadly on this definition, in 1997, T. Mitchell gave the definition of machine learning as:

"Improving some task T based on experience E with respect to performance measure P".

Machine learning has the ability to learn and provide a model even without being explicitly programmed. Based on definitions by Kevin P. Murphy and Christopher M. Bishop, machine learning can also be described as methods that automatically detect patterns or regularities from data and use these uncovered regularities or patterns to predict future data, predict other outcomes of interest or take actions.

The basic flow diagram of a machine learning system is given below (Figure 2.4). Generally, machine learning systems consists of two phases namely the testing and training phases and provides techniques that can learn and then predict using data. In the training phase, large amounts of data which in the case of NLP can be a word, a sentence or text is given as input. This input may or may not be pre-processed before converting the data to feature vectors. Now depending on the type of learning algorithm used, these feature vectors may or may not be associated with labels. The learning algorithm then builds a statistical based learning or prediction model. This model is thus essentially built by finding patterns using the large amounts of input data. During the testing phase a hitherto unseen data is taken, pre-processed if necessary and then converted to corresponding feature vectors and given to the model built during training phase. The learnt model then predicts the outputs such as class, sentiment, POS tag depending on the NLP task.

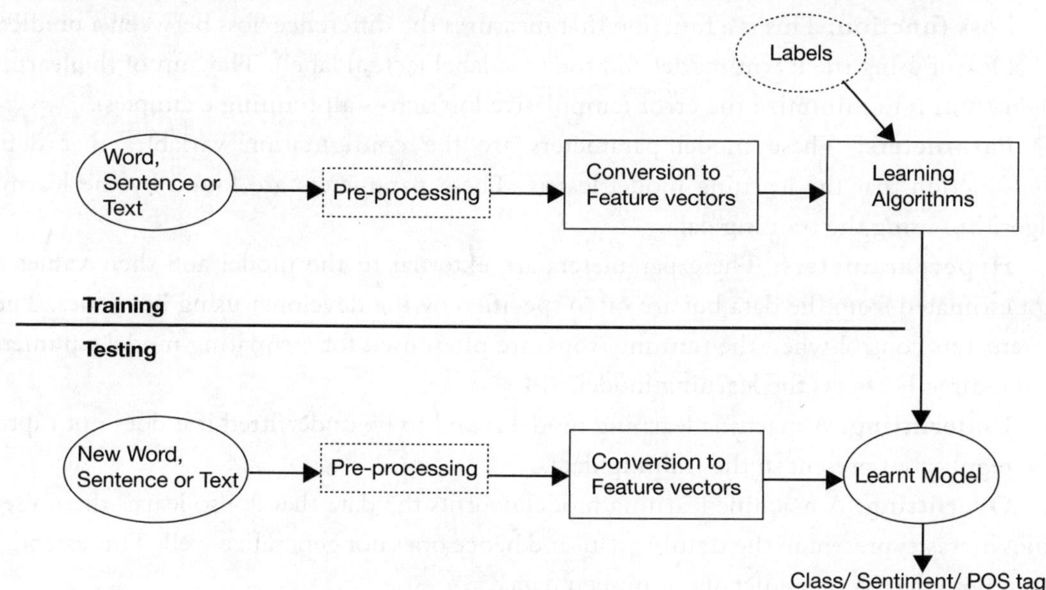

Figure 2.4: Machine Learning System

Machine learning essentially performs a particular task or reacts to environmental inputs. It carries out concept learning from data where it models concepts underlying data, predicts about unseen input, compacts knowledge representation and discovers knowledge.

2.5.1 Terminology Associated with Machine Learning

Now let us understand some terminology that is used in the context of machine learning:

Training Samples: Examples or data used to train a machine learning algorithm.

Features/Attributes/Independent Variables: Set of features represented as a vector associated with an example. The features to be used are decided by the developers and is designed to capture the features of the input that are expected to relate to the output predictions.

Feature Vector: The list of feature values representing the examples passed into a model.

Target/Dependent Variable: Values or categories assigned to data. The correct label for a training sample that is needed during training in the case of supervised learning.

Output: Prediction label obtained from input set of samples using a model learnt using machine learning algorithm

Model: Information that the machine learning algorithm learns after training. This model is used for predicting the output labels of new, unseen examples.

Loss function: This is a function that measures the difference/loss between a predicted label learnt using the learnt model and the true label (actual label). The aim of the learning algorithms is to minimize the error (cumulative loss across all training examples).

Parameters: These model parameters are the configuration variables that define the function that the learning model learns. These parameters are found by the learning algorithm using the training data.

Hyperparameters: These parameters are external to the model and their values are not estimated from the data but are often specified by the developer using heuristics. These parameters control when the training stops, are often used for estimating model parameters and indirectly affects the learning model.

Underfitting: A machine learning model is said to be underfitted if it does not capture the regularities present in the training data.

Overfitting: A machine learning model overfits the data that it also learns the noise or idiosyncrasies present in the training data and hence does not generalize well. This essentially it cannot effectively predict about unseen data.

2.5.2 Types of Machine Learning

Now we will briefly describe the different types of machine learning.

Supervised Machine Learning: In this type of learning the training data includes the desired output or labels. From one perspective, the supervised learning model discovers a mapping function between the input and desired output from the training data and then uses this mapping function to predict output of unseen data. A typical example of supervised learning in NLP is text classification where we know the correct output class associated with training text. The classification model predicts the class of a hitherto unseen text.

Unsupervised Machine Learning: In this type of learning the training data does not include the desired output or labels. Here the model discovers patterns from unlabelled data. A typical example in NLP is clustering similar documents based on text content.

Semi-supervised Machine Learning: In this type of learning the training data includes a few examples with desired data. One of the oldest methods of semi-supervised learning is self-training. The process starts by using the labelled data to train the model. The model is then used on unlabelled data. Next some of the unlabelled examples that are labelled with high probability by the model are then added to the labelled data and the process is repeated till a fairly good model is obtained.

Reinforcement Learning: In this type of learning, the model is trained to obtain the maximum reward possible from a sequence of actions of a process or a task. It is a general-purpose framework for sequential decision-making and is described as an agent interacting with unknown environment trying to select an action to maximize a future cumulative reward. Reinforcement learning derives its fundamentals from human psychology research, where generally good behaviour is rewarded, and bad behaviour patterns are punished. An example in NLP is the use of reinforcement learning for chatbots where we aim for optimized customer outcomes in dialogue generation.

2.6 Machine Learning for NLP

In this section we will briefly discuss how some typical machine learning algorithms that have been used for NLP. For a machine learning system to be successful when applied to NLP, the system needs to understand the biases and assumptions associated with NLP that may be based on linguistic theory or representations. The typical outputs of a machine learning based NLP systems are either a set of rules or a set of probability values.

Example

An example of a rule learned could be

"if the word to the left of the verb is a noun that has the animacy feature it is likely to be the agent of the action denoted by the verb".

The man repairs the car (*man* is the agent; animate)

The car repairs (*car* is not the agent; inanimate)

The same can be given as probability values.

P(agent|word) is to the left of verb and has animacy) > P(object|word) is to the left of verb and has animacy) etc.

The difference between machine learning approach to classical rule-based approach is that in classical approach the rules have to be given by the linguist while in the machine learning approach the rules and probability values are learnt from text corpora using machine learning algorithms. However, the selection of features associated with the training text corpora requires linguistic knowledge. The features used by machine learning includes frequencies of lexical units or terms such as word, phrase, etc., co-occurrence frequencies between all relevant types of units such as term–document, term–term, term–category, sense–term, etc., The representation used by machine learning could be sequences, feature sets or vectors.

The simplest example for the use of machine learning for NLP is classification where mapping function from an instance to a category is learnt. Here the set of categories is fixed. A large number of NLP tasks can be modelled as classification. Examples include text classification that is assigning a document to a thematic category and sentiment analysis that is assigning a word occurrence to a sense identifier.

As we have already discussed in chapter 1, ambiguity is a crucial issue of NLP. Ambiguity problems can also be modelled as classification.

She saw the band as she danced. ~~NN~~ NN ~~JJ~~ VB ~~VB~~ VB	Morpho-Syntactic Ambiguity	POS Tagging
She saw the board as she danced. ~~(like governing band)~~ (like bulletin band)	Semantic or Lexical Ambiguity	Word Sense Disambiguity
She saw the boy (with the telescope)$_{PP}$ attached as PP to saw not to boy.	Syntactic Ambiguity	PP Attachment Disambiguation

Figure 2.5: Ambiguity Resolution as Classification Problems

In Figure 2.5 we can see that the three ambiguity issues namely morpho–syntactic ambiguity (POS tagging), lexical semantic ambiguity (Word sense disambiguation) and syntactic ambiguity (PP attachment disambiguation) can be viewed as classification problems.

Machine Learning Algorithms for Classification: In this section we will discuss some of the machine learning algorithms used for classification problems in NLP. The details of text classification will be discussed in Chapter 3. Supervised learning algorithms which require hand–classified training data represented as feature vectors are commonly used for classification. These include k-Nearest Neighbors (simple, powerful), Naïve Bayes, Support Vector Machines (SVM) and Decision trees. Many commercial systems often use a mixture of these algorithms. **K-nearest neighbours (k-NN)** is a pattern recognition algorithm that uses training datasets to find the k closest neighbours and then label of closest matches to classify new samples. **Naïve Bayes algorithm** is a probabilistic classifier that is based on Bayes' theorem. Naïve Bayes uses probability to predict the tag of a text based on prior knowledge and the assumption of "naive" independence between the variables (features or in our case words). It calculates the probability of each tag for a given text, and then predicts the tag with the highest probability. **Support Vector Machines (SVM)** is a classification algorithm that determines the best decision boundary between vectors that belong to a given group (or category) and vectors that do not belong to it. **A decision tree** is a supervised learning algorithm that is good for classification problems as we can see *exactly* how decisions are made. Decision Trees are known for their simplicity and interpretation, but they are limited in their power to learn complicated rules and to scale to large data sets. We will be discussing how these, and other algorithms are used for text classification in Chapter 3.

Hidden Markov model (HMM) is typical machine learning algorithm used when NLP tasks use a sequence of words to discover a sequence of hidden states that is POS tags in the case of POS tagging or entity class in the case of Named entity recognition. We will take the example of POS tagging which is a task of labelling each word in a sentence with its appropriate part of speech. HMMs are so called because it relies on the assumption that the events we observe depend on some internal factors or states, which are not directly observable. In other words, HMM has two parts: hidden and observed. The hidden part consists of hidden states which are not directly observed, their presence is observed by observation symbols that hidden states emits. The Hidden Markov Model constructs an inference model based on the assumptions of a Markov process. The Markov process assumption simply states that the "future is independent of the past given the present". In other words, assuming we know our present state, we do not need any other historical information to predict the future state and this process explain how we model the changes of the hidden states through time. In POS tagging we predict a sequence of POS tags (hidden variables) based on the sequence of words (observed variables). We will discuss POS tagging and HMM in detail in succeeding chapters. Another class of NLP tasks is one where **probabilistic technique** are used to generate parse trees from a sequence of words and a grammar of the language. Probabilistic learning methods are also used to find the correspondence between words, sentences and paragraphs of a source text and its translation.

Unsupervised Machine Learning for NLP: Similar documents are grouped together using clustering techniques. Hierarchical classification can then be used to sort the clusters obtained based on importance or relevance. Latent Semantic Indexing (LSI) is another unsupervised machine learning technique developed in the 1980s in order to make information retrieval more accurate. It discovers statistical co-occurrence of words or phrases that frequently by identifying the hidden contextual relationships between words. We will discuss in detail some of the important machine learning techniques used for typical NLP tasks in the succeeding chapters.

2.7 Need for Deep Learning for NLP

In recent years, as far as NLP is concerned there has been a shift from paradigm shift from traditional machine learning methods to neural network based deep learning methods. Let us discuss the main reasons of why deep learning is suited for NLP, and some of the advantages and challenges in using Deep learning for NLP. In general, machine learning methods like Naive Bayes, SVM relied on the bag of words approach to represent text where neither the grammar nor the ordering of the words in the text are retained. The following are some of the reasons why deep learning is needed for NLP:

- **Learning Representation:** Machine Learning needs hand-crafted features which are often over specified and incomplete and whose generation is time consuming. Moreover, most features need to be redesigned for each specific domain. Therefore, moving from this requirement of hand-crafted features became a necessity with the overwhelming availability of text data. Deep learning provides a very flexible, fairly universal, learnable framework for representing both linguistic and world information. Thus, representation learning, a concept associated with deep learning attempts to automatically learn good features or representations and moreover these learned features are easy to adapt and fast to learn.

- **Need for Distributional Similarity and Distributed Representation:** Current NLP systems are incredibly fragile because of their atomic symbol representation where often one-hot encoding is used to represent the word from a fixed vocabulary and uses a bag-of-words to represent documents where the size of the vocabulary determines the length of the representation resulting in huge sparse vectors. These representations do not provide information about the interactions or similarities between the words. Learned word representations can help enormously in NLP and provide a powerful similarity model for words. While generalizing locally using nearest neighbour like approaches requires representative examples for all relevant variations, using neural networks that parameterize and learn a "similarity" kernel ensures efficiency and thus handle the curse of dimensionality. Distributional similarity-based word clusters greatly help many applications. Distributional representations can also represent multiple levels of similarity in a finite vector space. This distributional representation provides the opportunity for NLP systems to do more complex reasoning tasks.

- **Unsupervised Features and Weight Training:** NLP tasks that use traditional supervised machine learning techniques require labelled data. With the large amount of data now available, unsupervised learning assumes importance since it is often not practical to provide labels for the examples. Deep learning allows learning to be unsupervised. Deep learning helps to make classifications decisions based on models of observed data. Deep learning can learn unsupervised (from raw text) and supervised (with specific labels like positive/negative).

- **Learning Multiple Levels of Representation:** Learning multiple levels of representation to handle increasing complexity is one of the salient points of deep learning. Successive model layers learn deeper intermediate representations. Now, language is composed of words and phrases and recursion is important component of language where the same operator (word feature) may be applied repeatedly on different component (words in sentences). Deep learning is designed to handle recursive nature of input which is the case with human language. Deep learning, specifically recurrent neural models, has the ability to capture this recursive sequential aspect of language.

- **End-to-end Training:** Another major advantage of deep learning for NLP is that it is possible to carry out end-to-end training for an application. The rich representability and information in the data can be encoded in the deep neural network model. For example, by providing a parallel corpus, a neural machine translation model can be constructed almost without any human intervention.

- **Possibility of Multi-Modality:** Using deep learning, it is possible learn the representations of different types of data such as text, image and audio as real valued vectors which in turn makes it is possible to process multi-modal information.

- **Why the Time has come:** Though deep learning has been around for some time, it is only now that applications of deep learning for NLP has become successful. This is mainly because new methods of supervised pre-training, more efficient parameter estimation is available and there is better understanding of parameter regularization. Moreover, the vast amount of textual data enables better deep learning and faster machines with multicore CPUs and GPUs enabling massively parallel computations for faster deep learning.

Now let us discuss some advantages of deep learning methods for NLP. Deep learning is good for pattern recognition problems and is basically data-driven with high performance for many tasks. As discussed, end-to-end training with little or no domain knowledge is possible. Due to uniformity of representation learning, cross-modality is conceivable. After unsupervised representation learning, deep learning mainly uses supervised methods that are more tractable. However, there are many challenges associated with using deep learning for NLP. Basically, deep learning is not very suitable for problems involving inferencing and decision making. Deep learning cannot directly handle symbols — the fundamental unit of language and requires them to be converted to real valued vectors. Deep learning works well with abundant data, and hence does not work well with small data sets. Deep learning model is usually a black box and is difficult to interpret and the computational cost of learning is high. Moreover, unsupervised learning algorithms are still to be developed and theoretical foundations are still to be established.

2.8 Fundamentals of Deep Learning

Deep learning is very effective for pattern learning. Deep learning algorithms derive meaning out of data using a hierarchy of multi-layers that essentially mimic the neural networks of our brain. In other words, if deep learning is provided lots of information, it begins to understand it and respond in useful ways.

Let us first understand the difference between machine learning and deep learning. Machine learning algorithms require that data be described using features that the computer can understand. The machine learning algorithm's job is the optimization of the weights of these features. On the other hand, representation learning attempts to automatically learn good features or representations of increasing complexity or abstraction. The deep learning process learn multiple levels of representative features and then uses the training algorithm to produce the output. (Figure 2.6).

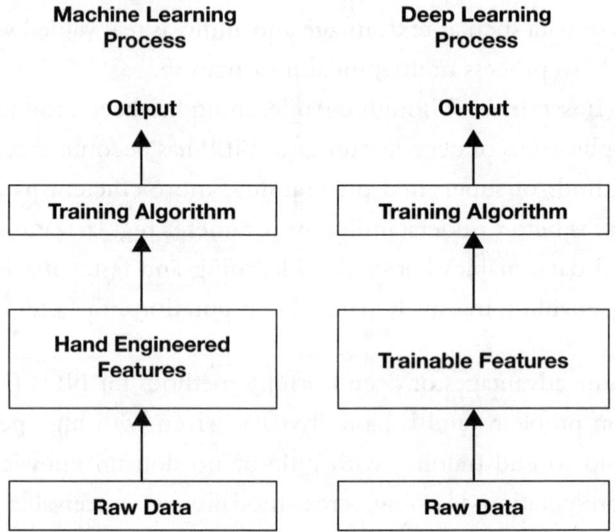

Figure 2.6: Machine Learning and Deep Learning Processes

Deep learning essentially consists of a neural network with several layers of nodes_between input and output. The series of layers between input and output do feature identification and processing in a series of stages, just as our brains seem to. Though neural networks have been around for a long time, it is only now that algorithms have been developed for training multi-layer neural networks and hence the evolution of deep learning. An artificial neuron contains a nonlinear activation function and has several incoming and outgoing weighted connections.

The weighted input is given to the neurons which are trained to filter and detect specific features or patterns, passing it to the outgoing connections. The error signal which is the difference between expected and predicted output is backpropagated to optimize the weights. The deep learning architecture consists of one input layer which essentially accepts the raw basic unit (for example, word), one output layer which essentially outputs the predictions and multiple fully connected hidden layers in between. (Figure 2.7). Each layer is represented as a series of neurons and each hidden layer progressively extracts higher and higher-level features of the input. Thus, deep learning is very good at tasks where the basic unit of information processing (word, pixel) has very little meaning in itself, but the combination of such units has a combined useful meaning. This is similar to how humans first learn simpler concepts and then compose them to represent more abstract ones. Features are automatically learnt and optimally tuned for desired outcome.

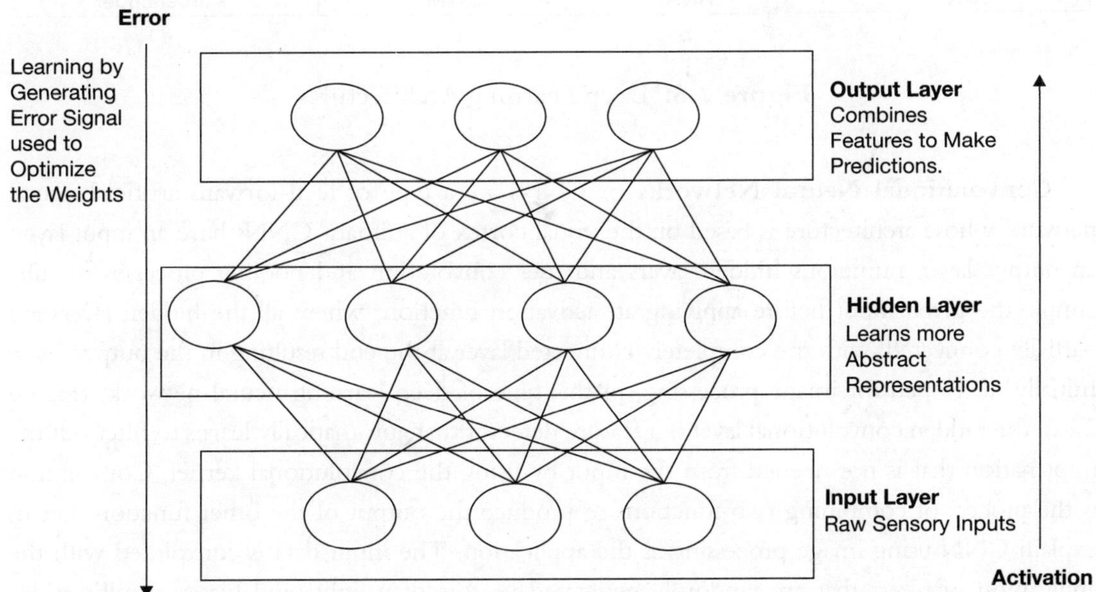

Figure 2.7: Deep Learning Architecture

2.8.1 Types of Deep Learning Models

Convolutional neural networks (CNN), recurrent neural networks (RNN), long short-term memory (LSTM) and autoencoders (Figure 2.8) are some of the deep learning models we will briefly discuss. We will discuss these models in detail in the chapters where these models are used for particular NLP tasks.

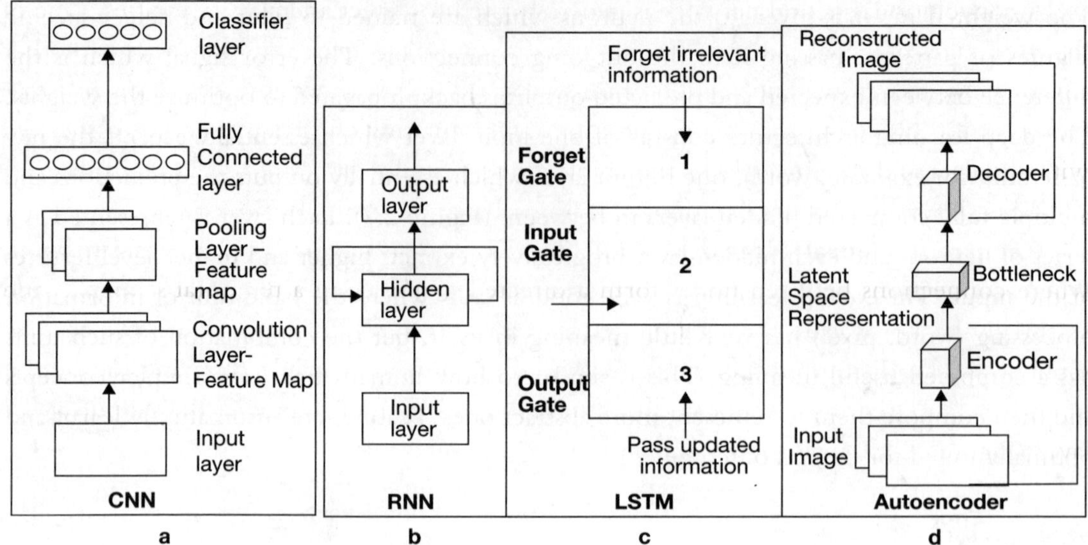

Figure 2.8: Deep Learning Architectures

Convolutional Neural Networks or CNNs are a type of feed-forward artificial neural network whose architecture is based on the visual cortex of animals. CNNs have an input layer, an output layer, numerous hidden layers and uses convolution and pooling processes to sub-sample the given input before applying an activation function, where all the hidden layers are partially connected, with the completely connected layer at the end resulting in the output layer. Initially developed for image processing, in this type of deep learning neural network, (Figure 2.8a), the hidden convolutional layer is a feature detector that automatically learns to filter out the information that is not needed from the input by using the convolutional kernel. Convolution is the process of combining two functions to produce the output of the other function. Let us explain CNN using image processing as the application. The input data is convoluted with the application of filters that are randomly generated vectors of weights and biases, resulting in a feature map. Instead of having individual weights and biases for each neuron, CNN uses the same weights and biases for all neurons. At each step during the convolution, the filter acts on a region in the input data and produces in a single number as output. Combining together the regions for the entire data results in the activation map. Pooling layers compute the maximum or average value of a particular feature over a region of the input data. These layers reduce the scope of mathematical work for future layers, whilst still retaining important information. After a collection of convolution and pooling layers, the last layer is joined and flattened out to be one long neural layer. This is then passed to a fully connected network (an MLP) to reach an output layer.

A convolutional neural network is generally used to detect and classify entities. One of the advantages of CNN is that it is highly accurate for image recognition problems. Another advantage is the automatic detection of important features without any human supervision. However, CNNs do not consider the position and orientation of particular entities associated with the data and moreover lacks the ability to be spatially invariant to the input data. In addition, CNNs need a large amount of training data.

Recurrent Neural Networks or RNNs are a type of feedforward neural network where connections between nodes form a directed graph along a temporal sequence and essentially backpropagate through time. This type of model can learn algorithms to map input sequences to output sequences. RNN works on the principle of saving the output of a particular layer and feeding this back to the input in order to predict the output of the layer (Figure 2.8b). In RNNs, the connections between nodes form a directed graph and can use the internal states (memory) of the nodes to process variable length sequences of inputs. The output vector is influenced by the entire history of inputs where the output from the previous step is fed as input to the current step. The hidden state of RNNs remembers some information about a sequence. Each node in the RNN model acts as a memory cell, continuing the computation and implementation of operations. RNNs use the same parameters for each input as it performs the same task on all the inputs or hidden layers to produce the output. This reduces the complexity of parameters, unlike other neural networks. If the network's prediction is incorrect, then the system self-learns and continues working towards the correct prediction during backpropagation.

Long Short-Term Memory: If the sequence considered is long, then RNN finds it difficult to carry information from a particular time instance to an earlier one because of the vanishing gradient problem. This problem is essentially a situation in which the recurrent neural network (RNN) does not have the ability to propagate useful gradient information from the output end of the model back to the layers near the input end of the model. In order to overcome this problem, the LSTM (Long Short-Term Memory) was designed. This model is a particular type of recurrent neural network composed of cells or LTSM units that consist of a forget gate, an input gate, and an output gate (Figure 2.8c). These cells give the network, memory cells with read, write and reset operations. During training, the network can learn when it should remember data and when data should be thrown away. The cell remembers values over arbitrary time intervals and the three gates regulate the stream of information that enters and exits the cell. This type of deep learning network is useful for modelling of time series data. Just like a simple RNN, an LSTM also has a hidden state where the hidden state of the previous timestamp goes through LSTM cell to obtain the hidden state of the current timestamp.

Deep Autoencoders: Autoencoders are a specific type of feedforward neural networks where the input is the same as the output. Autoencoders are an unsupervised learning technique in which we leverage neural networks for the task of representation learning. The neural network architecture imposes a bottleneck in the network which forces a compressed knowledge representation of the original input. In most situations where some sort of structure exists in the data (i.e., correlations between input features), this structure can be learned and consequently leveraged when forcing the input through the network's bottleneck. This model consists of two symmetrical deep belief networks (Figure 2.8 d). The encoding network learns to compresses the input to a condensed lower-dimensional vector called as latent–space representation. The decoding network can be used to reconstruct the data.

2.9 Deep Learning for NLP

The workflow of Deep learning for NLP is given in Figure 2.9. The words of the text are first converted to word embedding which is distributed representation. We will discuss word embedding representation in detail in subsequent chapters. The deep embedding text representation is taken by the hidden layers for processing to give the output which is then handled as per the NLP application. The behaviour of the hidden layers and output units depends on the deep learning model used.

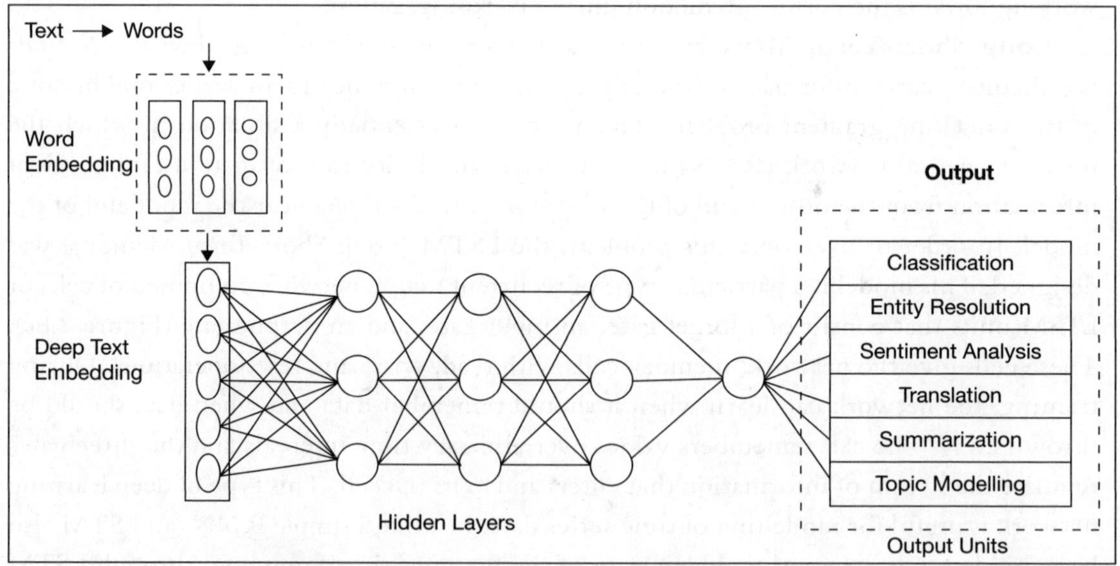

Figure 2.9: Workflow of Deep Learning for NLP

CNN for NLP: In a CNN, a feature function is applied to a sequence of words to extract higher-level features. With the advent of word embeddings with its ability to represent words in a distributed space, the extraction of higher-level features became even more important. The basic CNN can be enhanced to perform word-based predictions such as NER, and POS tagging. The sub-sentence or a window of neighboring words of fixed size is considered and a standalone CNN is applied with the objective of predicting the word leading to word-level classification. The abstract features that are extracted can then be used for various NLP tasks such as sentiment analysis, summarization, machine translation, and question answering.

In order to use CNN, sentences are first tokenized into words, and then into a word embedding matrix. Then, a feature map is produced by applying convolutional filters to all possible window sizes. A *max-pooling* operation that is application of max operation on each filter is carried out to obtain a fixed length output which reduces the dimensionality to obtain the sentence representation.

In general, CNN can cull out semantic clues present in windows of the context. However, they are unable to conserve the sequential order and cannot model long–distance context required for many NLP tasks. Moreover, they are very data heavy models since they include a large number of trainable parameters.

RNN for NLP: RNNs are specialized approaches effective at processing sequential information. A sequence is obtained by applying a complex computation recursively using randomly initialized weights and biases. This sequence is represented as a fixed size vector and fed to the recurrent unit sequentially.

RNNs are effective for processing sequential information thus making it suitable to capture the inherent sequential nature present in language, where the units of information processing are characters, words or even sentences. RNNs provide flexibility and better modeling capability to capture unbounded context, including very long sentences, paragraphs and even documents making it a suitable model for many NLP tasks. Many NLP tasks require semantic modeling over the whole sentence. This involves creating a gist of the sentence in a fixed dimensional hyperspace.

In general, RNNs have been found suitable for different NLP tasks such as language modeling machine translation, image captioning, etc. The ability of RNN to summarize text to a fixed vector made it suitable for tasks such as text summarization.

RNN is also able to perform distributed joint processing based on time and cater to many sequence labeling tasks such as POS tagging, multi-label text categorization, multimodal sentiment analysis and subjectivity detection.

RNN generally takes as input one–hot encodings or word embeddings, however they can also take as input abstract representations obtained from deep learning models such as

CNN. The vanishing gradient_problem is an issue associated with simple RNNs making it difficult to learn and tune parameters. One variant, the long short-term memory (LSTM) networks was introduced to overcome this limitation.

LSTM for NLP: LSTM (Long Short-Term Memory) is widely used for learning sequential data prediction problems. The basic operation of LSTM can be considered to hold the required information and discard the information which is not required or useful for further prediction. LSTMs are predominantly used to learn, process, and classify sequential data because these networks can learn long-term dependencies between time steps of data. LSTM models are widely used nowadays, as they are particularly designed to have a long-term "memory" that is capable of understanding the overall context better than other neural networks affected by the long-term dependency problem. Common LSTM applications include sentiment analysis, language modelling, speech recognition, and video analysis.

Generating natural language, considered a complex NLP task is a natural application of LSTMs. Deep LSTMs have the ability to generate fairly good task-specific text for applications such as machine translation, image captioning, etc. In general, transforming one sequence to another is carried out by the deep LSTM encoder-decoder framework. In this case, one LSTM is used to encode the "source" sequence as a fixed-size vector, which is then used as the initial state of the decoder LSTM. The decoder generates tokens one at a time, while updating its hidden state with the last generated token.

Autoencoders for NLP: An autoencoder is a neural network model that seeks to learn a compressed representation of an input. They are considered an unsupervised learning method, although technically, they are trained using supervised learning methods, referred to as self-supervised. Auto-encoders encode a variable-length input sequence x into a fixed-length vector representation c and to decode c into a variable length sequence y that is trained to resemble the initial input such as in applications such as machine translation.

One useful form is denoising autoencoder which is used to help the network learn representations of the data that are more meaningful to the underlying data's variability. Instead of simply training a network to recall the input it was given, random noise is applied to the input before passing it to the network — the network is still expected to recall the original input, which should force the network to stop picking up on minute details while focusing on the bigger picture. The random noise essentially prevents the network from learning the specifics, ensuring that it generalizes to the important characteristics. One possibility is to with probability p remove a word from the input sentence to minimize the contribution of a single word on the semantics of the sentence. The second is to with probability p add Gaussian noise to all the values of a vector. This trains the encoder to generalize a word to synonyms and other words that fit the context of the sentence.

2.10 Natural Language Processing Tools

Some of the tools used for natural language processing include the following:

- **NLTK** has open-source Python modules, linguistic data and documentation for research and development in natural language processing and text analytics with appropriate data sets and tutorials. The Tool kit has basic data-oriented classes to represent data for NLP and provides infrastructure in the form of task-oriented classes to encapsulate the resources and methods needed to perform a specific task. The Python library provides modules for processing text, classifying, tokenizing, stemming, tagging, parsing, etc.
- **Apache OpenNLP** (http://opennlp.apache.org/) is a machine learning toolkit that provides tokenizers, sentence segmentation, POS tagging, named entity extraction, chunking, parsing, coreference resolution, etc. OpenNLP provides maximum entropy and perceptron-based machine learning. One of the aims of OpenNLP is to provide both pre-built models and annotated text resources for a variety of languages.
- **Stanford NLP** (http://www-nlp.stanford.edu/software/) is a suite of NLP tools that provide word segmentation, part-of-speech tagging, named entity recognition, chunking, parsing, classification, coreference resolution system, sentiment analysis, etc.
- **MALLET –Machine Learning for Language Toolkit** (http://mallet.cs.umass.edu/) is a statistic-based Java package that provides latent dirichlet allocation, document classification, clustering, topic modeling, information extraction, etc.
- **LingPipe** (http://alias-i.com/lingpipe/) finds the names of people, organizations or locations in news, automatically classifies Twitter search results into categories and suggests correct spellings of queries.

Summary

- Introduced the basic approaches to natural language processing.
- Explained the different aspects of natural language analysis and applications.
- Explored the NLP viewed from the learning perspective.
- Outlined the need of machine learning and deep learning for NLP.
- Explained the basics of machine learning and deep learning and their use for NLP.
- Listed the various NLP tools.

Exercises

Suggested Activities

1. Fill the following table to list applications of Natural Language Processing:

Type of NLP task	NLP Units Needed	Mapping Description in Terms of Units	Basic Type of Task
Word sense disambiguation			
Sentiment analysis			
Chatbot			
Co-reference resolution			

2. Give and explain at least 10 NLP tasks required for an educational technology application.

Self-Assessment: Multiple Choice Questions

Give answers with justification for correct and wrong choices:

1. ______________ methods perform NLP tasks using deterministic approaches with fixed hard boundaries
    i.   Machine learning
    ii. Deep learning
    iii. Rule-based

2. ______________ methods are characterized by training using large amounts of labelled data and feature engineering
    i.   Machine learning
    ii. Deep learning
    iii. Rule-based

3. In these methods feature engineering is generally unsupervised
    i.   Machine learning
    ii. Deep learning
    iii. Rule-based

4. Given a string or text s, obtaining the topic of the text or document is
    i.   Text Classification
    ii. Sentiment analysis
    iii. Topic Modelling

5. Question answering can be explained as
    i.   Analyzing a sequence of words s, the appropriate tags t

    ii. Matching, where two strings s_1, s_2 are matched to obtain a real value r.

    iii. Identification of components in a string s_1 to map and link another string s_2.

6. Machine learning methods model language using statistical methods

    i. Able to handle the flexibility associated with the human language.

    ii. Able to learn without feature engineering.

    iii. Able to learn hierarchically.

7. Hyperparameters associated with machine learning

    i. configuration variables that define the function that the learning model learns

    ii. external to the model and their values are not estimated from the data but are often specified by the developer using heuristics.

    iii. set of variables represented as a vector associated with an example.

8. A machine learning model is said to be ______________ if it does not capture the regularities present in the training data.

    i. Overfitted

    ii. Underfitted

    iii. Learning

9. In ______________ learning, the model is trained to obtain the maximum reward possible from a sequence of actions

    i. Supervised learning

    ii. Semi–supervised learning

    iii. Reinforcement learning

10. ______________ is a classification algorithm that determines the best decision boundary between vectors that belong to a given group (or category) and vectors that do not belong to it.

    i. Support Vector Machines

    ii. Decision Trees

    iii. K-nearest neighbours

11. ______________ is designed to handle recursive nature of human language

    i. Decision trees

    ii. Machine learning

    iii. Deep learning

12. ______________ type of model can learn algorithms to map input sequences to output sequences.

    i. CNN

    ii. RNN

    iii. SVM

Self-Assessment: Match the Columns

No		Match	
1.	Machine learning	A	machine learning algorithm commonly used for POS tagging
2.	Deep learning	B	identification of components in a string to map and link to complex structures
3.	Semantic based analysis	C	lacks the ability to be spatially invariant to the input data
4.	Dependency parsing	D	robust, probabilistic based with soft boundaries where the relevant statistics or probabilities are learned from data
5.	Loss function	E	associated with vanishing gradient problem.
6.	Unsupervised learning	F	specific type of feedforward neural networks where the input is the same as the output
7.	Hidden Markov Model	G	named entity recognition, word sense disambiguation
8.	CNN	H	training data does not include the desired output or labels
9.	RNN	I	measures the difference between a predicted label learnt using the learnt model and the true label
10.	Autoencoders	J	learn important features directly from very large corpora thus avoiding feature engineering

Short Questions

1. Differentiate between rule–based, machine learning and deep learning approaches to NLP.
2. Explain the flow of an NLP system for Word Sense Disambiguation and Machine Translation.
3. Discuss the different units and features associated with NLP. Illustrate with any two examples.
4. Explain with mapping and NLP tasks how machine learning can be used for structured prediction.
5. Discuss in detail some examples of sequence labelling tasks of NLP.
6. Justify why machine learning is need for NLP.
7. Discuss the general flow of a machine learning system.

8. Differentiate between the different types of machine learning.
9. Discuss with examples three NLP tasks for which machine learning is suitable.
10. Outline in detail the need for deep learning for NLP.
11. Differentiate between machine learning and deep learning processes.
12. Describe a typical deep learning architecture.
13. Differentiate between CNN, RNN, and LSTM architectures.
14. Explain how LSTM and deep autoencoders are used for NLP tasks.
15. Discuss the salient features of any two NLP tools.

Text Classification

CHAPTER 3

3.1 Introduction – The Classification Problem

Classification from the NLP perspective can be defined as the assignment of documents, or a piece of text to a fixed set of categories. Text classification plays an important role in many NLP tasks. In fact, it is said that most tasks in NLP can be formalized as a classification problem. Typical problems tackled by text classification include assigning subject categories, topics or genres to web pages, spam filtering, prioritizing or folderizing emails, identifying authorship or age or gender of blogs, letters or books and identifying language and analyzing sentiment of reviews or social media text. With the advent of the internet and the ever increasing of text available, classification has become a preliminary step before processing any textual material.

In simple terms classification can be considered as a mapping h from input data x (drawn from the data instance space X) to a label or labels y drawn from the label space Y. In the case of text classification, X is the set of documents and Y is the set of categories where in the case of customer reviews can below to the enumerated set, Y = {very good, good, average, bad}. In this context, some typical text classification or categorization is given in Table 3.1

Task	X	Y
Newspaper Articles	Text	{Politics, Sports, Business, Entertainment}
Language Identification	Text	{English, Hindi, Tamil, Malayalam}
Movie Review Assignment	Text	{Very Good, Good, Average, Bad}
Spam Classification	Email	{Spam, Not Spam}
Web Page Genre Assignment	Web page	{Scientific Article, News Article, Blog}
Book Genre Identification	Text	{Romance, Mystery, Philosophy, History}
Authorship Attribution	Text	{Nora Roberts, Agatha Christie, James Patterson, ...}
Sentiment Analysis	Text	{positive, negative, neutral}

Table 3.1: Examples of Text Classification

Classification can be of three types. Binary classification where each input text is mapped to – exactly to one of two classes. Then we have multi-class classification where each input text is mapped to exactly one of K classes where $K > 2$. Finally, we have multi–label classification where each input text is mapped to N of K classes where $N \geq 1$.

3.2 Supervised Learning and Classification

Text classification is often carried out using supervised learning. Given training data in the form of $<x, y>$ pairs, we need to learn the classification function $f(x)$. Here x is the representation of the text and y is the category of the text. In the case of supervised learning the input is a set of documents along with the category or label and the model learns the function $y = f(x)$ and gives as output the category of a new document (Figure 3.1).

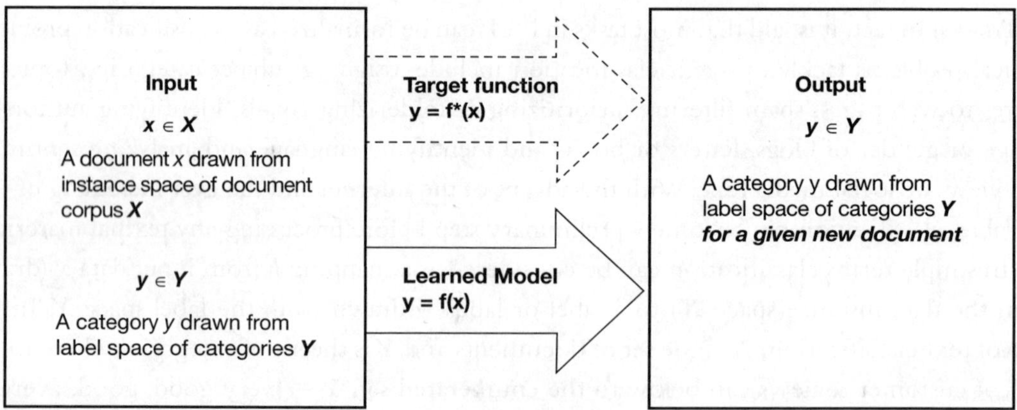

Figure 3.1: Text Classification as Supervised Learning

The classification function that we want to learn consists of the following two components:

- The representation of data
- The structure of the learning method that finds the relationship between the input data and the output category.

Both the above components depend on whether we are using machine learning techniques or deep learning techniques to carry out classification. In this chapter we will discuss vector representations of the text and discuss machine learning methods such as Naïve Bayes and logistic regression and one neural network-based machine learning method- the perceptron used for text classification. In subsequent chapters we will discuss other representations of text as well as deep learning methods for text classification.

Before we go further let us discuss some **NLP datasets.** These datasets include inputs which are usually text and outputs which are usually some sort of annotation. These labelled datasets called gold standard are used for supervised learning in natural language processing. There are many annotated datasets for text classification such as Stanford Sentiment Treebank for sentiment analysis, subjectivity/objectivity sentence classification, binary sentiment analysis of customer reviews and TREC question classification.

3.2.1 Simple Representation of Text

The document can be represented in a feature space as a vector. The simplest method of representing text is the **one-hot encoding** where words of the document are converted into a binary vector of dimension m where m is the number of distinct words in the document. The text is thus represented as a $n \times m$ two-dimensional array where n is the number of words in the text. One of the important disadvantages of one-hot encoding is the sparsity problem where most of the entries in the two-dimensional array are zero. Moreover, each sentence creates vectors of different size depending on the length of the document and there is no way to capture semantics associated with the documents.

The next most commonly used vector-based representation of text is the **Bag of Words** or **BoW** representation where the representation describes the occurrence of words within a document. It is one of the most used text vectorization techniques used in text classification tasks. Bag of Words is similar to one-hot encoding. In the Bag of Words approach we create a vocabulary for the document and we have a single fixed length vector corresponding to the words in a sentence and the entry of each word gives the count of the words in the sentence or document. This representation is called the "bag" of words because any information about order and structure or grammar of the words is the document is not considered. This model represents the presence and count of the known vocabulary words in the document but not where these words in the document. Bag of Words for a sentence and a document is shown in Figure 3.2. Figure 3.2 (a) shows the Bag of Words Vector for a sentence while Figure 3.2 (b) shows the terms or words X document matrix in Bag of Words representation assuming that each document consists of only one sentence. Here we assume that the vocabulary size is 17.

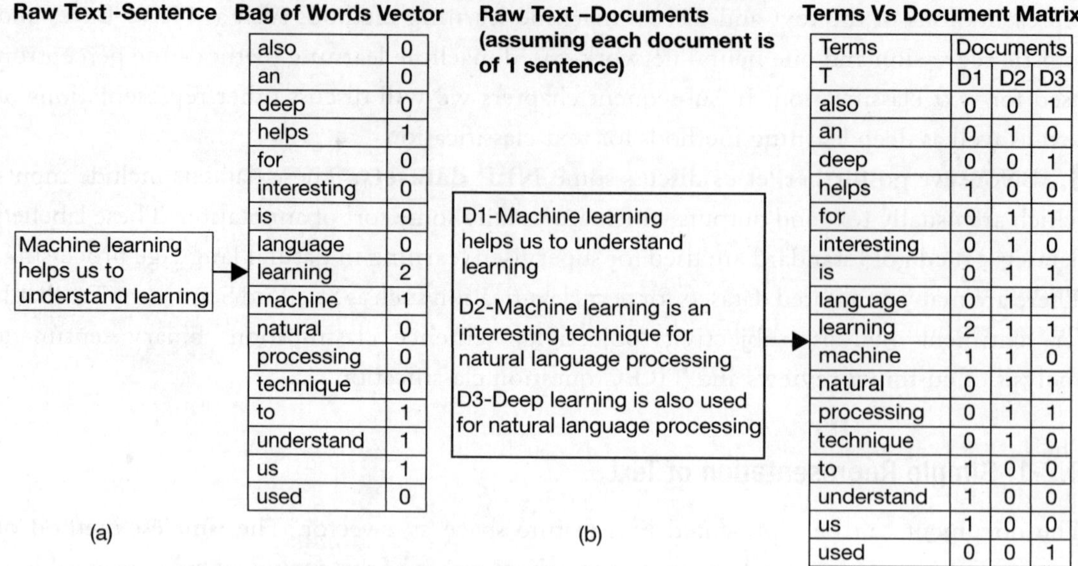

Figure 3.2: Bag of Words Representation

3.2.2 Basis of Supervised Learning Method

As already discussed, the supervised learning algorithm when given a collection of labelled documents, needs to build a model or function that maps hitherto unseen documents to the correct labels or classes. We first discuss two broad approaches to text classification namely generative approaches where a probabilistic model of the data is used and discriminative approaches based on optimizing some error-related criterion. Bayes theorem plays a crucial role in probabilistic learning for text classification. Bayes theorem plays a critical role in probabilistic learning and classification. Here a generative model is built that approximates the production of data. When no information about the words of text is available the categorization is done simply using *prior* probability of each category. Categorization produces a *posterior* probability distribution over the possible categories given the details of the words. Here, we will discuss three classification techniques namely:

- Probabilistic Naïve Bayes which assigns calibrated probability confidence scores to the predictions,
- Discriminative perceptron classification which essentially learns to discriminate correct and incorrect classes, and

- Logistic regression technique which is both discriminative and probabilistic and aims to directly compute the conditional probability of the class. Here we assume in all three cases the documents are represented as Bag of Words.

3.3 Naïve Bayes Algorithm for Text Classification

The Naïve Bayes is a probabilistic classifier where a probability model is defined and the parameters of the model are estimated based on Bayes theorem which is used to convert the observation probability into label probability. The parameters of the probability model are estimated using **maximum likelihood** that is by maximizing the likelihood of the dataset. For document classification Bayes theorem can be stated as given in Figure 3.3a. The posterior probability is determined given likelihood of the document feature vector based on given class, the prior probability of class and probability of the document feature vector. Naïve Bayes text classifier is multinomial that it is a distribution over vector of counts and naively assumes that all words are equally important. One assumption associated with this classifier is that normally the Bag of Words representation is used where the position of the words are not considered important. In addition, Naïve Bayes is called Naïve as it assumes **conditional independence** where the feature probabilities of each word $P(x_i|c)$ are considered independent given the class c.

The classification decision involves finding the class among all the set of classes C with the maximum posterior probability for the given document feature vector. This classification decision C_{MAP} is estimated using the Maximum A Posteriori or MAP (Figure 3.3 (b)). In order to find C_{MAP}, we find the class argmax $c \in C$ which gives the maximum posterior probability given the document feature vector. To find C_{MAP} we first apply Bayes rule and then drop the denominator (Equations 3.1 & 3.2).

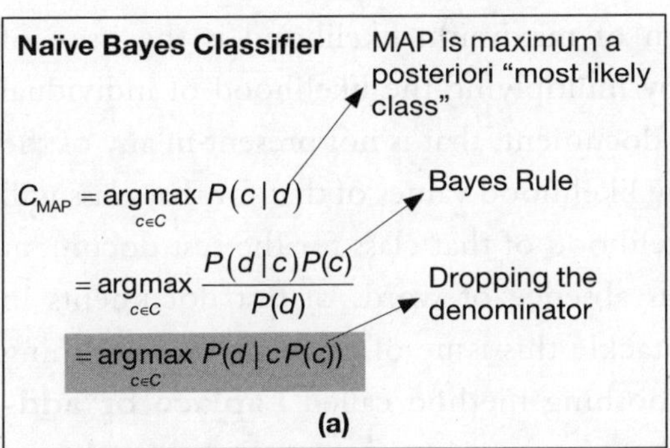

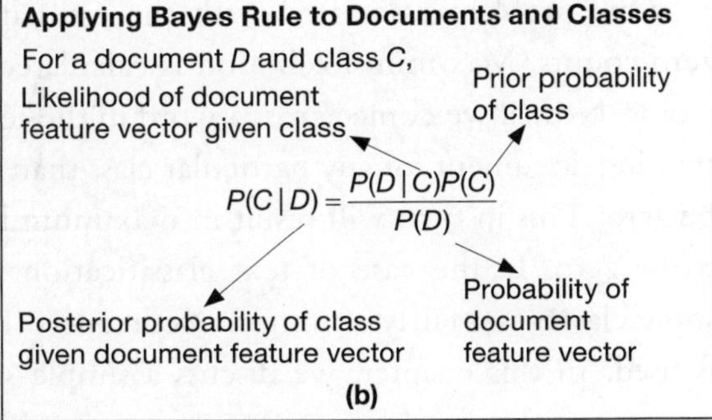

Figure 3.3: Naïve Bayes Classifier

Multinomial Naïve Bayes Classifier

$$C_{MAP} = \arg\max_{c \in C} P(x_1, x_2, \ldots x_n \mid c) P(c). \tag{3.1}$$

$$C_{NB} = \arg\max_{c \in C} P(c_j) \prod_{x \in X} P(X \mid c). \tag{3.2}$$

Multinomial Naïve Bayes Independence Assumptions $P(x_1, x_2, \ldots x_n \mid c)$.

Assumption: Bag of words, position doesn't matter

Conditional Independence: Assume the feature probabilities $P(x_i \mid c_j)$ are independent given the class c (Equation 3.3)

$$P(x_1, x_2, \ldots x_n \mid c) = P(x_1, x_2, \ldots x_n \mid c) \cdot P(x_1 \mid c) \cdot P(x_2 \mid c)$$
$$\cdot P(x_3 \mid c) \cdot \ldots .P(x_n \mid c) \tag{3.3}$$

In a simple case, for estimation of prior probability and maximum likelihood estimates, we use frequencies in the data. Hence the prior probability of a class c_j is defined as the number of documents whose class C is c_j out of the total number of N documents (Equation 3.4)

$$\hat{P}(c_j) = \frac{N(C = c_j)}{N} \tag{3.4}$$

Here the likehood of word (Equation 3.5)

$$\hat{P}(x_i \mid c_j) = \frac{N(X = x_j, C = c_j)}{N(C = c_j)}. \tag{3.5}$$

One problem associated with the estimation of maximum likelihood is the issue of zero counts. Maximim likelihood is calculated by multiplying the likelihood of individual words. Now if we come across a word in the test document, that is not present in any of the training document for any particular class than the likelihood values of that for that class will be zero. This in turn will result in maximum likelihood of that class for the test document to be zero. In the case of text classification this absence of words of test documents in some classes is a fairly common occurrence. To tackle this issue of zero counts smoothing is used. In this chapter, we discuss a simple smoothing method called **Laplace or add-one smoothing** where a value of one is added to any zero counts to avoid the value of maximum likelihood being zero.

Example 3.1 Text Classification Using Naïve Bayes Algorithm

Let us discuss this with a simple example where we deal with extermely small documents.

Document No.	Type	Text	Class
D1	Training	Good happy Good	Positive
D2	Training	Good good Service	Positive
D3	Training	Good friendly	Positive
D4	Training	Lousy good cheat	Negative
D5	Test	Good good good cheat lousy	??

Figure 3.4: Set of Training and Test Documents

Prior Probabilities of positive and negative docuements are (Figure 3.4):

P(pos) = Total number of postive documents / Total number of documents = 3/4 and

P(neg) = Total number of negative documents / Total number of documents = 1/4.

Now we have to find likelihood of each word in positive documents and negative documents respectively. Given the words in the test document *good, cheat and lousy*, we need to determine the likelihood for each of these words when the class is positive and negative, respectively. Here we add one to each value as a smoothing value which we will explain later. As seen in the above example, "cheat" and "lousy" are not present in any training document that is classified as positive. In this case the likelihood of the words "cheat" and "lousy" will be zero in positive case and these zero probabilities cannot be conditioned away where the resulting posterior probability of the postive case will be zero. In order to avoid this issue, in this example we have introduced the add-one smoothing.

The denominator in each case sums the total number of words in all positive/negative documents and the number of words in text document +one respectively.

- P(good/pos) = (5 + 1)/(8 + 6) = 3/7 and P(good/neg) = (1 + 1)/(3 + 6) = 2/9
- P(cheat/pos) = (0 + 1)/(8 + 6) = 1/14 and P(cheat/neg) = (1 + 1)/(3 + 6) = 2/9
- P(lousy/pos) = (0 + 1)/(8 + 6) = 1/14 and P(lousy/neg) = (1 + 1)/(3 + 6) = 2/9

Now we can calculate the posterior probability of the test document being positive

$$P(\text{pos}/D5) = P(\text{pos}) * (P(\text{good/pos}) * P(\text{cheat/pos}) * P(\text{lousy/pos})$$
$$= 3/4 * 3/7 * 1/14 * 1/14 = 0.0003$$

Similarly, we can calculate the posterior probability of the test document being negative

$$P(neg/D5) = P(neg) * (P(good/neg) * P(cheat/neg) * P(lousy/neg)$$
$$= 1/4 * 2/9 * 2/9 * 2/9 = 0.0001$$

The posterior probability of the class of the test document is the class that gives maximum value and in this case it is the positive class

3.3.1 Advantages and Disadvantages of Naïve Bayes Text Classifier

Naïve Bayes classifier is simple to implement since there is no numerical optimization or matrix operations involved. It is efficient to train and use, can be esily updated with new data and can tackle both binary and multi–class text classification. For the above reasons it is considered a dependable baseline for text classification. One of the main disadvantages of this classifier is the assumption that features are independent of each other.

3.4 Perceptron for Text Classification

Naïve Bayes naively ignores dependencies between words, and treats every word as equally informative but discriminative classifiers avoid this problem by not attempting to model the "generative" probability. Perceptron classifier is error–driven and do not make the independence assumption. The perceptron is a binary classifier that tries to find the hyperplane that separates instances of samples belonging to the two classes if such a hyperplane exists.

The perceptron learning process is as follows:

1. *The input used for training is a set of documents D_{train} = $\{(x_1, y_1), (x_2, y_2), \ldots \ldots (x_M, y_M)\}$ where $x_1, x_2, \ldots \ldots x_M$ are the documents and $y_1, y_2, \ldots \ldots y_M$ are the associated classes of the documents. Let us assume that $\phi(x_1), \phi(x_2), \ldots \ldots \phi(x_M)$ are the bag of words representing each document.*

2. *Initially we set weight $w = 0$*

3. *Then for each pair (x, y) we predict the class $y' = sign(w.\phi(x))$*
   If $y' \neq y$
   / if prediction is not correct, then decrease the weights for the features of the true label*/*
   then update $w = w - \phi(x)$
   / else if prediction is correct, increase the weights for the features of the predicted label*/*
   else update $w = w + \phi(x)$
   *return w /*Repeat until all training instances are correctly classified or we run out of time*/*

Perceptron is a type of classifier that can be viewed as the process of minimizing a loss function on the weights. Such a loss function should be a good proxy for the accuracy of the classifier and must be easy to optimize.

3.5 Logistic Regression for Text Classification

Logistic regression is a supervised machine learning algorithm used for classification. Two functions are normally used namely logistic function and sigmoid function. Logistic regression can be classified as binomial where the classes are only two, multinomial when there are three or more classes and ordinal when the categories are ordered such as "very good," "good," "poor," and "very poor."

As already discussed, logistic regression is a discriminative classifier and finds the class c among the set of all classes C that has the maximum posterior probability given the document d (Equation 3.6).

$$\hat{C} = \arg\max_{c \in C} P(c \mid d) \qquad\qquad 3.6$$

Logistic regression consists of two phases, the training phase where we learn weights w and the bias b using stochastic gradient descent and cross–entropy loss and the testing phase where given a test example t we compute the probability of the output label given the text sample t using learned weights w and bias b, and returns the output label which has the higher probability. As is the case with any text classification algorithm, we assume that the document is represented using bag of words or features. In logistic regression, for each feature x_i, the weight w_i gives the importance of feature x_i. Therefore, the logistic regression for one document x consists of

- Input observation: Feature vector $x = [x_1, x_2, ..., x_n]$ corresponding to one document
- Weights: one per feature: $\hat{W} = [w_1, w_2, ..., w_n]$ associated with each feature of the vector
- Output: a predicted class $\hat{Y} \in \{0,1\}$ in case of binary classification or $\hat{Y} \in \{0, 1, 2, ... m\}$ in case of multinomial logistic regression

In the case of binary classification, we will sum up all the weighted features and add the bias (Equation 3.7)

$$Z = \sum_{i=1}^{n} W_i X_i + b \qquad\qquad 3.7$$

$$z = w.x + b$$

If this sum z is high, we say $y = 1$; if low, then $y = 0$. However, this sum z is not a probability and needs to be converted to probability that we need to use a function of z that gives a value from 0 to 1.

After computing $z = w.x + b$ we pass it through a sigmoid function that is $\sigma\left(w.x + b\right)$ and treat it as a probability (Equation 3.8)

$$P\left(y = 1\right) = \sigma\left(w.x + b\right) = \frac{1}{1 + e^{-\left(w.x+b\right)}} \qquad 3.8$$

Now we need to turn the probability into a classifier with 0.5 being the decision boundary as (Equation 3.9):

$$\hat{y} = \begin{cases} 1 & if \ P(y = 1 \,|\, x) > 0.5 \\ 0 & otherwise \end{cases} \qquad 3.9$$

The sigmoid or logistic function and is shown in Figure 3.5

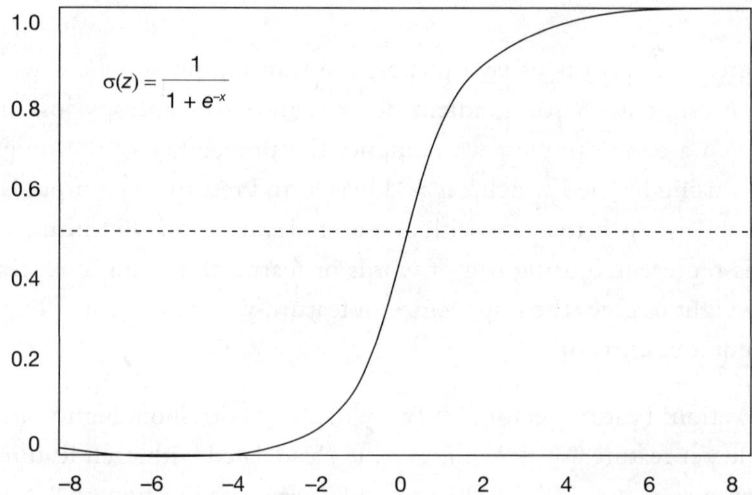

Figure 3.5: The Sigmoid or Logistic Function of the Probabilitic Classifier

In this supervised learning task, we are given the correct label y for each input value x, but however the method gave only an estimate of y, $\hat{y}$. Now we need to learn the parameters w and b in order to minimize the distance between our estimated value $\hat{y}$ and the true value y. Therefore, we need:

- A distance estimator that is a **loss function** or a **cost function** in our case we define the **cross–entropy loss** and
- An optimization algorithm to update w and b so as to minimize the loss. Here we use the **stochastic gradient algorithm** for optimization.

Cross-entropy Loss: In other words, the distance estimator defines how far the estimated classifier output $\hat{y} = \sigma(w \cdot x + b)$ is from the true output y (which is either 0 or 1). A measure of distance between the classifier prediction and true label for a given set of parameters is called the loss or cost function:

$L(\hat{y}, y)$ = how much $\hat{y}$. differs from the true y

A loss function that is used for logistic regression and many other neural network algorithms is the cross-entropy loss function based on the intuition of negative log likelihood loss. In other words, we want to maximize probability of the correct label $p(y|x)$ as (Equation 3.10)

$$\log p\left(y \mid x\right) = \log\left[\hat{y}^{y}\left(1 - \hat{y}\right)^{1-y} \right] = y \log \hat{y} + (1 - y)\log\left(1 - \hat{y}\right) \qquad 3.10$$

Now we flip the sign to turn this maximization into a loss that is converting it to a minimization requirement. This in turn is the **cross-entropy loss** which we need to minimize (Equation 3.11)

$$L_{CE}\left(\hat{y}, y\right) = -\log p\left(y \mid x\right) = -\left[y \log \hat{y} + \left(1 - y\right)\log\left(1 - \hat{y}\right) \right] \qquad 3.11$$

By substituting for $\hat{y}$ as. $\sigma(w \cdot x + b)$ we get the cross-entropy lost to minimize as (Equation 3.12)

$$L_{CE}\left(\hat{y}, y\right) = -\left[y \log \sigma\left(w.x + b\right) + \left(1 - y\right)\log\left(1 - \sigma\left(w.x + b\right)\right) \right] \qquad 3.12$$

Stochastic Gradient Optimization: Our goal is to minimize the loss. In the case of logistic regression having a convex loss function there is only one minimum. Gradient of a function is a vector pointing in the direction of the greatest increase in a function. After finding the gradient of the loss function at the current point, gradient descent strives to move in the opposite direction. Gradient function is always guaranteed to discover the minimum for a convex function such as logistic regression. The slope is the derivative of the cross-entropy loss given as (Equation 3.13):

$$\frac{\partial L_{CE}\left(\hat{y}, y\right)}{\partial w_j} = \left[\sigma\left(w.x + b\right) - y \right] x_j \qquad 3.13$$

The value of the gradient (slope in our example) $\dfrac{d}{dw} L\big(f\left(x; w \right), y \big)$ is usually weighted by a **learning rate** η. Higher the learning rate, the faster w moves.

Let us define the loss function as parameterized by weights $\theta = (w, b)$ and then represent output $\hat{y}$ as $f(x; \theta)$ thus showcasing the dependence on θ. Averaged over all the samples, the weights need to be selected so as to minimize the loss (Equation 3.14):

$$\hat{\theta} = \arg\min_{\theta} \sum_{i=1}^{m} L_{CE}\left(f\left(x^{(i)}; \theta \right), y^{(i)} \right)$$

3.14

The gradient is a vector that describes the direction of the sharpest slope of each dimension. In this way the direction of movement in the N-dimensional space of N parameters (θ) is determined.

Steps of the Stochastic Gradient Function

Given the set x of m training inputs $\{x^{(1)}, x^{(2)}, \ldots\ldots x^{(m)}\}$ and the associated set y $\{y^{(1)}, y^{(2)}, \ldots\ldots y^{(m)}\}$ of training m outputs or labels and defining L as the loss function and f as the function parameterized by θ, the stochastic gradient function returns θ.

1. *We first set $\theta \leftarrow 0$*
2. *For each training tuple $(x^{(i)}, y^{(i)})$ taken in random order*

    a. *Compute $\widehat{y(i)} = f(x^{(i)}, \theta)$*   */* computing estimated output */*

    b. *Compute the loss $L\,(\widehat{y(i)},\, y^{(i)})$ /* the difference between the estimated output*

    $\widehat{y(i)}$, *and the true output $y^{(i)}$ */*

    c. *$g \leftarrow \nabla_{\theta}\, L(f(x^{(i)}, \theta),\, y^{(i)})$*   */* How should we move θ to maximize loss */*
    d. *$\theta \leftarrow \theta - \eta\, g$*   */* Move in the opposite direction */*
3. *Now we consider the next training tuple until we have considered all training samples.*
4. *Finally return θ.*

The stochastic gradient function starts with an initial value of θ and an input to find and computes an estimated output. It then computes the loss between this estimated output and the true output and then determines the direction we need to move θ to maximize loss. We now move in the opposite direction with a learning rate η. We continue until all the training samples have been tackled and then return the final θ.

3.6 Evaluation of Text Classification

Normally in the evaluation setup for text classification, the data is split into separate sets such as training, and test sets. However, a better method is to have k-fold cross validation where the data is split into k disjoint sets of equal size. Then k experiments are carried out using set I of class c to test and remainder which is a union of all equivalent classes of c to train. This gives the average, maximal and minimal accuracies. When there is a need to compare the performance of classifiers it is important to use the same test and training data with the same classes.

3.6.1 Evaluation Metrics

There are some common metrics used for evaluating text classification.

Given the input data, the job of classification is to predict the class labels associated with the documents. While in binary classification, we deal with only two possible output classes, in multiclass classification, we deal with more than two possible classes. Accuracy, confusion matrix, precision and recall are some of the most common metrics used for document classification.

We will first describe the confusion matrix which is a $n \times n$ matrix (where n is the number of classes) based on which the performance of a classification model can be described given test documents and associated known true output. Each row in the confusion matrix represents an actual class whereas each column represents a predicted class. A confusion matrix for two classes (binary classification) C and $\neg C$ (is shown in Figure 3.6. Here we assume that the documents belong to class C or not.

Suppose we are classifying documents as belonging to class C or not belonging to class C. When performing classification predictions, there are four types of outcomes that could occur (Figure 3.7):

True Positive (TP): When you correctly predict a document belongs to class C and it actually does belong to that class.

True Negative (TN): When you correctly predict a document does not belong to class C and it actually does not belong to that class.

False Positive (FP): When you falsely predict that a document belongs to class C but it actually does not belong to that class.

False Negative (FN): When you falsely predict that a document does not belong to class C but it actually does belong to that class.

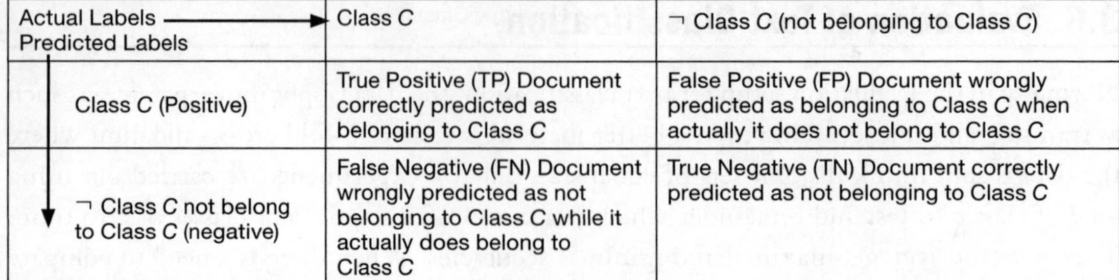

Actual Labels ⟶ Predicted Labels	Class C	¬ Class C (not belonging to Class C)
Class C (Positive)	True Positive (TP) Document correctly predicted as belonging to Class C	False Positive (FP) Document wrongly predicted as belonging to Class C when actually it does not belong to Class C
¬ Class C not belong to Class C (negative)	False Negative (FN) Document wrongly predicted as not belonging to Class C while it actually does belong to Class C	True Negative (TN) Document correctly predicted as not belonging to Class C

Figure 3.6: Confusion Matrix – Binary Classification Example

Now given the above confusion matrix, we will discuss the various evaluation metrics.

Accuracy

The first metric is accuracy. Accuracy focuses on True positive and True Negative and gives the fraction of predictions that are correct. Formally, accuracy is defined as given in equation:

Accuracy = Number of correctly classified documents / Total number of documents

In terms of confusion matrix, accuracy is defined as given in Figure 3.7

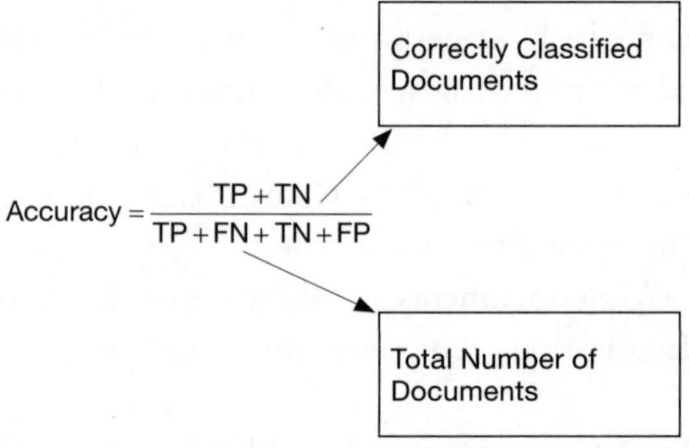

Figure 3.7: Accuracy

Thus, accuracy defines the fraction of documents in the test set that are classified correctly.

Recall (True Positive Rate)

Recall gives the fraction we correctly classified as belonging to class C out of all documents actually belonging to class C (given in Figure 3.8) or in other words indicates how precise we are during classification.

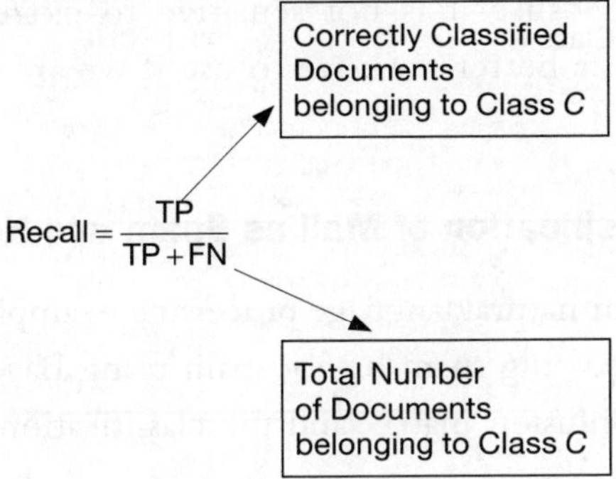

$$Recall = \frac{TP}{TP + FN}$$

Figure 3.8: Recall

Precision

Precision gives the fraction we correctly classified as belonging to class C out of all documents that were classified as belonging to class C by the classification algorithm (given in Figure 3.9) or in other words indicates how good we are at classification.

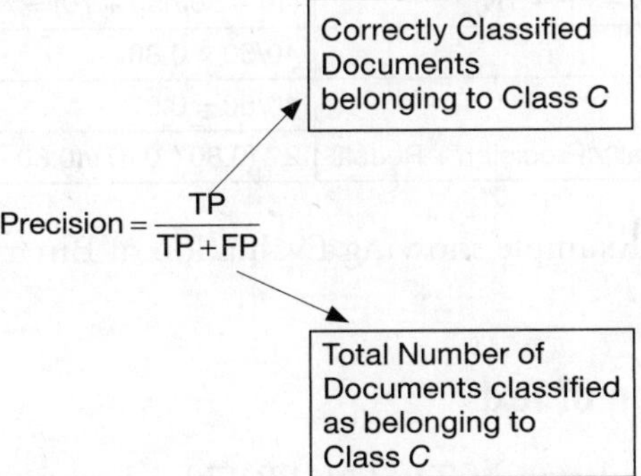

$$Precision = \frac{TP}{TP + FP}$$

Figure 3.9: Precision

F1 Score

When we want to compare different models with different precision-recall values, we need to combine precision and recall into a single metric to compute the performance. F1 Score is defined as the harmonic mean of precision and recall and is given in Figure 3.10.

$$F1\ Score = 2 * \frac{Precision * Recall}{Precision + Recall}$$

Figure 3.10: F1 Score

Harmonic mean is used because it is not sensitive to extremely large values, unlike simple averages. F1 score is a better measure to use if we are seeking a balance between Precision and Recall.

Example 3.2 Binary Classification of Mail as Spam and Not Spam

Let us consider a very popular natural language processing example of text classification where we need to classify a mail as being spam or not spam using Bayes theorem stated in Figure 3.3a. The corresponding confusion matrix and the classification metrics is shown in Figure 3.11.

Example 3.2		Actual Values		
Predicted Classification		Spam	Not Spam	Total
	Spam	TP = 40	FP = 20	(TP + FP) 60
	Not Spam	FN = 10	TN = 50	(FN + TN) 60
	Total	(TP + FN) 50	(FP + TN) 70	120
Email Classification as Spam and not Spam – Evaluation Metrics				
Accuracy = (TP + TN)/(TP + FN + FP + TN)		(40 + 50)/(50 + 70) = 75%		
Recall = TP/(TP + FN)		40/50 = 0.80		
Precision = TP/(TP + FP)		40/60 = 0.67		
F1 Score = 2 * (Precision * Recall)/(Precision + Recall)		2 * (0.80 * 0.67)/(0.80 + 0.67) = 0.73		

Figure 3.11: Example showing Evaluation of Binary Classification

3.6.2 Multi-Classification of Text

Let us now discuss the calculation of TP, TN, FP, FN values for a particular class in a multi class scenario. Here **TP** is the value in the cell of the matrix when actual and predicted class are the same. **FN** is the sum of values of corresponding rows of the class except the TP value while FP is the sum of values of corresponding column except the TP value. On the other hand, **TN** is the sum of values of all columns and row except the values of that class that we are calculating the values for.

Example 3.3 Multi-Classification of Movie Reviews

Let us consider an example where texts about movie reviews are to be classified to indicate movies as Good, Average and Poor. The corresponding confusion matrix and the classification metrics is shown in Figure 3.12.

Example 3.3		Actual Classes		
		Good	Average	Poor
Predicted Classes	Good	25	20	5
	Average	5	50	10
	Poor	5	20	20
Multi-Classification Values				
Good	TP = 25	FN = 20 + 5 = 25	FP = 5 + 5 = 10	TN = 50 + 10 + 20 + 20 = 100
Average	TP = 50	FN = 5 + 10 = 15	FP = 20 + 20 = 40	TN = 5 + 5 + 10 + 20 = 40
Poor	TP = 20	FN = 5 + 20 = 25	FP = 5 + 10 = 15	TN = 5 + 5 + 50 + 20 = 80
Multi-Classification of Movie Reviews-Evaluation Metrics				
	Accuracy = (TP + TN)/ (TP + FN + FP + TN)	Recall = TP/(TP + FN)	Precision = TP/(TP + FP)	F1 Score = 2 * (Precision * Recall)/(Precision + Recall)
Good	78.13%	0.5	0.71	0.59
Average	62.07%	0.77	0.55	0.64
Poor	71.43%	0.44	0.57	0.51

Figure 3.12: Confusion Matrix and Multi-Classification Metrics of Movie Reviews

3.6.3 Macro-Average and Micro-Average

There are two methods of aggregating precision and recall across classes. In the **macro–average** we average the precision or recall over all K classes without taking into consideration how common each class is. Macro–average is useful if performance of all classes is considered equally significant.

Example 3.4 Macro-Average and Micro-Average

Considering example 3.2 and the corresponding evaluation metrics shown in Figure 3.12, macro–average recall and macro–average precision are as follows:

$$\textbf{Macro–average Recall} = (0.5 + 0.77 + 0.44)/3 = 0.57$$
$$\textbf{Macro–average Precision} = (0.71 + 0.55 + 0.57)/3 = 0.61$$

In the case of **micro–average,** we average the precision over all the items without taking into consideration the class that the items belong to. Micro–average is useful if performance of all items is considered equally significant. As before, taking example 3.2 and the corresponding evaluation metrics shown in Figure 3.12, micro–average recall and macro–average precision are as follows:

Micro-average Recall = Sum of TP of all items / Sum of (TP +FN) of all items
$$= 25 + 50 + 20/((25 + 50 + 20) + (25 + 15 + 25)) = 95/160 = 0.59$$

Micro-average Precision = Sum of TP of all items / Sum of (TP +FP) of all items
$$= 25 + 50 + 20/((25 + 50 + 20) + (10 + 40 + 15)) = 95/160 = 0.59$$

Summary

- Introduced the basic concept of classification.
- Explained the different aspects of supervised learning for text classification.
- Described some simple representations of text.
- Outlined the Naïve Bayes algorithm for text classification.
- Explained the use of perceptron for text classification.
- Discussed how logistic regression is used for text classification and how stochastic gradient is used for optimization in this context.
- Outlined the different measures used for evaluating text classification.

Exercises

Suggested Activities

1. Fill the following table to list the context where text classification can be used.

Type of NLP Task	NLP Units Considered	Description of Text Classification Task
Word sense disambiguation		
Sentiment analysis		
Chatbot		
Question Answering		
Information Retrieval		

2. Give and explain at least 5 specific Text Classification tasks used in each of the following text classification tasks:
   a. Educational Technology
   b. Banking
   c. Human Resource Management

3. Case Study- Sentiment Analysis on Movie Reviews: Using IMDb movie reviews (https://www.kaggle.com/datasets/lakshmi25npathi/imdb-dataset-of-50k-movie-reviews), classify movie reviews as positive or negative sentiment using bag-of words and a Naïve Bayes classifier.

Self-Assessment: Multiple Choice Questions

Give answers with justification for correct and wrong choices:

1. ______________ is an annotated dataset available for text classification.
   i. Stanford Sentiment Treebank
   ii. Amazon Mechanical Turk
   iii. Penn Treebank

2. ______________ is a vector-based representation of text.
   i. One-hot embedding
   ii. Bag of words
   iii. Rule-based

3. Characteristics of Bag of Words representation
   i. Fixed length, maintains order of words.
   ii. Variable length, does not maintain order of words.
   iii. Fixed length, does not maintain order of words.

4. Probabilistic Naïve Bayes
    i. learns to discriminate correct and incorrect classes.
    ii. assigns calibrated probability confidence scores to the predictions.
    iii. directly computes the conditional probability of the class.

5. Perceptron
    i. learns to discriminate correct and incorrect classes.
    ii. assigns calibrated probability confidence scores to the predictions.
    iii. directly computes the conditional probability of the class.

6. The parameters of the probability model of Naïve Bayes model are estimated
    i. using maximum a priori
    ii. using only prior probability of class
    iii. using likelihood of the document feature vector

7. The perceptron is a binary classifier that
    i. makes the conditional independence assumption.
    ii. fits a probability model to the instances of the classes
    iii. finds the hyperplane that separates instances of samples belonging to the two classes.

8. The sum of the weighted features and the bias is converted to a probability using
    i. Tan function
    ii. Linear function
    iii. Sinusoid function

9. An optimization algorithm to update w and b so as to minimize the loss in the case of logistic regression is
    i. Linear Programming
    ii. Stochastic Gradient Descent
    iii. Simulated Annealing

10. Cross-entropy loss is a distance measure used by
    i. Logistic Regression
    ii. Naïve Bayes
    iii. Perceptron

11. Gradient descent finds the gradient of the
    i. loss function at the current point and moves in the same direction.
    ii. loss function at the current point and moves in the opposite direction.
    iii. gain function at the current point and moves in the opposite direction.

12. In a confusion matrix, False Positive (FP) is
    a. When you predict that a document belongs to class C but it actually does not belong to that class.

    i. When you predict that a document does not belong to class C but it actually does belong to that class.

    ii. When you predict a document does not belong to class C and it actually does not belong to that class.

13. Recall

    i. gives the fraction of correctly classified documents as belonging to class C out of the total number of documents.

    ii. gives the fraction of correctly classified as belonging to class C out of all documents that were classified as belonging to class C by the classification algorithm.

    iii. gives the fraction of all documents correctly classified as belonging to class C out of all documents actually belonging to class C.

14. Precision

    i. gives the fraction of correctly classified documents as belonging to class C out of the total number of documents.

    ii. gives the fraction of correctly classified as belonging to class C out of all documents that were classified as belonging to class C by the classification algorithm.

    iii. gives the fraction of all documents correctly classified as belonging to class C out of all documents actually belonging to class C.

15. Macro–average is

    i. useful if performance of all classes is considered equally significant.

    ii. useful if performance of all items is considered equally significant.

    iii. useful if performance of one class is considered significant.

Self-Assessment: Match the Columns

No		Match	
1.	Text Classification	A	assigns ranked probability confidence scores to the classes
2.	Authorship Attribution	B	average the precision over all the items without taking into consideration the class that the items belong to
3.	BoW Representation	C	defined as the assignment of documents, or a piece of text to a fixed set of categories
4.	Naïve Bayes	D	finds the class c among the set of all classes C that has the maximum posterior probability given the document d
5.	Laplace Smoothing	E	is an example of Multiclass classification

No		Match	
6.	Perceptron Classifier	**F**	gives the fraction we correctly classified as belonging to class C out of all documents actually belonging to class C
7.	Logistic Regression	**G**	a single fixed length vector giving the count of the words in the text without considering the order
8.	Cross-entropy Loss	**H**	adds a value of one to any zero counts to avoid the value of maximum likelihood being zero
9.	Recall	**I**	is error-driven and do not make the independence assumption
10.	Micro-averaging	**J**	is a distance estimator between our estimated label and the true label

Short Questions

1. How do we define text classification? Give an illustrative example.
2. What are the components of a text classification function? Discuss.
3. Describe and outline the characteristics of Bag of Words representation using an illustrative example.
4. Explain the Naïve Bayes algorithm for text classification.
5. Given the following, find the class of the test document using Naïve Bayes.

Document No.	Type	Text	Class
D1	Training	Bed TV kitchen	Home
D2	Training	TV bed bed printer	Home
D3	Training	Kitchen cook TV computer	Home
D4	Training	Desk printer printer computer	Office
D5	Training	Computer desk desk printer	Office
D6	Test	Bed kitchen desk desk computer printer	??

Figure 3E3.1

6. Why do we need smoothing?
7. Discuss the advantages and disadvantages of using Naïve Bayes algorithm for text classification.
8. Outline the perceptron learning process for text classification.
9. Explain the logistic regression techniques used for text classification.
10. Outline in detail the stochastic gradient optimization procedure.

11. Describe the confusion matrices used for binary classification and multi-classification.

12. Discuss in detail the evaluation metrics - accuracy, recall, precision, and F1-score used for text classification.

13. Explain Macro-Averaging and Micro-Averaging.

14. (a) The following table is given regarding movie reviews (binary – Positive and Negative). Find accuracy, recall, precision, and F1-score measures.

Example E3.2		Actual Values	
		Spam	Not Spam
Predicted Classification	Positive	TP = 70	FP = 30
	Negative	FN = 20	TN = 70

Figure 3E3.2

(b) The following table is given regarding grades (Good, Average and Poor) of students. Find accuracy, recall, precision, and F1-score measures for each of the three classes. Also, find the Macro-average Recall, Macro-average Precision, Micro-average Recall and Micro-average Precision.

Example E3.3		Actual Classes		
		Good	Average	Poor
	Good	45	30	10
Predicted Classes	Average	35	55	15
	Poor	20	10	20

Figure 3E3.3

Language Modelling

4.1 Introduction

A probabilistic approach to model a sequence of words is called a language model. This model indicates the plausibility of occurrence of a specific word sequence. The validity in this context does not refer in any way to grammatical validity but the way people use language, and the language models attempt to learn this usage of language. The job of language models is to find the probability of occurrence of a sentence or a sequence of words, and the purpose is to assign high weights to plausible sequences and can be used to score or rank possible sentences (Equation 4.1):

$$P(W) = P(w_1, w_2, w_3, w_4, \dots w_n) \qquad 4.1$$

Examples include–

- Machine Translation: P(strong winds tonight) > P(large winds tonight)
- Spelling Correction: You are twenty minutes late. P(are twenty minutes late) > P(are twenty minutes lite)

A related task of generating strings can also be defined as (Equation 4.2)

$$P(w_5 \mid w_1 w_2 w_3 w_4) \qquad 4.2$$

A language model uses machine learning to learn the probability distribution over the sequence of words. Language models can also be defined as models that analyze bodies of text data to provide a basis for their word predictions. Learning from a corpus of text and language models can be used for generating original text, predicting the next word in a text and for applications such as machine translation and question answering.

Language models form the backbone of Natural Language Processing. They are a way of transforming qualitative information about text into quantitative information that machines can understand. They have applications in a wide range of core NLP tasks as well as in industries like tech, finance, healthcare, military, etc., and an integral part of any natural language processing application.

There are two types of language models namely probabilistic language models and neural language models. In this chapter we will be dealing with probabilistic language models while in a subsequent chapter we will discuss neural language models. Creating a perfect "language model" is not possible but however approximate probabilistic language models can be constructed which are suitable for many NLP applications.

4.2 Probabilistic Language Modelling

Estimating the probability of a sequence of words is thus the fundamental problem of language modelling. This can be stated as follows (Equation 4.3) where W is the sequence.

$$P(W) = P\left(w_1, w_2, w_3, w_4, \ldots w_n\right) \qquad 4.3$$

Here we assume that the words are taken from a vocabulary consisting of a finite set of discrete symbols such as words or characters.

4.2.1 Estimation of $P(W)$

Now we need to estimate $P(W)$ for which we use the chain rule associated with probability. Conditional probability states that

$P(A_2|A_1) = P(A_1,A_2)/P(A_1)$ for two variables, from which we can derive the joint probability of two variables as $P(A_1,A_2) = P(A_1)\ P(A_2|A_1)$. The above definition can be extended, say for example to four variables as (Equation 4.4)

$$P(A_1,A_2,A_3,A_4) = P(A_1)\ P(A_2|A_1)\ P(A_3|\ A_1,A_2)\ P(A_4|A_1,A_2,A_3) \qquad 4.4$$

Generalizing this concept to n variables we get the chain rule as

$$P(a_1, a_2, a_3, \ldots\ldots\ldots a_n) = P(a_1)\ P(a_2\mid a_1)\ P(a_3\mid a_1, a_2)\ldots\ldots P(a_n\mid a_1, a_2 \ldots\ldots a_{n-2}, a_{n-1})$$

Applying the above chain rule, we can calculate the joint probability of a sequence of n words as (Equation 4.5)

$$P(w_1^n = P\left(w_1\right)P\left(w_2\mid w_1\right)P\left(w_3\mid w_1^2\right)\ldots P\left(w_n\mid w_1^{n-1}\right)$$

$$= \prod_{k=1}^{n} P(w_k\mid w_1^{k-1}) \qquad 4.5$$

How do we estimate these probabilities? One simple way to think of this is by counting the occurences and dividing as follows

Example 4.1:

$$P\left(\text{language}\,|\,\text{unigram is the simplest type of}\right)=\dfrac{\text{Count}\left(\begin{array}{l}\text{unigram is the simplest}\\\text{type of language}\end{array}\right)}{\text{Count}\left(\begin{array}{l}\text{unigram is the simplest}\\\text{type of}\end{array}\right)}$$

Example 4.2:

$$P(\text{India}|\,\text{lotus is the national flower of})=\dfrac{\text{Count}\left(\text{lotus is the national flower of India}\right)}{\text{Count}\left(\text{lotus is the national flower of}\right)}$$

This method of counting is not realistic since generally we would not have sufficient examples to estimate. Now we discuss a simple assumption that language models make – that is the **Markov assumption** or the independence assumption. This assumption states that the conditional probability of a word is determined by the probability of a limited number of previous words that is instead of considering all previous words when predicting a word, we only consider a shorter history. A Markov assumption technically means assuming conditional independence (Equation 4.6).

$$P\left(w_1 w_2 \ldots w_n\right) \approx \prod_i P(w_i \mid w_{i-k} \ldots w_{i-1}) \qquad 4.6$$

In other words, the Markov assumption approximates each component in the product as follows (Equation 4.7)

$$P\left(w_i \mid w_1 w_2 K w_{i-1}\right) \approx P(w_i \mid w_{i-k} w_{i-1}) \qquad 4.7$$

4.3 *N-gram Language Models*

Now we describe the *N*-gram approach to language models which estimate the probability distribution for a sequence. A simple probabilistic language model can be described by finding the probabilities of *n*-grams that is the probability of a word is conditioned on some number *n* of previous words. An *n*-gram is defined by a sequence of *n* words, where *n* is an integer greater than zero. The probability of the *n*-gram is defined as the conditional probability of the nth word which is decided by the previous *n*–1 words or the *n*−1 gram. This concept as described above is a Markov assumption. The *n* can be any number, and essentially defines the size of the "gram", or sequence of words being assigned a probability. In the context of NLP, *n*-gram is a subsequence of *n* items from a given sequence and the item can be phonemes, syllables, characters, words or any other entity depending on the application. Basically, n can be thought of as the amount of context or history that the model is considering. Counting frequencies followed by normalization can be used for the training of N-gram models. Maximum likelihood estimation (MLE) is an intuitive manner to estimate the following probability of n-gram (Equation 4.8)

$$P(w_n \mid w_1, w_2 \dots w_{n-1}) \qquad 4.8$$

Maximum likelihood estimates the model parameters such that the probability is maximized.

To find the probability of generating a training set T, given a model M, we need to estimate the parameters of the model M that maximizes the likelihood of the training set T. The relative frequency of the word sequences estimates the ***maximum likelihood estimates*** since they maximize the probability that model M will generate the training corpus T. In practice, we simply count the occurrence of word patterns to calculate the maximum likelihood estimation of $P(w_n \mid w_1, w_2 \dots w_{n-1})$. Therefore, for n gram model the estimate is given as follows (Equations 4.9 and 4.10)

Given that $C\left(w_1 w_2 \dots w_n\right)$ is the frequency of $w_1 w_2 \dots w_n$ in the training text where N is the total number of training n-grams, then

$$P_{\text{MLE}}\left(w_1 w_2 \dots w_n\right) = C\left(w_1 w_2 \dots w_n\right) / N \qquad 4.9$$

$$P_{\text{MLE}}\left(w_n \mid w_1 w_2 \dots w_{n-1}\right) = C\left(w_1 w_2 \dots w_n\right) / C\left(w_1 w_2 \dots w_{n-1}\right) \qquad 4.10$$

Unigram Language Model: The unigram is the simplest type of language model where conditioning context is not used. This is essentially the bag of words model and is mostly used in information retrieval. It evaluates each word or term independently (Equation 4.11).

$$P\left(w_1 \dots w_n\right) = P\left(w_1^n\right) = P\left(w_1\right) \prod_{k=2}^{n} P\left(w_k\right) \qquad 4.11$$

Given a large corpus, unigram just estimates the count of unique words in it.

Bi-gram Language Model: Bi-grams estimate the probability of two words coming together in the corpus. In the bi-gram model, the conditional probability of a word is dependent only on the preceding word. The model is as follows (Equation 4.12)

$$P\left(w_1 \dots w_n\right) = P\left(w_1^n\right) = P\left(w_1\right) \prod_{k=2}^{n} P\left(w_{k-1}\right) \qquad 4.12$$

The probability of bi-grams can be estimated as given below (Equation 4.13) where C denotes count.

$$P\left(w_n \mid w_{n-1}\right) = \frac{P\left(w_{n-1},w_n\right)}{P\left(w_{n-1}\right)} = \frac{\dfrac{C\left(w_{n-1},w_n\right)}{N_{pairs}}}{\dfrac{C\left(w_{n-1}\right)}{N_{words}}} = \frac{C\left(w_{n-1},w_n\right)}{C\left(w_{n-1}\right)} \qquad 4.13$$

Example 4.3:

Consider the following set of sentences:

Children are very beautiful.

Children like to eat ice-creams very much.

Children like to dance well.

Children like to play much.

$P(\text{are}|\text{children}) = 1/4$ $P(\text{to}|\text{like}) = 3/3$, etc.

Tri-gram Language Model:

Similarly, trigram model considers previous 2 words and is given as follows (Equation 4.14).

$$P\left(w_1 \ldots w_n\right) = P\left(w_1^n\right) = P\left(w_1\right)\prod_{k=2}^{n} P(w_k \mid w_{k-1}, w_{k-2}) \qquad 4.14$$

4.3.1 Advantages and Disadvantages of *N*-gram Models

Language models have certain advantages. First and foremost is that the model is easy to understand and easy and cheap to build especially with modern hardware. It works well for some NLP applications. However, language models assume a fixed known vocabulary of words. The Markov assumption which is the basis of language model only captures short distance context which is linguistically inaccurate since a lot of natural language phenomena have long distance dependencies. Language models are also associated with the data sparseness problem although smoothing helps to generalize to new data to a certain extent.

4.4 Issues Associated with *N*-gram Models

Drawbacks of Overfitting: The main problem associated with *n*-grams is that they work best when the test corpus is similar to the training corpus, or in other words when the learning model overfits the training data. However, this is rarely true and leads to the sparseness problem. Therefore, we need to train models that are robust and can generalize.

Sparseness Problem: The sparseness problem associated with language modelling occurs when new words or out of vocabulary words for which n-grams have not been calculated are encountered. Zipf's empirical law states most phenomena follow an inverse relationship between number of events and frequency. Collecting statistics for high frequency can be done in less time, however, collecting statistics for low frequency takes an arbitrarily long time. This essentially means that the zero-probability calculated by n-gram models are often associated with low frequency events. Since there are a combinatorial number of possible word sequences, many rare (but not impossible) combinations never occur in training, so maximum likelihood estimation incorrectly assigns zero to many parameters because of this rare data. If a new combination occurs during testing, it is given a probability of zero and the entire sequence gets a probability of zero since this is computed by multiplying the probabilities of subparts.

4.5 Smoothing Techniques

As already discussed even if one n-gram is unseen in the sentence, probability of the whole sentence becomes zero and to avoid this, some probability mass has to be reserved for the unseen words. The zero-probability problem is solved using smoothing techniques that is we redistribute probability mass. Smoothing is the task of adjusting the maximum likelihood estimate of probabilities to produce more accurate probabilities. Smoothing techniques tend to make distributions more uniform, by adjusting low probabilities such as zero probabilities upward, and high probabilities downward. Smoothing not only prevents zero probabilities but also attempts to improve the accuracy of the model. In other words, smoothing or discounting techniques allocate some probability mass for the missing n-grams. Therefore, smoothing techniques adjust parameter estimates to account for unseen but not impossible events.

Discounting is the central idea in all smoothing algorithms. To assign some probability mass to unseen event, we need to take away some probability mass from seen events. **Discounting** is the lowering of each non-zero count c to c^* according to the specific smoothing algorithm. Thus, for a word that occurs c times in training set of size N (Equation 4.15)

$$P^{\text{MLE}}(w) = \frac{c}{N} \text{ and } P^{\text{smoothed}}(w) = \frac{c^*}{N} \tag{4.15}$$

Add–one Smoothing (Laplace Correction): In this type of smoothing, we add 1 to all counts resulting in no zeros and then normalize by count and vocabulary size. This increases the total number of words N in the corpus by the vocabulary V. Here, we assume that the vocabulary size V is fixed and known.

For the case of unigram, the probability is as given below (Equation 4.16):

$$P_{\text{LAP}}\left(w_i\right) = \frac{1 + c\left(w_i\right)}{V + N} \qquad 4.16$$

For the case of bigram, the probability is as given below (Equation 4.17):

$$P_{\text{LAP}}\left(w_i \mid w_{i-1}\right) = \frac{1 + c\left(w_{i-1}, w_i\right)}{V + c(w_{i-1})} \qquad 4.17$$

In general, for the case of n-gram, the probability is as given below (Equation 4.18):

$$P_{\text{LAP}}\left(w_n \mid w_1, \ldots., w_{n-1}\right) = \frac{1 + c\left(w_1, \ldots., w_n\right)}{V + c(w_1, \ldots.., w_{n-1})} \qquad 4.18$$

The problem with add–1 smoothing is that it tends to reassign too much of the probability mass to unseen n-grams. Here w_i indicates a particular word at position i.

Additive Smoothing: In add-one smoothing, unnecessary probability is redistributed to unseen n-grams. To avoid this issue, rather than one we add a fraction λ a value less than 1. The important question that arises is the amount of smoothing to be carried out or the choice of the value of λ. For estimating the value of λ, the data is divided into three parts namely training, held-out and test data. Initially, the n-gram probabilities are learnt using the training data. Now the held-out data is trained with different values of λs and the λ that gives the maximum probability is chosen. However, in both the above methods of smoothing, the vocabulary must be known.

Good-Turing Smoothing: This smoothing method does not assume that the vocabulary is known but however assumes that the words follow a binomial distribution. The probability mass of n-grams with zero (or low) counts is redistributed by considering the frequencies of occurrence of n-grams with higher counts. These frequencies are used for calculating the maximum likelihood estimate for estimating the probabilities of unseen n-grams.

For example, consider calculating the probability of a bigram B from a given corpus. If this bigram has never occurred in the corpus, the probability without smoothing would turn out to be zero. As per the Good-Turing Smoothing, the probability of B will depend upon the number of bigrams which occurred exactly one time among the total number of available bigrams. However, in case, the bigram B has occurred in the corpus with low frequency c times say c, the probability will depend upon number of bigrams which occurred more than one time of the count of current bigram B $(c+1)$, total number of bigrams which occurred same number of times as the current bigram and total number of bigrams. We partition the type of vocabulary into classes (novel, singletons, doubletons, …) by how often they occurred in training data and then use observed total probability of class $r+1$ to estimate total probability of class r as given below (Equation 4.19):

$$r / N = (N_r * r / N) / N_r \rightarrow (N_{r+1} * (r+1) / N) / N_r \qquad 4.19$$

can be calculated for n-grams with zero or low frequency.

Kneser–Ney Smoothing: This smoothing technique gives a better estimate for probabilities of lower-order unigrams. Now instead of finding the probability of a word in the corpus, we find $P_{continuation}(w)$ that is the probability of a word appearing in a novel continuation. In other words, for each word, we count the number of bigram *types* it completes is given below as (Equation 4.20):

$$P_{CONTINUATION}(w) \propto \left| \{ w_{i-1} : c(w_{i-1}, w) > 0 \} \right| \qquad 4.20$$

4.6 Backoff and Interpolation

Backoff and interpolation are other methods to handle some of the issues associated with language models. These models carry out conditioning on limited context for situations where training data does not contain samples with more context.

Backoff: The intuition of backoff is that short n-grams occur more frequently and can be more reliably estimated than longer n-grams. However, using only very simple n-grams can lead to inaccuracy. Backoff provides a solution by allowing longer n-grams to be included if good evidence is available, otherwise we use n-1 gram and so on until we finally end up with using only unigrams. Here, we try to fill any gap in n-grams at level n by looking 'back' to level n-1. For example, if a particular trigram "language models provide" has zero frequency, then we can try for example the bigram "language models" has a non–zero count, at worst, we back off all the way to unigrams such as "language", "models", and finally we carry out smoothing, if required. The concept here is that lower-order models play a part in case data for higher-order models is unavailable, that is we recursively back-off to weaker models until data becomes available.

Interpolation: In interpolation, a mixture of unigrams, bigrams, trigrams, etc., are used, and often interpolation works better. The weightage to be considered for tri-gram, bi-gram and unigram are given by λ_1, λ_2, λ_3, respectively, as given for below simple interpolation for trigram (Equation 4.21):

$$\check{P}\left(w_n \mid w_{n-2}w_{n-1}\right) = \lambda_1 P\left(w_n \mid w_{n-2}w_{n-1}\right) + \lambda_2 P\left(w_n \mid w_{n-1}\right) + \lambda_3 P\left(w_n\right) \qquad 4.21$$

where $\displaystyle\sum_i \lambda_i = 1$

As we did in the case of Good-turing method of smoothing, the values of λ_i is determined by maximizing the likelihood of an independent held-out corpus.

4.7 Evaluation of Language Models

We normally train parameters of our model on a training set. Now the question is how we evaluate the performance of our learnt model. For this purpose, we need to find the performance of our model on new data that is on data not yet seen, which we call a as test set. There are two methods of testing the performance of the language model in fitting to a new corpus namely intrinsic evaluation and extrinsic evaluation.

Intrinsic Evaluation: For intrinsic evaluation, two measures are used namely perplexity and entropy. Here we evaluate on ability to model test corpus (*intrinsic*), this evaluation is less realistic but cheaper. However, we need to check whether intrinsic evaluation correlates with an extrinsic one. Both perplexity and entropy are information theoretic measures.

Perplexity: Perplexity essentially measures of how well a model "fits" the test data. It uses the probability that the model assigns to the test corpus. At each choice point in a language model, we determine the average number of choices that can be made, weighted by their probabilities of occurrence. In other words, the probability a language model (LM) assigns to the sentences of a corpus, compared to another language model. Perplexity normalizes for the number of words in the test corpus and takes the inverse. It measures the weighted average branching factor in predicting the next word (Equation 4.22) and lower the value, the better is the model.

$$PP\left(W\right) = P\left(w_1 w_2 \ldots w_N\right)^{\frac{-1}{N}}$$

$$= \sqrt[N]{\frac{1}{P\left(w_1 w_2 \ldots w_N\right)}} \qquad 4.22$$

Using chain rule, we have (Equation 4.23)

$$PP(W) = \sqrt[N]{\prod_{i=1}^{N} \frac{1}{P(w_1 \mid w_1 \dots w_{i-1})}}$$

4.23

For bigrams, the perplexity is given as (Equation 4.24):

$$PP(W) = \sqrt[N]{\prod_{i=1}^{N} \frac{1}{P(w_1 \mid w_{i-1})}}$$

4.24

In this scenario, maximizing probability requires minimizing penalty. Perplexity can also be viewed as a weighted branching factor.

Example 4.4:

Let us consider a sentence consisting of random digits. Determine the perplexity of the sentence according to a given model that assign $P = 3/10$ to each digit.

$$PP(W) = P(w_1 w_2 \dots w_N)^{-\frac{1}{N}}$$

$$= \left(\frac{3}{10}^N \right)^{-\frac{1}{N}}$$

$$= \frac{3}{10}^{-1}$$

$$= 3.33$$

Example 4.5:

A dice has 6 faces: 1, 2, 3, 4, 5, 6 which appear with the following probabilities. Using a unigram model, what is the perplexity of the sequence (1, 2, 1, 4)?

$P(1) = 2/6$, $P(2) = 1/6$, $P(3) = 1/6$, $P(4) = 1/6$, $P(5) = 1/6$, $P(6) = 0$

$$PP\,(1, 2, 1, 4) = \left(\frac{2}{6} \times \frac{1}{6} \times \frac{2}{6} \times \frac{1}{6} \right)^{-\frac{1}{6}}$$

Higher the probability indicates lower perplexity, the more the information available, the lower is the perplexity, and the lower perplexity indicates a better model and a model closer to the true model.

Information Entropy: Information entropy measures information that fits model to data. The goal of any language is to convey information. To measure the average amount of information conveyed in a message, we use a metric called "entropy", proposed by Claude Shannon. Conceptually, lower bound of entropy indicates lesser number of bits to encode. Entropy is given as (Equation 4.25):

$$H(X) = -\sum_{x \in X} p(x) \log_2 p(x)$$

4.25

The entropy of a random variable that ranges over all finite sequences of words of length n in some language L can be states as follows (Equation 4.26):

$$H(w_1, w_2 \ldots w_n) = -\sum_{w_{1:n} \in L} p(w_{1:n}) \log p(w_{1:n})$$

4.26

Using this definition of entropy, cross-entropy can be defined. The cross-entropy can be used to estimate the probability distribution p that generated some data. A model m of p, or in other words the approximation of p can be defined as the cross-entropy of m on p is defined by (Equation 4.27)

$$H(p, m) = \lim_{n \to \infty} -\frac{1}{n} \sum_{W \in L} p(w_1 \ldots w_n) \log m(w_1 \ldots w_n)$$

4.27

For any model m, $H(p) \leq H(p,m)$. According to this statement simpler models can be utilized to estimate the true entropy of a sequence of symbols drawn according to probability p. The smaller the difference between the simpler model and the true model, the smaller will be difference in cross-entropies. In other words, the accuracy of a model is determined by finding the difference between $H(p,m)$ and $H(p)$. An approximation of the cross-entropy of a model M on a sequence of words W can be approximated as (Equation 4.28)

$$H(W) = -\frac{1}{N} \log P(w_1 w_2 \ldots w_N)$$

4.28

The perplexity of a model P on a sequence of words W is now formally defined as 2 raised to the power of this cross-entropy (Equation 4.29):

$$\text{Perplexity}(W) = 2^{H(W)}$$

$$= P(w_1 w_2 \ldots w_N)^{\frac{-1}{N}}$$

$$= \sqrt[N]{\frac{1}{P(w_1 w_2 \ldots w_N)}}$$

$$= \sqrt[N]{\prod_{i=1}^{N} \frac{1}{P(w_1 \mid w_1 \ldots w_{i-1})}}$$

4.29

This gives us the relation between the two intrinsic measures namely cross-entropy and perplexity.

Extrinsic Evaluation: Ideally, evaluate use of model in end application (*extrinsic, in vivo*) which is realistic but expensive. This type of evaluation is considered as the best evaluation to compare two models M1 and M2. Here, each model is used in a NLP task such as spelling correction, machine translation, etc. We carry out the concerned task and determine the accuracy for each of the two models by determining the percentage of misspelt words corrected properly in the case of spelling correction or percentage of words translated correctly. Based on these the accuracies of the two models are determined. The main problem associated with extrinsic evaluation is that it is too time consuming and requires building models for the specific application and obtaining appropriate test data.

Summary

- Introduced the concept and need for language modelling.
- Explained the probabilistic approach to language modelling.
- Explored the *n*-gram language model and its advantages and disadvantages in detail.
- Discussed some issues associated with *n*-gram models.
- Explained the different smoothing techniques.
- Outlined the backoff and interpolation methods.
- Discussed the different methods of evaluating language models.

Exercises

Suggested Activities

1. Fill the following Table for applications of language modelling assuming a noisy channel model

Problem	Input	Output	Language Model	Channel Probability
Part of Speech Tagging				
Question Answering				
Information Retrieval				
Handwriting Recognition				
Sentiment Analysis				

2. Discuss some issues associated with *n*-gram models with illustrative examples.

3. Case Study – Document Categorization: Using 20 Newsgroups dataset (https://www.kaggle.com/datasets/crawford/20-newsgroups), classify documents into predefined categories after constructing TF–IDF weighted N-gram language models for each category. Use the probability of N-grams in a document belonging to each category to make predictions. Logistic regression Classifier can be used.

Self-Assessment: Multiple Choice Questions

Give answers with justification for correct and wrong choices:

1. What is a language model?
    i. A sequential model
    ii. Probability of a word
    iii. Probability distribution over word sequences
2. When language model is used as a generative model, then it is defined as
    i. Discovering new knowledge from large corpora
    ii. Computing the probability of an upcoming word given the previous words.
    iii. Probability of one sequence of words
3. In language modelling, to find a probability of a sequence of words, we use
    i. Bayes Theorem
    ii. Chain Rule
    iii. Subtraction Rule
4. Markov assumption states that
    i. the probability of a word depends only on the probability of a limited history.
    ii. probability of a word is dependent only on the previous word.
    iii. probability of a word is independent of its context.

5. Maximum Likelihood Estimates indicates the relative frequencies of word sequences

    i. Since they maximize the probability that the model M will generate the training corpus T

    ii. Since they minimize the probability that the model M will generate the training corpus T

    iii. Since they give the probability that the model M will generate the training corpus T

6. Bi-gram Language model uses

    i. the conditional probability of only one succeeding word.

    ii. the conditional probability of only two preceding words.

    iii. the conditional probability of only one preceding word.

7. The zero-probability problem of language modelling is handled by

    i. using smoothing techniques that is we redistribute probability mass.

    ii. replacing zero probability by a small random probability.

    iii. increasing probability of all words.

8. In Laplace smoothing, we assume that

    i. The vocabulary is not known.

    ii. The size of the vocabulary is fixed and known.

    iii. The new words are introduced.

9. Good-Turing smoothing assumes that words have a

    i. Poisson distribution

    ii. Binomial distribution

    iii. Geometric distribution

Self-Assessment: Match the Columns

No		Match	
1.	Markov Assumption	**A**	measures information that fits model to data
2.	Tri-gram Model	**B**	evaluate use of model in end application
3.	Perplexity	**C**	use n gram if good evidence is available, otherwise we use $n-1$ gram till we finally end up with unigram
4.	Entropy	**D**	states that the probability of a word depends only on the probability of a limited number of previous words
5.	Good-Turing Smoothing	**E**	Uses a mixture of unigrams, bigrams, trigrams, etc.
6.	Backoff	**F**	approximates the probability of a word given all the previous words by using the conditional probability of only two preceding words

No		Match	
7.	Interpolation	**G**	re-estimate the probability mass of n-grams with zero (or low) counts by considering n-grams with higher counts
8.	Extrinsic Evaluation	**H**	measures the weighted average branching factor in predicting the next word and lower the value, the better is the model

Self-Assessment: Problems

1. Consider the following corpus:

   Sentence 1: You have ten minutes more till the end of the test.

   Sentence 2: You have finished the test.

   Sentence 3: You are given ten marks for the right answer.

   Choose the sentence 2 of the given corpus is the test. Determine the perplexity of the test?

2. A coin has two faces: Head, Tail which appear with the following probabilities. Using a unigram model, what is the perplexity of the sequence (Head, Head, Tail)?

   P (Head) = ½ and P (Tail) = ½

3. Consider the following set of sentences

   S1: I am Dinesh

   S2: Dinesh I am

   S3: I swim

   Estimate unigram, bigram, trigram probabilities.

Short Questions

1. Give a brief note on the need for language modelling.
2. What is the Probabilistic language model? Discuss.
3. Given an example of a 4-gram language model.
4. Give an example of a tri-gram language model where the terms are characters.
5. Discuss in detail some of the issues associated with n-gram models.
6. Discuss in detail three types of smoothing techniques clearly bringing out the differences between them.
7. What is the difference between backoff and interpolation? Indicate which is better and why?
8. Bring out the differences between extrinsic and intrinsic evaluation.
9. How in perplexity used in evaluating language models?
10. Bring out the link between perplexity and cross-entropy when used for evaluating language models.

Words, Morphology and Semantics

5.1 Morphology

Morphology can be defined as the study of the internal structure of words. It deals with the structure of complex words and components of words as well as the semantics of their lexical meanings. The components or parts of words are called **morphemes**. Understanding the basic structure of words, how they are formed and the properties conveyed by the structure enables the understanding of words and their meaning in context. Therefore, morphology involves the study of two aspects of words– their internal structure as well as the method or rules associated with the forming of words as shown in Figure 5.1. Morphology formulates rules based on part of speech of root word (basic word in the lexicon) and the ending letters of the words.

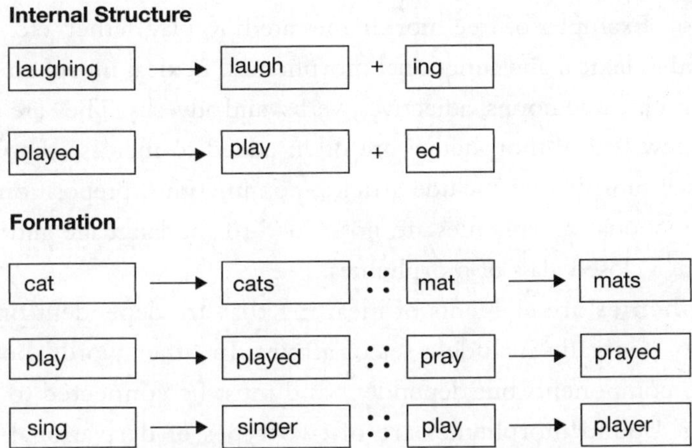

Figure 5.1: Structure of Words

5.1.1 Morphemes

Morphemes are the minimal unit of meaning or grammatical function that constitute a word. Morphemes explain the minimal pairings of form and meaning. Morphemes can be roots or affixes. Roots are the core of the word that carries the basic meaning while affixes (prefixes, suffixes, infixes or circumfixes) are morphemes that are added to the root or stem. Morphemes of English like languages usually consist of root or stem and affixes most commonly prefixes or suffixes. A simple example is shown in Figure 5.2.

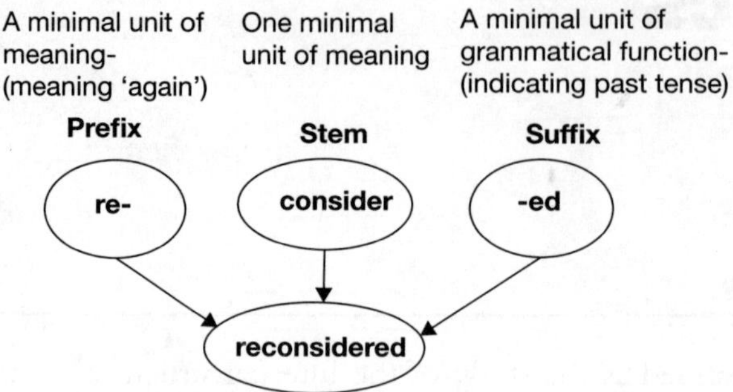

Figure 5.2: Example of Morphemes of a Word

Categories of Morphemes

Morphemes are broadly classified as free and bound morphemes.

Free morphemes are considered as independent words which carry meaning. When free morphemes are used with bound morphemes, the basic free morpheme word–form is called as the stem or the root. Examples of free morphemes are boy, play, father, etc. Free morphemes are further classified as lexical and functional morphemes. Lexical morphemes are considered as content words and include nouns, adjectives, verbs, and adverbs. They are also an open class of words because new lexical morphemes are often added to increase the vocabulary of the language. Functional morphemes include articles, conjunctions, prepositions, and pronouns. In general, new functional morphemes are not added to the language and hence functional free morphemes are a closed class of morphemes.

Bound morphemes are elements of meaning that are dependent on the words they are added to. They generally include a set of affixes. In other words, bound morphemes are not standalone components but dependent and must be connected to free morphemes to attain meaning. Bound morphemes are of two types of derivational morphemes and inflectional morphemes. Derivational morphemes are prefixes and suffixes that are added to lexical morphemes or stems to make new words of a different grammatical category from the stem. Inflectional morphemes are a category of bound morphemes that are used to indicate aspects of the grammatical function of a word, e.g., plural, singular, tense, comparative, or possessive form.

5.1.2 Types of Morphology

Bound morphemes join with stems by means of three connection processes namely **derivation, inflection,** and **compounding** and hence morphology are of the following three types:

Derivational Morphology: This describes how words are created from existing words often changing the grammatical category. Often the meaning of the derived word is not exactly predictable and depends on usage.

Writer – one who writes, **painter** – one who paints, cutter – (instrument used to cut?) Derivational morphology also describes the change in meaning of the root word.

This morphology is considered less productive compared to inflectional morphology. Table 5.1 shows the affixes of English derivational morphology.

Category Changing Derivational Suffixes		
Suffix	**Functions**	**Examples**
Suffix- able	Derives adjective from a verb	Eat – eat–able (able to be eaten)
Suffix-er	Derives a noun from a verb – a human agent or an inanimate instrument	Speak – speak-er (one who speaks)
Suffix – ful	Derives adjective from noun – indicates addition / abundance	care-care-ful – full of care
Suffix-less	Derives adjective from noun – indicates subtraction/ reduction	Care-care-less – with no care
Suffix- ure and –age	Derive noun from a verb	Fail- fail-ure, Marry – marri-age
Suffix- –hood and – ness	Derive abstract noun from concrete noun	Quick – quick-ly
Suffix – ly	Derive adverb from adjective	fast – fast-er
Suffix – ing	Derives a noun from a verb	Write – writ-ing
Semantic Changing Prefixes		
Prefix-pre	Means before	Pre-fix
Prefix-un	Means negative	Un-happy, Un-cover
Prefix-re	Means do again	Re-consider
Prefix – de	Conveys a sense of subtraction	De-fame
Prefix-dis	Sense of negativity	Dis-place

Table 5.1: The Affixes of English Derivational Morphology

Verb Inflectional Suffixes		
Suffix	**Functions**	**Examples**
Suffix- s	Present Simple as the third person of verb	to play – he play-s
Suffix-ed	Past simple tense marker in regular verbs	to play – play-ed
Suffix – ed (regular verbs & - en (for some regular verbs)	Past participle & marking of perfect aspect	To play – played play-ed To eat – ate eat-en
Suffix-ing	Present participle, gerund & in marking continuous aspect	To play – play-ing To eat – eat-ing
Noun Inflectional Suffixes		
Suffix- s	plural of nouns	girl – girl-s
Suffix- s	Possessive Marker	Geetha-'s pen
Adjective Inflectional Suffixes		
Suffix – er	Comparative marker	fast – fast-er
Suffix – est	Superlative marker	fast – fast-er

Table 5.2: Suffixes of English Inflectional Morphology

Inflectional Morphology: This morphological process describes how features relevant to the syntactic context of a word indicating grammatical functions such as number (like singular and plural), tense (present and past) and in some languages gender, person, case, etc., are added to the base morpheme. This type of morphology results in words of the same grammatical category. Table 5.2 shows the suffixes of English inflectional morphology.

Compounding Morphology: This describes how new words are created by combining existing words with or without spaces.

5.1.3 Spelling Rules

Normally when bound morphemes are combined with lexical morphemes there may be some spelling changes which may vary from language. Here, as an example we consider the English language where the rules are simple. When the inflectional suffix -s is added to nouns in some cases there are spelling rules to be applied. Nouns ending in –s, -z, -sh and sometimes –x require suffix –es to be added instead of suffix -s., examples include dress**es**, qui**zz**es, dish**es** and box**es.** In case of example "quiz" a repetition of last consonant z is followed by the suffix-es. Nouns ending in –y if preceded by a consonant change the –y to -i before adding suffix-es. Examples ba**by** – bab**ies** and flop**py** – flopp**ies.** Other languages often have more complex spelling rules.

The spelling changes for regularly inflected verbs are similar to nouns where if the verb ends with y, then it is changed to –i before adding inflectional suffixes –es and –ed. For the verbs ending in –se when –ing participle is added the –e is removed. For verbs ending with –b, the consonant –b is repeated before adding suffixes –ing and –ed. Now in the English language, there are some irregularly inflected verbs especially as far as the past form and the –ed participle is concerned. Examples include eat – which is ate and eaten and bring is brought and brought in the past form and the –ed participle forms.

5.2 Morphological Processing for NLP

Most languages are not isolating **(a morpheme is a word with no inflectional morphology)** but are agglutinative (words contain different morphemes to determine their meanings, but all of these morphemes including stems remain unchanged after their concatenation), fusional (where a single inflectional morpheme denotes multiple grammatical, syntactic, or semantic features) and templatic (word structure represented by a template in which roots are accompanied by a sequence of slots in fixed positions, filled by mutually exclusive systems of contrasting affixes). All these languages present challenges for most NLP tasks. Particularly challenging is extending morphological techniques for morphologically rich languages like Indian and Arabic languages.

5.2.1 Importance of Morphology Processing for NLP

Morphological analysis is very meaningful for the determination of part–of–speech structure in syntactic parsing, and for the semantic analysis of words and hence the sentence. Information regarding the various affixes are important for the concept of word ordering. Morphological analysis is used to reduce the size of lexicon since only the root words needs to be stored. Morphological analysis provides the information of the word such as number, gender etc and in more morphologically rich languages additionally person, mood and aspect for verb and case affixes for noun. Machine translation uses this information so that the correct form of the word or in some cases groups of words can be generated for the target language. In the case of morphologically rich languages the spell checker is based on morphological processing since the large number of inflections of each word would otherwise require large space. Morphological analysis and generation improves the result of the search engine. Output of the search engine depends on stored index words. Suppose the query word is in inflected form but is not an index word, the search results will be affected. Morphological analysis of the query word can be carried out to obtain the root form which can then be searched in the stored index. It is often desirable to remove inflectional morphology since inflectional morphology does not change the meaning or the part of speech of the word. However, it is better to leave the derivational morphology as it is since most lexicons do contain the derivationally formed word too. As an example, in a search engine, if we search *reconsider*, we want the search engine to return pages containing *reconsidered, reconsiders, reconsidering* but not the stem *consider* obtained from derivational morphology. Inflectional morphology makes instances of the same word appear in different forms increasing sparsity and is a challenge for many NLP tasks such as information extraction and information retrieval. However, both inflectional and derivational morphology encode information that is important for NLP tasks such as machine translation and discourse analysis.

5.3 Stemming and Lemmatization

In order to help such NLP tasks, it is necessary to normalize the data. This is carried out in two ways namely stemming and lemmatization and both these tasks are language dependent. In the simpler task of **stemming**, the inflectional suffixes are just crudely sliced off to yield the stem. It is to be noted this stem may not be a valid word – example fried – chopping off the inflection suffix -ed yields fri (the stem) which is not a valid dictionary word. However, in **lemmatization** after slicing off the suffix, one more step is carried out using the spelling rules to obtain the correct headword form or dictionary form of the word. Therefore, lemmatization reduces inflections or variant into base form that is available in the dictionary. Examples cries, cried, crying → cry and are, am, is → be

5.3.1 Porter Stemmer

Porter Stemmer is the most widely used stemming algorithm for English. Now it has been adapted to many languages including Russian, Danish, French, Finnish, German, Italian, Hungarian, Portuguese, Norwegian, Swedish, and Spanish. Porter stemmer is a rule-based algorithm and is *heuristic*, in that it is a practical method but not guaranteed to be optimal. The Porter Stemmer uses a sequence of steps to strip off successive layers of affixes. In each step the first matching rule is always applied. Steps, rules, and examples are shown in Table 5.3. Some later steps are used to clean any unfortunate side effects.

Step	Rule	Example
Step 1a	sses → ss	busine**sses** → busine**ss**
	ies → i	pon**ies** → pon**i**
	ss → ss	business → business
	s → φ	cats → cat

Step 1b	(*v*)ing → ϕ	**(walk)**ing → (*a*) ing → walk
		s(ing) → sing
	(*v*)ed → ϕ	(plaster)ed → (*v*)ed → plaster
Step 2	ational → ate	relational → relate
	izer → ize	digitizer → digitize
	ator → ate	operator → operate
Step 3	al → ϕ	revival → reviv
	able → ϕ	adjustable → adjust
	ate → ϕ	activate → activ

Table 5.3: Rules of Porter Stemmer

5.4 Morphological Analysis and Morphological Generation

Let us first understand morphological analysis or morphological parsing.

Example 5.1

Leaves → {leaf +N + Pl}, {leave + V + 3P + Sg}
Boys → {boy + N + Pl}
Play → {play + N + Sg}, {play + V + 3P + Pl}

Here (Example 5.1), input is the word (called surface form) while output is the word's stem (s) and features expressed by other morphemes (called as underlying form). For carrying out morphological analysis we need the lexicon containing the list of stems and suffixes along with basic information about them, the details about the morphotactics which is the model of morpheme ordering that explains which classes of morphemes can follow other classes of morphemes and finally the orthographic or spelling rules that model the changes that occur when morphemes combine.

Morphological analysis involves going from the surface to the lexical form while morphological generation is the opposite process, going from lexical form to surface form. In both the above cases we often proceed through an intermediate form. This intermediate form corresponds to the morphemes present before any orthographic rules are applied. Morphological analysis task takes the surface form of the word, splits it into stem and affixes that is the intermediate form and then outputs the semantic or grammatical function of the different components of the word (lexical form). An example is shown in Figure 5.3.

<table>
<tr><td>Input: Word</td><td>Disrespectfully - surface form</td></tr>
<tr><td></td><td>dis + respect + ful + ly - intermediate form</td></tr>
<tr><td></td><td>prefix + stem + suffix + suffix</td></tr>
<tr><td>Output:</td><td>NEG + respect + N + ADJ + ADV - - - - - - - - - - - lexical form</td></tr>
</table>

Figure 5.3: The Input and Output of Morphological Analysis – An Example

From the morphological generation perspective, when given lexical form is given as input, the intermediate form and then the surface form is generated.

5.4.1 Finite State Methods

Finite state methods provide a simple and powerful method for morphologically analyzing and generating words.

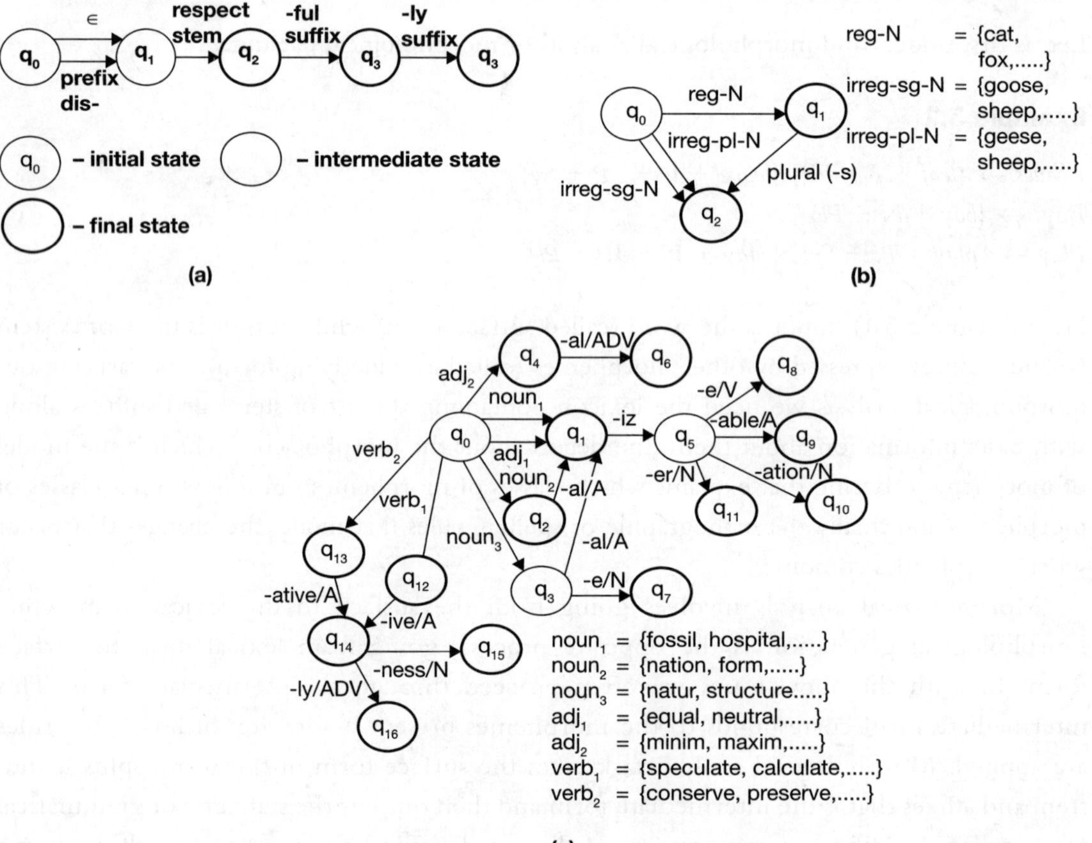

Figure 5.4: FSA for English Morphology

A Finite State Automata (FSA) FSA is said to emit or recognize strings. FSA consists of states which can be initial, intermediate, or final states, alphabets consisting of symbols including null symbol ε and transitions. These transitions occur between states and starts from initial state and on seeing symbols on the edges of the FSA moves to next state till final state is reached and the next symbol of the string seen does not indicate any transition. We will first show some examples of finite state automata that describes English morphology. Figure 5.4 (a) describes a specific case of FSA for the word *disrespectfully*. Figure 5.4 (b) shows a sample inflectional morphology for verb while Figure 5.4 (c) shows a FSA of sample derivational morphology.

5.4.2 Finite State Transducer

Now let us understand finite state transducer (FST) which is based on the concept of finite state automata. While finite state automata can be used to recognize or accept a string, it cannot indicate the internal structure. FST defines a relation between two regular languages. One important FST operation is inversion T^{-1} where the inversion $(T^{-1})$of a transducer switches input and output labels and hence can be used to switch from analysing words to generating words. For this purpose, we need a system that maps or transducer the input string to an output string and vice versa that also encodes its structure (Figure 5.5).

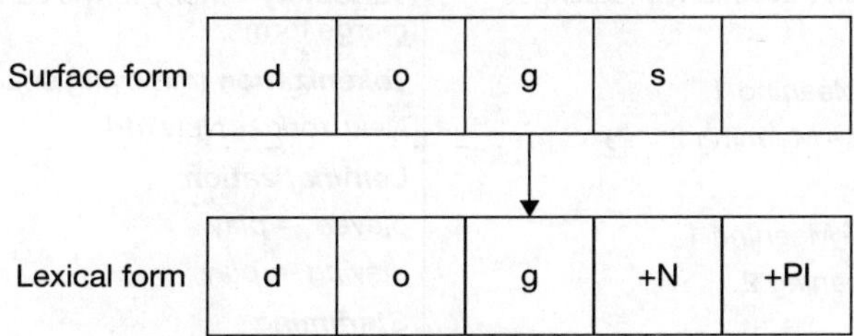

Figure 5.5: Example of FST

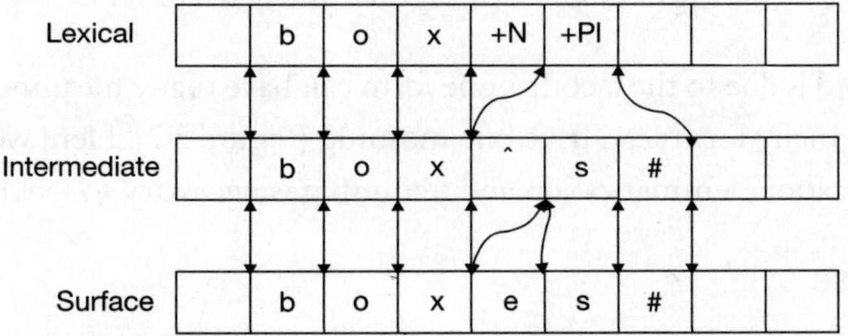

Figure 5.6: Two level FST for Morphology

Another important FST operation is composition ($T \circ T'$) also called cascading where for example two transducers $T = L1 \times L2$ and $T' = L2 \times L3$ can be composed into a third transducer $T'' = L1 \times L3$. In general for morphological analysis of NLP, we have a two level FST, using the concept of composition where one level mapping is from surface form to intermediate form and another level mapping from intermediate form to lexical form. In general, an intermediate representation captures morpheme boundaries (^) and word boundaries (#). Intermediate-to-surface generally handles spelling rules as seen in Figure 5.6, for example, if plural '*s*' follows a morpheme ending in '*x*','*z*' or '*s*', insert '*e*'.

5.5 Lexical Semantics – The Lexicographic Approach

We first discuss lexical semantics which is essentially the study of word meaning. There are basically two approaches to lexical semantics namely the lexicographic approach which we will discuss in this chapter and the distributional approach which we will discuss in succeeding chapters. We differentiate between **lemma** where words with same lemma have same stem, part of speech, rough semantics while **wordform** is the inflected form of the word as it appears in text. As we have already discussed in previous chapters, one of the reasons for the difficulty in processing natural language is semantics of words or in other words the ambiguity and variability associated with the linguistic expression of words.

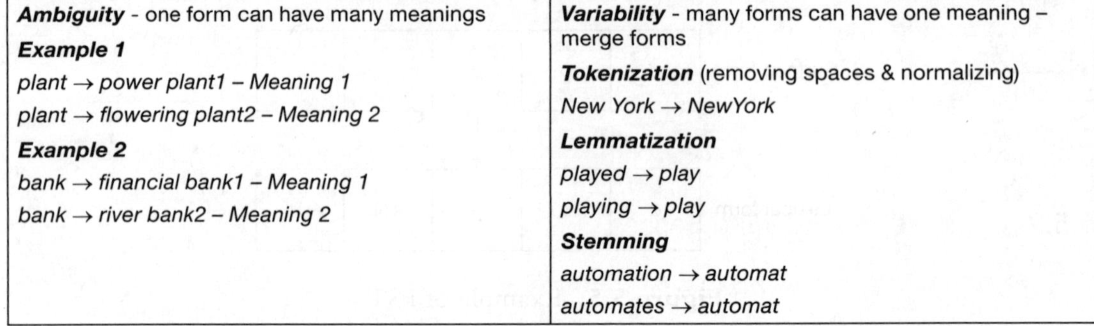

Figure 5.7: Ambiguity and Variability

Ambiguity of a word is due to the fact that one form can have many meanings while variability is due to the fact that many forms can have one meaning (Figure 5.7). Here we show that merging forms using tokenization, lemmatization and stemming is necessary to tackle variability.

5.5.1 Word Sense

Word Sense is one distinct accepted meaning of a word. The lexicographic approach uses lexicons, thesauri and ontologies and assumes that words have discrete word senses.

Example 2: Word senses of the lemma or word "bank"

- *financial bank* – Indian banks have increased interest rates.
- *particular branch of a financial institution* – The bank on Mount Road closes at 6 PM.
- *river bank* – The bank of River Cauvery is heavily populated.
- *repository* – You can approach the blood bank for blood in the case of emergency.

A single lexeme or root word can be associated with many meanings which is generally listed in the dictionary. The entries of a typical lexicon are given in Figure 5.8 and consists of lexemes, word senses, glossary, and examples of the use of the sense associated with the word.

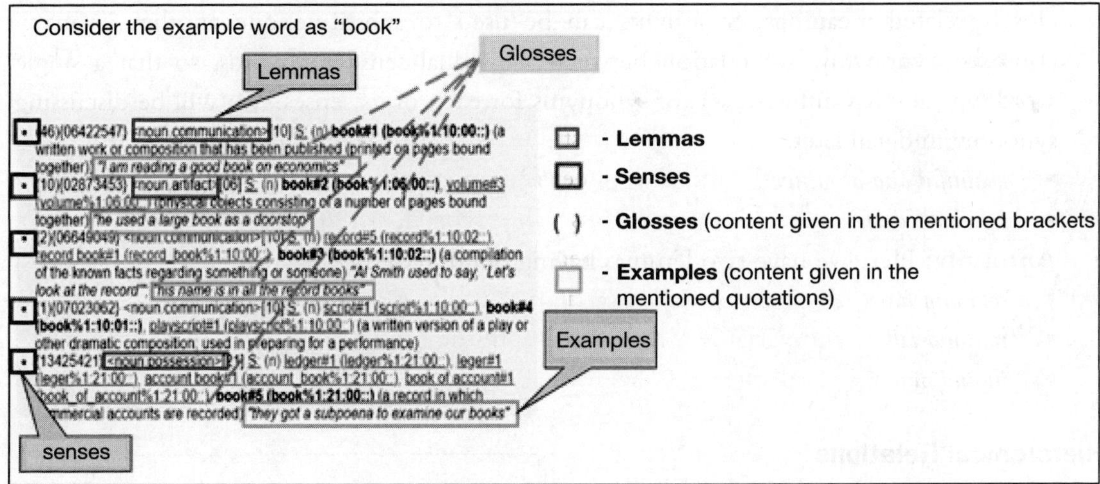

Figure 5.8: An Example of a Lexical Entry

5.5.2 Categorization of Word Senses

One broad method to categorize the patterns of multiple meanings are:

- **Homonymy:** Here unrelated senses have the same orthographic form
    - *bank* having sense of *financial bank* as well as *river bank*
    - *bat* having sense of club for hitting a ball as well as *a nonturnal flying mammal*
- **Homophony:** Here unrelated senses have same pronounciation but have different spelling
    - *wright/right, piece/peace*
- **Polysemy:** Here we have related but distinct senses, The senses are strongly related in a systematic way.
    - *financial bank, blood bank* and *tree bank* – all mean they are related as they store things but are also distinct

- **Metonymy: Here** a single characteristic or name of an object is used to identify an entire object or related object.
    - *crown (For the power of a king.)*
    - *dish (To refer an entire plate of food.)*

Another way of categorizing word senses is based on whether the relations are symmetric or hierarchical.

Symmetric Relations

- **Synonmy:** Here the **semantic** qualities or sense relations exist between lemmas with closely related meanings. Synonyms can be used to substitute one another in many contexts. Synonymy is a relation between individual senses of words, so that a single word typically has different sets of synonyms for each of its senses. We will be discussing synonmy in detail later.
    - *beautiful and attractive*
    - *sofa and couch*
- **Antonmy:** Here we have two lemmas having opposite senses.
    - *cold and hot*
    - *rise and fall*
    - *in and out*

Hierarchical Relations

- **Hypernymy and Hyponymy:** Here in both the cases, the lemmas belong to a set and are related in a hierarchical manner. Hypernyms are lemmas having a broader, superordinate label or category that applies to many members of a set, while the members of the set are themselves called hyponyms. Hyponyms are lemmas whose senses are included in the sense of another lemma.
    - Hypernym- hyponym: Examples
        - tree – oak, music – opera, drink – tea, group - family
  Hyponymy is a hierarchical relationship, and may consist of a number of levels.
        - For example, *dog* is a hyponym of *animal*, but it is also the hypernym of *poodle, alsatian, terrier, beagle*, etc.
- **Meronymy and Holonomy:** Here we have two lemmas that denotes a constituent part or a membership relation. This part-to-whole relationship is called *meronymy*. The opposite of meronymy is holonomy—the name of the whole of which the meronym is a part.

- ■ Meronym - Holonom
  - ♦ Examples: feather - bird, wing – bird, eyes - face
- ■ Meronymy is not just a single relation but a bundle of different part-to-whole relationships.
  - ♦ Example: Finger - hand – body – nail

There are many subtypes of meronym relations.

- ■ Component-of: kitchen–apartment
- ■ Member-of: soldier–army
- ■ Portion-of: slice–pie

5.6 Perspectives of Word Meaning

There are basically three ways of understanding word meaning. They are as follows:

Decompositional Semantics: This approach understands meaning of a word by dividing the meaning of the word into components.

Example 5.2

boy {+human, –female, –adult}
girl {+human, +female, –adult}
man {+human, –female, +adult}
woman {+human, +female, +adult}

In decompoential semantics each word is associated with a bundle of semantic features. Let us consider two words *cat* and *tiger*. We first need to decide on the componential attributes. Let us assume that the designed attributes and the values for the examples are as given in Table 5.4:

Attributes	Furry	Carnivorous	Heavy	Domesticable
Example: Cat	Y	Y	N	Y
Example: Tiger	Y	Y	Y	N

Table 5.4: Examples of Decomponential Semantics

The issue associated with decompoential semantics is that it is difficult to design a complete and correct set of attributes and hence this approach to semantics is the.

Ontological Semantics: This approach understands meaning of a word by its relationship to the meanings or senses of other words or making use of relational semantics. The basic

S.no	Name of Relation	Explanation	Example
1.	Synonymy	Equivalence	<small, little>
2.	Antonymy	Opposition	<hot, cold>
3.	Hyponymy	Subset	<chair, furniture>
4.	Hypernymy	Superset	<furniture, chair>
5.	Meronymy	Part-of relation	<heart, body>
6.	Holonymy	Has–a relation	<body, heart>

Table 5.5: List of Ontological Relations

Distributional Semantics: This approach understands meaning of a word by the context in which the word is found, relative to other words. Normally, a large corpus of raw text is used to learn the meaning of words from the contexts in which they occur. The approach maps words to vectors that capture corpus statistics and hence is also called vector semantics. We will discuss vector semantics in detail in the succeeding two chapters. ontological semantic relations have already been discussed in the section on word senses. The list of the ontological relations are as given in Table 5.5. Here when synonymous words are put together, a unique meaning often emerges. This is the basic principle used by the lexical resource WordNet. We will discuss WordNet in detail in the next section.

5.7 WordNet – The Lexical Resource*

WordNet is a very large, publicly available (https://wordnet.edu/) lexical database or electronic thesaurus that organizes words according to their semantic relations. This lexical knowledge base is based on conceptual lookup since it organizes concepts in a semantic network. It organizes lexical information in terms of word meaning rather than word form. WordNet was first created for English in 1985, at the Cognitive Science Laboratory of Princeton University. WordNet consists of three separate databases; one for nouns, one for verbs, and one for adjectives and adverbs put together. Currently the English WordNet has about 1,00,000 nouns, 11,000 verbs, 20,000 adjectives, and 4,000 adverbs. The definitions of words in the WordNet are not like definitions in a dictionary. Various WordNet interfaces are available. Many programming language interfaces are listed at https://wordnet.princeton.edu/related-projects while there is a Python based interface from NLTK which returns a list of synset objects.

5.7.1 Components of WordNet

The basic building block of WordNet are synsets. Synsets are groups of word senses that are associated to one another since they are synonymous. Each synset or set of cognitive synonyms represents an underlying lexical concept and express a distinct meaning. Please note that Many words are members of multiple synsets, which can be thought of as separate "senses" of the word.

Examples of Synsets (5.3)

- **Verb:** {*write*, *compose, pen, indite*}
- **Noun:** {*car*, *auto, automobile, machine, motorcar*}
- **Adjective:** {*lovely*, *adorable, endearing*}, **Adverb:** {*slowly*, *slow, easy, tardily*}

Each lexeme in the WordNet has a POS tag and is associated with one or more-word senses. Each word sense is represented as a synset. The actual form of a WordNet entry is given in Figure 5.9 (a) and its components such as synsets, gloss and example are explicitly shown in Figure 5.9 (b)

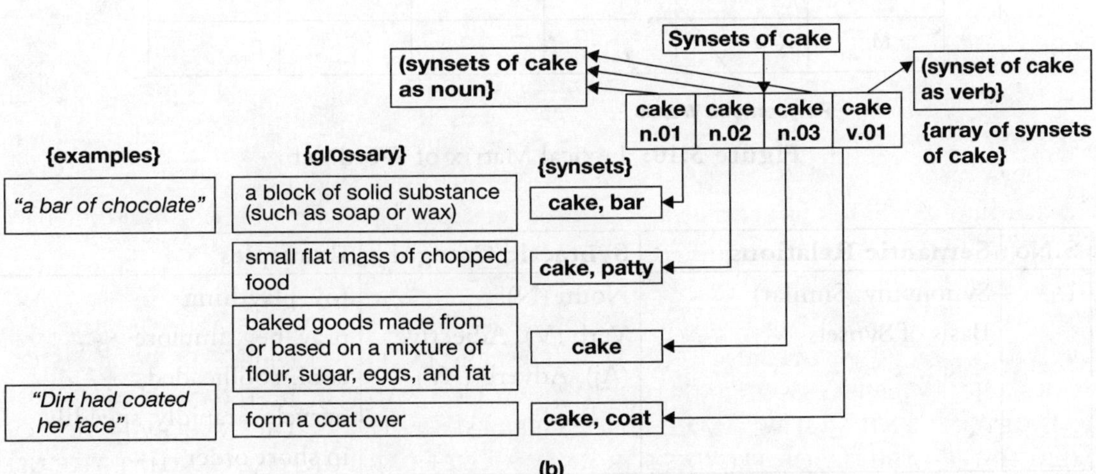

Figure 5.9: An Example of a Synset of WordNet

A WordNet has more information than a thesaurus since WordNet brings together specific word senses. Synsets are linked to other synsets by conceptual-semantic and lexical relations a form networks. Generally, semantic relations are contained within each word class and there are no links between word classes. The lexical matrix of WordNet can be visualized as given in Figure 5.10. The nodes of WordNet are synsets. Links between two nodes are either **conceptual-semantic** (bird, feather) or **lexical** (feather, feathery) relations Lexical links subsume conceptual-semantic links. These relations are based on concepts and therefore, give us valuable information about words. For example, the verbs (communicate, talk, whisper) are all about talking but the manner goes from general to specific. A similar example with nouns would be (furniture, bed, bunkbed). An example of a part-whole relation is (leg, chair). These sorts of relations are captured in WordNet. The complete set of semantic relations captured by WordNet is given in Table 5.6. The first four relations have already been described earlier in the chapter. Troponymy is the main relation linking verbs in the WordNet semantic network and describes the manner relation between two verbs. Entailment refers to a relation between a pair of facts where the truth of second fact necessarily follows the truth of the first fact.

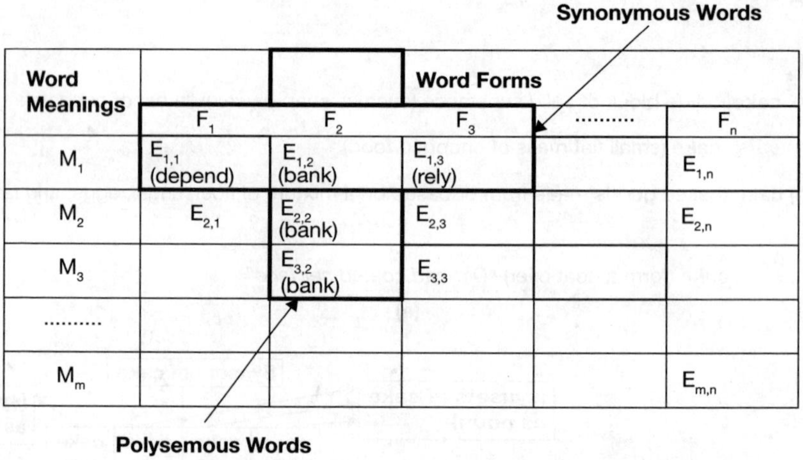

Figure 5.10: Lexical Matrix of WordNet

S.No	Semantic Relations	Syntactic Category	Examples
1.	Synonymy (Similar) Basis of Synsets	Noun (N), Verb (V), Adjective (Aj), Adverb (AV)	toy, plaything pray, beg, implore cool, coolheaded, nerveless rapidly, speedily, in short order

2.	Antonymy (opposite)	Aj Av	beautiful, ugly slowly, fast
3.	Hyponomy (subordinate)	N	red, colour rose, flower
4.	Meronymy (part or member)	N	nail, finger wheel, automobile ship, fleet
5.	Troponomy (manner)	V	limp, walk glare, see
6.	Entailment	V	divorce, marry snore, sleep

Table 5.6: Semantic Relations of WordNet

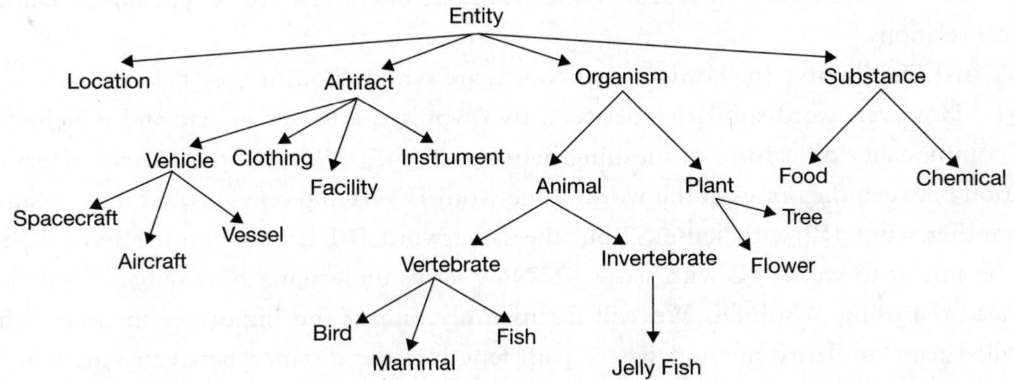

Figure 5.11: Part of WordNet Hierarchy

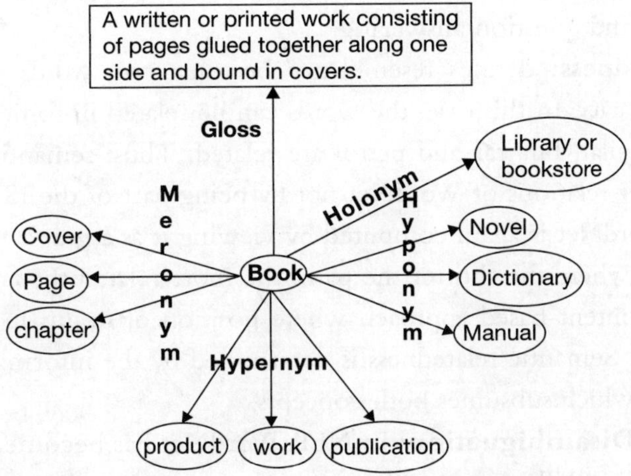

Figure 5.12: Sample sub-net of WordNet for "Book"

The synsets of WordNet are connected in a hierarchy or network based on the hypernym/hyponym (IS-A) relation and the holonym/meronym (HAS-A) relation. A sample view of a WordNet IS-A hierarchy for noun is shown in Figure 5.11. A small sub-net of WordNet with many relations is shown in Figure 5.12

5.7.2 WordNet and NLP

WordNet is extensively used by those working in the areas of AI and NLP. Some of the applications include word sense disambiguation, information retrieval, automatic text classification, automatic text summarization, and machine translation. A direct application is the use of WordNet as a thesaurus where words are organized by concept and semantic or lexical relations.

Word Similarity: In WordNet two words are synonymous if they belong to the same synset. However, word similarity between two words is a looser metric and is defined as the commonality of features of meaning between them. In WordNet, similarity refers to a relation between the senses of the words. One word $W1$ having one sense $S1$ may be similar to another word $W2$ with sense $S2$ but the same word $W1$ having another sense $S2$ may not be similar to word $W2$ with sense $S2$. Now let us understand how semantic similarity is measured using WordNet. We will discuss only one of the important methods which is called path similarity method where path length is the distance between synsets in the WordNet hierarchy treated as a graph. Concepts are nodes and semantic relations between these concepts can be treated as edges. In this case, the path similarity between two words is the shortest distance between the two words. Word similarity measures can be used in spelling checking and question answering.

Word Relatedness: defines resemblance between two words and is a more general concept than similarity. In this case, the words can be related in some way. For example, car and bicycle are similar, but car and petrol are related. Thus, semantically related words are connected by other relations of WordNet not by being part of the IS-A hierarchy. Semantic Relatedness in WordNet is again computed by viewing it as a graph and finding path length between concepts where the shorter the path, the more related the concepts are. Another is the information content-based approach where position of nouns in *is-a* hierarchy is taken into consideration. Semantic relatedness is determined by the information content of lowest common concept which subsumes both concepts.

Word Sense Disambiguation: In NLP, WordNet has become a useful tool for word sense disambiguation. When a word has multiple senses, WordNet can help in identifying the correct sense. WordNet's symbolic approach complements statistical approaches.

There are many approaches to word sense disambiguation which we will discuss in detail in succeeding chapters.

5.7.3 Limitations of WordNet

However, Wordnet does not completely solve the issue of representing meanings of words. First of all, Wordnet has limited coverage and is available only for a small set of languages. Moreover, Wordnet only conveys whether two-word forms are similar or not but not the extent of similarity or dissimilarity. WordNet can be used to limited extent noun–noun or verb-verb similarity but however we cannot use WordNet to compare nouns and verbs, or use other parts of speech.

5.8 Thematic Roles

Another perspective of semantics is the relations of words in the sentence or arguments of the verb present in it. Semantic or thematic roles are defined as roles that participants play in events or situations represented in the sentence. In other words, thematic roles are semantic relationships that a participant or entity has with the main verb in a clause or sentence. In 1968, Fillmore defined thematic roles as Case Roles (Fillmore, 1968, The Case for Case). Some basic thematic roles with examples are given in Table 5.7. We will be discussing thematic roles in detail when we discuss semantic role processing in later chapters.

S.No	Thematic Roles	Definition	Examples
1.	Agent or Actor	The initiator of some action who does the action by free will	**The boy** ate the mango
2.	Patient or Theme	The entity affected by the action or entity undergoing state change	The girl cut **the apple** Ram kicked **the ball**
3.	Experiencer	The entity which is aware of the action or state described by the predicate but which is not in control of the action or state	**Sita** saw the cow
4.	Beneficiary	The entity for whose benefit the action was performed	The girl sang for **her friend**
5.	Instrument	The means by which an action is performed	The man cut the apple with **a knife**

6.	Location	The place in which something takes place	The peacock danced in the **forest**
7.	Time	The time at which something takes place	The boy left at **5.00 AM**
8.	Source	The entity from which something moves, either literally or metaphorically.	The boy travelled from **Delhi**
9.	Goal or Destination	The entity towards which something moves, either literally or metaphorically.	The man travelled to **Mumbai**

Table 5.7: Thematic Roles with Examples

We will be discussing other aspects of semantic processing in detail in succeeding chapters.

Datasets associated with Thematic Roles: The two important lexicons containing case frames or thematic grids for each verb are Proposition Bank (PropBank) and FrameNet.

PropBank (https://home.propbank.app/) has a set of verb-sense specific "frames" with informal English glosses describing the roles. It is a basically an annotation of the predicate-argument structure. PropBank commits to annotating all verbs in a corpus. The syntactic tree-based Penn Treebank which we discuss later is labelled with these verb-sense specific semantic roles. PropBank does not annotate events or states of affairs described using nouns. PropBank was developed with the idea of serving as training data for machine learning-based semantic role labeling systems. It requires that all arguments to a verb are associated with syntactic constituents. Moreover, different senses of a word are distinguished only if the differences affect the arguments. The arguments are numbered and required for the valency of the predicate (Table 5.8(a)). The semantic classification of modifiers of predicates is given in Table 5.8(b). Though there may be slight variations based on the usage of the predicate, the arguments in general correspond to the list given in Table 5.8(b). The semantic roles of arguments in the predicate dictionary are as given in Table 5.8 (c). It is to be noted that sentences are annotated with reference to this dictionary and actual arguments are just numbered. Figure 5.13(a) shows the arguments of different senses of the verb "break". The argument labels are consistent irrespective of the different syntactic realizations of the same verb (Figure 5.13 (b)).

Semantic Roles and Argument Number	
ARG0	agent
ARG1	patient
ARG2	instrument, benefactive, attribute

Semantic Roles and Argument Number	
ARG3	starting point, benefactive, attribute
ARG4	ending point
ARG5	modifier

(a)

Semantic Classification of Modifiers of Predicates			
ARGM-COM	comitative	ARGM-CAU	cause
ARGM-LOC	locative	ARGM-DIS	discourse
ARGM-DIR	directional	ARGM-ADV	adverbials
ARGM-GOL	goal	ARGM-ADJ	adjectival
ARGM-MNR	manner	ARGM-MOD	modal
ARGM-TMP	temporal	ARGM-NEG	negation
ARGM-EXT	extent	ARGM-DSP	direct speech
ARGM-REC	reciprocals	ARGM-LVB	light verb
ARGM-PRD	secondary predication	ARGM-CXN	construction
ARGM-PRP	purpose		

(b)

Semantic Roles of Arguments in the Predicate Dictionary (Sentences – annotated with reference to dictionary entry and arguments are just numbered)	
ARGn-PAG	proto–agent
ARGn-PPT	proto–patient
ARGn-PRD	secondary predication
ARGn-GOL	goal, recipient, beneficiary
ARGn-DIR	direction
ARGn-MNR	manner, instrument
ARGn-PRP	purpose
ARGn-VSP	verb-specific

(c)

Table 5.8: Arguments of PropBank

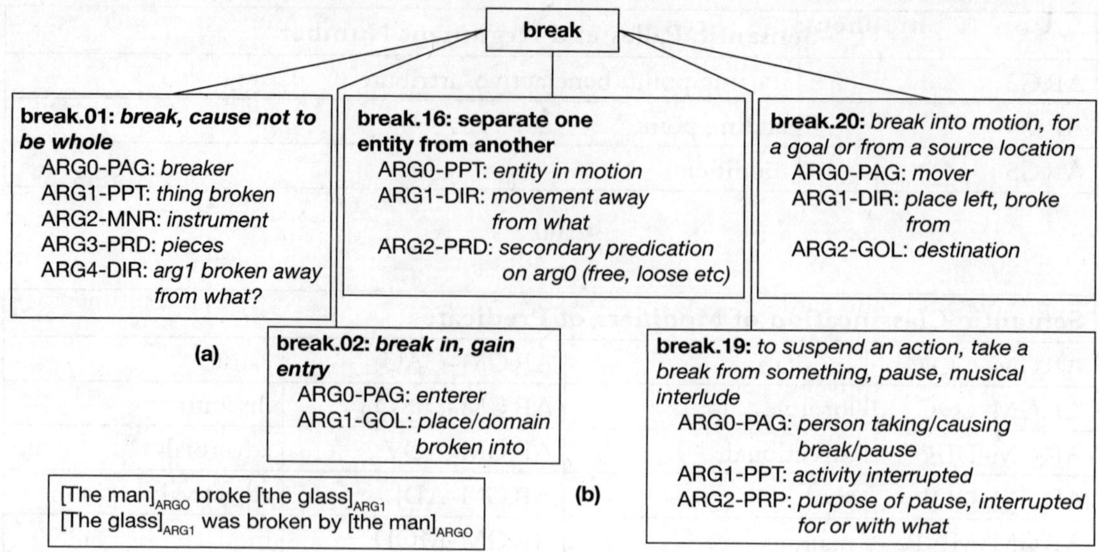

Figure 5.13: Sample Senses of Verb "Break"

- **FrameNet** (http://www.icsi.berkeley.edu/~framenet/) is based on frame specific thematic roles or Frame Semantics. The central idea of Frame Semantics is that word meanings must be described in relation to semantic frames – schematic representations of the conceptual structures and patterns of beliefs, practices, institutions, images, etc. that provide a foundation for meaningful interaction in a given speech community. (Fillmore 2003). The FrameNet project has been in operation at the International Computer Science Institute in Berkeley since 1997. The FrameNet project builds a lexical database of English that is both human and machine-readable, based on annotating examples of word usage in actual text corpora. From a NLP perspective FrameNet provides the more than 200,000 manually annotated sentences linked to more than 1,200 semantic frames provide a unique training dataset for an important aspect of NLP; semantic role labelling, which in turn is used in many applications such as information extraction, machine translation, event recognition, sentiment analysis, etc. Essentially FrameNet describes the frames or or conceptual structures and records the different ways in which the associated frames are expressed in actual text. The important aspects of FrameNet project are the characterization of frames, fitting words to the frames, development of a descriptive terminology, and extraction and annotation of appropriate sentences.

Core Components of FrameNet: FrameNet is a linguistic knowledge graph containing information about lexical and predicate argument semantics of the English language. FrameNet is based on frame semantics, a theory of meaning derived mainly from the work of Fillmore. The fundamental concept is that meanings of words can be understood in terms of a semantic frame, which is essentially a description of a certain kind of event, connection, or item and its actors. For example, the "Gardening" frame involves elements that represent different aspects of the activity, such as the person doing the gardening (Gardener), the plants being cultivated (plants), the place where gardening takes place (location), and the tools used for implementation (tools). FrameNet is similar to PropBank but however abstracts from specific verbs so that semantic frames now enclose a number of verbs having similar description of roles. FrameNet contains two distinct entity classes: semantic frames and lexical units, where a semantic frame represents conceptual structures or schemas and a lexical unit (LU) represents the linguistic expressions associated with the frame. Moreover, semantic frames of FrameNet can be associated with not only verbs but also nouns and adverbs. In FrameNet, the role names are called frame elements or FEs and are local to particular frames. While some roles are general in nature, others are specific to a small family of lexical items. For example, there are abstract frames (such as the "Communication" frame), as well as specific frames (such as the "Meeting" frame). Each sense of a word in this example "bat", is associated with its own frame (Figure 5.14). The FrameNet project is dedicated to producing valency descriptions of frame-bearing lexical units from both semantic and syntactic point of view based on word usage obtained from a large text corpora. In addition, FrameNet is a linguistic knowledge graph and includes inheritance and causation relationships among frames. Two frames are in an inheritance relation if one of them has all of the properties of the other plus additional information.

One word has many frames: For example: "BAT"

Animal: A living creature that is not a human being.
    Example: "I saw a bat flying in the night sky."
Sports equipment: Equipment used in sports or recreational activities.
    Example: "He swung the bat and hit the ball."
Hitting: Striking an object with force.
    Example: "The batter batted the ball out of the park."
Visual Perception: The ability to see or perceive objects and their attributes.
    Example: "I saw the bat hanging upside down."

Figure 5.14: FrameNet- Example

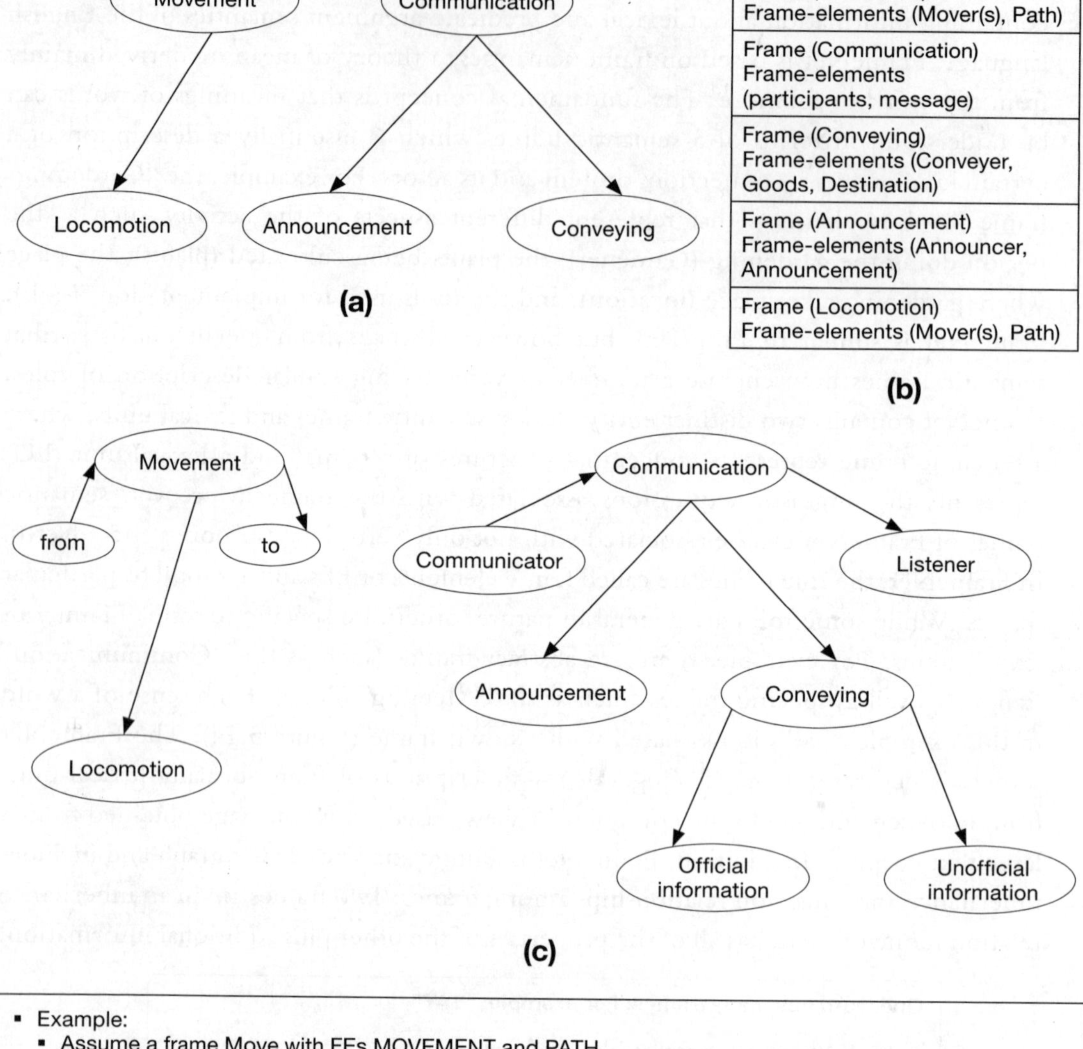

Figure 5.15: Hierarchical Structures between Frames that Resemble Ontologies

Example 5.4

Decision Making is the parent frame for Choose (Selecting options) and Opt Out (not participating). Given these relations, it is possible to build hierarchical structures between frames that resemble ontologies (Figure 5.15 (a) and Figure 5.15 (b)). Multiple inheritance is also permitted and hence FrameNet structures forma graph (Figure 5.15(c)). Often, when describing complex situations, it is necessary to embody existing subframes and FrameNet (Figure 5.15(d)).

Summary

- Introduced the basic concepts of morphology and its types.
- Discussed the morphological processing aspects from an NLP perspective.
- Explained the difference between stemming and lemmatization and described the Porter stemmer.
- Outlined the steps of both morphological analysis and morphological generation including finite state methods.
- Introduced the concept of the lexicographic approach to lexical semantics.
- Explained the three perspectives of understanding word meaning.
- Described the components of the lexical resource WordNet.
- Outlined the important aspects of thematic roles and two lexical resources PropBank and FrameBank based on thematic roles.

Exercises

Suggested Activities

1. Fill the following table with appropriate example words (not mentioned in the chapter) and sample sentences using them:

Category of Word Sense	Example Word	Example Sentence
Homonymy		
Homophony		
Polysemy		
Metonymy		
Synonymy		
Antonymy		
Hypernymy		
Hyponymy		
Meronymy		
Holonomy		

2. Explain 3 different NLP applications where the following lexical resources are be used:
   a. WordNet
   b. PropBank
   c. FrameNet

3. Using either a language or software of your choice (like Python, NLTK) with each of following lexical resources, classify at least a set of 100 newspaper articles:
   a. WordNet
   b. PropBank
   c. FrameNet

   Comment on the results.

4. Case Study – Morphological Analysis: Using Morpho Challenge dataset https://k4all.org/project/morpho-challenge-2010-semi-supervised-and-unsupervised-analysis/), analyze the morphological structure of words and perform tasks like morphological inflection or generation using morpheme-based models to learn morphological patterns with training carried out on annotated data using any supervised learning technique.

Self-Assessment: Multiple Choice Questions

Give answers with justification for correct and wrong choices:

1. Morphemes are
    i.   the minimal unit of meaning or grammatical function that constitute a word
    ii. the minimal unit of meaning
    iii. the maximal unit of meaning
2. Morphemes are broadly classified as
    i.   Prefixes and suffixes
    ii. Bag of words
    iii. Free and bound
3. The morphology of how words are created from existing words often changing the grammatical category is called
    i.   Inflectional morphology
    ii. Derivational morphology
    iii. Compounding
4. In agglutinative languages
    i.   a morpheme is a word with no inflectional morphology
    ii. a single inflectional morpheme denotes multiple grammatical, syntactic, or semantic features
    iii. words contain different morphemes to determine their meanings, but all of these morphemes including stems remain unchanged after their concatenation
5. Languages in which word structure represented by a frame in which roots are accompanied by a sequence of slots in fixed positions, filled by mutually exclusive systems of contrasting affixes are called
    i.   fusional
    ii. isolating
    iii. templatic
6. In lemmatization
    i.   inflectional suffixes are just sliced off
    ii. after slicing off the inflectional suffix, correct headword form is obtained
    iii. the word is completely analyzed
7. The morphologically analysed output of "tries" is
    i. $\{try + N + Pl\}$, $\{try + V + 3P + Sg\}$
    ii. $\{try + N + Pl\}$
    iii. $\{try + V + 3P + Sg\}$

8. Porter stemmer
    i. rule-based algorithm and is heuristic
    ii. all steps are carried out in parallel
    iii. statistical methods
9. Finite State Transducer
    i. Emits or recognizes strings
    ii. Defines a relation between two languages
    iii. Defines a relation between two regular languages
10. Ambiguity of a word is due to the fact that
    i. many forms can have one meaning
    ii. one form can have many meanings
    iii. many forms can have many meanings
11. The word pair knight–night exhibit
    i. Polysemy
    ii. Homophony
    iii. Homonymy
12. When a single characteristic or name of an object is used to identify an entire object or related object, it is called
    i. Synonymy
    ii. Meronymy
    iii. Metonymy
13. The basic building block of __________ are synsets.
    i. WordNet
    ii. Lexicon
    iii. FrameNet
14. The approach that understands meaning of a word by its relationship to meanings or senses of other words is called
    i. Ontological semantics
    ii. Distributional semantics
    iii. Decomponential semantics
15. PropBank is based on
    i. frame semantics of verbs
    ii. a set of verb–sense specific frames
    iii. lexicon

Self-Assessment: Match the Columns

No		Match	
1.	Destination	A	requires that all arguments to a verb are associated with syntactic constituents
2.	WordNet	B	abstracts from specific verbs so that semantic frames now enclose a number of verbs having similar description of roles
3.	Two level FST	C	when bound morphemes are combined with lexical morphemes
4.	Meronym	D	need the lexicon containing the list of stems and suffixes along with basic information about them
5.	Morphological Analysis	E	mapping from surface form to intermediate form and from intermediate form to lexical form
6.	Spelling Rules	F	approach that understands meaning of a word by the context in which the word is found, relative to other words
7.	Inflectional Morphology	G	morphological process which describes how features relevant to the syntactic context of a word indicating grammatical functions
8.	FrameNet	H	conveys whether two-word forms are similar or not but not the extent of similarity or dissimilarity
9.	Distributional Semantics	I	Component-of, Member-of and Portion-of
10.	PropBank	J	The entity towards which something moves, either literally or metaphorically

Short Questions

1. How do we define morphology and why is it important?
2. What are morphemes? Give the different types of morphemes with examples.
3. Describe the three types of morphology using illustrative examples.
4. Give some examples of spelling rules with examples for English language.
5. Why is morphological processing important for NLP? Discuss.
6. Describe the Porter Stemmer.

7. Discuss how morphological analysis takes the surface form, outputs the intermediate form and then the lexical form for the words "computational", "ungracefully" and "interestingness".

8. Give the finite state automata for adjectives of English.

9. Discuss the two level FST used for morphology and show the same for the example "knives".

10. Outline the categorization of word senses.

11. Describe the confusion matrices used for binary classification and multi–classification.

12. What are the three ways of understanding word meaning? Discuss.

13. Outline the core components of WordNet.

14. Describe with examples the semantic relations used by WordNet.

15. What are thematic roles? Describe the roles commonly used.

16. Describe the components of PropBank.

17. How is FrameNet different in comparison to WordNet and PropBank?

Representation of Text – Basic Vector Models

6.1 Representation of Text

One of the important requirements of machine learning approaches to NLP is the mathematical or numerical representation of the text that we can use as input to our machine learning models. These numerical representations are usually vectors. Unlike image representation where the RGB matrix gives a numerical representation, there is no apparent way to directly obtain numerical or vector representation of text. There are basically two approaches for representing words, both based on the underlying theory of Distributional Hypothesis (Harris 1954 & Firth 1957) which states that "similar words occur in similar contexts". In other words, vector representation encodes information about the distribution of contexts a word appears in. Words that appear in similar contexts have similar representations and hence similar meaning as stated by distributional hypothesis. The first approach called **distributional semantics** is count-based and has been used since the 1990s and includes Tf-idf, PPMI methods and class-based models such as brown clusters. The second and more recent approach is the distributed prediction-based embedding approach called **word embeddings** which has been inspired by deep learning. We will discuss aspects of distributional semantics in this chapter and word embeddings in the next chapter.

6.1.1 One-Shot Vector Representation of Words

Before we go further, vector model, let us discuss the simplest vector model for words. In this model, words are treated as atomic symbols. Viewed from one level it is a vector of weights. In the simple 1-of-N or one-hot encoding, every element in the vector is associated with a word in the vocabulary. For encoding a word, the corresponding element in the vector is set to one, and all other elements set to zero. Suppose our vocabulary has only 5 words then the encoding of the word "Apple" is as given in Figure 6.1.

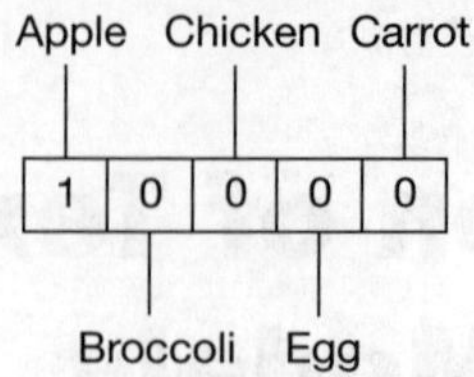

Figure 6.1: One Hot Encoding

One major limitation of one–hot encoding is that the vocabulary size must be determined in advance. The representation cannot scale to large vocabularies. Moreover, the method is computationally expensive with large input vectors which in turn results in having to learn too many parameters. Another limitation is the need to handle "Out-of-Vocabulary" (OOV) problem or the handling of words hitherto unseen. One naïve method to tackle this problem is to use a special symbol to represent low-frequency or unseen words. Another disadvantage of one–hot encoding is that the word vectors are not comparable, and at most they can be used for checking equality.

6.2 Distributional Semantics

As discussed in the previous chapter there are some obvious issues associated with resources such as WordNet. For example, nuances in the meaning of words are usually missing – example "shining" is the synonym of "brilliant" but however this is true only in some contexts. These resources are not always current and hence do not include new meanings of words. The building of the resources requires intense human effort. Moreover, these resources cannot be used accurately to compute word similarity. In traditional NLP, normally word meaning is represented by an index to the vocabulary.

The intuition behind distribution models is that linguistic items having similar distributions that are having similar contexts are similar (Figure 6.2). In this context, the meaning of the word is a vector of numbers and is represented as an embedding in vector space.

INTUITIONS OF DISTRIBUTIONAL MODELS

Suppose I have you the following corpus:
   I have **a book** on my shelf.
   Everyone loves reading **books.**
   Books can transport you to different worlds.
   We learn from **books.**
What is **book?**
From context, we can infer that **books** are objects used for reading and acquiring knowledge.
Intuition: two words **(book, knowledge)** are similar if they have similar word contexts.

Why do we need vector models of word?

To compute the similarity between words

Tasty is similar to **Delicious**
Question Answering

Q: How **tasty** the food is?
A: The food is very **delicious**

Figure 6.2: Intuitions of Distributional Models

There are many methods to encode the notion of "context" and obtain the word vectors. Some methods are based on counts, some based on prediction or learning, some are sparse while others are dense, and some have interpretable dimensions while some do not. Distributional semantics can thus be classified as being a sparse representation which include count based representation such as TF–IDF and PPMI and dense representations which include dimensionality reduction techniques such as Singular Value Decomposition (SVD), classed based Brown clusters and distributed prediction–based neural network based embeddings such as skip-grams and CBOW and finally distributed contextual embeddings obtained from language models such as BERT and Elmo (Figure 6.3).

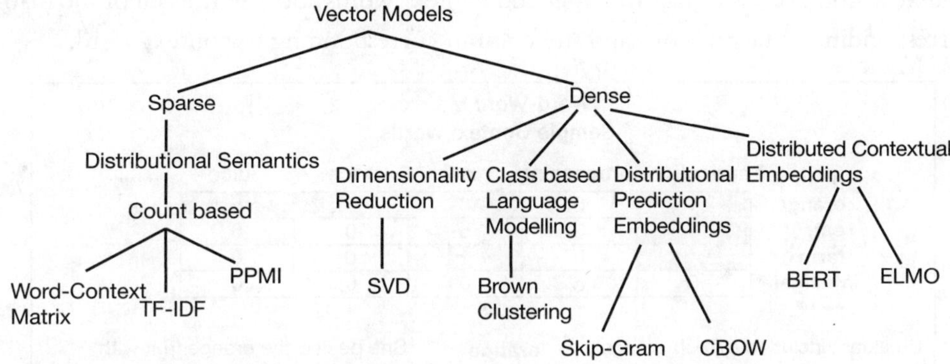

Figure 6.3: Distributed Vector Space Models

6.3 Count Based Distributional Vector Models

The simplest way to create the word vectors is to count the occurrences of context words. We can represent the frequency of occurrence of words in a document (here document is the context) to obtain term–document matrix. Another way is to represent the frequency of a word co–occurring with another.

6.3.1 Word-Context Matrix

A vector for the word "mango" has count of words in the context of "mango" in a dataset. There will be one entry in the vector for each unique context word. Then given the vocabulary V consisting of set of all words W, the vectors of all words are stacked to obtain the count matrix C which is called the word–context matrix or the term–term matrix or the word–co–occurrence matrix and is a matrix of size $|V| \times |V|$. In the word-context matrix, rather than using entire documents as contexts, smaller contexts are used such as a paragraph, a sentence or a window of n words where n usually is small and varies from 1 to 10 words (Figure 6.4). Figure 6.4 (a) shows an example where the matrix is of size 4×5. In reality, this matrix is very large such as 50,000 $\times$ 50,000 and hence is very sparse. The size of the window to be used depends on the purpose and affects the vector representation (Figure 6.4 (b)). In general, shorter windows of size 1–3 convey syntactic information for English like languages while longer windows of size 4–10 convey more semantic information. Considered from another viewpoint the co-occurrence between two words can be first-order that is the words are typically near each other, or can be second order that is they have similar neighbors. To construct the word–context matrix we first build the $|V| \times |V|$ matrix, with all entries initialized to zeros. Then we move a window of size $\pm n$ across the text. The central word is the target word and other words surrounding it are the context words. For every pair of target and context words add 1 in the cell of the matrix for row corresponding to target word and the column corresponding to context word.

Word-Word Matrix
Sample Context words

	agriculture	processing	fruit	price	juice	....
orange	1	0	3	1	6	
eat	1	0	5	0	0	
farm	4	0	1	0	0	
intelligent	0	6	0	0	0	

....

Breakfast included a fresh orange juice.	**orange**	She peeled the orange fruit with delight.
It's important to eat a balanced diet.	**eat**	We love to eat at that restaurant.
They grow vegetables on the family farm	**farm**	Cows grazed peacefully on the sunny farm
The AI system demonstrated highly intelligent behavior.	**intelligent**	The novel features an intelligent and resourceful protagonist.

Figure 6.4(a): Word Context Matrix

Sample: The cat sat on the mat	**Sample:** The sun sets behind the mountains
	Window Size 2
Window Size 1	**The:** none
Mr Dr Ms Miss prof	**sun:** The, sets
cat sat on the mat	**sets:** sun, The, behind, the
her him you we they	**behind:** sun, sets, the, mountains
	mountains: behind, the
More syntactic, and same part-of-speech-tag	More semantic, and mix of part-of-speech-tags

Figure 6.4(b): Examples of Word Context Matrix

6.3.2 Term Frequency–Inverse Document Frequency (TF-IDF)

TF-IDF representation is based on Bag of Words (BoW). Term–Document matrix is used to represent the document matrix whose size is determined by the size of the vocabulary obtained after removing stop words (row) and the size of the corpus (column) (Figure 6.5). BoW has already been discussed in Chapter 3. The columns of the Term–Document Matrix represent the document vectors while the rows represent the term vector. Each value in the cell of the matrix gives the frequency of a term in the that document. Two documents can be compared by comparing their document vectors. TF-IDF captures importance of a word in a document.

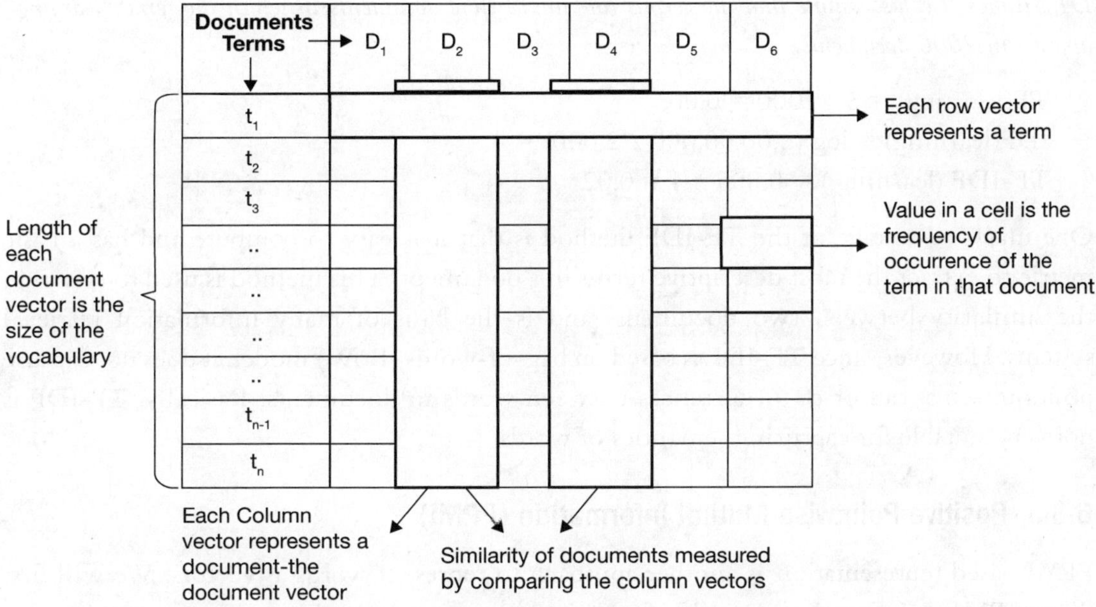

Figure 6.5: Term Document Matrix

relative to the corpus. BOW basically gives count of occurrences of a word or term in a document and the importance of a term increases proportionally to the number of times a word appears in the document but is inversely proportional to the frequency of the word in the corpus. These aspects are captured by term frequency (TF) and inverse document frequency (IDF) and is given as in Equation (6.1), Equation (6.2) and Equation (6.3)

$$\text{Term Frequency of a term } t = \text{TF}(t) = \frac{\text{No. of times term } t \text{ appears in a document } d}{\text{Total No. of terms in the document)}} = tf_{t,d} \qquad 6.1$$

Inverse Document Frequency of term = inverse fraction of number of Documents D_t containing term t among total number of documents in the collection

$$N = \text{IDF}(t) = \frac{\log(\text{Total No of documents})}{\text{No. of document with term } t \text{ n it}} = \frac{\log N}{D_t} \qquad 6.2$$

Then $\text{TF} - \text{IDF}(t) = \text{TF}(t) * \text{IDF}(t) = tf_{t,d} * \dfrac{\log N}{D_t}$

Example 6.1

Let us assume that a document D1 contains 1000 words. The term "learning" appears in document D1 5 times. Let us assume that the corpus contains 2 crore documents in which the term "learning" appears in 2000 documents.

    TF(learning) = 5 / 1000 = 0.005
    IDF(learning) = log (2,00,00,000 / 2,000) = 4
    TF-IDF (learning) = 0.005 * 4 = 0.02

One major advantage of the TF-IDF method is that it is easy to compute and has a basic metric to extract the most descriptive terms in a document. This method is used to compute the similarity between two documents and is the basis of many information retrieval systems. However, since TF-IDF is based on bag-of-words (BoW) model, it does not capture position, semantics or co-occurrences between words in documents. Basically, TF-IDF is not very suitable for capturing semantics of words.

6.3.3 Positive Pointwise Mutual Information (PPMI)

PPMI based representation is another approach to represent words as vectors. We will first discuss PMI or Pointwise Mutual Information (Equation 6.4) where rather than using raw counts of words based on frequency, we determine whether a word w_1 and w_2 co-occur more than if they were independent.

$$\text{PMI}(w_1, w_2) = \log_2 \frac{P(w_1, w_2)}{P(w_1)P(w_2)} \qquad 6.4$$

The value of PMI ranges from $-\infty$ to $+\infty$. However, the interpretation of negative values is that words are co-occurring less than we expect by chance, but this is unreliable unless we have an enormous corpus. Therefore, we replace negative PMI value by 0 and hence we have positive PMI or PPMI defined as follows:

Positive PMI that is PPMI can be derived from PMI as follows (Equation 6.5):

$$\text{PMI}\left(w_1, w_2\right) = \max\left(\log_2 \frac{P\left(w_1, w_2\right)}{P\left(w_1\right)P\left(w_2\right)}, 0\right)$$

6.5

Now let us discuss (Equations 6.6–6.10) the computing PPMI on a word–context matrix X having W words as rows and C columns as contexts.

Let X_{ij} = number of times word w_i occurs in context c_j

Probability of occurrence of w_i occurs in context c_j out of occurrences of each word in each context

$$p_{ij} = \frac{X_{ij}}{\sum_{i=1}^{W}\sum_{j=1}^{C} X_{ij}}$$

6.6

Probability of occurrence of all words out of occurrences of each word in each context

$$p_w = \frac{\sum_{j=1}^{C} X_{ij}}{\sum_{i=1}^{W}\sum_{j=1}^{C} X_{ij}}$$

6.7

Probability of occurrence of all words out of occurrences of each word in each context

$$p_c = \frac{\sum_{i=1}^{W} X_{ij}}{\sum_{i=1}^{W}\sum_{j=1}^{C} X_{ij}}$$

6.8

The pointwise mutual information (PMI) $pm_{ij} = \log_2 \dfrac{p_{ij}}{p_w \star p_c}$

6.9

Positive pointwise mutual information (PPMI) $ppm_{ij} = \begin{cases} pm_{ij} & \text{if } pm_{ij} > 0 \\ 0 & \text{otherwise} \end{cases}$

6.10

Contexts

Words		agriculture	processing	fruit	price	juice
	orange	1	0	3	1	6
	eat	1	0	5	0	0
	farm	4	0	3	2	0
	intelligent	1	6	0	0	0

$$P(W = \text{orange}, C = \text{agriculture}) = \frac{1}{33} = 0.030$$

$$P(W = \text{orange}, C = \text{fruit}) = \frac{3}{33} = 0.090$$

$$P(W = \text{orange}, C = \text{price}) = \frac{1}{33} = 0.030$$

Likewise for all words and contexts it should be determined.

$$P(W = \text{orange}, C = \text{juice}) = \frac{6}{33} = 0.181$$

$$P(W = \text{eat}, C = \text{agriculture}) = \frac{1}{33} = 0.030$$

$$P(W = \text{eat}, C = \text{fruit}) = \frac{5}{33} = 0.151$$

P(W, Context)

	agriculture	processing	fruit	price	juice	**P(w)**
orange	0.030	0	0.090	0.030	0.181	**0.331**
eat	0.030	0	0.151	0	0	**0181**
farm	0.121	0	0.090	0.060	0	**0.271**
intelligent	0.030	0.181	0	0	0	**0.211**
P(context)	**0.211**	**0.181**	**0.331**	**0.090**	**0.181**	

$$\text{PMI}(\text{farm}, \text{agriculture}) = \log_2 \frac{0.121}{0.211 * 0.271} = 0.326$$

$$\text{PMI}(\text{farm}, \text{fruit}) = \log_2 \frac{0.090}{0.331 * 0.271} = 0.0048$$

$$P(\text{intelligent}, \text{agriculture}) = \log_2 \frac{0.030}{0.211 * 0.211} = -0.166$$

$$P(\text{intelligent}, \text{processing}) = \log_2 \frac{0.181}{0.211 * 0.181} = 0.677$$

Figure 6.6: Example– PPMI Calculation (*Continued*)

PMI (*W*, Context)

	agriculture	processing	fruit	price	juice
orange	−0.36	0	−0.08	0.014	0.480
eat	−0.105	0	0.401	0	0
farm	0.326	0	0.004	0.397	0
intelligent	−0.166	0.677	0	0	0

PPMI (*W*, Context)

	agriculture	processing	fruit	price	juice
orange	0.00	–	0.00	0.014	0.480
eat	0.00	–	0.401	–	–
farm	0.326	–	0.004	0.397	–
intelligent	0.00	0.677	–	–	–

Figure 6.6: Example- PPMI Calculation

Figure 6.6 shows an example of PPMI calculation.

6.4 Sparse versus Dense Vectors

Traditional distributional vector representations of words are sparse vectors. Each dimension of the word represents one specific context and, in each case, whether term–term matrix or term–document matrix, the vector entries are based or term–context co–occurrence. The vectors representing words are long (normally is the size of the vocabulary) and sparse where most elements are zero. An alternative to the methods one-short encoding, word–context matrix, TF–IDF, and PPMI based word–context matrix discussed in Section 6.2, where the representation is long and sparse, we can learn vectors which are comparatively short and dense. Short vectors are often easier to use as features since there are less parameters to tune. Moreover, dense vectors may generalize better when compared to storing explicit counts. These representations are often better at capturing semantic concepts such as synonymy and in general work better.

6.5 Short Dense Vectors using Singular Value Decomposition

The intuition behind dimensionality reduction is that we approximate an N-dimensional dataset using fewer dimensions or fewer axes of data. This is carried out by rotating the axes into a new space where the higher order dimension captures the maximum variance present in the original dataset, the next higher dimension is the direction orthogonal to the first in which the points show second highest variance, and so on. Many dimensionality reduction methods such as Principal Components Analysis (PCA), Factor analysis and Singular Value Decomposition (SVD) are based on the above intuition. In this chapter, we will be describing SVD. In essence, it is a method for transforming correlated variables into a set of uncorrelated ones exposing relationship among the original data items. SVD accomplishes this by identifying and ordering the dimensions along which data points exhibit the most variation.

Let us discuss the SVD technique applied to a term–document matrix as shown in Figure 6.7. I – Input Data Matrix of dimension $m \times n$ (m - documents and n - terms) having rank r which is decomposed into three matrices,

W – Left Singular Matrix of dimension $m \times r$ (m- documents and r – concepts),

Σ – Singular Values Diagonal matrix of dimension $r \times r$ (strength of each concept) where r is the rank of matrix I, and

C – Right Singular Matrix of dimension $n \times r$ (n – terms and r concepts) where t his decomposition gives an approximation of the original input matrix I.

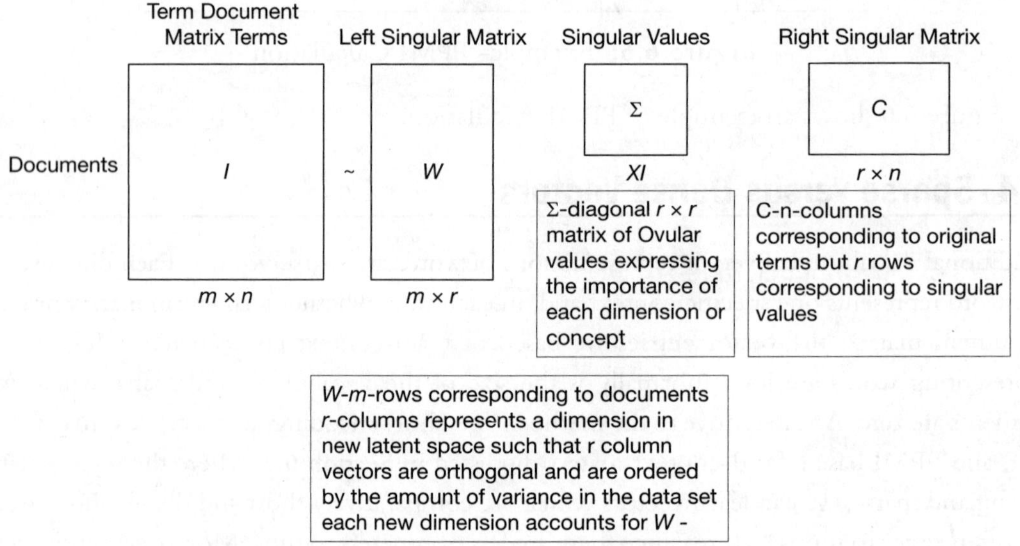

Figure 6.7: Singular Value Decomposition

Let I^T be the transpose of input matrix I with dimension $n \times m$. Now, II^T and $I^T I$ have the same set of eigen vectors $\lambda_1, \lambda_2, \dots\dots \lambda_r$. Then there is a singular value decomposition (SVD) of input matrix $I = U\Sigma C^T$. W, the left singular matrix consists of the eigenvectors of the matrix II^T, C, the right singular matrix holds the eigenvectors of the matrix $I^T I$, and Σ is a diagonal matrix having the diagonal formed by the square roots of the eigenvalues of either the matrix II^T or the matrix $I^T I$. The singular values in Σ are non–negative and sorted in decreasing order($\sigma_1 \geq \sigma_2 \geq\dots\dots\geq 0$).

6.6 Short Dense Vectors using Class based Brown Clustering

Brown clustering is a greedy method of hierarchical clustering of words based on the contexts in which they occur that is based on distributional similarity. The intuition behind the method is that similar words appear in similar contexts and have similar distributions of words to their immediate left and right. Brown clustering is a class–based model that is one where probabilities of words are based on the classes or clusters of previous words. In essence, Brown clustering is based on the simple bigram class–based language model.

The word clusters obtained from brown clustering can be represented as a vector and can be used to address the data sparsity problem. Brown clustering consists of the following steps:

Brown Clustering Algorithm

Input: *A large corpus having T words* w_1, w_2, w_3,........ w_T *and having vocabulary V*

Output: *A partition of words divided into word clusters and a generalized hierarchical word clustering*

Assumption: *Objective is to obtain a partition of m clusters* $C \to \{1,2,3....m\}$

Step 1: *Sort the words W in the collection by frequency.*

Step 2: *Consider the top m most frequent words. Each word of these m words initially forms its own cluster that is m clusters* c_1, c_2, c_3, ... c_1

Step 3: *Repeat merge step (m+1)-|V| times*

Create a new cluster c_{m+1}

Choose two clusters from the now present m+1 clusters and merge based on maximum quality (Q) and obtain m clusters. Quality Q is defined as a merging of two words that have the most similar probabilities of preceding and succeeding words. Given that

$$Quality(C) = \prod_{i=1}^{n} p(w_i \mid C(w_i))p(C(w_i) \mid C(w_{i-1}))$$

where $p(C(w_i) \mid C(w_{i-1}))s$ *is the probability of cluster of* w_i *to follow the cluster of* w_{i-1}

$$p(w_i \mid C(w_i)) = \frac{count(w_i)}{\sum_{x \in C(w_i)} count(x)}$$

$$p(w_1, w_2, ...w_T) = \prod_{i=1}^{n} p(w_i \mid C(w_i))p(C(w_i) \mid C(w_{i-1}))$$

We select a merging that maximizes the quality of the partition.

Step 4: *Carry out m-1 final merges to obtain the final hierarchy.*

Brown Clusters as Vectors: The order in which the clusters are merged is traced and a binary tree is constructed from bottom to top. Each word is represented by a binary string which is the path from the root to leaf of this binary tree. Each intermediate node in the tree is a cluster. The output can also be thought of as a sequence of merges finally ending up with a big class of all words.

An example of the vector representation is given in Figure 6.8.

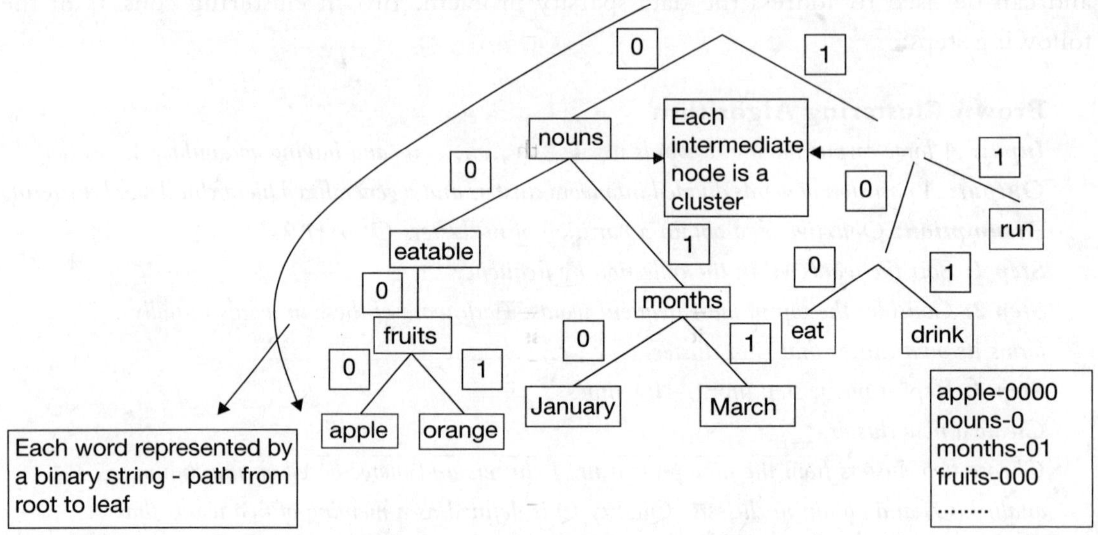

Figure 6.8: Brown Clustering and Vector Formation

We will discuss the other distributed dense representations in the succeeding chapters.

6.7 Measuring Similarity

Distributional similarities use the representation of the set of contexts in which words appear to measure similarity. Each word is represented as a vector in an n–dimensional vector space. As discussed in the previous sections, each dimension in the vector space corresponds to a particular context and each element captures the degree to which the word is associated with a context. The similarity between two words is then given by the similarity between their corresponding vectors. The most common method to measure similarity between two vectors is based on **dot product or inner product**. The dot product is given by (Equation 6.11):

$$u.v = \sum_{i=1}^{d} u_i v_i \qquad \text{6.11}$$

The value of dot product is dependent on the size of the vector which in turn is longer if they have higher values in each dimension. Hence frequent words having larger counts results in larger dot product. Therefore, the issue with using dot product as a similarity metric is that it is sensitive to word frequency. A method to overcome the above issue is to normalize by dividing the dot product by the length of the vectors. This is nothing but the **cosine** of the angle between the vectors (Equation 6.12).

$$\cos\theta = \frac{\vec{x}.\vec{y}}{|\vec{x}||\vec{y}|} \qquad \text{6.12}$$

The cosine similarity metric value of –1 indicates that the vectors point in opposite directions while a value of + 1 indicates that the vector point in the same direction. Since word counts are non–zero the cosine ranges from 0 to 6. Higher value of cosine between two–word vectors indicate high similarity between the words. Figure 6.9 shows an example of the calculation of cosine similarity between two words.

	agriculture	processing	fruit	price
orange	1	0	3	1
farm	4	0	3	2
intelligent	1	6	0	0
computer	0	5	0	4

$$\text{cosine similarity}(\text{orange, farm}) = \frac{4+0+9+2}{\sqrt{1+0+9+1}\sqrt{16+0+9+4}} = \frac{15}{\sqrt{11}\sqrt{29}} = 0.839$$

$$\text{cosine similarity}(\text{orange, intelligent}) = \frac{1+0+0+0}{\sqrt{1+0+9+1}\sqrt{1+36+0+0}} = \frac{1}{\sqrt{11}\sqrt{37}} = 0.049$$

$$\text{cosine similarity}(\text{orange, computer}) = \frac{0+0+0+4}{\sqrt{1+0+9+1}\sqrt{0+25+0+16}} = \frac{4}{\sqrt{11}\sqrt{41}} = 0.188$$

$$\text{cosine similarity}(\text{farm, intelligent}) = \frac{4+0+0+4}{\sqrt{16+0+9+4}\sqrt{1+36+0+0}} = \frac{8}{\sqrt{29}\sqrt{37}} = 0.244$$

$$\text{cosine similarity}(\text{farm, computer}) = \frac{0+0+0+8}{\sqrt{16+0+9+4}\sqrt{0+25+0+16}} = \frac{8}{\sqrt{29}\sqrt{41}} = 0.232$$

$$\text{cosine similarity}(\text{intelligent, computer}) = \frac{0+30+0+0}{\sqrt{1+36+0+0}\sqrt{0+25+0+16}} = \frac{30}{\sqrt{37}\sqrt{41}} = 0.770$$

Figure 6.9: Cosine Similarity between Word Vectors

Other distance measures such as Euclidean distance and Manhattan distance can also be used to measure similarity between two word vectors as given below (Equation 6.13, Equation 6.14):

$$\text{Manhattan distance}\left(L1\ norm\right) = dist_{L1}\left(\vec{x}, \vec{y}\right) = \sum_{i=1}^{N}\left|x_i - y_i\right| \qquad 6.13$$

$$\text{Euclidian distance}\left(L2\ norm\right) = dist_{L2}\left(\vec{x}, \vec{y}\right) = \sqrt{\sum_{i=1}^{N}\left(x_i - y_i\right)^2} \qquad 6.14$$

6.8 Evaluation

The representation of word vectors is evaluated basically in two ways. One is extrinsic evaluation where the evaluation is carried out by task based end-to-end evaluation where the NLP tasks can be question answering, essay writing, etc. On the other hand, intrinsic evaluation determines the relatedness correlation using Spearman or Pearson correlation between vector similarity of a pair of words represented using the model and the similarity as judged by humans.

Summary

- Introduced the basic concepts of numerical representation of text including one-shot vector representation.
- Discussed the concept of distributional semantics.
- Explained count-based distributional vector models including word–context matrix, term–document matrix and PPI.
- Compared sparse and dense vector representations.
- Outlined two types of sparse vector representations that used single value decomposition and class based brown clustering.
- Explained the various methods of measuring similarity between distributed representations.
- Briefly discussed the evaluation of representation of word vectors

Exercises

Suggested Activities

1. Take two sample documents that are similar and build TF–IDF and PPMI representations and compare their similarity using cosine similarity.
2. Explain 3 NLP applications that uses similarity between documents.
3. **Case Study 1: Spam Email Detection:** Using Enron email dataset (https://www.cs.cmu.edu/~enron/) classify emails as spam or non-spam using TF–IDF words and a SVM classifier
4. **Case Study 2: Sentiment Analysis:** Using Amazon product reviews dataset (https://www.kaggle.com/datasets/saurav9786/amazon-product-reviews) determine the sentiment of text data. The data has to be converted into numerical vectors using any of the techniques discussed in this chapter. The training can be carried out using any of the supervised learning techniques. Evaluate performance using metrics like accuracy, precision, recall, and F1-score.

Self-Assessment: Multiple Choice Questions

Give answers with justification for correct and wrong choices:

1. Distributional Hypothesis states that
    i. Similar words occur in similar contexts
    ii. Similar words are distributed throughout the document
    iii. Similar words are distributed syntactically
2. Brown Clusters are
    i. Short vectors
    ii. Dimensionality reduction techniques
    iii. Class-based models
3. A major limitation of one-hot encoding is
    i. Fixed size dense vector
    ii. Vocabulary size must be known in advance
    iii. Variable size sparse vector
4. Shorter windows of size 1–3 in word context matrix
    i. Convey semantic information
    ii. Convey syntactic information for English like languages
    iii. Convey POS tagging information for English like languages

5. TF-IDF is based on
   i. Phrases
   ii. Independent Document Frequency
   iii. Bag of Words
6. IDF is defined as
   i. Inverse fraction of number of documents containing the term among total number of documents in the collection
   ii. Independent function of number of a particular term among total number of terms in the collection
   iii. Inverse fraction of number of a particular term among total number of terms in the collection
7. Pointwise Mutual Information is based on whether
   i. A word w1 and w2 co-occur more than if they were independent
   ii. Words are mutually exclusive
   iii. Raw counts of words are frequent
8. The intuition behind dimensionality reduction is
   i. Randomly removing some less important dimensions
   ii. Approximating N–dimensional dataset using fewer dimensions
   iii. Rotating the axes into a new space where the higher order dimensions capture the maximum variance present
9. Brown clustering is a
   i. Greedy method of hierarchical clustering of words based on the contexts in which they occur
   ii. Greedy method of clustering of words based on the contexts in which they occur
   iii. Lazy method of hierarchical clustering of words based on the phrases in which they occur
10. Cosine of the angle between the vectors is
   i. The dot product between the two vectors divided by the angle of the vectors
   ii. The dot product between the two vectors divided by the length of the vectors
   iii. The dot product between the two vectors

Self-Assessment: Match the Columns

No		Match	
1.	Distributional Hypothesis	A	method for transforming correlated variables into a set of uncorrelated ones exposing relationship among the original data items

No		Match	
2.	"Out-of-Vocabulary" (OOV) problem	B	determines the relatedness correlation using Spearman or Pearson correlation
3.	The co-occurrence between two words is of second order	C	similar words occur in similar contexts
4.	TF-IDF	D	class-based model that is one where probabilities of words are based on the classes or clusters of previous words
5.	Dense Vectors	E	carried out by task based end-to-end evaluation
6.	Singular Value Decomposition	F	One-shot encoding
7.	Brown clustering	G	measure similarity between two vectors
8.	Inner product	H	They have similar neighbors
9.	Extrinsic evaluation carried out by task based end-to-end evaluation	I	importance of a term increases proportionally to the number of times a word appears in the document but is inversely proportional to the frequency of the word in the corpus
10.	Intrinsic evaluation	J	generalize better when compared to storing explicit counts

E.6.4 Short Questions

1. Explain the role played by distributional hypothesis in the representation of text.
2. Discuss the limitations of one-shot encoding.
3. Give three examples that explain the intuition of distributional models.
4. Give a classification diagram of the different types of distributed vector models. Explain each type in a sentence or two.
5. What is word context matrix? Discuss with an illustrative example.

6. Let us assume that a document D1 contains 5000 words. The term "representation" appears in document D1 20 times. Let us assume that the corpus contains 1 crore documents in which the term "representation" appears in 1000 documents.

7. Explain how the concepts of PMI and PPMI are used to represent words as vectors.

8. Discuss the application of dimensionality reduction of a term–document matrix using SVD technique.

9. Explain in detail the Brown clustering algorithm.

10. Given the following table, show the calculation of cosine similarity between the words.

	work	sports	stove	cricket	food
cook	1	0	5	0	4
play	3	5	0	6	2
recipe	0	0	3	0	6
tournament	1	6	1	5	2
score	3	5	0	4	1

Neural Language Models - I

7.1 N-Gram Language Model – A Recap

In chapter 4, we discussed n-gram language models where words were represented in discrete space based on vocabulary. Here again we will discuss the construction of word representations in continuous space using vector models. Reviewing the goal of language models which is that of learning a function that returns a joint probability. Language models are used to compute the probability of a sentence or sequence of words (Equation 7.1):

$$P(W) = P(w_1, w_2, w_3, \ldots, w_n) \tag{7.1}$$

The language model is also used to predict the probability of a succeeding word as in Equation 7.2:

$$P(w_5 | w_1, w_2, w_3, w_4) \tag{7.2}$$

Therefore, by calculating the product of the probability of each word given its previous words in case of a sentence or by calculating the probability of each sentence in the document given the previous sentences, the likelihood of a sentence or whole document can be computed.

Given a document or sentence $w_1, w_2, w_3, \ldots\ldots w_T$

$$P(w_1, w_2, w_3, \ldots, w_n) = \sum_{t=1}^{T} P(w_t | w_{t-1}, \ldots, w_2, w_1) \tag{7.3}$$

7.1.1 Limitations of N-gram Model

- N-gram language modelling needs too many parameters to accurately estimate the required joint probability distribution or the model is associated with the **curse of dimensionality** or sparse statistics. The curse of dimensionality is described mathematically as an increase in volume in Euclidean space when the dimension increases. In the context of machine learning, when the number of features or attributes used to describe the data increases, the number of data points required for effective machine learning increases exponentially. When we consider language models, the curse of dimensionality arises when we model the full joint distribution of say 10 consecutive words, considering vocabulary size to be 1,00,000 words, then we have approximately $1,00,000^{10} \approx 10^{50}$ parameters that we need to estimate. N-gram models simplify the above problem by predicting a word based on limited context usually the preceding word only. N-gram models generally do not take into account contexts farther than 1 or 2 words. However, this limits the possibility of extending this representation for hitherto unseen n-grams. Partial solution to this issue is the adding of a small value as count to every word in the vocabulary with the process of smoothing.

- Another issue associated with n–gram models is the need to store the count of all possible n–grams.

- Moreover, n-gram based models treat all words / prefixes independently of each other and hence fail to generalize to already observed related words or word sequences since they assume that each word depends only on preceding n–1 words.

- N-gram models consider the identity of the previous words but does not take into account any other information such as grammatical roles or semantics about the sequence preceding the words. In other words, n-gram models do not consider the similarity between words. Figure 7.1 shows the example of two sentences, where given the first sentence, the model should be able to generalize for the second sentence since the–a, boy–girl, and fruit–mango have similar semantic and grammatical roles.

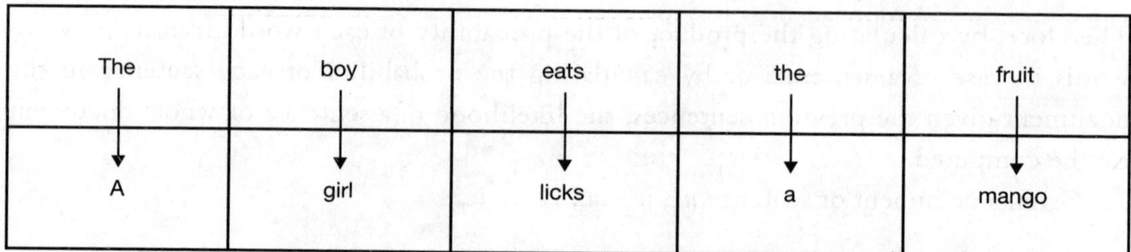

Figure 7.1: Sentences having Similarity

7.2 Neural Language Models

Bag-of-Words representation is normally used for representation of words by N-gram models. In this representation each word is represented by a vector of size V, where V is the size of the vocabulary, and this is vector of zeros with a single 1 indicating the word's index in the vocabulary. Using this representation all words are equally similar or dissimilar. This one-hot representation is simple but however, words which are semantically similar do not have similar representations.

7.2.1 Basics of Neural Language Models

A language model that exploits the ability of neural networks to learn distributed representations can be used to reduce the impact of the curse of dimensionality. The model simultaneously learns a distributed representation for each word and the probability function for word sequences, expressed in terms of these representations. It is possible to A sequence of words hitherto never observed can become highly probable because it is composed of words that fall near words already seen in feature space thus achieving generalization. The first neural language model based on simple feedforward neural networks was introduced by Bengio et.al in 2003 where they discuss many important aspects of neural language modelling. However, current neural language models use more powerful neural network architectures such as recurrent networks and transformer networks. In the next section we will discuss Feedforward Neural Language Models.

7.2.2 Advantages and Disadvantages of Neural Language Models

Some of the advantages of neural language models over n-gram language models are that they can handle longer histories, can generalize better over contexts of similar words, and can predict words more accurately. However, since neural net language models are complex, they are slower and are more computing intensive to train and are less interpretable than n-gram models.

7.3 Feedforward Neural Language Model (LM)

Feedforward neural language model is a feedforward network that takes as input takes a distributed representation of some number of prior words (w_{t-1}, w_{t-2}, etc.) and outputs a probability distribution over possible next word. However, just as is the case with n-gram language models, the feedforward neural LM approximates the probability of a word given the entire prior context by approximating based on the $N-1$ previous words (Equation 7.4):

$$P(w_t \mid w_1, \ldots w_{t-1}) \approx P(w_t \mid w_{t-N+1}, \ldots w_{t-1}) \tag{7.4}$$

In the model introduced by Bengio, et.al (Bengio et al 2001, Bengio et al 2003), the probabilistic prediction $P(w_t \mid w_{t-n+1}, \dots w_{t-1})$ is obtained by first obtaining the embedding layer or the embeddings of the context words. Thus, instead of using word identity as is done by n-gram models, prior context represented by their embeddings (distributed representations) are used by neural language models. This usage of embeddings allows neural language models to generalize better when unseen data is encountered.

7.3.1 Concepts of Feedforward Neural Language Model

The training set to the neural model is a sequence $w_1, \dots \dots w_T$ of words where $w_t \in V$, the vocabulary which is a large finite set. The objective of the neural model is to learn the function (Equation 7.5):

$$f\left(w_t, \dots, w_{t-n+1}\right) = P(w_t \mid w_1^{t-1}) \tag{7.5}$$

This function can be decomposed into two parts:

- A mapping C from any element i of V to a real vector $C(i) \in \mathfrak{R}^m$. This represents the **distributed feature vectors** associated with each word in the dictionary.
- The probability function over words expressed with the feature vectors C with a function g that maps an input sequence of feature vectors for words context (Equation 7.6)

$$C\left(w_{t-n+1}\right), \dots, C\left(w_{t-1}\right) \tag{7.6}$$

to a conditional probability distribution over words in V for the next word w_t. The output of the function g is a vector whose i-th estimates the probability (Equation 7.7)

$$P(w_t = i \mid w_1^{t-1}) \tag{7.7}$$

Therefore, the function f is a composition of the two mappings C which is shared across all words in the context and the mapping g as follows (Equation 7.8):

$$f\left(i, w_{t-1}, \dots, w_{t-n+1}\right) = g\left(i, C\left(w_{t-1}\right), \dots, C\left(w_{t-n+1}\right)\right) \tag{7.8}$$

7.3.2 Distributed Representation of Context Words

Neural language models use continuous representations or sometimes called embeddings of words to make their predictions that is we associate with each word in the vocabulary a distributed *word feature vector* (a real valued vector in R^m). In this model each word in the vocabulary is associated with a distributed real-valued word feature vector instead one-hot vectors. This feature vector represents different aspects of the word and is associated with a point in the continuous vector feature space. The number of features associated with the distributed representation varies between 30 to 100 and is much smaller than the size of the vocabulary which is often in lakhs.

Each word in the dictionary is represented using a continuous–valued vector having say m dimensions (often with values 30, 60 or 100). A semantic or grammatical characteristic of the word is associated with each dimension of this m dimensional space. In this new feature space functionally, similar words are likely to be closer to each other along at least some of these dimensions. The feature vector representation distributes the representation along all dimensions of an embedding vector (we will discuss this embedding vector soon) and are able to model similarity between words. They distribute probability mass where it matters rather than uniformly in all directions around each training point and therefore, allow generalization across sentences . In the following examples we will show a 4–gram example, so we will use the neural net to estimate the probability that is previous context consists of 3 words (Equation 7.9):

$$P(w_t \mid w_{t-3}, w_{t-2}, w_{t-1}) \tag{7.9}$$

This component of the neural network model is shown in Figure 7.2.

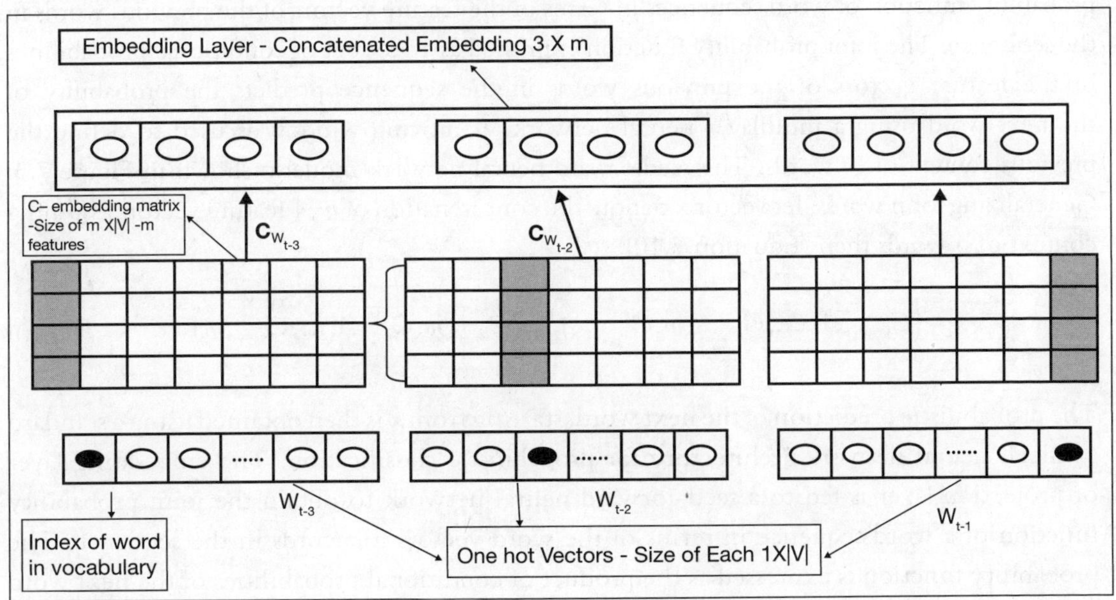

Figure 7.2: Distributed Representation of 3 Context Words

The previous context in this case the three previous words are each represented as one hot vector of size $|V|$ where V is the vocabulary and $|V|$ is the number of unique words in the vocabulary. These one–hot vectors are mapped into a low-dimensional real-valued space using the shared weight matrix C of size $m \times |V|$ where m is the number of features used to represent the word. The shared embedding or weight matrix C basically acts as a lookup table for the words in the vocabulary and consists of pre-computed embeddings of the words. We will discuss later the building of this weight matrix C. Each column is a representation or encoding for each word in the vocabulary, each vector being of m dimensions. This column can be viewed as an embedding since it indicates a location in a high-dimensional space with words that are closer being semantically closer and can also be viewed as a feature vector since it can be used just like any feature vector for making predictions . Thus, we get the low-dimensional real-valued vector or embedding of size m associated with each context word and concatenating the representations of the context words we get a one-dimensional embedding layer of size 3m. This layer is followed by the hidden layer and the output layer.

7.3.3 Feed-Forward Neural Network for Prediction

During the forward pass of the network a probability distribution over possible outputs that is the next words is produced. This is called forward inference. Here we express the joint probability function of word sequences in terms of the feature vectors of the previous words in the sequence. The joint probability function expressed as a product of conditional probabilities of the feature vectors of the previous words in the sequence predicts the probability of the next word using a multilayer neural network. A moving window is used to define the previous context of N words. The feedforward neural network model is shown in Figure 7.3. Generalizing for n words, let vector x denote the concatenation of $n-1$ feature vectors assuming context of n words then (Equation 7.10)

$$x = \left(C_{w_{t-n+1}}, 1, ..., C_{w_{t-n+1}}, m, C_{w_{t-n+2}}, 1, ..., C_{w_{t-2}}, m, C_{w_{t-1}}, 1, ..., C_{w_{t-1}}, m \right) \tag{7.10}$$

The probabilistic prediction of the next word, starting from x is then obtained using a standard artificial neural network architecture for probabilistic classification. The embedding layer or projection layer is fed to a feed-forward neural network to obtain the joint probability function of a word sequence in terms of the word vectors for words in the sequence. The probability function is expressed as the product of conditional probabilities of the next word given the previous word (Equation 7.11).

$$\hat{P}\left(w_t \mid w_{t-1}, ..., w_{t-n+1} \right) \tag{7.11}$$

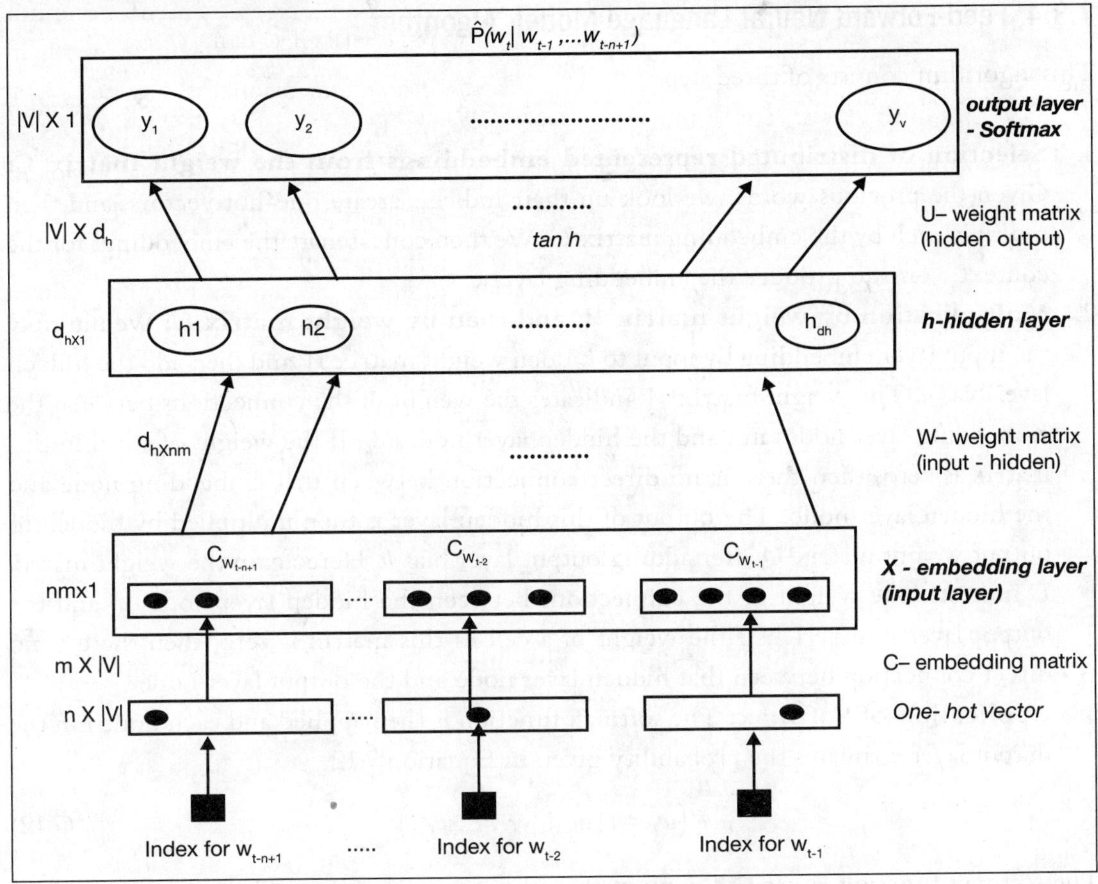

Figure 7.3: Prediction with Feedforward Neural Language Model

The feedforward model thus takes as input the sequence of embedded context words (the vector of concatenated embeddings – the embedding layer) and 2 other layers – the hidden layer which uses tanh as the activation function and the output layer which uses the softmax function. The role of activation function in the neural network is to derive output from a set of input values fed to a layer. In the neural language model, the tanh function is used by the hidden layer and has the S–shape with output range being –1 to 1. The softmax function is used to transform the resulting vector into a probability distribution.

The probability function is expressed as a product of conditional probabilities of the next word given the previous ones, using a multilayer neural network to predict the next word given the context. This function has parameters that can be iteratively tuned in order to **maximize the log-likelihood of the training data** or a regularized criterion, e.g. by adding a weight decay penalty. The feature vectors associated with each word are learned, but they could be initialized using prior knowledge of semantic features.

7.3.4 Feed-Forward Neural Language Model- Algorithm

This algorithm consists of three steps:

1. **Selection of distributed represented embeddings from the weight matrix C:** Given the previous words, we look up their indices, create one–hot vectors, and then multiply each by the embedding matrix C. We then concatenate the embeddings for the context words to produce the embedding layer e.

2. **Multiplication by weight matrix W and then by weight matrix U:** We multiply the input layer embedding by input to hidden weight matrix W and then add the hidden layer bias d. The weight matrix W indicates the weight of the connections between the embedding layer nodes nm and the hidden layer nodes d_h. If the weight of a cell in this matrix is zero, then there is no direct connection between that embedding node and the hidden layer node. The output of this hidden layer is then multiplied by hidden to output weight matrix U after adding output layer bias b. Here again the weight matrix U indicates the weight of the connections between the hidden layer nodes d_h and the output layer nodes $|V|$. If the weight of a cell in this matrix is zero, then there is no direct connection between that hidden layer node and the output layer node.

3. **Application of Softmax:** The softmax function is then applied and each node i in the output layer estimates the probability given in Equation 7.12

$$P\left(w_t = i \mid w_{t-N+1}, \ldots, w_{t-1}\right) \tag{7.12}$$

The softmax function is used to convert the output to probability vales and is given as in Equation 7.13

$$softmax\left(x\right) = \frac{e^x}{\sum_j e^{x_j}} \tag{7.13}$$

where x is a vector x, x_j is dimension j of x where each dimension j of the softmaxed output represents the probability of class j

In the case where we assume context of three, this equation is then (Equation 7.6)

$$P(w_t = i \mid w_{t-3}, w_{t-2}, w_{t-1})$$

In summary, the equations for a neural language model with a window size of 3, given one-hot input vectors for each input context word (Equation 7.11), and the output is as given in Equation 7.14:

$$e = \left[C_{X_{t-3}}, C_{X_{t-2}}, C_{X_{t-1}}\right]$$

$$y = b + Wx + U\tanh\left(d + Hx\right) \qquad (7.14)$$

Here, x is the word features layer activation vector, which is the concatenation of the input word features from the matrix C and the hyperbolic tangent $\tan h$ is applied element by element. In the above model, the number of free parameters **only scales linearly** with V, the number of words in the vocabulary and **only scales linearly** with the order n.

7.3.5 Example to Explain Neural Language Models

Given a d-dimensional vector representation x of a prefix, we do the following to predict the next word. First, we project it to a V-dimensional vector using a matrix–vector product (a.k.a. a "linear layer", or a "feedforward layer"), where V is the size of the vocabulary. Next, we apply the softmax function to transform the resulting vector into a probability distribution. the We carry out the *forward pass* to compute the prediction of the next word given an existing neural language model which **compose** word embeddings into vectors for phrases, sentences, and documents.

Let us assume we know the composed prefix vector (here "girls booted their") (Figure 7.4 (a)).

Here each dimension of x corresponds to a *feature* of the prefix. However, we cannot easily *interpret* these features. Now we need to predict the next word from composed prefix representation (Figure 7.4(b)).

In general, we need to learn the probability distribution over the entire vocabulary which we will explain in the next section. For now let us assume we know the probability distribution over the entire vocabulary. For our example, we assume we have a tiny vocabulary having only 4 words namely "laptops", "books", "houses" and "lamps" and we have the probability distribution over these four words.

W is a *weight matrix*. It contains *parameters* that we can *update* to control the final probability distribution of the next word. Each column of **W** contains **feature weights** for a corresponding word in the vocabulary. We assume we have the weight matrix for our tiny vocabulary (Figure 7.4 (d)). We will now project our 3-d prefix representation to 4-d with a matrix–vector product (Figure 7.4(e)) so we get:

$$W_x = \left\langle 10.93, -10.12, -0.90, 1.13 \right\rangle$$

Now from this 4-d vector, we need to convert to a probability distribution using softmax function.

$$softmax\left(W_x\right) = \left\langle 0.73, 0.006, 0.02, 0.24 \right\rangle$$

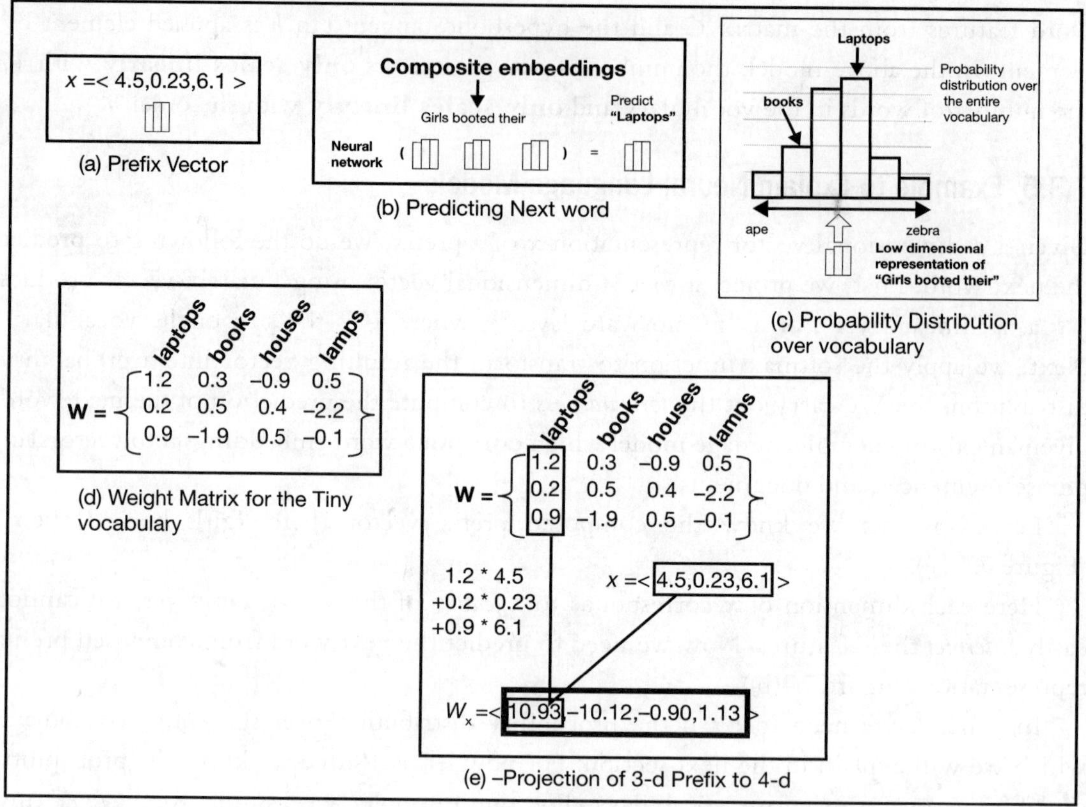

Figure 7.4: (a)–(e) – Example of Neural Language Model

Accordingly, for this output, the word predicted after "girls booted their" is "computers".

7.3.6 Training the Neural Language Model

Neural language models use a neural network as a probabilistic classifier, to compute the probability of the next word given the previous n words. The feedforward neural net is an instance of supervised machine learning in which we know the correct output y for each observation x. The system produces output y' the estimate of the true y. The goal of the training procedure is to learn parameters C, W, b, U, d that makes output y' for each training observation as close as possible to the true y.

Training Procedure: As already discussed, for some tasks, we assume that the embedding matrix C is frozen with predefined values then matrix C is assumed to be set while we only modify W, U, b, and d, i.e., we do not update C during language model training.

Starting with Embedding Matrix C having Random Weights: Generally, it is preferred to learn the embeddings simultaneously while training the network. This is useful when the task the network is designed for (like sentiment classification, translation, or parsing) places strong constraints on what makes a good representation for words. In this case, we train the entire model including C, that is learn to set all the parameters $q = C$; W; U; b; d. We want one single embedding weight matrix C that is shared among the context words because over time many different words will appear as context, and therefore the words are represented with one common vector whatever context position it appears in. In this case, training proceeds by taking as input a very long text, concatenating all the sentences, starting with random weights, and then iteratively moving through the text predicting each word w_t. Since the feedforward neural net model is an instance of supervised machine learning we know the correct output for each observation.

Calculating the Loss: We calculate the resulting loss between system output and the actual output and backpropagate the error. In general, we use logistic regression, where we need a loss function that models the distance between the system output and the gold output and we use the loss function used for logistic regression, the cross-entropy loss. At each word w_t, we use the cross-entropy (negative log likelihood) loss where the error is backpropagated. For language modelling, the classes are the words in the vocabulary, essentially, we want the model to assign the appropriate probability to the correct next word. The architecture for training a neural language model, needs to set the parameters $q = C$; W; U; b; d.

Iterative Procedure to Minimize Loss: Then to find the parameters that minimize this loss function, gradient descent optimization algorithm is used. This gradient descent requires knowing the gradient of the loss function, for which we use error backpropagation or backward differentiation. Gradient descent is used where error backpropagation on the computation graph is used to compute the gradient.

Result: This language model produces a model for language modelling (in essence a word predictor) and in addition a new set of embeddings C that can be used as word representations for other tasks. Training thus not only sets the weights W and U of the network, but also simultaneously when predicting upcoming words, learns the embeddings C for each word that best predict upcoming words.

The feedforward neural language models achieve better perplexity scores than n-gram language models. They can scale to larger orders of n. This is achievable because parameters are associated only with individual words, and not with n-grams. Moreover, they generalize across contexts. For example, by observing the words appear in similar contexts, the model will be able to assign a reasonable score to a similar example even though it was never observed in training. Another important advantage of this model is that word embeddings are obtained as a by-product during training. However, feedforward neural language model has several limitations which we will discuss in the next section.

7.3.7 Limitations of Feedforward Neural Language Model

- Computationally Expensive to Train
  - Bottleneck: need to evaluate probability of each word over the entire vocabulary.
  - Very slow training time (days, weeks).
- Ignores Long-range Dependencies
  - Fixed window used are too small. Enlarging the windows is not a solution since windows can never be large enough. Many NLP tasks require access to information arbitrarily distant from the point at which a decision is made.
  - Continuous version of n-grams and actually shares the weakness of Markov approaches since the context is limited by window size.
- Ignores Recency of Context
  - There is no knowledge built in that most recent context word should generally be more informative than earlier ones –this has to be learned.
- Ignores Strength among Synonymous Words
- Cannot Condition on Context with Intermediate Words
- No Sharing of Weights across Context
- Architectures are non–intuitive.
  - Parameters of the model are hard to interpret.

In order to tackle some of the limitations of the feedforward neural language model, we consider the Recurring Neural Network (RNN) Language Model.

7.4   RNN Language Model

Simple RNN is a network that contains a cycle where the hidden layer activation depends on the input layer and the activation of the hidden layer from the previous timestep (Figure 7.5). Here the hidden layer from the previous timestamp acts as a type of memory (or context). In other words, this allows the encoding of processing carried out in the previous timestamp which in turn effects the decision made in the future. Moreover, the information included extends back to the beginning of the sequence due to propagation through timestamps. The feedforward process is like that of feedforward neural language model but however P

determines how the RNN language model should make use of the past context (Figure 7.6) as given below as given below (Equation 7.15).

$$h_t = g\left(Ph_{t-1} + Wx_t\right)$$

$$y_t = f\left(Uh_t\right)$$

$$y_t = softmax\left(Uh_t\right) \tag{7.15}$$

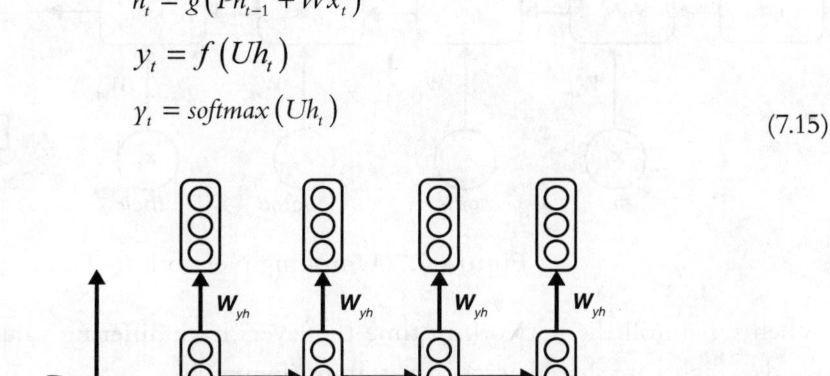

Figure 7.5 RNN Language Model

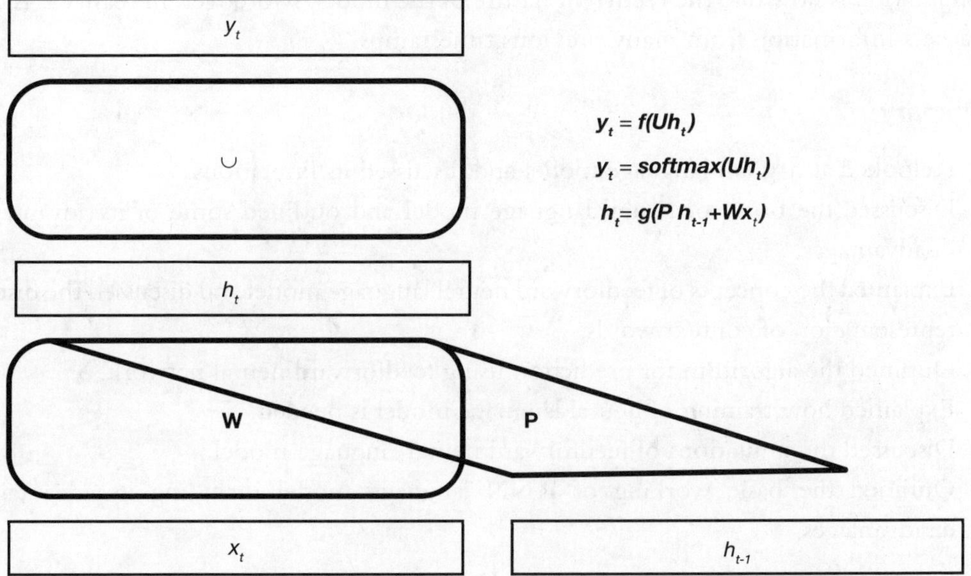

Figure 7.6 RNN Language Model Using Past Context

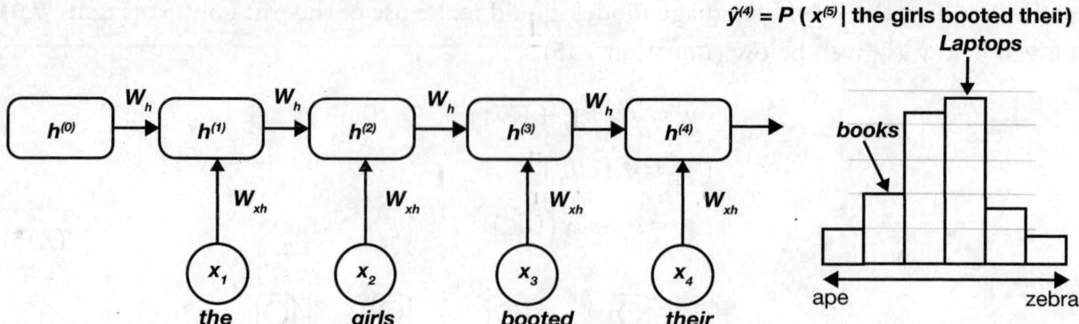

Figure 7.7 Unrolling Network In Time

When we unroll the network in time the layers have differing values over time, in other words weights are shared across timestamps (Figure 7.7).

7.4.1 Advantages and Limitations of RNN Language Model

The RNN language model can process input of any length without increase in model size. Computation at any step t can in principle use information from many previous steps. More importantly weights are shared across timestamps or in other words, representations are shared. However, some of the disadvantages of RNN language model include the fact that computation is slow due the recurrent nature of the model. Moreover, in reality it is difficult to access information from many previous timestamps.

Summary

- Relooked at n–gram language model and discussed its limitations.
- Discussed the basics of neural language model and outlined some of its advantages and disadvantages.
- Explained the concepts of feedforward neural language model and discussed the distributed representation of context words.
- Outlined the algorithm for prediction using feedforward neural network.
- Explained how training of neural language model is needed.
- Discussed the limitations of feedforward neural language model.
- Outlined the basic working of RNN language model including its advantages and disadvantages.

Exercises

Suggested Activities

1. Given the fact that we are using 5 context words, embedding space with dimensional 300, vocabulary size 10,000, redraw Figure 7.3. Indicate any assumptions made.

2. Case Study – Language Modelling: Using WikiText-2 dataset (https://www.kaggle.com/datasets/aliakay8/penn-treebank-dataset), predict the next word in a sequence of text by training using CNN based feedforward neural network to learn the probability distribution of words given the previous context.

Self-Assessment: Multiple Choice Questions

Give answers with justification for correct and wrong choices:

1. In the context of n-gram language models, the curse of dimensionality problem comes from huge number of
   i. different combinations of values of the input variables
   ii. possible sequences of words
   iii. parameters

2. To model the full joint distribution of 10 consecutive words with vocabulary size of 1,00,000 we need approximately __________ parameters.
   i. 10^{50}
   ii. 10^{10}
   iii. 10^{40}

3. The neural network language model learns
   i. probability function for word sequences
   ii. simultaneously a distributed representation for each word
   iii. simultaneously a distributed representation for each word and the probability function for word sequences

4. The neural network language model can
   i. *handle much longer histories*
   ii. interpret better than n-gram models
   iii. predict better with contexts of dissimilar words

5. In the feedforward neural network language, each word in the vocabulary is represented as
   i. binary vector
   ii. distributed feature vector
   iii. one hot vector

6. Given an input, running a forward pass on the feedforward network to produce a probability distribution over possible output is called
   i. forward inference
   ii. training
   iii. learning
7. The hidden layer of feedforward neural language model uses
   i. Cosine function
   ii. RELU function
   iii. Tanh function
8. The softmax function is used by feedforward neural language model
   i. To embed the context information
   ii. To transform the output to a probability distribution
   iii. To convert the word based on which to predict
9. The loss function generally used by feedforward neural language model is
   i. Mean squared error
   ii. Cross-entropy loss
   iii. Likelihood loss
10. One of major limitations of feedforward neural language model is
    i. Ignores long-range dependencies
    ii. Has fast training time
    iii. Considers recency of context
11. RNN language model makes use of
    i. activation of the hidden layer from the future timestep
    ii. activation of the hidden layer depends on current context
    iii. activation of the hidden layer from the previous timestep
12. The RNN language model can
    i. process input of any length but with increase in model size
    ii. process input of any length without increase in model size
    iii. process input of only limited length

Self-Assessment: Match the Columns

Order		Match	
1.	*n*-gram	A	Sequence of words that has never been seen before gets high probability if it is made of words that are similar in feature space to the words forming an already seen sentence
2.	Curse of dimensionality	B	Negative log likelihood
3.	Neural language model	C	Used to predict the probability of a succeeding word as: $P(w_5|w_1, w_2, w_3, w_4)$
4.	Generalization	D	The first neural language model was introduced by Bengio et.al in 2003
5.	Based on simple feedforward neural networks	E	The feedforward model is associated with 3 layers
6.	Distributed feature vectors	F	Accurately estimate the required joint probability distribution
7.	Varies between 30 to 100	G	Feature vectors of the previous words in the sequence
8.	Express the joint probability function of word sequences	H	A mapping C from any element i of V to a real vector $C(i) \in \mathfrak{R}^m$
9.	Embedding, hidden and output layers	I	The accurate estimation of the joint probability distribution in *n*-gram model
10.	Cross-entropy	J	The number of features associated with the distributed representation

Short Questions

1. What are the limitations of n–gram models?
2. How does neural language models reduce the impact of curse of dimensionality?
3. Discuss some advantages and disadvantages of neural language models.
4. Give the objective of the feedforward neural language model. Explain.
5. Discuss the distributed representation of context words.
6. Explain how feedforward neural network for prediction.

7. Discuss the three steps of feed-forward neural language model algorithm.

8. Give a new example to explain neural language models.

9. Describe the training of feedforward neural network in the context of neural language model.

10. What are the limitations of feedforward neural language model? Discuss.

11. Explain the RNN language model.

12. List the advantages and disadvantages of RNN language model.

Vector Models – Word Embedding

8.1 Distributed Representation – A Recap

In chapter 6 and 7, we discussed distributed representation where rather than a one-hot representation, a vector is used to represent a word or concept. Each single component of the vector representation does not convey any meaning on its own but the meaning is distributed across the dimensions of the vector. The interpretable features such as the contexts of the word are hidden and distributed across the dimensions. As discussed earlier, the basis of distributed representation is distributed semantics where linguistic terms with similar distributions (for example context words) have similar meanings. The distributional property is usually induced from document, sentence or textual vicinity using sliding windows. The distributed hypothesis states that the meaning of a word w is described by the words that frequently appear close to it. When the word w appears in a text, its context is the set of words that appear close by where the context is defined by a window. By finding the number of times the word w occurs in a text and then using the many contexts of w, the dense vector for w is generated (Figure 8.1). Distributed representation is the basis of word embedding.

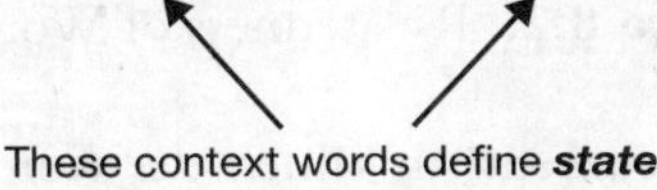

Figure 8.1: Many Contexts of Word "state"

8.2 Word Embedding

The basic idea behind word embedding is that running text provides implicitly supervised training data. The concept actually is derived from neural language modelling (Bengio et al. 2003) discussed in Chapter 7 and the neural language models used to build distributed descriptions described by Collobert et al. in his paper titled Natural Language Processing (Almost) from Scratch (Collobert et al. 2011). Word embedding can be defined as any technique but the meaning is distributed across the dimensions of the vector, in other words one embeds the word in a different space. This embedding or vector is based on three main ideas. One, similarity in meaning is indicated by similarity of vectors where mathematics is used to encode the meaning. Two, as indicated by the distributional hypothesis (Harris, 1954) which states that "words are characterized by the company they keep", the context of the word determines its meaning and finally three, a large corpus of billions of words is used since neural models the core of word embedding require large amounts of data for training the models. The word embeddings assumes that the more often two words co-occur, the closer their associated vectors. In other words, embeddings are used to convert items such as words, short text, long text, images, entities, audio into real-valued and dense vector representations whose dimensions are much smaller than the number of items.

Now let us understand the notion of relatedness for words from different perspectives as shown in Figure 8.2.

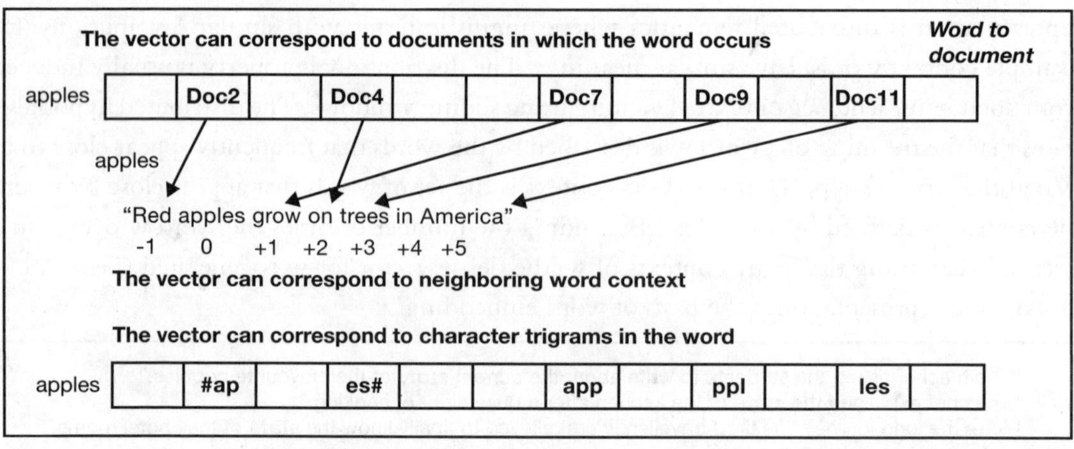

Figure 8.2: Relatedness of Words

The vector can correspond to documents in which the word occurs indicating the notion of relatedness as distributional topical similarity of the word "apples". The vector can correspond to neighbouring word context as in word context vectors that is a distributed context of words. Her we assume "apples" is at location 0 and the left context indicated by negative inter-word distance while right context is indicated by positive inter-word distance. The vector can also correspond to character trigrams in the word. These vector representations group the items together with semantically similar items in a vector space. Two words will have closer meanings if their local neighborhoods are similar. The vector representation enables the system to detect similarities between words mathematically. The relationships between words correspond to the mathematical difference between vectors or in other words the displacement (vector) between the points of two words represents the word relationship (Figure 8.3).

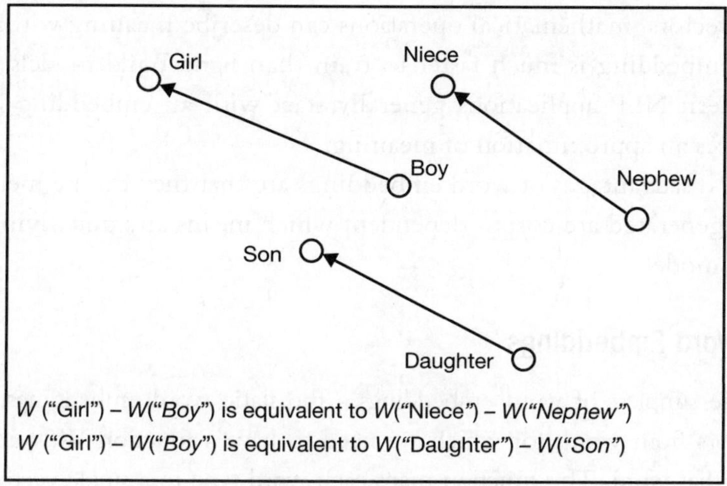

Figure 8.3: Word Relationships

If the words have the same relationship they are associated with the same vector. We use another example to show relatedness between documents in one case and words in the other. Note that the same words with different inter-word distance are represented separately in the vector representation (Figure 8.4).

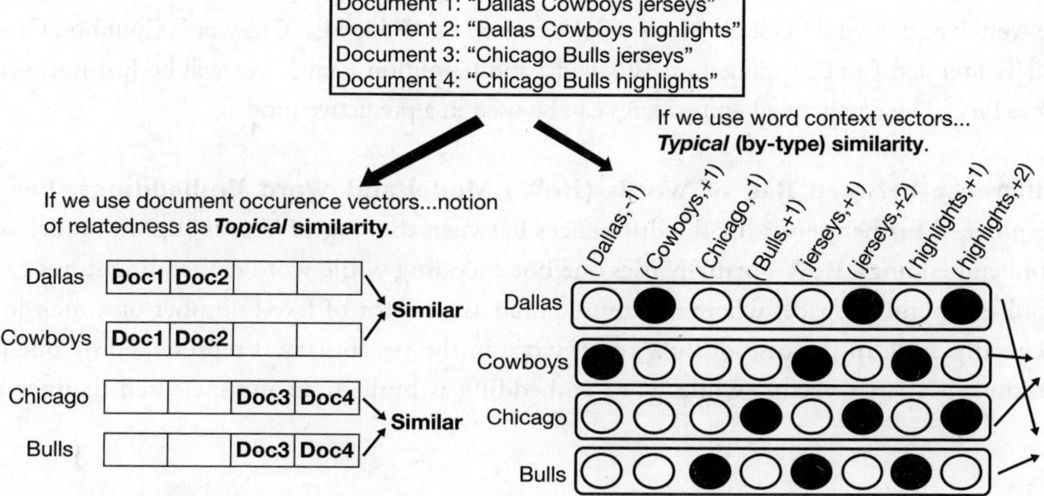

Figure 8.4: Representation of Words with Different Inter-word Distance

8.2.1 Advantages and Disadvantages of Word Embeddings

Depending on the model, word embeddings do not infer meaning only from global statistics, but local contexts which are more precise. The distance between the vectors can be used to understand the meaning or association between the words. Due to the fact that meanings are represented by vectors, mathematical operations can describe meaning within the semantic models. Word embedding is much faster to train than hand build models like WordNet. Almost all modern NLP applications generally start with an embedding layer and these embeddings stores an approximation of meaning.

Some of the disadvantages of word embeddings are that they can be memory intensive, and the vectors generated are corpus dependent which means any underlying bias can have an effect on the model.

8.2.2 Static Word Embeddings

Let us discuss the simplest of word embeddings – the static word embeddings. Here we learn embedding vectors from words for which we need to have a function W(word) that returns a vector encoding that word. This function maps each word type to a single vector based on their occurrence with other words in a large corpus. These vectors are typically dense and have much lower dimensionality than the size of the vocabulary. This mapping function does not consider the fact that the same lexeme 'bank' can exhibit diverse meanings (financial institution vs the side of a river) or functions as different parts of speech (a bank account vs to bank on a curve). This type of embedding assumes a fixed size vocabulary and hence we may have to deal with words that are unknown. Word Embeddings can be trained on large collection of unlabeled text (Wikipedia, news, Twitter, books) preferably in the domain required. Examples of pretrained word embeddings are word2vec trained on Google News, GloVe trained on Wikipedia, Gigaword, Common Crawl and Twitter and FastText trained on Wikipedia and Common Crawl. We will be first discussing Word2Vec. These pretrained embeddings can be used in a predictive model.

Difference between Bag of Words (BoW) Model and Word Embeddings: Before we proceed further, let us list the differences between the Bag of Words (BoW) model and word embeddings. BoW normally uses one hot encoding while word embedding stores each word as a point in space, where it is represented as a vector of fixed number of dimensions (generally 300). In the case of BoW, each word in the vocabulary is represented by one bit position in a large vector, while word embedding is built in an unsupervised manner by reading a huge corpus. In the case of BoW, context information is not utilized but in the case of word embedding, the dimensions are basically projections along different axes and represents a mathematical concept.

8.3 Word2Vec

Word2Vec (Mikolov et al. 2013) is the first really influential dense word embedding. Word2Vec is inspired by neural network models. It is based on prediction based neural network model where vector weights are directly set to optimally predict the contexts in which the corresponding words tend to appear and in doing so learn dense embeddings for the words in the training corpus.

Word2Vec can be viewed from two perspectives – that it is a simplification of neural language models and is a binary logistic regression classifier. The methods use a binary classifier to predict which words appear in the context of a target word. The parameters of that classifier provide a dense vector representation of the target word (embedding). Since similar words appear in similar contexts, the system naturally learns to assign similar vectors to similar words. Instead of entire documents, word2vec uses words k positions away from each center word where these words are called **context words**.

Example for $k = 3$:

"On a clear and chilly April **morning**, the clocks rang out their chimes." Here center word also called focus word is in bold and all other words are context words or target words. Word2Vec considers all words as center words, and all their context words.

Word2vec Learning: When given a set of positive and negative training instances, and an initial set of embedding vectors, the goal of learning is to adjust those word vectors such that we **maximize** the similarity of the target word, context word pairs (w, cpos) drawn from the positive data and **minimize** the similarity of the (w, cneg) pairs drawn from the negative data.

These models can be trained on large amounts of raw text and moreover pre-trained embeddings can be downloaded. The steps associated with word2vec modelling are:

- A large corpus of text documents is used to train a neural network model maximizing the conditional probability of context given the word.
- Every word in a fixed vocabulary is assigned a vector.

- Go through each position t in the text, which has a centre word w and outside or context words c.
- The similarity of the word vectors for w and c are used to calculate the probability of c given w.
- The word vectors are continuously adjusted by optimizing the parameters θ to maximize the conditional probability of the context c given the word w. D is the set of all (w, c) pairs (Equation 8.1).

$$\arg\max_{\theta} \prod_{(w,c) \in D} p(c \mid w; \theta)$$

(8.1)

- The trained model is then applied to each word to get its corresponding vector (Figure 8.5(a)).
- Then the vectors of sentences are calculated by averaging the vector of their words (Figure 8.5(b)).
- Then similarity matrix between sentences is constructed (Figure 8.5(c)).
- PageRank (L.Page, et.al 1998) is then used to score the sentences in graph.

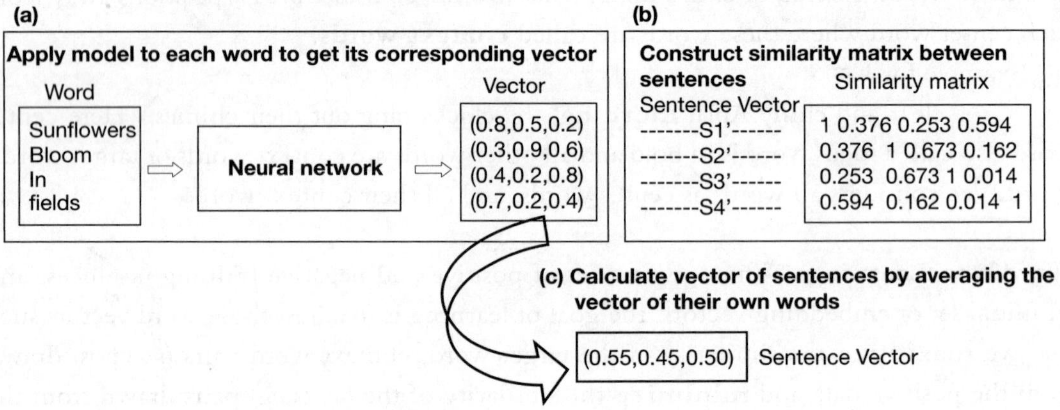

Figure 8.5: Vector of Sentences and their Scores

Working of Word2vec: Each word is represented as a d dimensional vector. Similarly, each context is also represented as a d dimensional vector. All vectors are initialized to random weights. The two vectors are arranged as two matrices W and C. The neural network representation is given in Figure 8.6.

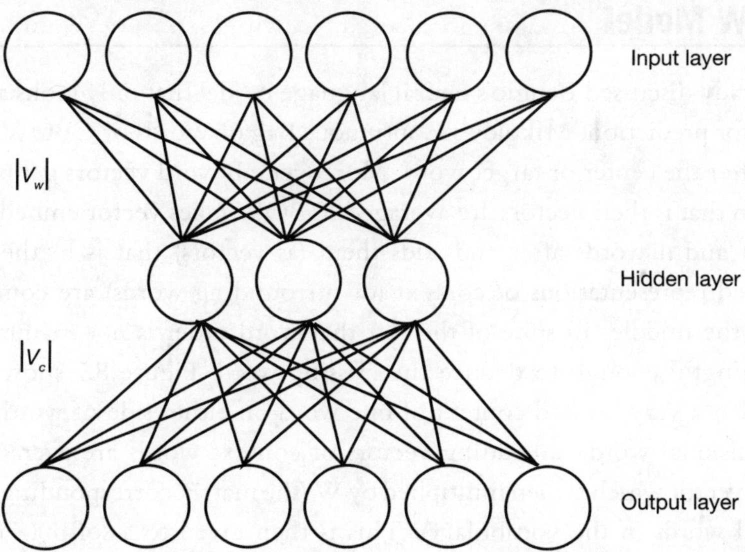

Figure 8.6: Word2Vec Neural Network Representation

One question that remains is why we should use separate vectors – the center or word vector and the context vector. The reason is that this use of two vectors makes optimization easier. However, our final vector is the average of the context and word vectors.

word2vec is **not** a single algorithm but represents words as vectors and contains the following:

- Two distinct models – CBoW and Skip-Gram
- Various training methods – Negative Sampling and Hierarchical Softmax
- A rich preprocessing pipeline – Dynamic Context Windows, Subsampling and Deleting Rare Words

Thus, there are basically two variants of Word2Vec based on two different context representations namely CBOW or Skip-Gram which uses two different optimization objectives: namely negative sampling (NS) or hierarchical softmax. The advantages of these prediction-based models are that they are fast and easy to train and are available online in the word2vec package including sets of pretrained embeddings. These methods use neural networks to train word or context classifiers consisting of feed-forward neural nets. They use local context windows (environment around any word in a corpus) as inputs to the neural networks. There are two main models namely Continuous bag-of-words (CBOW) and Skip-gram (SG).

8.4 CBOW Model

We have already discussed Bengio's neural language model that only looks at previous words as a context for prediction. Mikolov's Continuous Bag of Words or CBOW looks at n words before and after the center or target word. Moreover, all word vectors get projected into the same position that is their vectors are averaged. CBOW takes vector embeddings of n words before target and n words after and adds them (as vectors) that is in the CBOW model, the distributed representations of context (or surrounding words) are combined to predict the word in the middle. In spite of the fact that word order is not maintained, the vector sum is meaningful enough to deduce the missing word. Figure 8.7 shows the case where we assume that a very limited context of one word on either side of word w is considered. The d-dimensional word embedding vectors of context words are averaged, to get the d dimensional vector which is then multiplied by W (the matrix corresponding to d dimensional vectors of all words in the vocabulary). This is then given to a softmax function and the probability of the next word is obtained.

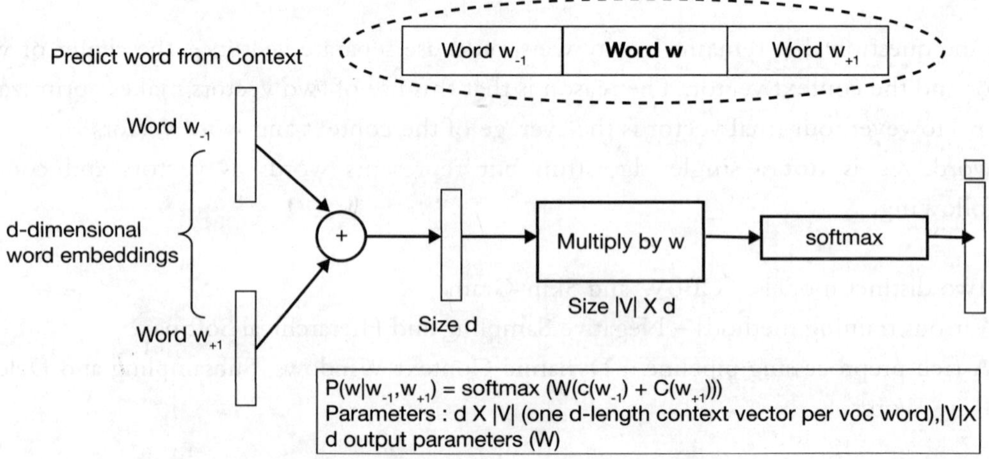

Figure 8.7: Simple CBOW Model

In the generalized model given a window of 2m words as context, we predict the word in the centre. Objective function is task of maximizing the probability of correct center word given the context words. The steps are as follows:

1. We generate the one hot word vectors corresponding to the context as given in Equation 8.2

$$\left(x^{(c-m)},\ldots,x^{(c-1)},x^{(c+1)},\ldots,x^{(c+m)}\right) \tag{8.2}$$

2. If a word is to be associated with a dimension, its one–hot vector has 1 in that dimension and zero everywhere else. These vectors are embedded using n dimensions say 300. Let V be the vocabulary of all words (Equation 8.3)

$$\left(v_{c-m} = \gamma x^{(c-m)}, v_{c-m+1} = \gamma x^{(c-m+1)}, \ldots, v_{c+m} = \gamma x^{(c+m)} \right) \qquad (8.3)$$

3. The context vectors are averaged before using in prediction as given in Equation 8.4

$$\hat{v} = \frac{v_{c-m} + v_{c-m+1} + \ldots + v_{c+m}}{2m} \qquad (8.4)$$

4. Generate a score vector $z = U \hat{} v$
5. Turn the scores into probabilities $\hat{} y = \text{softmax}(z)$
6. We desire our probabilities generated, $\hat{} y$, to match the true probabilities, y, which also happens to be the one hot vector of the actual word.

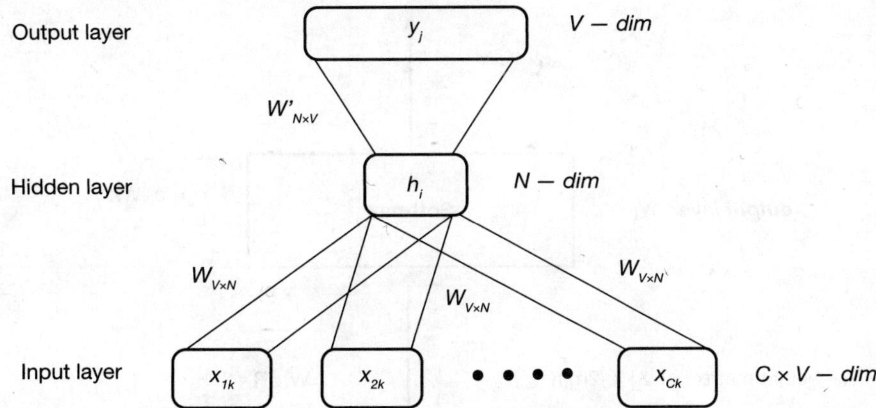

Figure 8.8: General CBOW Model

The general model is shown in Figure 8.8. Each word is represented with two different vectors (context vector, output vector). Each vector is N dimensions. The model parameters are the word vectors, and we need to learn $2 \times V \times N$ parameters. We create two matrices, $V \in R^{n \times |V|}$ and $U \in R^{|V| \times n}$ where n is an arbitrary size which defines the size of the embedding space. V is the input word matrix such that the i-th column of V is the n-dimensional embedded vector for word w_i when it is an input to this model. We denote this $n \times 1$ vector as v_i. Similarly, U is the output word matrix. The j-th row of U is an n-dimensional embedded vector for word w_j when it is an output of the model. We denote this row of U as u_j. Note that we do in fact learn two vectors for every word w_i (i.e., input word vector v_i and output word vector u_j).

Now, we need to understand the learning of the two matrices V and U. For this we need to create an objective function When we are learning a probability from some true probability, we information theory to give us a measure of the distance between two distributions. Here, we use a popular choice of distance/loss measure, cross entropy as given in Equation 8.5.

$$H(\hat{y}, y) \tag{8.5}$$

Let us look at CBOW from the perspective of neural language model (Figure 8.9). In this model we use 2m words $w_{t-m},..., w_{t-1},...w_{t+m}$ as context . Let n be the dimension of the embedding space C with $C \in R^{|V| \times n}$. The projection layer averages the input, and the input is (Equation 8.6)

$$x = average\left(C\left(w_{t-m}\right),...,C\left(w_{t-1}\right),...C\left(w_{t+m}\right)\right) \tag{8.6}$$

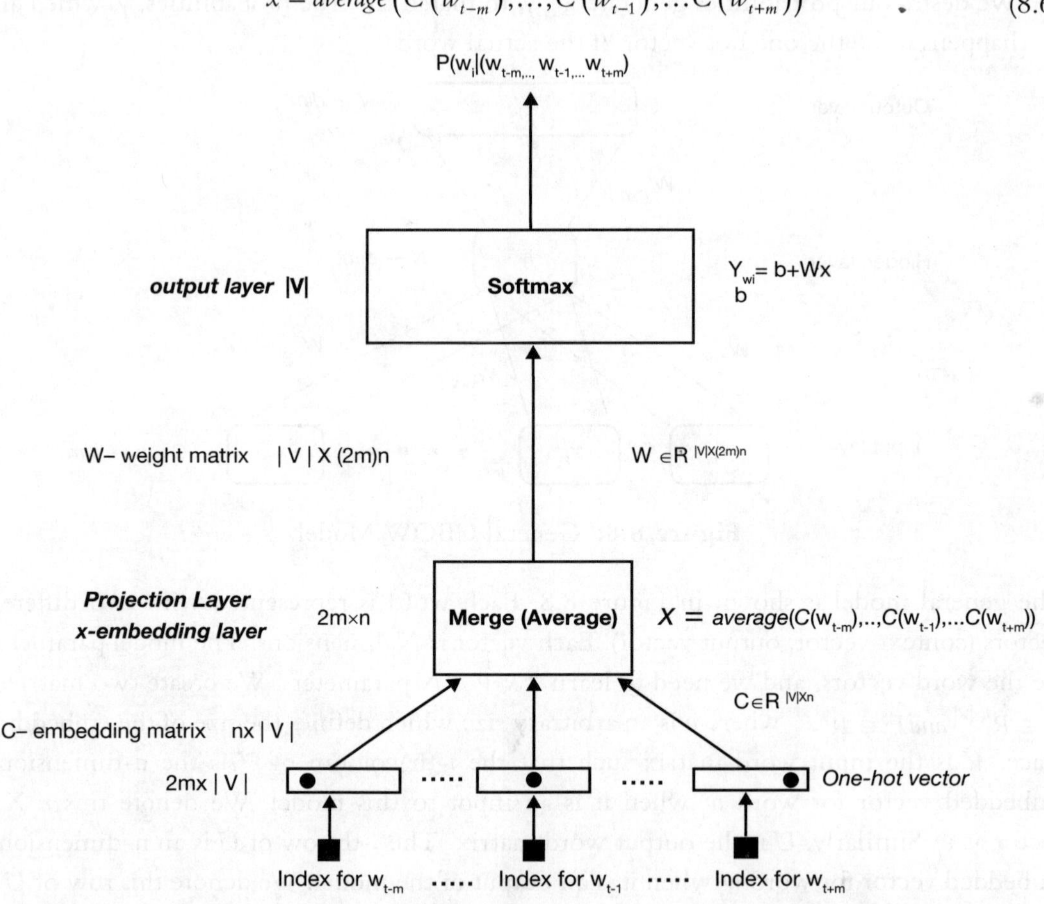

Figure 8.9: CBOW Model from Perspective of Neural Language Model

The weight matrix W has dimension $|V| \text{X} (2m)n$ with $W \in R^{|V|\text{X}(2m)n}$. The softmax uses a parameter b and the hence the total parameters $\theta = (b, W, C)$. The output is as given below (Equation 8.7)

$$y_{wi} = b + Wx \tag{8.7}$$

After applying softmax (Equation 8.8),

$$y_j = \frac{e^j}{\sum_{j=1}^{V} e^j} \tag{8.8}$$

the probability of output w_i is as follows (Equation 8.9)

$$P(w_i \mid w_{t-m}, \ldots, w_{t-1}, \ldots, w_{t+m}) \tag{8.9}$$

Summarizing, CBOW predicts the current word based on the context, is in general faster to train than the skip-gram model and predicts frequent words better.

CBOW with Hierarchical SoftMax: Instead of using softmax, CBOW can use hierarchical softmax to obtain probability. The issue associated with regular softmax is that for each sample, we need to normalize over the whole large vocabulary. Hierarchical softmax (H-Softmax) is an approximation inspired by binary trees that was proposed by Morin and Bengio (2005) [3]. Hierarchical-Softmax essentially replaces the flat softmax layer with a hierarchical layer that has the words as leaves, as can be seen in Figure 8.10. This allows us to decompose calculating the probability of one word into a sequence of probability calculations, which saves us from having to calculate the expensive normalization over all words. In hierarchical softmax, we first Huffman encode the vocabulary building a binary tree and use binary classifiers to decide which branch of the binary tree to take. Here, the leaves are words and there is a unique path from root to each word. There is no output representation for words but however every intermediate node has a vector representation. In this model, the probability of a word w given a vector wi, $P(w|wi)$, is equal to the probability of a random walk starting in the root and ending in the leaf node corresponding to w. The main advantage in computing the probability this way is that the cost is only $O(\log(|V|))$, corresponding to the length of the path (Equation 8.10).

$$P(w|w_i) = \prod_{j=1}^{L(w)-1} \sigma\left(\left[n(w, j+1) = ? \, LeftChild(n(w, j)) \right] . v_{n(w,j)}^T v_{wi} \right) \tag{8.10}$$

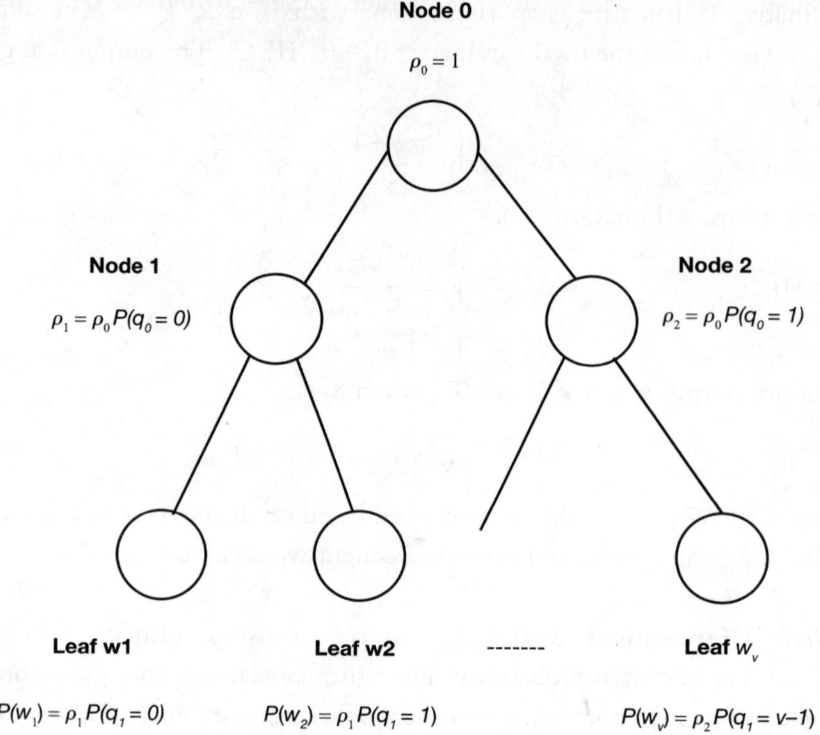

Figure 8.10: Hierarchical–Softmax

where $L(w)$ it the length from root to word w, $n(w, j)$ is the node on distance j–1 from the root on the path of word w, $[x] = 1$ if x is true, and –1 if false. The condition here means whether the next node on the path to w goes to be left child or not, σ is the sigmoid function and $v_n^t(w, j)$ is the vector corresponding to the intermediate node.

The objective is still to minimize the negative log likelihood. However, instead of updating output vectors of words, we update the vectors of nodes on the path to the word.

8.5 Skip Gram Model

Skip–Gram model is an alternative to CBOW model where we start with a single word embedding and try to predict the surrounding words that is the distributed representation of the input word is used to predict the context. This is a much less well-defined problem but works better in practice since it scales better. The Skip–Gram model approach can be explained as follows:

1. It is required to predict if candidate word c is a "neighbor" of a given target word t.
2. The target word t and a neighboring context word c are treated as positive examples.

3.   Now other words in the lexicon are sampled randomly to obtain negative examples.

4.   Then logistic regression is used to train a classifier to distinguish the two types of cases.

5.   The learned weights are used as embeddings.

Let us first understand a simple Skip-Gram Classifier assuming a context size of 2 that is a +/-2 word window. We predict each neighboring word in a context window of $2C$ words from the current word. So, for $C = 2$, we are given word w_t and predicting these 4 words (Equation 8.11):

$$[w_{t-2}, w_{t-1}, w_{t+1}, w_{t+2}] \tag{8.11}$$

Example

...lemon, a [tablespoon of apricot jam, a] pinch...

c1 c2 [target]c3 c4

Goal: train a classifier that is given a candidate (word, context) pair

(apricot, tablespoon), (apricot, of) (apricot, jam), (apricot, a) are positive examples.

(apricot, aardvark), (apricot, space)......etc, pairs randomly taken using the lexicon are negative samples.

Each pair is assigned a +/– probability:

$$P(+|w, c)$$

Similarity is computed from dot product, i.e., Similarity$(w, c) \propto w \cdot c$. It is necessary to normalize to get a probability. Therefore, to summarize the probabilistic classifier is defined such that given a test target word w and its context window of L words $c1{:}L$, assigns a probability that w occurs in this window.

To compute this probability, we need embeddings for all the words in the vocabulary. Now let us discuss the Skip-Gram where a word predicts context, a range before and after the current word with the concept of embedding such that less weight is given to more distant words. The log-linear classifier with continuous projection layer is used. In other words, walking through the given corpus, let us assume the target word is $w(t)$, whose index in the vocabulary is j, that is w_j (where $1{<}j{<}|V|$). We want to predict $w(t+1)$, whose index in the vocabulary is k (where $1{<}j{<}|V|$). Thus, the task is computing the probability of $P(w_k \mid w_j)$.

Figure 8.11 shows the case where we assume that a very limited context of one word on either side of word w is considered. The d-dimensional word embedding vector of the word w is multiplied by W (the matrix corresponding to d dimensional vectors of all words in the vocabulary). This is then given to a softmax function, and the probability of the context word is obtained.

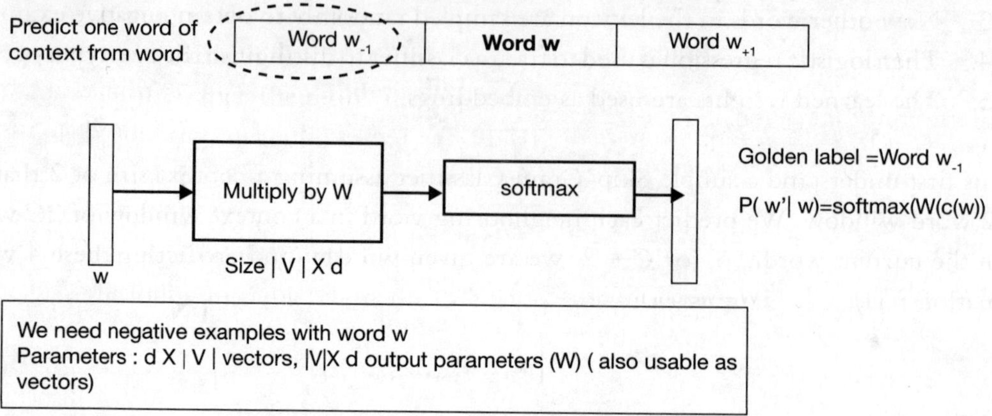

Figure 8.11: Simple Skip-Gram Model

The general model of Skip-Gram is shown in Figure 8.12. The input vector for the word w is represented as a one–hot vector of $|V|$ dimensions with a one corresponding in the index corresponding to word w. The hidden layer weight matrix W of dimension $nX\,|V|$ consisting of n linear neurons corresponding to the n-dimensional embedding space for each of the $|V|$ words in the vocabulary. The output layer is a softmax classifier consisting of $|V|$ words with n features and gives the probability that a word at a randomly chosen nearby position is w_1, …..$w_{|V|}$. It is essentially a word vector lookup table of dimension $nX|V|$. Note that there is no activation function on the hidden layer neurons, but the output neurons use softmax.

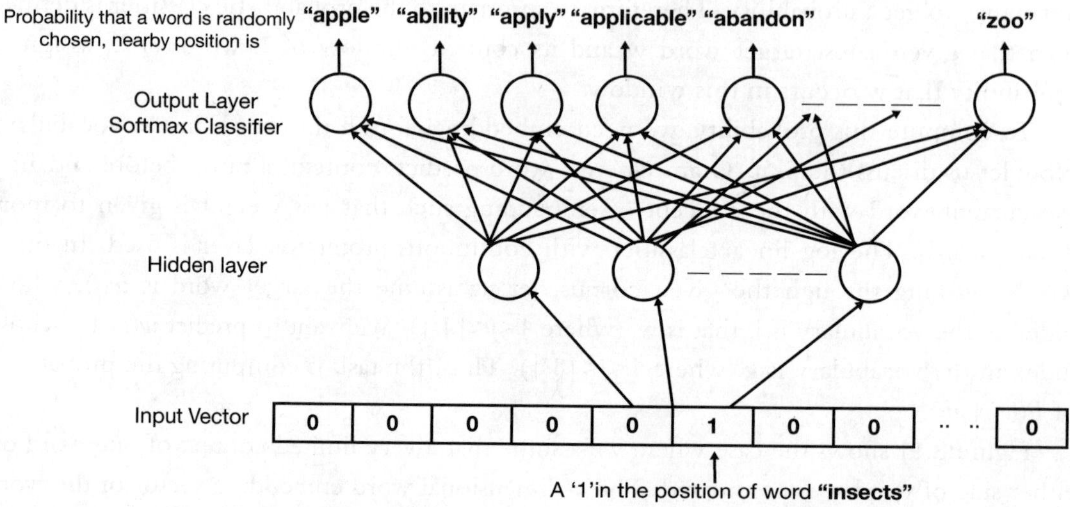

Figure 8.12: General Model of Skip-Gram

Let us look at Skip-Gram model from the perspective of neural language model (Figure 8.13).

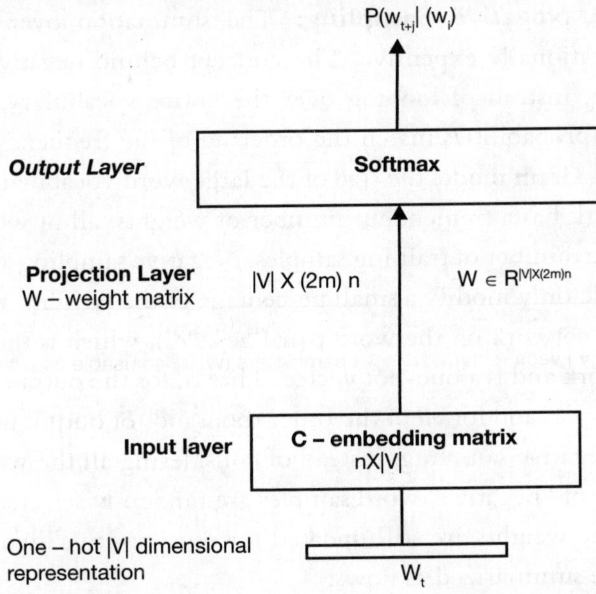

Figure 8.13: Skip–Gram Model from Perspective of Neural Language Model

In this model the input is the one hot $|V|$ dimensional vector of word w_t. This word is then mapped to the embedding matrix C. Let n be the dimension of the embedding space C with $C \in R^{|V|Xn}$. The input layer is the word and the input is (Equation 12)

$$x = C\,(w_i).\qquad(8.12)$$

The weight matrix W has dimension $|V|X\,n$ with $W \in R^{|V|Xn}$. The softmax uses a parameter b where $b \in R^{|V|}$. and the hence the total parameters $\theta = (b, W, C)$. The output is as given below (Equation 8.13)

$$y_{wi+j} = b + Wx\qquad(8.13)$$

After applying softmax (Equation 8.8):

$$y_j = \frac{e^j}{\sum_{j=1}^{V} e^j}$$

the probability of output w_i is as follows (Equation 8.14):

$$P(w_{i+j} \mid w_i)\qquad(8.14)$$

Skip-Gram with Negative Sampling: The summation over |V| in the objective function is computationally expensive. The concept behind negative sampling is that, for every training step, instead of looping over the entire vocabulary, just "sample" from a distribution whose probabilities match the ordering of the frequency of the vocabulary. In the context of Skip-Gram model the size of the large word vocabulary means that our skip-gram neural network has a tremendous number of weights, all of which would be updated slightly, by the huge number of training samples. Negative sampling addresses this by having each training sample only modify a small percentage of the weights, rather than all of them. When training the network on the word pair ("w", "c"), which is the positive sample is the output of the network and is a one-hot vector. That is, for the output neuron corresponding to "c" has to output a 1, and for *all* of the other thousands of output neurons the output is to be set to 0. With negative sampling, instead of considering all the words of the vocabulary, just a small number of "negative" word samples are randomly selected (let's say 5) to update the weights for. The weights are still updated for our "positive" word. The steps of Skip-Gram model can be summarized as flows:

- Treat the target word and a neighbouring context word as positive examples.
- Randomly sample other words in the lexicon to get negative samples. The random samples are selected by sampling from uniform distribution.
- Use logistic regression to train a classifier to distinguish those two cases.
- Use the learned weights as the embeddings – we do not use the actual classifiers.

8.6 FastText and GloVe Word Embeddings

8.6.1 FastText

FastText is another word embedding method that is an extension of the word2vec model. Here instead of learning vectors for words directly, FastText represents each word as an n-gram of characters. For example, take the word, "*machine*" with n=3, the FastText representation of this word is <*ma, mac, ach, chi, hin, ine, ne* >, where the angular brackets indicate the beginning and end of the word. This method helps in capturing the meaning of shorter words and allows the embeddings to understand suffixes and prefixes. Once the word has been represented using character n-grams, a skip-gram model is trained to learn the embeddings. This model is considered to be a bag of words model with a sliding window over a word because no internal structure of the word is taken into account. As long as the characters are within this window, the order of the n-grams is ignored. FastText works well with rare words since even though a word is not seen during training, it can be broken down into n-grams to get its embeddings.

8.6.2 GloVe

While word2Vec is a predictive model — learning vectors to improve the predictive ability, GloVe is a count-based model. Global Vectors (GloVe) exploits the global statistical information regarding word co-occurrences. GloVe is based on two concepts – global matrix factorization and local context window. Global matrix factorization is the process of using matrix factorization methods to reduce large term frequency matrices. These matrices usually represent the occurrence or absence of words in a document. Local context window methods are CBOW and Skip–Gram. As already discussed, Skip-Gram works well with small amounts of training data and works for even rare words, whereas CBOW trains several times faster and has slightly better accuracy for frequent words.

Instead of extracting the embeddings from a neural network that is designed to perform a different task like predicting neighbouring words (CBOW) or predicting the focus word (Skip-Gram), the embeddings are optimized directly, so that the dot product of two word vectors equal the log of the number of times the two words will occur near each other. This forces the model to encode the frequency distribution of words that occur near them in a more global context.

The steps can be summarized as follows:

- Count-based models learn vectors by doing dimensionality reduction on a co-occurrence counts matrix.
- This matrix is factorized to yield a lower-dimensional matrix of words and features, where each row yields a vector representation for each word.
- The counts matrix is preprocessed by normalizing the counts and log-smoothing them and a log-bilinear model with a weighted least-squares objective is used.
- The model generates two sets of word vectors, W and $\tilde{W}$. W and $\tilde{W}$ are equivalent and differ only as a result of their random initializations. The two sets of vectors should perform equivalently. The average of the two vectors can be used.

8.7 Applications of Word Embeddings

- The use of word representations has become a key secret weapon for the success of many NLP systems in recent years, across tasks including named entity recognition, part-of-speech tagging, parsing, and semantic role labeling.
- Learning a good representation on a task A and then using it on a task B is one of the major contributions of deep learning.
  o Examples include pretraining, transfer learning, and multi-task learning.

- Can allow the representation to learn from more than one kind of data and learn to map multiple kinds of data into a single representation.
  - E.g., bilingual English and Mandarin Chinese word-embedding (Socher *et al.* 2013a). With such embeddings we know that words that are known as close translations should be close together. However interestingly, words we did not consider as translations ended up close together in embedding space where structures of two languages influence the alignment.
- . Can apply to get a joint embedding of words and images or other multi-modal data sets.
  - New classes map near similar existing classes: e.g., if 'cat' is unknown, cat images map near dog.

Summary

- Relooked at distributed representation of a word.
- Discussed the basic concept of word embedding.
- Listed some advantages and disadvantages of word embeddings.
- Explained the difference between Bag of Words and word embeddings.
- Introduced Word2Vec and how it is learnt.
- Described a simple CBOW model.
- Explained CBOW from the perspective of neural language model.
- Discussed the concept of hierarchical softmax.
- Described a simple skip-gram model.
- Explained skip-gram from the perspective of neural language model.
- Discussed the concept of negative sampling.
- Outlined FastText and GloVe Word Embeddings.
- Listed some common applications of word embeddings.

Exercises

Suggested Activities

1. List a set of 5 NLP tasks or applications that can use Word2Vec. Implement any one of them using appropriate datasets.

2. **Case Study –Text Clustering:** Using 20 Newsgroups dataset (https://www.kaggle.com/datasets/crawford/20-newsgroups), cluster similar documents together based on their content. Convert text documents into document embeddings using word embeddings. Apply clustering K–means clustering algorithm to the document embeddings. Evaluate clustering performance using metrics like silhouette score or purity.

Self-Assessment: Multiple Choice Questions

Give answers with justification for correct and wrong choices:

1. In vector representation the meaning is distributed
   - **i.** as boolean values along the vector
   - **ii.** across the dimensions of the vector
   - **iii.** such that each dimension corresponds to a specific component

2. Distributional property is usually induced from document using
   - **i.** sliding windows
   - **ii.** bag of words
   - **iii.** fixed window

3. The dense vector for a word w is generated by finding
   - **i.** the frequency of occurrence of the word
   - **ii.** the number of times the word occurs in a text and then using the many contexts of the word
   - **iii.** the context of the word

4. The basic idea behind word embedding is based on
   - **i.** *WordNet*
   - **ii.** lexical semantics
   - **iii.** neural language models

5. Word2Vec was developed by
   - **i.** Mikolov et al.
   - **ii.** Bengio et al.
   - **iii.** Collobert et al.

6. Distributional hypothesis states
    i. "words are distributed across text"
    ii. "words are characterized by the company they keep"
    iii. "words have distributed meanings"
7. The word embedding vector can correspond to documents in which the word occurs indicating
    i. distributed character similarity
    ii. distributional semantic similarity
    iii. distributional topical similarity
8. In word embedding, two words will have closer meanings
    i. if the local neighborhoods are similar
    ii. if the documents are similar
    iii. if they have same lexical meaning
9. Word embeddings infer meaning
    i. from global statistics
    ii. from dictionary
    iii. from local contexts
10. Disadvantage of word embeddings is that
    i. they are not dependent on corpus used
    ii. they are memory intensive
    iii. they are local context based
11. In static word embedding, function maps each word type to a single vector
    i. based on their occurrence with other words in a large corpus
    ii. based on their occurrence with other words in a lexicon
    iii. based on their occurrence across documents
12. Word2Vec is basically a
    i. high dimensional word embedding
    ii. dense word embedding
    iii. lexical word embedding
13. Word2Vec can be viewed from one perspective as a
    i. multi-classifier
    ii. k-way clustering
    iii. binary logistic regression classifier
14. Word2Vec learning involves training a neural network model
    i. to maximize the conditional probability of context given the word
    ii. to minimize the conditional probability of context given the word
    iii. to maximize the conditional probability of semantics given the word

15. In Word2Vec learning, ________ is used to score the sentences in graph.
    i. PageRank
    ii. Logistic Rank
    iii. Dynamic Rank

16. CBOW looks
    i. at n words before and after the center or target word and averages their vectors
    ii. at n words before and after the center or target word and projects their vectors to n dimensional space
    iii. at n words before the center or target word and averages their vectors

17. In CBOW model , objective function is task of
    i. maximizing the probability of correct center word given the context words
    ii. maximizing the probability of correct context words given the center word
    iii. minimizing the probability of correct center word given the context words

18. In Skip-Gram model,
    i. distributed representation of the context is used to **predict the target word**
    ii. distributed representation of the input word is used to **predict the context**
    iii. distributed representation of the historical context is used to **predict the target word**

19. In negative sampling,
    i. For positive samples, samples from a distribution whose probabilities match the ordering of the frequency of the vocabulary
    ii. Random samples are taken
    iii. For negative samples, samples from a distribution whose probabilities match the ordering of the frequency of the vocabulary

20. Hierarchical-Softmax
    i. decreases calculating the probability to just probability of the leaves of the binary tree
    ii. decomposes calculating the probability of one word into a sequence of probability calculations
    iii. decomposes calculating the probability of one word into just a random sample of probability calculations

Self-Assessment: Match the Columns

No		Match	
1.	Collobert et al. 2011	A	Approximation inspired by binary trees that was proposed by Morin and Bengio (2005)
2.	Distributed vector representation	B	Natural Language Processing (Almost) from Scratch

No		Match	
3.	Bengio et al. 2003	C	Learn vectors that represents each word as an n-gram of characters
4.	Harris, 1954	D	Word2Vec
5.	Distributional topical similarity	E	The meaning is distributed across the dimensions of the vector
6.	Mikolov et al. 2013	F	Start with a single word embedding and try to predict the surrounding word
7.	CBOW	G	Neural language modelling
8.	Hierarchical softmax	H	Word vectors of context get projected into the same position that is their vectors are averaged
9.	Skip-Gram	I	Word embedding can correspond to documents in which the word occurs
10.	FastText	J	Words are characterized by the company they keep

Self-Assessment: Sequencing

Order	Please arrange in descending order (Timeline from latest to earliest)
1.	The counts matrix is preprocessed by normalizing the counts and log-smoothing them and a log-bilinear model with a weighted least–squares objective is used.
2.	Count-based models learn vectors by doing dimensionality reduction on a co–occurrence counts matrix.
3.	The model generates two sets of word vectors, W and $\tilde{W}$. W and $\tilde{W}$ are equivalent and differ only as a result of their random initializations. The two sets of vectors should perform equivalently. The average of the two vectors can be used.
4.	This matrix is factorized to yield a lower-dimensional matrix of words and features, where each row yields a vector representation for each word.

Order	Please arrange in descending order (Timeline from latest to earliest)
1.	The context vectors are averaged before using in prediction.
2.	Scores are obtained as probabilities.

3.	If a word is to be associated with a dimension, its one-hot vector has 1 in that dimension and zero everywhere else. These vectors are embedded using n dimensions say 300.
4.	We generate the one hot word vectors corresponding to the context.
5.	Probabilities generated match true probabilities.
6.	A score vector is generated.

Short Questions

1. Discuss the basic concepts of word embedding.
2. What are advantages and disadvantages of word embedding?
3. Differentiate between Bag of Words (BoW) model and word embeddings.
4. Discuss Word2vec learning.
5. Bring out the differences between CBOW model and Skip-gram models.
6. Describe the steps of a generalized CBOW model.
7. Discuss how CBOW model can be viewed from the perspective of neural language model.
8. Describe the steps of a generalized Skip-gram model.
9. Discuss how Skip-gram model can be viewed from the perspective of neural language model.
10. Discuss the concepts of negative sampling and hierarchical softmax in the context of Word2Vec.

Transformers and Pre-trained Models

CHAPTER
9

9.1 RNN Language Models – Issues

In chapter 7, we discussed RNN Language models where the basic concept was to condition the neural network on all previous words in the sequence of words and tie the weights at each time step. This language model produces context-specific word representations at each position. The major bottleneck is that the current hidden representation must encode all the information about the text observed so far. This becomes difficult especially with longer sequences. As we already discussed RNNs are unrolled from left to right which means that the model encodes linear locality that is nearby words are the ones that often affect each other's meanings which is a useful characteristic. However, this linear interaction distance means that it takes O(sequence length) steps for the distant word pairs to interact. These long-distance dependencies are harder to learn due to gradient problem. Moreover, the linear order of words that is the linear structure does not fully convey the meaning. As we know RNN models have forward and backward passes each associated with O(sequence length) operations, however these passes are unparallelizable. This is because future RNN hidden states cannot be computed in full before past hidden states have been computed. This in fact inhibits training on very large datasets and is even more true when we are dealing with increasing sequence lengths.

RNN and LSTM (long short-term memory networks) neural models were designed to process language and carry out tasks like classification, summarization, translation, and sentiment detection. In both models, layers get the next input word or a context of previous words, and thus use the left context of the word. Word embeddings were used where the meaning of each word was represented as a real vector of fixed size between 100 and 300. This fixed representation of words (e.g., word2vec) are associated with two issues. The first issue is that a word type has the same representation irrespective of the context in which the word occurs and this is not amenable to fine-grained word sense disambiguation. In addition, this one representation for a word does not consider the different aspects of a word such as semantics, syntactic behavior, and connotations. Thus, use either the left context or right context. This unidirectionality is needed to generate a well-formed probability distribution. However, language understanding is basically bidirectional. To summarize, the recurrence aspect of these language models gives rise to issues with learnability due to vanishing gradients, remembering long history and scalability due to sequential nature and not being parallelizable. The solution points towards doing away with recurrence and instead introducing attention.

9.2 Attention – The Basics

In many deep learning models, data passes through multiple layers of neural networks layers where it becomes increasingly complex to correctly identify the relevant information. **Attention mechanisms** were introduced as a way to address this limitation. In attention-based models, the model can selectively focus on certain parts of the input when making a prediction. In language models, attention mechanisms allow the models to concentrate on a particular portion of the observed context at each time step. Encoding a sentence using a single vector is too restrictive and therefore we produce a vector for each word or input in the sentence. But finally, we need a single vector which we can obtain by summing or averaging all the vectors which in essence gives equal importance to each input. However, it is possible to dynamically decide the importance of each input for a particular task by having a weighted sum to reflect this variation – the attention.

9.2.1 Attention Mechanisms in Neural language Models

The attention mechanism allows the neural language model to focus on the most relevant information when making predictions. In other words, the attention mechanism is another layer in the neural network that dynamically highlights the pertinent features of the input and can be applied directly to the input or to any higher-level representation. Associating a weight distribution to the input sequence such that higher weights are assigned to more relevant elements is the central idea behind attention. Training of the attention layer to discover what is *relevant* is simultaneously carried out when the other part of the network is being trained.

9.2.2 Simple Encoder-Decoder Model

In order to explain the attention mechanism, let us consider an encoder-decoder sequential model. The encoder-decoder architecture is powerful for sequence-to-sequence-based prediction for neural machine translation, summarization, and image caption generation (Figure 9.1). The encoder is a kind of network that extracts features from given input data. The encoder reads the input sequence, and summarizes the information in the form of a fixed length context vector. The decoder is responsible for interpreting this context vector. The entire encoder-decoder model is trained in its entirety and not separately element by element. One of the main drawbacks of this encoder-decoder network is the inability to extract strong contextual relations from long semantic sentences, the basic seq2seq model cannot identify those contexts and therefore, affects model performance and eventually decreases accuracy.

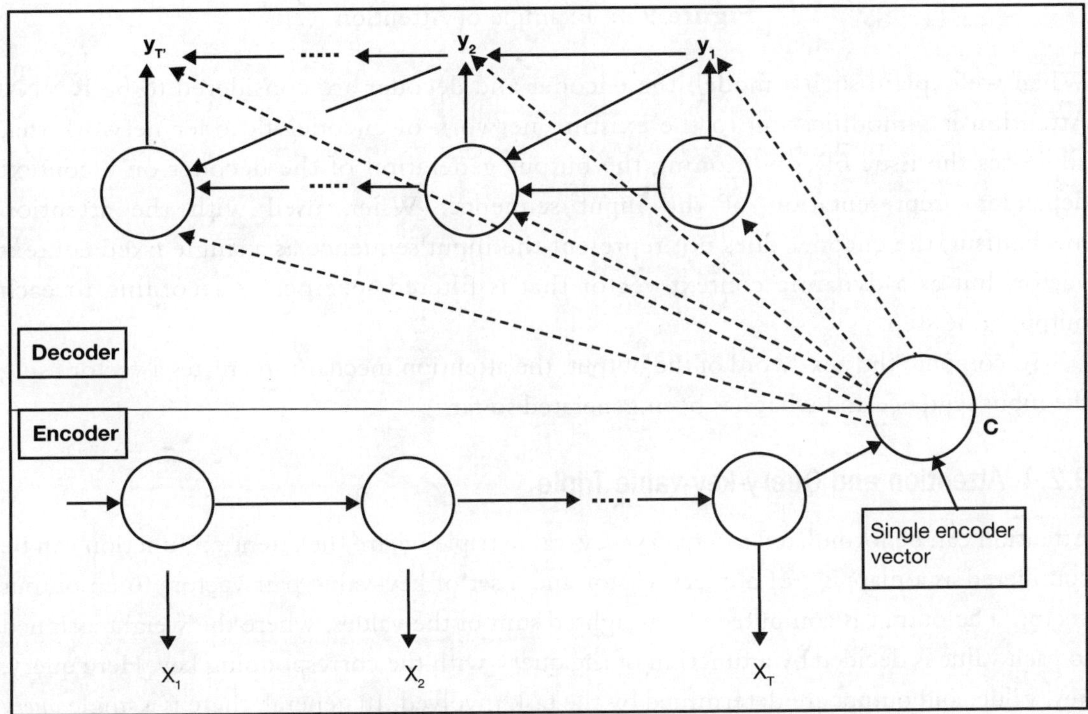

Figure 9.1: Simple Encoder–Decoder Model

9.2.3 Encoder-Decoder Model with Attention

A more general view of seq2seq model can be viewed as follows: any function of the encoder's output can be utilized as a representation of the context on which we want to condition the decoder. Moreover, we can feed the context not only at the beginning of the decoding process but at any time step during decoding. While processing a word w, attention enables the model to focus on words closely related to the word *w* that is there in the input. In the example given in Figure 9.2, "frock" is closely connected to "pink" and "liked" while it is not related to "girl".

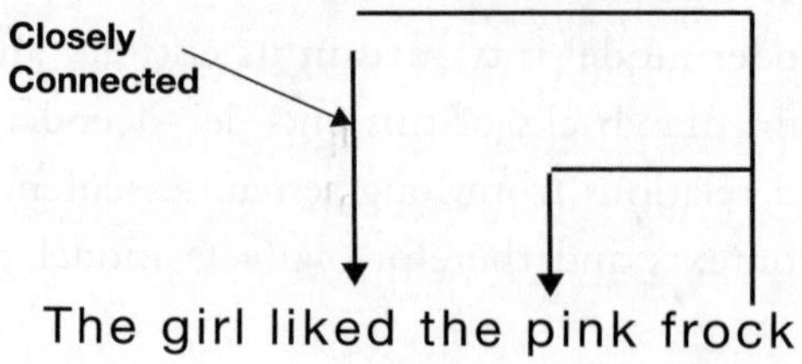

Figure 9.2: Example of Attention

When we explain such a model, the encoder and decoder are considered to be RNNs. Attention is a modification to the existing network of encoder–decoder network that addresses the issue of conditioning the output generation of the decoder on a context dependent representation of the input sequence. When used with the attention mechanism, the encoder does not represent the input sequence as a single fixed context vector, but as a dynamic context vector that is filtered specifically according to each output time step.

To compute the next word of the output, the attention mechanism creates a vector using the input sentence and what has been generated so far.

9.2.4 Attention and Query-key-value Triple

Attention can be formulated as a query–key–value triple where the attention function can be considered as a mapping of a query vector and a set of key-value pair vectors to an output vector. The output is computed as a weighted sum of the values, where the weight assigned to each value is decided by a function of the query with the corresponding key. Here query, key, value, and output are determined by the task involved. In general, there is a single *query* vector and multiple *key* vectors. Encoder outputs an explicit "key" and "value" at each input time where key is used to evaluate the importance of the input at that time, for a given output. Key is used to evaluate the importance of the input at that time, for a given output. Decoder outputs an explicit "query" at each output time. Query is used to evaluate which inputs to pay attention to. Here three vectors are created as abstractions. These are calculated by multiplying the input vector(X) with weight matrices that are learnt during training as given below:

- ***Query Vector***: $q = X * Wq$. This can be viewed as the current word.
- ***Key Vector***: $k = X * Wk$. This can be viewed as an indexing mechanism for Value vector.
- ***Value Vector***: $v = X * Wv$. This can be viewed as the information in the input word.

A dot product for q and k is carried out to find the key k most similar to query q where the closest query–key product is indicated by the highest value. A softmax function ensures that this product value lies between 0 and 1. The value vectors with higher values will get more attention. These aspects are represented by the hidden states h.

9.2.5 Attention in the Encoder-Decoder Model

During the prediction of the output sequence, attention enabled the focus to be on certain portions of the input sequence. During decoding, attention is added to the decoder by feeding at each time step, a d–dimensional vector representation of the entire (arbitrary-length) input sequence into the decoder. A weighted average of the encoder's representation of the input (i.e. hidden states) can be used as the representation of the input. The averaging weights associated with each encoder element specifies how much attention to pay to that element. Since different parts of the input may be more or less important for different parts of the output, we want to vary the weights over the input during each time step of the decoding process.

The output generation of the decoder needs to be conditioned on a context dependent representation of the input sequence. The attention layer is trained to decide what is *relevant* at the same time as the rest of the network is being trained. In general, this encode–decoder model works by providing a more weighted context from the encoder to the decoder and a learning mechanism where the decoder can interpret where to actually give more 'attention' to the subsequent encoding network when predicting outputs at each time step in the output sequence. The steps of this model are as follows (Figure 9.3):

1. The encoder network is first utilized to obtain the hidden state of the decoder at the current time step.
2. Next, we calculate the attention scores. Attention scores indicates the match between each encoded input and the current output of the decoder. For the calculation of this attention score the output of the decoder from the previous time step is required which will be 0 initially. Attention scores is the dot product of the hidden states of the encoder.

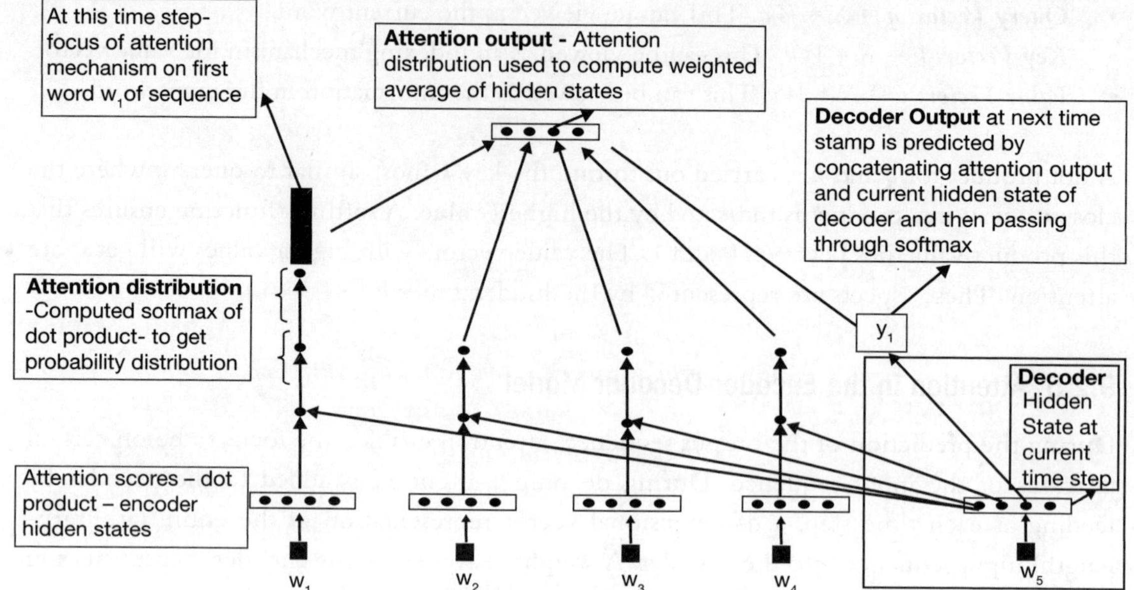

Figure 9.3: Encoder–Decoder Model with Attention Mechanism

3. Next, the attention scores are normalized to a probability distribution (Equation 9.1) using a softmax function.

$$\text{Probability distribution } \alpha^{(t)} = \left(\alpha_1^{(t)} \dots\dots\dots\dots \alpha_s^{(t)} \right) \tag{9.1}$$

This probability distribution α is described over S elements of the input sequence that depends on the output at current time step t. The scores are normalized so that they represent probabilities and essentially gives the likelihood of relevance between each encoded input time step (annotation) and current output time step. In other words, attention computes a probability distribution over the hidden states of the encoder which depends on the current hidden state of the decoder. This probability distribution is freshly computed for each output symbol.

4. Then this attention distribution is used to compute a weighted average of the hidden state vectors of the encoder as attention output (Equation 9.2)

$$c^{(t)} = \sum_{s=1\dots S} \alpha_s^{(t)} h^{(s)} \tag{9.2}$$

where $c^{(t)}$ is the weighted average of the encoder, and $h^{(s)}$ are the hidden states of the encoder.

5. The attention output and current hidden state of the decoder is concatenated and then passed through softmax layer to obtain the output of the decoder at next time stamp.

Thus, attention allows the decoder to consult with both the final hidden layer, produced by the encoder, and a selected portion of the original encoder input using another layer for example tanh (Equation 9.3).

$$o^{(t)} = \tanh\left(W_1 h^{(t)} + W_2 c^{(t)}\right)$$

(9.3)

where $c^{(t)}$ the weighted average of the encoder, and $h^{(t)}$ the hidden states of the encoder at time t are used to compute the output $o^{(t)}$.

One value at a time is outputted by the decoder. These values may be passed onto in more layers before a prediction of the output for the current output time step is obtained.

9.3 Transformers

Transformers are neural networks that learn context and understanding through sequential data analysis. Transformers draw inspiration from the encoder–decoder architecture found in RNNs because of their attention mechanism. Transformers were introduced in 2017 by Vaswani et al., and this architecture was found to be outstanding in handling inherently sequential text data. They take a text sequence as input and produce another text sequence. Transformers are a sequential transduction model which does not perform data processing in sequential order but however uses attention mechanism to learn contextual relations between words. It is a pure attention–based model with no convolutions or recurrence.

9.3.1 Challenges of RNNs Tackled by Transformer Models

- **Long-range dependencies:** RNNs suffer with issues like long-range dependencies. Transformer networks almost exclusively use attention which helps to draw connections between any parts of the sequence, so long-range dependencies are not a problem anymore. With Transformers, long-range dependencies have the same likelihood of being taken into account as any other short-range dependencies. Transformers capture more long-range dependencies with fewer parameters.
- **Gradient vanishing and gradient explosion:** This problem associated with RNNs is not associated with transformer models since in transformer models the entire sequence is trained simultaneously and have only fewer layers.
- **Larger training steps:** RNNs need large training steps to reach a local/global minima. since the size of the network depends on the length of the sequence. This gives rise to many parameters, and most of these parameters are interlinked with one another. As a result, the optimization requires a longer time to train and a lot of steps. However, Transformers require fewer steps to train compared to RNNs.

- **No parallel computation:** RNNs work as sequence models, that is, all the computation in the network occurs sequentially and therefore cannot be parallelized. There is no recurrence in the Transformer networks therefore they are easier to parallelize and faster to train than RNNs.

9.3.2 Applications of Transformers

Transformers were found to be suitable for many NLP tasks such as language models and text classification. Transformers were used for NLP applications such as machine translation, text summarization, question-answering, speech recognition, etc., which are essentially based on sequence–to–sequence modelling. Transformers are important since they form the basis of important pre-trained models such as BERT and GPT.

9.3.3 Architecture of Transformer

Transformers use stacked self-attention and position–wise, fully connected layers for the encoders and decoders (Figure 9.4). Embedding layers and an output layer to generate the final output is associated with each of the encoder and decoder stacks. The encoder reads the text input and the decoder produces a prediction for the task. The model uses self-attention to represent input/output without using recurrence.

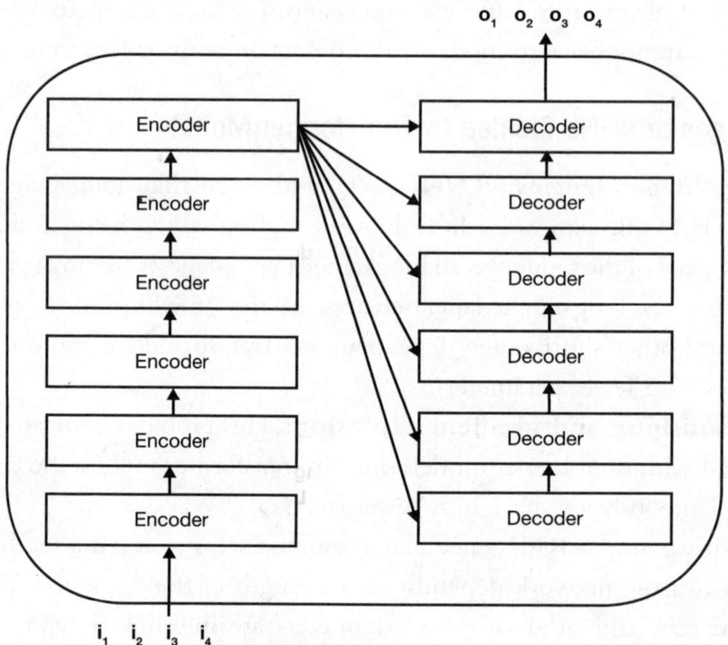

Figure 9.4: Stacked Encoder-Decoder Model

9.3.4 Training and Inference – Transformer

By utilizing both the input and target sequence, the transformer needs to learn how to output the target sequence. The working of the transformer varies a little during training and inference phases. During the training phase (Figure 9.5 (a)), before being fed to the encoder, the input sequence is represented as embeddings incorporated with position encoding. This input is processed by the stack of encoders to produce an encoded representation of the input sequence. During training the target sequence is prefixed with a start–of–sentence token and similar to input sequence represented as embeddings incorporated with position encoding and fed to the decoder. This embedded target sequence along with the encoded representation from the encoder is then processed by the stack of decoders to obtain the encoded representation of the target sequence. This target sequence is converted into word probabilities and finally, the output sequence by the output layer. The loss function associated with the transformer compares model's predicted output sequence with the desired target sequence from the training data. The gradients of this loss function were used to train the transformer during back-propagation and parameters updated in the direction so as to reduce the loss.

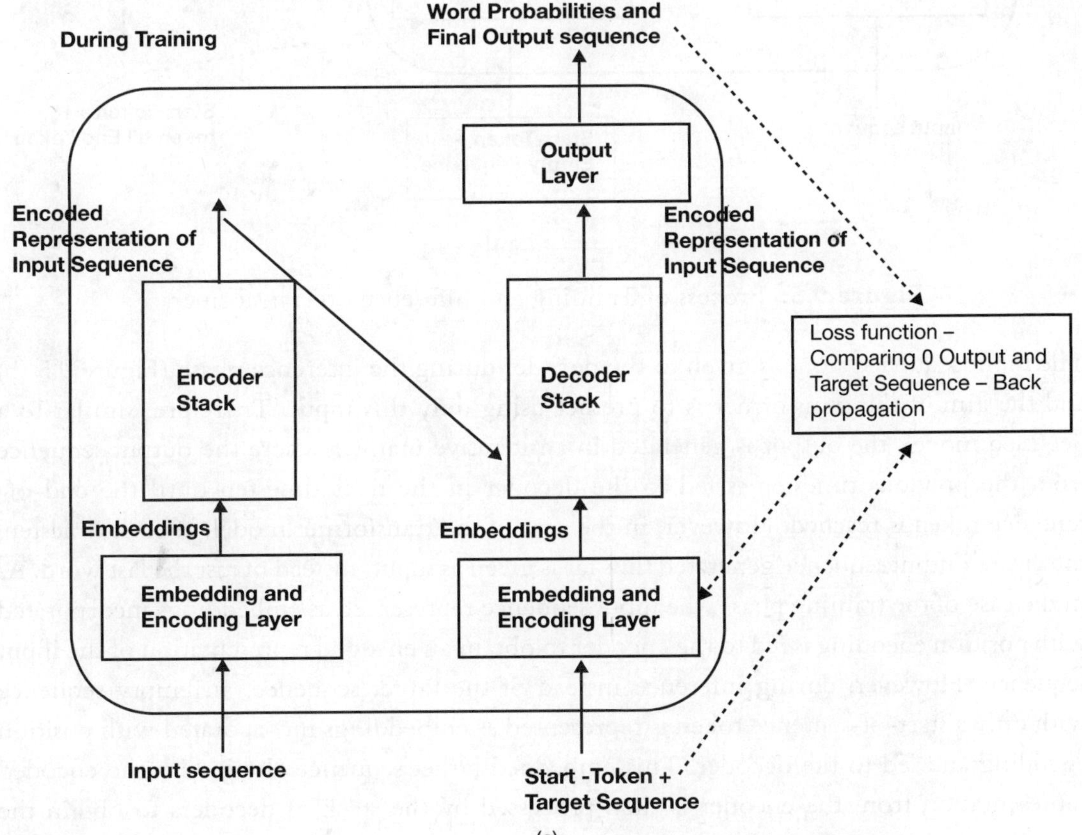

(a)

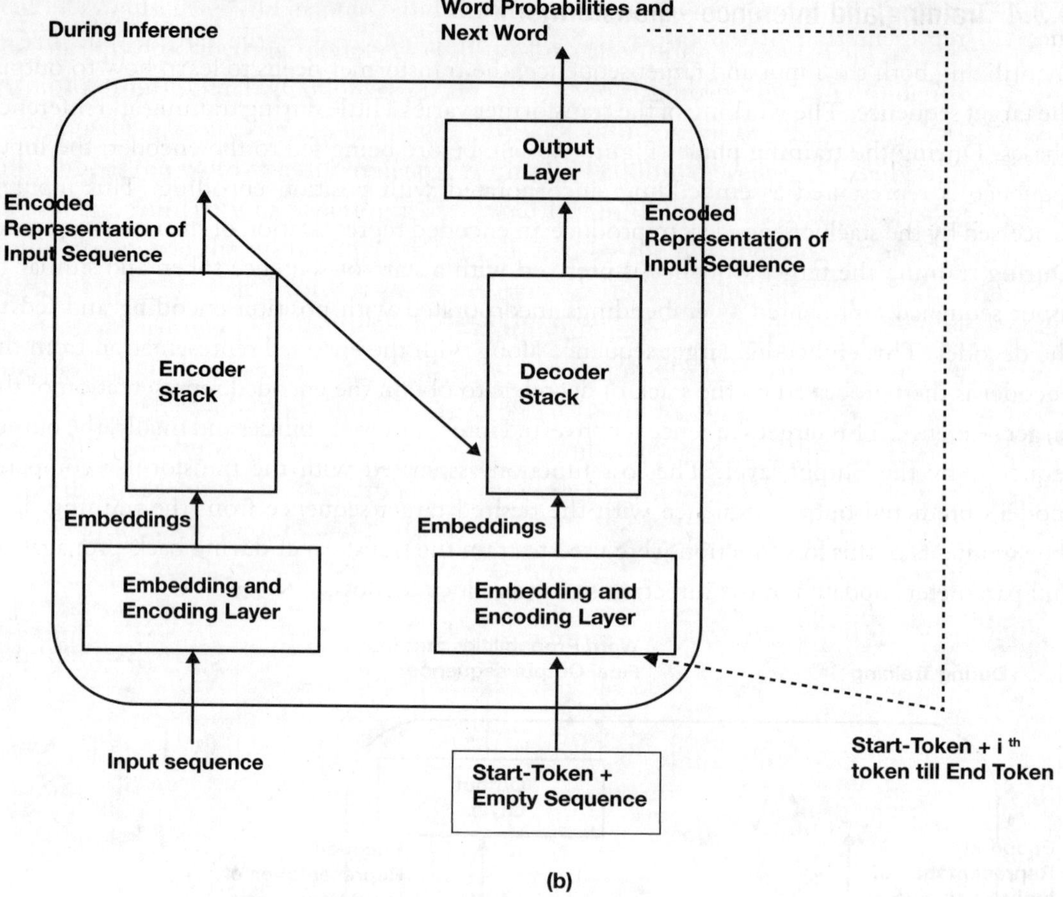

Figure 9.5: Process of Training and Inference of Transformers

The input sequence alone is given to the decoder during the inference phase (Figure 9.5 (b) and the aim of the transformer is to predict using only this input. Therefore, similar to a Seq2Seq model, the output is generated in an iterative manner where the output sequence from the previous timestep is fed to the decoder in the next timestep until the end-of-sentence token is reached. However, in the case of the transformer model, at each timestep, the entire output sequence generated thus far is given as input, instead of just the last word. As in the case of the training phase, the input sequence represented as embeddings incorporated with position encoding is fed to the encoder to obtain an encoded representation of the input sequence. However, during inference instead of the target sequence, an empty sequence with only a start-of-sentence token is represented as embeddings incorporated with position encoding and fed to the decoder. This embedded target sequence along with the encoded representation from the encoder is then processed by the stack of decoders to obtain the encoded representation of the target sequence. The last word of the output sequence is considered as the predicted word. The predicted word is now made to occupy the second position of the decoder input sequence, which during this time step contains a start-of-sentence token and the first word. Now as before the new decoder sequence is fed into the model. Then the second word of the output is suffixed to the decoder sequence. This process is repeated until the end-of-sentence token is predicted. Since the encoder sequence does not change for each iteration, we do not repeat the associated encoding steps. Thus, like in a Seq2Seq model, we generate the output in an iterative manner.

As already discussed, at each timestep, the entire output sequence generated thus far is given as input, instead of just the last word and this approach of training is known as **teacher forcing**. During inference by similarly by feeding the target sequence generated so far to the decoder, we are giving it a clue, just as a teacher would. The transformer is able to consider all the words in parallel and hence speeds up the training process.

9.3.5 Components of the Transformer

Now let us discuss the various components of the transformer model in detail (Figure 9.6). There are several (usually six) sequentially connected encoders and decoders associated with the encoder and decoder stacks respectively. Each encoder of the encoder stack contains the multi-head attention layer and the feed-forward layer. The embeddings incorporated with position encoding are given as input to the first encoder in the stack. The other encoders in the stack receive their input from the previous encoder. The multi-head self-attention layer receives its input from the encoder. The feed-forward layer receives its input from the self-attention layer, and in turn passes its output to the next encoder. Each of the decoders in the stack receive their input from the preceding decoder. Each decoder in the decoder stack receives the final encoded representation of the input sequence from the last encoder in the encoder stack. The structure of the decoder is similar to the encoder, but however there are some important changes. Each decoder in the decoder stack contains one masked multi-head attention layer (not present in the case with encoder), another encoder-decoder multi-head attention layer and a feed-forward layer. Similar to encoder stack, the embeddings associated with the previous time-stamp output of the decoder stack incorporated with position encoding is given as input to the first decoder in the stack. The masked multi-head self-attention layer receives its input from decoder. The encoder-decoder multi-head self-attention layer receives its input from the masked multi-head self-attention layer. The output of the self-attention is passed to a feed-forward layer, which then sends its output to the next decoder. Each of the decoders in the stack receive their input from the preceding decoder. A residual skip-connection, followed by a layer-normalization is associated with each of the sublayers of both the encoder and decoder stacks.

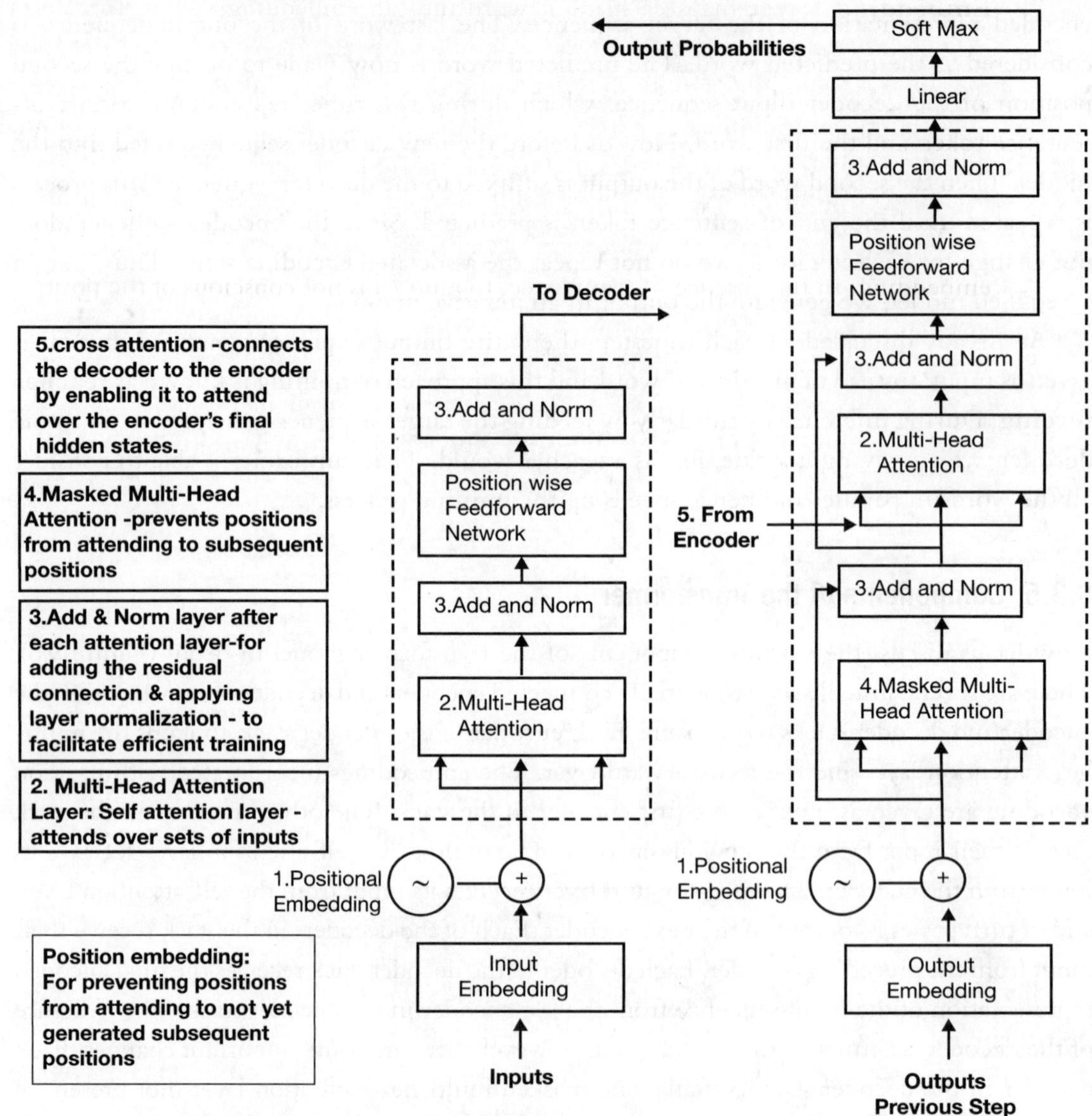

Figure 9.6: Components of Encoder–Decoder

Like any NLP model, the transformer requires the meaning of the word and its position in the sequence. Now let us describe the functions of each component of the transformer model.

- **Embedding and Encoding layer:** The input data for both the encoder and decoder stack contains the embedding layer which essentially encodes the meaning of the word. Here, the text sequence is mapped to numeric word IDs using the vocabulary.

o   **Embedding Layer** maps each input word into an embedding vector. In case of encoder, the input sequence is fed to the input embedding layer. In case of decoder, the target sequence is fed to the output embedding layer after shifting the targets right by one position and inserting a start token in the first position. During Inference, the initially empty output sequence is fed to this output layer iteratively.

o   **Position Encoding Layer** fulfills the need for information about the positions and order of tokens in a sentence. Position embeddings are added to each word embedding. In the absence of recurrence, the model is not conscious of the position of the word in the input sequence. One position encoding layer each is associated with the encoder part and the decoder part respectively. This encoding is dependent only on the maximum length of the sequence independent of the actual input sequence. computed independently of the input sequence and are fixed values that depend only on the max length of the sequence. In other words, we have a constant code associated with each position which are computed using the equation given below (Equation 9.4):

$$PE_{(pos,2i)} = \sin\left(pos\ /\ 10000^{2i/s-length}\right)$$

$$PE_{(pos,2i+1)} = \cos\left(pos\ /\ 10000^{2i/s-length}\right) \tag{9.4}$$

where *pos* is the position of the word in the sequence embedding vector, *s-length* is the length and *i* is the index value into this vector.

- **Multi-Head Self-Attention Layer** in the encoder allows the input sequence to pay attention to itself. In self-attention each element attends to every other element. For computing a representation of a sequence, the attention mechanism relates the different positions of the sequence. In the self-attention of the encoder, the input is passed by the self-attention layer of the encoder to all three parameters, query, key, and value. Each element becomes query, key, and value from the input embeddings by a weight matrix multiplication. The linear layers that is the weight matrices without biases are stacked and are independent for the queries, keys, and values. The output of the attention heads is concatenated to form the output.

    Two sources of inputs, namely the output from the masked self-attention layer below it as well as the output of the encoder stack are combined by the encoder–decoder multi-head attention layer of the decoder. This layer of the decoder is called cross attention layer since this layer links the decoder to the encoder and allows the final hidden states of the encoder to be provided with attention.

- **Multi-head attention** allows the model to focus on different positions of the sequence and attend to them differently by giving attention layer multiple representation subspaces.

Intuitively, multiple attention heads enable attending to parts of the sequence differently. Provided with the same set of queries, keys, and values, the model has the capability to capture different ranges of the same dependencies (e.g., shorter-range vs. longer-range) within a sequence. This requires the attention mechanism to jointly utilize different representation subspaces of queries, keys, and values, by transforming them using h independently learned linear projections. In Transformer, the attention module repeats its computations multiple times in parallel. Each of these modules is called an Attention Head. The Attention module splits its Query, Key, and Value parameters N-ways and passes each split independently through a separate Head. All of these similar attention calculations are then combined together to produce a final attention score. This is called multi-head attention and gives the Transformer greater power to encode multiple relationships and nuances for each word.

- **Add and Norm Layer:** Efficient training is facilitated by providing a residual skip-connection, followed by a layer-normalization with each of the sublayers of both the encoder and decoder stacks. Residual connections, which mean that we add the input to a particular block to its output, help improve gradient flow.

- **Feed-Forward Layer:** A feed-forward layer on top of the attention-weighted averaged value vectors allows us to add more parameters / nonlinearity.

- **Masked Multi-Head Self-Attention Layer** of the decoder works differently when compared with both the multi-head self-attention layers used by encoder and decoder. By masking or restricting future positions, this layer is permitted to attend to only preceding positions in the sequence. Masked Multi-Head Attention in the decoder enables the target sequence to pay attention to the preceding positions of the input sequence but prevents attending to subsequent positions. This masking, and by off-setting output embeddings by one position, predictions for a word at position i depend only on known output words at positions before i.

- **Output Layer of the Decoder:** The output layer generates the final output, and contains the linear layer and a softmax layer.

9.4 Pre-Trained Language Models

Before we discuss pre-trained models, we should remember that some of the representations used by neural language models such as word2vec were also pre-trained representations which are built in a context free manner. However, pre-trained models use these pre-trained representations for transfer learning. The classification of pre-trained representations is as shown in Figure 9.7. The pre-trained representations used by pre-trained models are contextual in nature.

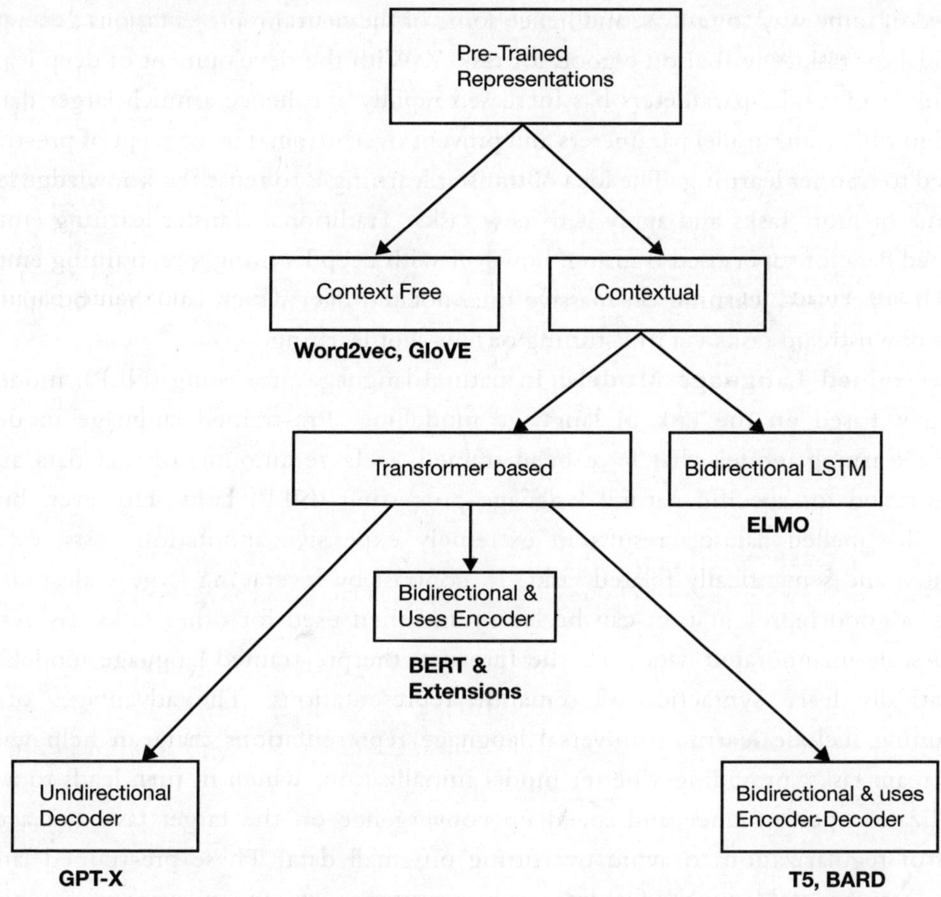

Figure 9.7: Classification of Pre-trained Representations

Contextual representations are further classified as unidirectional and bidirectional. While GPT considers unidirectional context, BERT, T5, BARD and ELMO consider bidirectional context, however ELMO does so in a shallow manner. Another dimension of the classification of contextual models are transformer based and LSTM based models. While GPT models use only the decoder of transformers, BERT uses only encoder of transformers, T5 and BARD use the encoder-decoder of transformers, however ELMO is not based on transformer at all but uses the LSTM model.

Pre-Trained Models: The current rapid increase in NLP adoption is because of the concept of transfer learning enabled through pretrained models. Pre-training in AI refers to training a model with one task to help it form parameters that can be used in other tasks. Pre-training is described as modelling on a large dataset for a particular task X, and then fine-tuning the learned model on a smaller dataset for task Y. Here, we assume that the task Y

is related in some way to task X, and hence some of the neural representations generated by the model for task X will also be good for task Y. With the development of deep learning, the number of model parameters has increased rapidly and hence a much larger dataset is needed to fully train model parameters and prevent overfitting. The concept of pre-training is related to transfer learning. The idea of transfer learning is to reuse the knowledge learned from one or more tasks and apply it to new tasks. Traditional transfer learning employed annotated data for supervised training, however with deep learning, pre-training employed with self-supervised learning on massive unannotated data which can then be applied to various downstream tasks via fine-tuning or few-shot learning.

Pre-trained Language Models: In natural language processing (NLP), model pre-training is based on the task of language modelling. Pre-trained language models are machine learning models that have been trained on large amounts of text data and can be fine-tuned for specific natural language processing (NLP) tasks. However, building large-scale labelled datasets results in extremely expensive annotation costs, especially for syntax and semantically related tasks. In contrast by leveraging large-scale unlabelled corpora a good representation can be learnt and then used for other tasks. By resorting to web-scale unannotated data from the Internet, the pre-trained language models could automatically learn syntactic and semantic representations. The advantages of using pre-training include learning universal language representations that can help with the downstream tasks, providing a better model initialization, which in turn leads to a better generalization performance and speed up convergence on the target task and acting as a kind of regularization to avoid overfitting on small data. These pre-trained language models learn general language features, such as grammar, syntax, and semantics, which can be adapted to various NLP tasks, such as sentiment analysis, named entity recognition, and text summarization. Pre-trained language models have resulted in a paradigm shift from supervised learning to pre-training followed by fine-tuning. The language model is first fed a large amount of unannotated data (for example, the complete Wikipedia dump). This lets the model learn the usage of various words and how the language is written in general. The model is now transferred to an NLP task where it is fed smaller task-specific datasets, which are used to fine tune and create final models capable of performing the specific tasks (Figure 9.8). Fine-tuning the pre-trained representations adjusts the language model parameters by the learning signal of the end-task. These pre-training-based models are better than task-focused models because a model which trains only on the task-specific dataset needs to both understand the language and the task using a comparatively smaller dataset. The language model on the other hand already understands the language since it has 'read' large language dumps during pre-training.

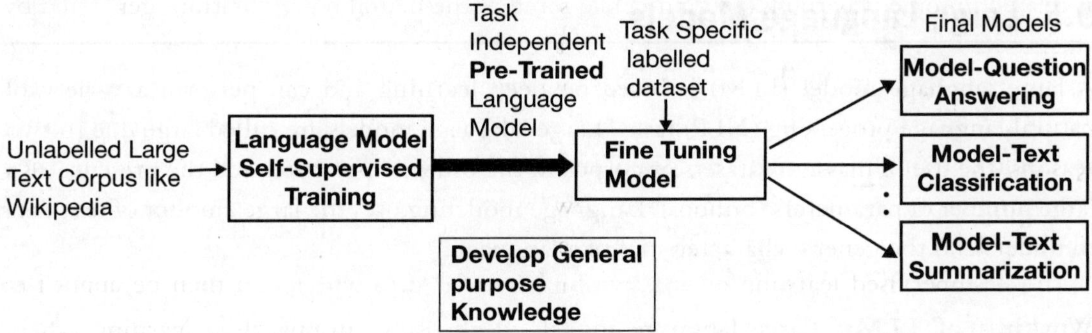

Figure 9.8: Framework of Pre-Training

In general, the goal of language modelling is to predict the next token, given a history of unannotated texts. The first neural language modelling models n-gram probabilities through distributed representations of words and feed–forward neural networks. In neural language modelling, distributed word representations the "word embeddings" were learned with models such as Word2Vec and GloVe as discussed in Chapter 8. RNN and LSTM are popular deep learning methods used for training language models. Transformer models enabled the building of stronger and more efficient language models. These models used self-supervised learning where the learning paradigm is same as supervised learning, but the labels of training data are generated automatically. Self-supervised learning is a technique used to train models in which the output labels are a part of the input data, thus no separate output labels are required. Although static word embeddings could improve the performance of downstream NLP tasks, they. Context–aware language modelling, which uses unannotated data to improve sequence learning with recurrent networks allowed the representation of different meanings of words in context. Later contextualized word vectors were proposed, which were derived from an encoder that is pre-trained on machine translation and then transferred to a variety of downstream NLP tasks. This "pre-training then fine-tuning" paradigm led to many other pre-trained models. Generative pre-training (GPT) was the first model to use unidirectional transformers as the backbone for the GPT of language models. Bidirectional Encoder Representations from Transformers (BERT) was the first model to leverage bidirectional transformers to learn bidirectional contexts by means of conditioning on both the left and the right contexts in deep stacked encoder layers. T5 was another model based on encoder-decoder model of transformers but rather than predicting the complete input, a prefix of every input is provided to the encoder. We will next discuss Large Language Models.

9.5 Large Language Models

A large language model (LLM) is based on deep learning and can perform a variety of natural language processing (NLP) tasks. Large language models are called large due to two reasons, the use of massive datasets or corpus in the order of petabytes and the presence of a large number of parameters (billions). Language modeling uses the large amount of text data to understand the general characteristics of a language.

Working of LLMs: Large language models work using unsupervised learning where the model is trained on a large amount of data without any specific labels or targets. The goal is to learn the underlying structure of the data and use it to generate new data that is similar in structure to the original data. LLMs rely on complex deep learning semi-supervised algorithms that shift through massive datasets with optimization of large number of parameters and are usually general-purpose models trained for relatively simple tasks, like predicting the next word in a sentence. This enables recognition of patterns at the word level and the learning of many of the general characteristics of language, such as grammar, syntax, and semantics. This process helps the LLMs better understand natural language and how it is used in context and then make predictions related to various NLP tasks such as text generation, summarization, translation, text classification, and even answering questions with a high degree of accuracy. This is a path breaking approach to NLP applications, where earlier specialized language models were trained to perform specific tasks. On the contrary, many emergent abilities of LLMs were observed, abilities that they were never trained for. For instance, LLMs have been shown to perform multi-step arithmetic, unscramble a word's letters, and identify offensive content in spoken languages.

Building Blocks of LLMs: LLM models generally refer to any model trained on broad data that can be adapted to a wide range of downstream tasks. LLMs are composed of several key building blocks (some of these concepts have been discussed in previous chapters and some in the preceding sections of this chapter) that enable them to efficiently process and understand natural language data. Modern LLMs use transformer models based on of encoder-decoder architecture (discussed earlier in the chapter) to recognize, translate, predict, or generate text or other content. The various key blocks are discussed below.

- **Tokenization:** Tokenization as already discussed is the process of converting a sequence of text into individual words, sub-words, or tokens. In LLMs, tokenization is usually performed using sub-word algorithms which split the text into smaller units that enables then to represent any text sequence, but with limited vocabulary size.

- **Embedding:** Embeddings are continuous vector representations learnt during the training process of LLMs where the vector representations capture complex relationships between words, such as synonyms or analogies.

- **Attention:** Attention mechanisms in LLMs, particularly the self-attention and multi-head mechanism used in transformers, allow the model to weigh the importance of different words or phrases in a given context enabling the model to focus on the most relevant information while ignoring less important details. This ability to selectively focus on specific parts of the input is crucial for capturing long-range dependencies and understanding the intricacies of natural language.

- **Pre-training:** LLMs takes a foundation (pre-training)–fine-tuning approach. A large volume of data (typically petabytes in size) is used to train the foundational layer of an LLM. The training normally consists of multiple steps. Generally, the initial step is an unsupervised learning approach trained with easily available unstructured and unlabeled data. During pretraining, the model learns general language patterns, relationships between words, and other foundational knowledge. Relationships between different words and concepts are generally learnt by this unsupervised model. For some LLMs, next training and fine-tuning is carried out utilizing a self-supervised learning approach where identification of different concepts is more accurately learnt. Finally, a deep learning architecture such as transformer is used. Using a self-attention mechanism, this architecture enables learning of relationships and connections between words and concepts. Once the training of the foundational model of the LLM is completed, fine-tuning techniques are applied for the foundation model to adapt to a broad range of different NLP applications.

- **Transfer learning:** Transfer learning is the technique of leveraging the knowledge gained during pretraining and applying it to a new, related task. In the context of LLMs, transfer learning involves fine-tuning a pre-trained model on a smaller, task-specific dataset thereby significantly reducing the amount of labeled data and training time required to achieve high performance on various NLP tasks.

Advantages and Challenges of LLMs: The advantage of LLMs is the use of a combination of general-purpose foundation model and application specific fine-tuning that enables extensibility and adaptability. LLMs provide foundation models that can be fine-tuned for customized use cases, for varied NLP tasks and deployments across organizations, users, and applications. The training of LLMs on huge widely available unlabeled data ensures that these models are high-performing with great accuracy, easily fine-tunable. However, LLMs are also associated with several challenges and limitations including high development and operational costs, high complexity, the probability of bias in the unlabeled training data and the lack of explainability.

Medium and Very Large LLMs: LLMs are of different sizes, where medium-size models include GPT-1, BERT and its extensions and T5 Models. These medium sized models will be discussed in detail in this chapter. Today very large LLMs exist where models are associated with more than 100 billion parameters. Depending on different sizes of LLMs there are different ways these models adapt and use the pre-trained models or foundation models such fine-tuning, few-shot and zero-shot prompting and instructor prompting.

Medium sized LLMs use the transfer learning approach of fine-tuning in which weights of a pre-trained model are further trained on new data. Generally, a new set of weights connects the final layer of the language model to the output of the downstream task. Fine-tuning is generally accomplished using supervised learning with a much smaller set of labeled data specific to the task. The many pre-trained models and their usage discussed in this chapter involve fine-tuning. However, as LLMs started to grow bigger, simpler techniques like prompting were used to leverage LLMs for specific tasks. In this approach, the problem to be solved is presented to the model as a text prompt that the model must solve by providing a completion. Few-shot prompting or in-context learning is a prompting technique that allows a model to process examples before attempting a task by including few examples of problem and solution pairs, known as shots. Zero-shot model is a large, generalized model trained on a voluminous size generic corpus of data provides moderately accurate result for general use cases, without the need for additional training. Instructor tuning is a form of fine-tuning where the language model is trained on many examples of tasks formulated as natural language instructions and appropriate responses. The reinforcement learning from human feedback (RLHF) is one of the techniques of instructor tuning used by popular models like ChatGPT and Sparrow. The most popular and pathbreaking application of very large LLMs are conversational AI and chatbots that can enable a conversation with a user in an effective and natural way in comparison to previous generations of AI technologies. ChatGPT, developed by OpenAI is now the most popular LLM based AI chatbot. ChatGPT currently is based on the GPT-3.5 model, and the newer GPT-4 LLM. We will be discussing this application of LLMs in detail in a subsequent chapter. However, in the following sections we will be discussing the pre-trained LLMs such as GPT, BERT, T5 and BARD models.

9.6 Generative Pre-trained Transformer (GPT)

OpenAI's General Pretrained Transformers or GPT as they are called is based on the transformer architecture which excels at processing sequential data (such as sentences, phrases, paragraphs and so on). GPT uses the pretrained decoder architecture from the standard transformer network as an independent language modelling unit and then uses them as generators.

Before GPT, language models (LMs) were typically trained on a large amount of accurately labelled data, which was hard to come by. These LMs offered great performance on supervised tasks that they were trained for, but were unable to handle domains adapt to other specific tasks. GPT works through a two-step process: pre-training and fine-tuning.

Pre-Training: GPT was designed to comprehend and create human-like text based on the patterns it picks up after learning from vast amounts of text dataset during the pre-training phase. The pre-training phase called generative pretraining, is an important part of GPT. In this phase, the model learns language by predicting the next word in sentences and gaining an understanding of general aspects of language. Pre-training is typically an unsupervised learning process, where models learn from unlabelled text data without explicit guidance or labels. This phase uses masked language models which are trained to predict missing or masked words within sentences, learning contextual relationships and capturing linguistic patterns.

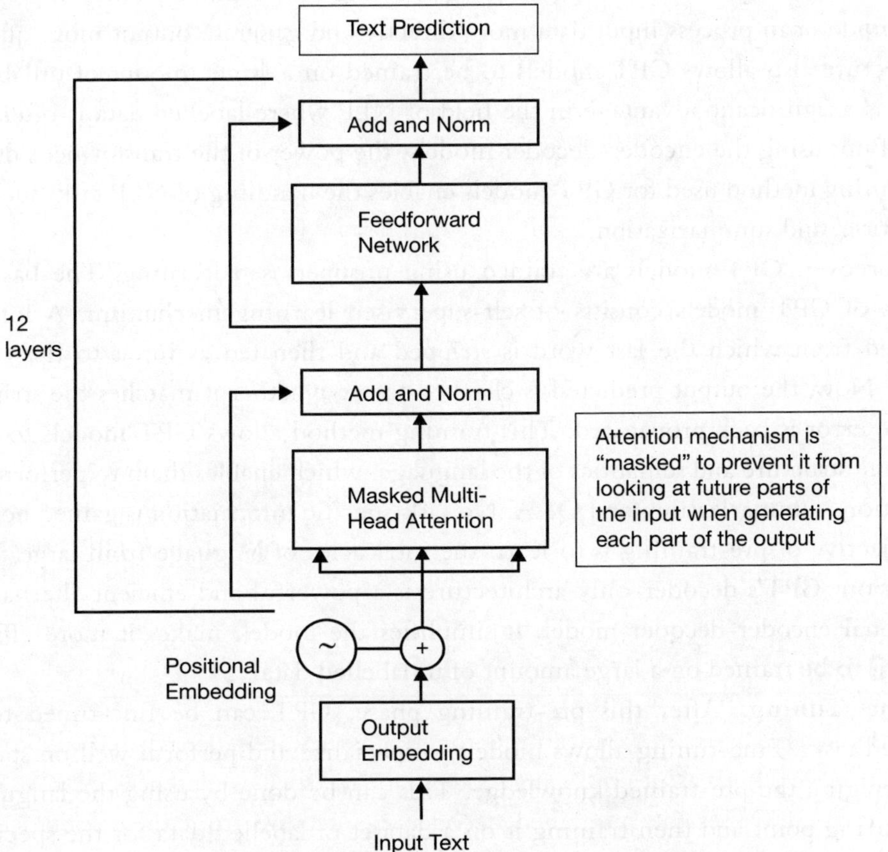

Figure 9.9: GPT Decoder Architecture

Use of Decoder Component of Transformer: As discussed earlier, pre-training often employs the decoder components of transformer-based architectures, which excel in capturing long-range dependencies and contextual information. The decoder in a GPT model uses a specific type of attention mechanism known as masked self-attention. In a traditional transformer, the attention mechanism allows the model to focus on all parts of the input when generating each part of the output. However, in a decoder-only transformer like GPT, the attention mechanism is "masked" to prevent it from looking at future parts of the input when generating each part of the output. This is necessary because GPT models are trained to predict the next word in a sentence, so they should not have access to future words. The decoder-only architecture normally with 12 layers simplifies the model (Figure 9.9) and makes it more efficient for certain tasks, like language modelling. Despite not having an encoder, GPT models are still capable of performing tasks typically associated with encoder-decoder models because the transformer's decoder uses self-attention, which allows it to focus on different parts of the input when generating the output. By removing the encoder, GPT models can process input data more directly and generate output more quickly. This architecture also allows GPT models to be trained on a large amount of unlabelled data, which is a significant advantage in the field of NLP where labelled data is often scarce. In spite of not using the encoder-decoder models, the power of the transformer's decoder and the training method used for GPT models enables the handling of NLP tasks such as Q&A, translation, and summarization.

Moreover, GPT models are trained using unsupervised learning. The basic training process of GPT models consists of self-supervised learning mechanism. A lot of text is gathered from which the last word is stripped and then fed as input to the transformer model. Now, the output predicted is checked to see whether it matches the stripped word and the error is back propagated. This training method allows GPT models to learn a lot about the structure and semantics of the language, which enables them to perform tasks like translation, summarization, and Q&A. No task-specific information is gained here, overall, the objective of pre-training is to learn the intricacies of language from large datasets. In conclusion, GPT's decoder-only architecture is a powerful and efficient alternative to the traditional encoder-decoder model. It simplifies the model, makes it more efficient, and allows it to be trained on a large amount of unlabelled data.

Fine Tuning: After this pre-training phase, GPT can be fine-tuned to perform specified tasks. Fine-tuning allows models to specialize and perform well on specific tasks by leveraging the pre-trained knowledge. This can be done by using the language model as a starting point and then training it on a dataset of labelled data for the specific task or domain. After pre-training, models are fine-tuned on task-specific labelled data to adapt their knowledge to a particular downstream task.

Fine-tuning is designed to improve the performance of the language model on the specific task or domain by adjusting the weights of the model to better fit the data. Supervised Fine-Tuning (SFT) is a type of fine-tuning that uses labelled data to train the LM. The labelled data consists of pairs of input and output data. The input data is the data that the LM will be given, and the output data is the data that the LM is expected to generate. Fine-tuning leverages transfer learning, where models transfer the learned representations from pre-training to the target task. Models are trained on labelled data that is specific to the target task, such as sentiment-labelled sentences or question-answer pairs. Fine-tuning typically involves gradient-based optimization techniques to update the model's parameters based on the task-specific data. SFT is a relatively simple and efficient way to fine-tune an LM. Reinforcement Learning from Human Feedback (RLHF) is a type of fine-tuning that uses human feedback to train the LM. Human feedback can be collected in a variety of ways, such as through surveys, interviews, or user studies. RLHF is a more complex and time-consuming way to fine-tune an LM, but it can be more effective than SFT. The best method for fine-tuning an LM depends on a number of factors, such as the availability of labelled data, the time, and resources available, and the desired performance. If you have labelled data available, SFT is a good option. If you do not have labelled data available, or if you need to improve the performance of the LM then RLHF is a good option.

There are a number of benefits of fine-tuning an LM. Fine-tuning helps in adapting the foundation model for a specific task or domain. Fine-tuning can also make the LM more interpretable, which can be helpful for debugging and understanding the behaviour of the model.

During fine-tuning, the model is trained on specific tasks or domains to make it more specialized. Given a prompt, GPT uses its learned patterns to generate coherent and contextually appropriate text ranging from a few words to entire paragraphs. Based on the prompts, GPT can produce responses based on various tones and styles, variations, or a continuation of the prompt. Even a slight change in the prompt guarantees a different response generated by GPT because GPT's generational capability stems from the context it detects from the prompt.

Examples of the Use of GPT: GPT's capabilities are really amazing. Here are just some examples of what it can do. The most obvious use of GPT is to generate content- whether it's generating information on topics or writing articles and blog posts from scratch, GPT can do it all within seconds, thereby saving time and effort. Owing to its human-like conversational style, GPT-powered chatbots and virtual assistants allow for engaging conversations that can assist or simply entertain users which we will be discussing Open ChatGPT in detail in a subsequent chapter. As it understands the relationships between words after comprehending chunks of data, GPT is capable of completing sentences and elaborating on or summarizing texts. GPT can also suggest, rephrase, or directly edit text, increasing readability and aiding users to improve their writing. GPT can break down language barriers thanks to its ability to easily translate text between languages. The examples of innovative uses will continue to grow. We will discuss more advanced models of GPT and Open ChatGPT in subsequent chapters.

9.7 Bidirectional Encoder Representations from Transformers (BERT)

Generally, only the left context or right context are used by language models, however human language understanding is bidirectional. Google's BERT is the first, deeply bidirectional, unsupervised language representation, pre-trained using only a plain text corpus.

BERT uses **WordPiece** a sub-word tokenization algorithm developed by Google for pre-training Sub-word tokenization lies between word and character-based tokenization. This tokenization solves issues of word-based tokenization such as very large vocabulary size, large number of out of vocabulary words, and similar words having different semantics and that of character tokenization such as very long sequences and less meaningful tokens. WordPiece starts with a small vocabulary and special tokens used by the model and the initial alphabet. For BERT the algorithm identifies sub-words by adding a prefix "##". Initially each word is split by the prefix between each character.

Example the word "dance" is split as "##d ##a ##n ##c ##e.

Then the WordPiece algorithm learns the rules for merging characters (pairs) where merging is carried by the score calculated as given below (Equation 9.5)

Score = (frequency of pairs)/((frequency of first element) X (frequency of second element))

This score ensures that merging of pairs where the individual elements are less frequent in the vocabulary is given priority.

BERT's fine-tuning methodology is based on transformers where every output element is connected to every input element, and the attention mechanism enables weights between these connections to be dynamically determined. In contrast to viewing a text sequence in a single direction, either from left to right, BERT applies bidirectional training to language modelling allowing better understanding of language context and stream. Therefore, BERT is able to give state-of-the-art performance for a varied set of both sentence-level as well as token-level NLP tasks. BERT has been pre-trained on BooksCorpus (800 million words) and English Wikipedia (2,500 million words).

The bi-directional based transformer enables learning of contextual relations between words in a text with the encoder that reads the text input, the decoder that carries out prediction and its attention mechanism. BERT being a language model only uses the encoder component of the transformer but however the model learns the context of a word based on all of its surroundings (left and right of the word) by reading the entire sequence of words simultaneously.

To overcome the limited context-learning challenge of most language models where generally the next word is predicted, BERT is pre-trained on two different, but related, unsupervised NLP tasks namely Masked Language_Modeling (MLM) and Next Sentence Prediction (NSP). Both MLM and NSP are trained together, token representations are pre-trained for MLM while the class [CLS] is pre-trained for NSP.

Masked Language Model (MLM): The objective of Masked Language Model (MLM) training is the prediction of a masked (hidden) word in sentence based on its context. Masking a certain percentage of randomly chosen input tokens of sentences, a deep learning based bidirectional representation is first learnt and then the masked tokens are predicted.

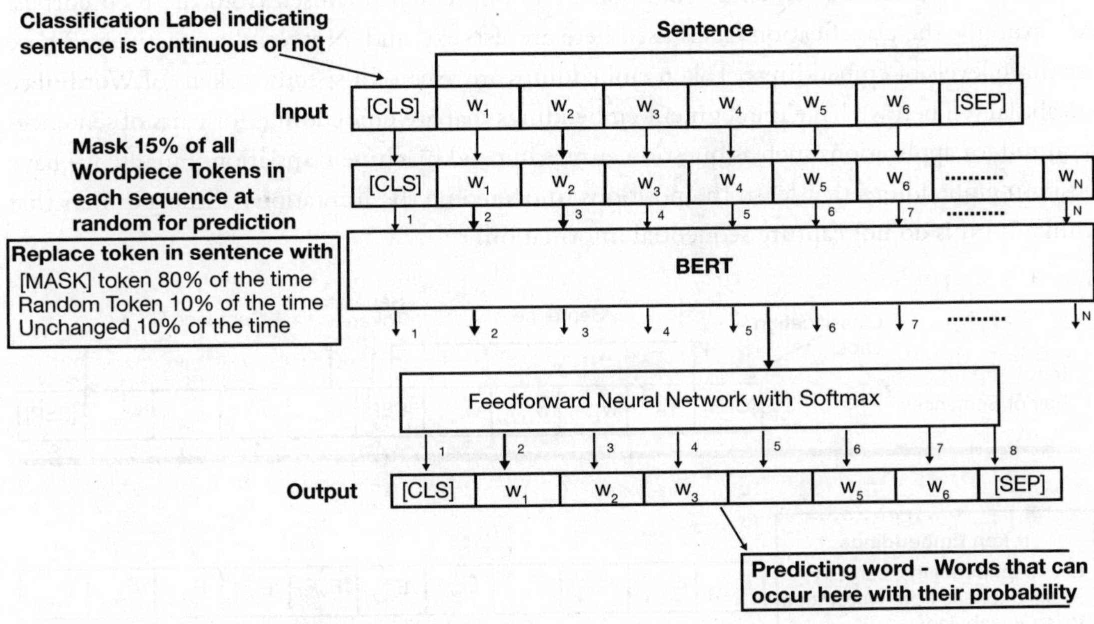

Figure 9.10: Masked Language Model

Masked Language Model is shown in Figure 9.10. First the sentence is prefixed with a classification label to indicate whether the sentence is continuous or not. These word sequences are altered by randomly replacing 15% of the words in each sequence with a [MASK] token 80% of the time, with random token 10% of the time and 10% of the time the input words are left unchanged before being given as input to the BERT model. In this way, the model is not allowed to build strong representations. Based on the context provided by non-masked words in the sequence, the BERT model tries to predict the original value of the masked words. In order to transform the output vectors into vocabulary dimensions, these vectors are multiplied by the embedding matrix. Finally, the probability of each word in the vocabulary is calculated using softmax as is done in a standard language model. The prediction of the masked values alone is considered during optimization of the BERT model.

Next Sentence Prediction (NSP): The objective of Next Sentence Prediction training is to have the program predict whether two given sentences have a logical, sequential connection or whether their relationship is simply random. In other words, Next Sentence Prediction learns relationships between sentences, predicting whether a sentence B is the actual sentence that follows sentence A, or a random sentence. A text dataset of 50,000 pairs of sentences is used as training data (Figure 9.11). During pre-training for 50% of the pairs, the second sentence would be the sentence that actually follows the first sentence while for the other 50% of the pairs, the second sentence would be a random sentence chosen from the used corpus. Accordingly, the classification labels used here are 'IsNext' and 'NotNext' respectively. There are three levels of embeddings. Token embeddings are learnt for specific tokens of WordPiece vocabulary. Then we have the segment embeddings that are embeddings for pairs of sentences required for applications such as question answering and machine translation. Finally, we have position embeddings that learn the positions to overcome the limitations of transformers that unlike RNNs do not capture sequential information.

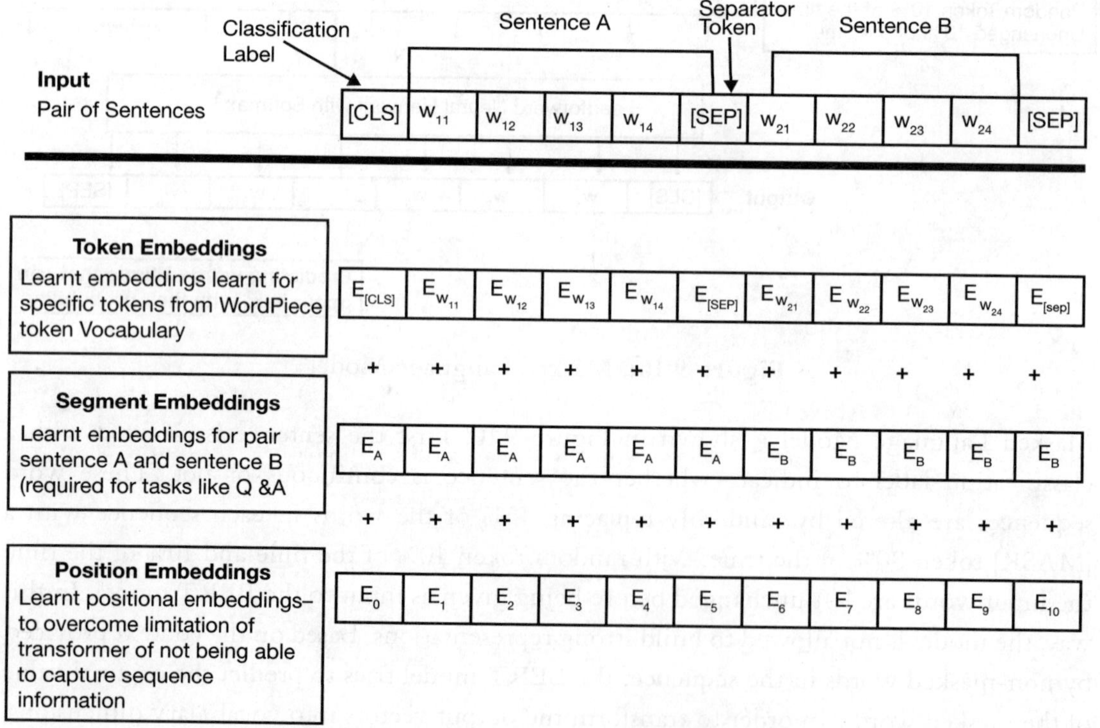

Figure 9.11: Next Sentence Prediction

Fine-Tuning BERT for NLP Tasks: We discussed the pre-training component of BERT; however, we need to comprehend how the pre-trained model learnt in an unsupervised manner can be adopted to different NLP tasks using fine-tuning. Fine-tuning is the supervised process of fine-tuning model parameters using labelled data from downstream application-oriented tasks (Figure 9.12). These tasks can be classified as sentence level tasks, token-level tasks, and sentence pair level tasks. For sentence level tasks, a single sentence is the input and the original BERT parameters, and the new classifier parameters will be learned together. For token level tasks where each token or element in the sequence will have a corresponding label in the output, a linear classifier is added over the hidden representations. For sentence pair tasks, segment embeddings for the two sentences separated using [SEP] is used along with a linear classifier on top of BERT that introduces C x h new parameters where C is the number of classes and h is the size of the hidden layer.

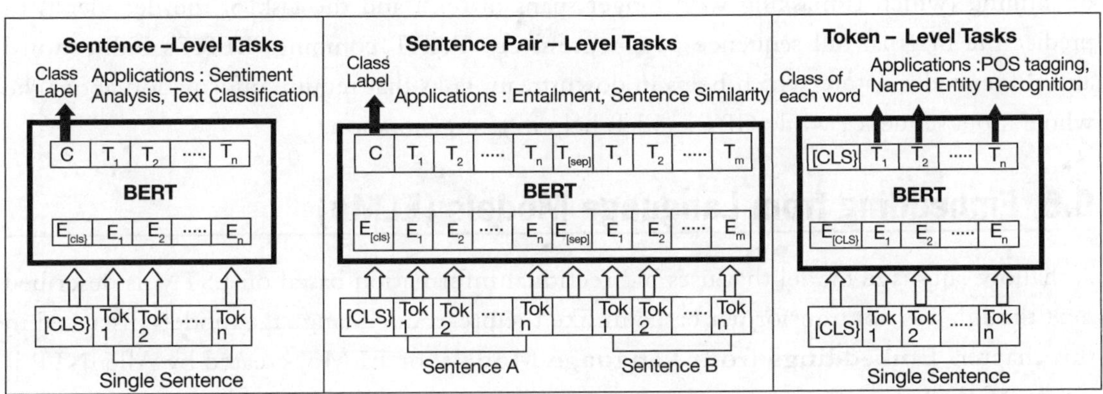

Figure 9.12: Fine-Tuning BERT for NLP Tasks

9.8 T5 and BART Models

T5: T5, or Text-to-Text Transfer Transformer, is a Transformer based encoder – decoder. architecture that uses a text-to-text approach. Every task such as translation, question answering, and classification is cast as feeding the model text as input and training it to generate some target text that as sequence-sequence tasks. It contains 12 transformer blocks with a total of 220 million parameters. The model was pre-trained on a C4 dataset (Colossal Clean Crawled Corpus) with 750 GB of English text. Like Bert, T5 uses MLM, and it learns to predict target words. The main difference between Bert and T5 is in the size of tokens (words) used in prediction. Bert predicts a target composed of a single word (single token masking), on the other hand, T5 can predict multiple words. It gives the model flexibility in terms of learning the model structure. With T5, all NLP tasks are reframed into a unified text-to-text format where the input and output are always text strings. This framework provides a consistent training objective both for pre-training and fine-tuning. Specifically, the model is trained with a maximum likelihood objective regardless of the task. To specify which task the model should perform, a task-specific textual prefix is added to the original input sequence before feeding it to the model. This allows using the same model, loss function, and hyperparameters on both discriminative and generative NLP tasks, such as classification, machine translation, document summarization, question answering tasks.

BART: BART developed by Facebook has an architecture similar to T5 and combines the bidirectional encoder similar to BERT with unidirectional auto-regressive encoder similar to GPT. The pre-training modifies the encoder input by masking, deletion, rotation, permutation, or infilling (which is masking with longer spans of text) and the task of the decoder is to predict the original full sequence auto-regressively. BART combines BERT's bidirectional and autoencoder nature which helps in downstream tasks that require information about the whole input sequence while GPT models help in text generation.

9.9 Embedding from Language Models (ELMo)

A shallow language model that uses bidirectional information based on LSTM is described next though it is not transformer based unlike the pre-trained language models discussed in this chapter. **Embeddings from Language Models**, or **ELMo**, created by AllenNLP is a state-of-the-art pre-trained model that provides contextualized word embeddings whose vector representation for a word differs from sentence to sentence. Other models such as word2vec, Fasttext, Glove, etc., generates the embeddings of words, but however ELMo provides contextualized word embedding of a word where a word may have a different meaning depending on the context in which it is used. ELMo is a way of representing deep contextualized word embeddings that models both complex characteristics of word use such as syntax and semantics, and how these uses vary across linguistic contexts for example to model polysemy. The ELMo vector assigned to a token or word is actually a function of the entire sentence containing that word and hence, the same word can have different word vectors under different contexts.

For example, considering two sentences,

- I *run* the computer every day.
- I liked the way he scored the run.

The verb "run" in the first sentence is a verb while it is a noun in the second sentence. This is a case of polysemy wherein a word could have multiple meanings or senses. Traditional word embeddings have the same vector for the word "run" in both the sentences without considering the context of the word and hence cannot distinguish between the polysemous words. ELMo word representations take the entire input sentence into consideration for calculating the word embeddings. Hence, the term "run" would have different ELMo vectors under different contexts.

ELMo word vectors are learned functions of the internal states of a deep bidirectional LSTM language model, which is pre-trained on a large text corpus. The pre-trained embeddings are fed into architectures that handle specific tasks. The weights of the task specific network are updated keeping the parameters of ELMo frozen. Then during fine-tuning the task specific network will backpropagate well into ELMo.

Character Embedding: In traditional neural language models, each token in the first input layer is converted into a fixed-length word embedding before being passed into the recurrent unit by initializing a word embedding matrix. However, in the case of ELMo language model, rather than simply looking up an embedding in a word embedding matrix, each token is first converted to an appropriate representation using character embeddings enabling the gathering of n-gram features that help to build more powerful representations. This allows morphological features to be picked up that are likely to be missed by word-level embeddings and hence mitigate the out-of-vocabulary (OOV) problem, because it can represent words that is has not seen during training. This character embedding representation is then run through a convolutional layer using some number of filters, followed by a max-pool layer. ELMo word representations are contextual and depend on the entire context in which a word is used, deep and combine all layers of a deep pre-trained neural network and is task-specific and is a linear combination of corresponding hidden layers — a downstream task learns weighing parameters.

ELMo ARCHITECTURE: ELMo architecture trains a language model using a 2-layer bi-directional LSTM (biLMs) where it uses all its layers in prediction but is actually a shallow concatenation of independently trained left-to-right and right-to-left multi-layer LSTMs and therefore strictly not bidirectional (Figure 9.13). ELMO uses the contextualized word representations to learn word vectors using long text instead of a context window. ELMO word vectors are computed on top of the two-layer bidirectional language model (biLM). Raw strings are converted into word Vectors by Character level Convolution neural network (CNN) and a highway network over characters whose output is fed to the first layer of biLM. The highway network is an architecture designed to ease gradient-based training of very deep networks by allowing unimpeded information flow across several layers on "information highways". The architecture is characterized by the use of gating units which learn to regulate the flow of information through a network and can be trained directly using stochastic gradient descent and with a variety of activation functions.

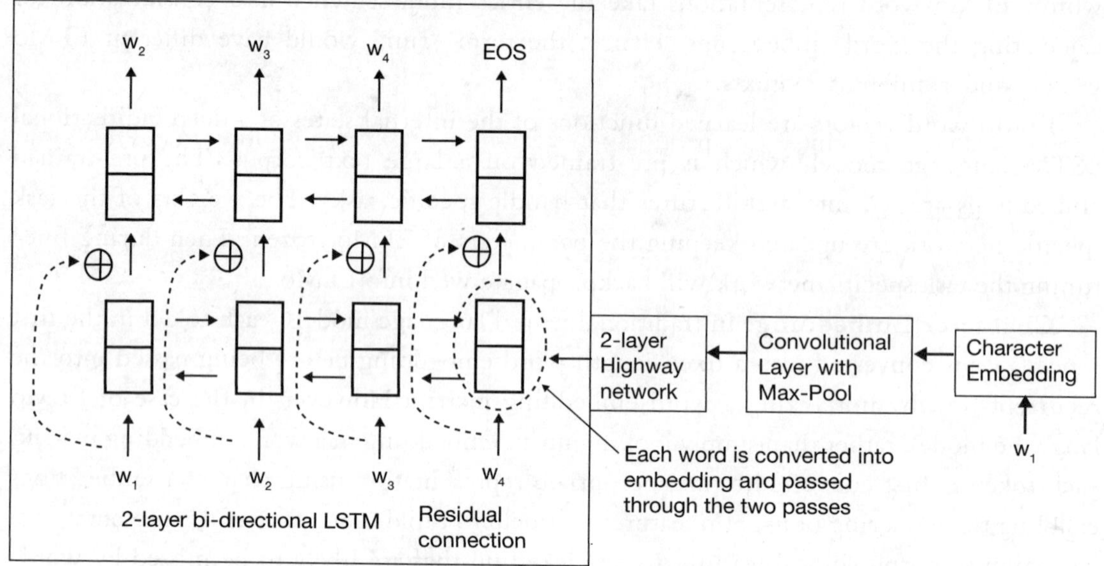

Figure 9.13: ELMo Architecture

The biLM model has two layers stacked together where each layer has 2 passes— forward pass and backward pass. Two passes are important to model both left and right context since bidirectionality is very crucial in language understanding tasks. Forward pass of biLm layer associates details of a word including the preceding context. The backward pass is similar to the forward pass contains details of a word and the context after it. Forward and backward pass both together form the intermediate word vector. This intermediate word vector is inputted to the second layer of biLm. The final representation (ELMo) is the weighted sum of the raw word vectors and the 2 intermediate word vectors. A residual connection to help deep models train successfully is added between the first and second LSTM layers where the input to the first layer is added to its output before being passed on as the input to the second layer. The final representation (ELMo) is the weighted sum of the raw word vectors and the 2 intermediate word vectors. As the input to the biLM is computed from characters rather than words, it captures the inner components of the word. The biLM thus understands that for example terms like *plenty* and *plentiful* are related at some level without even looking at the context they often appear in.

Summary

- Discussed issues associated with RNNs.
- Outlined the basics of Attention mechanism and the encoder–decoder models with attention.
- Explained in detail the transformer architecture and its applications.
- Outlined the concepts of pre-trained language models.
- Described the details of general Large Language Models (LLMs).
- Explained the architecture, pre-training, fine-tuning and use of Generative Pre-Trained Transformers (GPTs).
- Outlined the important aspects of Bidirectional Encoder Representations from Transformers (BERT) including architecture, pre-training with Masked Language Model (MLM) and Next Sentence Prediction (NSP) and fine-tuning BERT for NLP tasks.
- Explained T5 and BARD models briefly.
- Described the details of Embeddings from Language Models (ELMo).

Exercises

Suggested Activities

1. Explain 3 different NLP tasks that can be fine-tuned, assuming a pre-trained model is available. Explain the labelled dataset to be provided for each task.

2. Using either a language or software of your choice and available tools use pre-trained models to carry out text classification, sentiment analysis and question answering.

3. **Case Study – Fake News Detection:** Using Fake news dataset (https://www.kaggle.com/c/fake-news/data) available on Kaggle classify real and fake news articles using word embeddings and BERT model

Self-Assessment: Multiple Choice Questions

Give answers with justification for correct and wrong choices:

1. RNN models have forward and backward passes that are
   i. Parallelizable
   ii. Unparallelizable
   iii. Can be done together

2. In both RNN and LSTM, layers get the context of previous words
   i. the context of previous words
   ii. the context of future words
   iii. the context of both previous and future words

3 Attention mechanisms allow
   i. allow language models to focus on a particular part of the observed context
   ii. allow language models to focus on a particular part of the observed context at each time step
   iii. allow language models to fix attention only to a portion of the context at all times

4. Attention mechanism in neural language models is another layer in the neural network that dynamically highlights the relevant features and can be applied
   i. *only directly to raw input*
   ii. *directly to raw input* or to a higher level representation
   iii. *only* to a higher level representation

5. One of the main drawbacks of the encoder–decoder network is the
   i. inability to extract strong contextual relations from short semantic sentences
   ii. ability to extract strong contextual relations only long semantic sentences
   iii. inability to extract strong contextual relations from long semantic sentences

6. The encoder–decoder model is first used
    i. to obtain the hidden state of the encoder at the current time step.
    ii. to normalize attention scores to a probability distribution
    iii. to obtain the hidden state of the decoder at the current time step.

7. Transformer architecture excels
    i. at handling text data which is inherently sequential
    ii. at handling text data which is a bag of words
    iii. at handling a pair of text data

8. Transformer networks therefore they are easier to parallelize and faster to train than RNNs because
    i. there is no recurrence in transformer models
    ii. there is recurrence in transformer models
    iii. parameters are interlinked with one another

9. The goal of the transformer is to learn how to output the target sequence
    i. by using only the input sequence
    ii. by using both the input and target sequence
    iii. by using a permutation of target sequences

10. Position embeddings are added to each word embedding of the transformer model in order to make the model aware of the position of a word in the sequence since
    i. there is no recurrence
    ii. there is attention
    iii. there is encoder and decoder

11. Multiple attention heads
    i. enable attending to same parts of the sequence differently
    ii. enable attending to parts of the sequence differently
    iii. enable attending to parts of the sequence in the same manner

12. The multi–head self-attention layer of the encoder of the transformer model
    i. relates different positions of a single sequence in order to compute a representation of the same sequence
    ii. combines different positions of input and output sequences to compute a representation of the input
    iii. relates different positions of different sequences in order to compute a representation of the input sequence

13. Masked multi–head self-attention layer of the decoder of the transformer model
    i. prevents positions from attending to preceding positions
    ii. allows positions from attending to subsequent positions
    iii. prevents positions from attending to subsequent positions

14. The following pre-trained languge models consider unidirectional context
    i. GPT and BARD
    ii. GPT
    iii. BERT and T5
15. Large language models are so called because
    i. use of massive datasets in order of petabytes
    ii. presence of billions of parameters
    iii. use of massive datasets in order of petabytes and presence of billions of parameters
16. GPT uses
    i. the pretrained decoder architecture from the standard transformer network
    ii. the pretrained encoder architecture from the standard transformer network
    iii. the pretrained encoder and decoder architectures from the standard transformer network
17. BERT uses the encoder of the transformer model to learn
    i. the context of a word based on both the left and right context of the word
    ii. the context of a word based on only the left context of the word
    iii. the context of a word based on only the right context of the word
18. Masked Language Model
    i. hides a word in a sentence and then predicts the next word in the sentence based on the context of the hidden word
    ii. hides a word in a sentence and then predicts the masked word based on the context of the hidden word
    iii. hides a word in a sentence and then predicts the sentence based on the context of the hidden word
19. Next Sentence Prediction
    i. predicts whether two given sentences have a logical, sequential connection
    ii. predicts the occurrence of a sentence based on the last word of the previous sentence
    iii. predicts the occurrence of a sentence based on the title of the document
20. Embedding from Language Models is a
    i. shallow language model that uses bidirectional LSTM
    ii. shallow language model that uses bidirectional Transformer
    iii. deep language model that uses bidirectional LSTM

Self-Assessment: Match the Columns

No		Match	
1.	RNN language models	A	is another layer in the neural network that dynamically highlights the relevant features of the input data

No		Match	
2.	Attention mechanism	B	is an attention mechanism relating different positions of a single sequence in order to compute a representation of the same sequence
3.	Encoder–decoder architecture	C	first, deeply bidirectional, unsupervised language representation, pre-trained using only a plain text corpus
4.	Issues like long–range dependencies and no parallel computations	D	produces context-specific word representations at each position
5.	Transformers	E	predict whether two given sentences have a logical, sequential connection or whether their relationship is simply random
6.	Position Encoding Layer	F	hide a word in a sentence and then have the program predict what word has been hidden based on the context of the hidden word
7.	Multi-Head Self-Attention Layer in the encoder	G	are learned functions of the internal states of a deep bidirectional LSTM language model, which is pre-trained on a large text corpus
8.	Masked Multi-Head Attention in the decoder	H	are associated with RNNs
9.	Large Language Models	I	fulfills the need for information about the locations and order of tokens in a sentence
10.	GPT	J	typically involves gradient–based optimization techniques to update the model's parameters based on the task–specific data
11.	Fine-tuning	K	enables the target sequence to pay attention to the input sequence
12.	BERT	L	is powerful for sequence-to-sequence-based prediction for neural machine translation, summarization, and image caption generation
13.	Masked Language Model (MLM)	M	learn how to output the target sequence, by using both the input and target sequence

No		Match	
14.	Next Sentence Prediction	N	the use of massive datasets in the order of petabytes and the presence of a large number of parameters (billions)
15.	ELMo word vectors	O	pre-training employs the decoder components of transformer-based architectures

Short Questions

1. What are the issues associated with RNN language models?
2. What is the concept of attention in language model?
3. Describe the simple encoder–decoder model.
4. Discuss how attention can be formulated as a query–key–value triple.
5. How is attention mechanism incorporated into the encoder–decoder model?
6. What are the challenges of RNNs that are tackled by Transformers?
7. Describe the transformer architecture and training and inference is carried out.
8. Discuss in detail the various components of the transformer.
9. What are classes of pre-trained representations? Discuss.
10. Differentiate between pre-trained models and pre-trained language models.
11. Describe the framework of pre-trained language models.
12. Write a brief note on Large Language Models.
13. Describe the GPT decoder architecture.
14. Discuss how GPT models are fine-tuned.
15. Briefly describe the BERT model.
16. Explain how BERT is pre-trained using Masked Language_Modeling (MLM) and Next Sentence Prediction (NSP).
17. Explain the fine-tuning of BERT for NLP tasks.
18. Describe T5 and BARD models.
19. Explain the ELMo pre-training.
20. Describe ELMo architecture in detail.

POS Tagging and Sequence Labelling

10.1 Parts-of-Speech - Introduction

Parts-of-Speech or POS are also known as lexical categories or tags, word classes and morphological classes. POS categories of words are defined distributionally by the morphological and syntactic contexts that they appear in. In other words, each category occurs in the same contexts and has the same syntactic functions. Moreover, they also associated with morphological criteria in that the same category in general allows the same suffixes or prefixes. The reason for having POS tags is that there are too many words in any language and categorization helps to understand and study them by allowing a generalization of models. Though POS categories are commonly used, within the linguistic and cognitive community, the number, nature, and universality of these are still under discussion. This debate about the number of such POS categories exists across languages too. However, in English language the traditional and broad categories are as given in Figure 10.1

Open Classes

Noun: name of a person, place, thing or idea Noun - N – table, girl, frequency, singing
Verb: indicates action or state of being Verb—V- write, play, sleep, be
Adjective: describes, modifies or gives more information about a noun or pronoun Adjective –ADJ- red, big, beautiful, young, two
Adverb: modifies a verb, adjective or another adverb- tells how, where or when Adverb –ADV- gradually, unluckily, very, too

Closed Classes

Pronoun: used in place of noun or noun phrase to avoid repetition Pronoun –Pro- I, me, we, he
Preposition: shows relationship of noun or pronoun to another word Preposition –P – at, on, in, about
Conjunction: joins two words, ideas or phrases together & shows how they are connected Conjunction –C – and, but, or
Determiner: modifies, describes, or introduces a noun Determiner –DET– the, a, this, these, that
Auxiliary Verb: used along with a main verb to express tense, mood, or voice Auxiliary Verb - AUX – can, may, should

Figure 10.1: Traditional Parts-of-Speech of English

POS tags are generally classified as open and closed classes. Open class categories have large number of words and new ones are often created. These include Noun, Verb, Adjective and Adverbs – examples of new words include Noun (Google, microfinance), Verb (delist, googling), Adjective (geeky, client-side) and Adverb (landside). Many new words are often added mainly to the Noun category. Nouns are often further classified as proper nouns (India, TCS, Ram), count nouns (those that can be counted – cat, girl, country) and mass nouns (those that cannot be counted – sand, snow) and common nouns which include all the other nouns. Verbs in English are associated with morphological suffixes to indicate tenses and may have differing patterns of regularity. Adverbs are further classified as directional or locative (here, downward, behind), degree (very, extremely, entirely, slightly) and manner (perfectly, quickly, painfully). There are mainly four types of adjectives namely quality (clever, great, blue, big), quantity (few, whole, numerous, all), number (first, last, ten) and pronominal (this, my, which).

Closed class categories are composed of a small, fixed set of grammatical function words for a given language. These include Pronouns, Prepositions, Conjunctions, Determiners and Auxiliary verbs.

10.2 Parts-of-Speech (POS) Tagging

The process of assigning a POS to each word in a sentence is called as POS tagging. An example of a simple POS tagging is shown in Figure 10.2. It is assumed that an initial tokenization process separates sentences and words Thus the input to the POS tagging task is a sequence of word tokens w and output is a sequence of POS tags t, one per word. The complexity of POS tagging is that a word in isolation can be associated with multiple parts of speech especially if the POS tag set is large. The attributes that can be used for disambiguation include lexical identity of the word, context, morphology (suffixes, prefixes), capitalization (not all languages have this aspect – example most Indian Languages), gazetteers (dictionaries) etc.

Word	The	man	cut	the	mango	with	a	Knife
POS	DET	N	V	DET	N	PREP	DET	N

Figure 10.2: Example of POS Tagging

Need for POS Tagging: POS tagging is one of the first steps in the NLP pipeline, immediately after tokenization and segmentation. It is a foundation step for a variety of practical NLP tasks that is it is viewed as a prerequisite for harder disambiguation tasks such as lemmatization, multi-word extraction, syntactic parsing, semantic analysis, and applications such as speech synthesis, speech recognition, information extraction, sentiment analysis and machine translation (Figure 10.3).

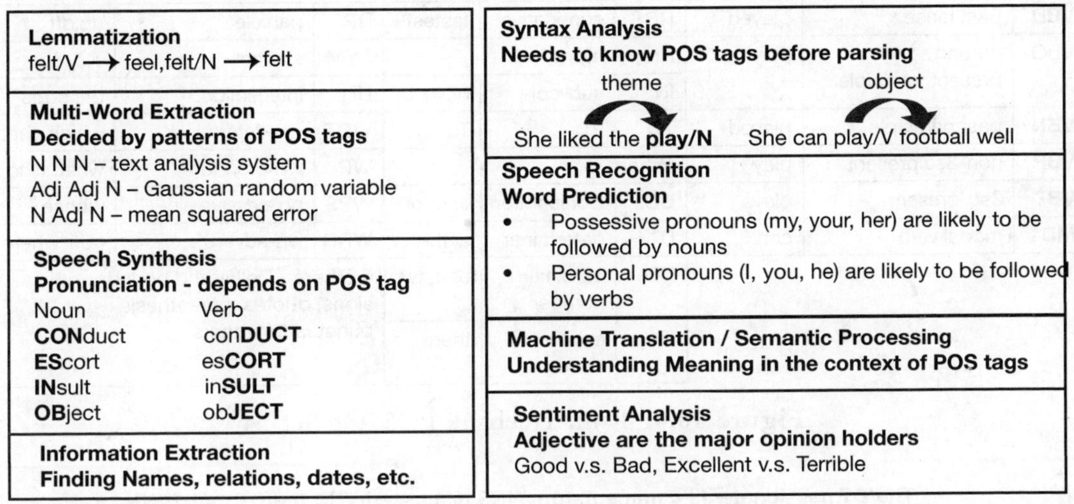

Figure 10.3: Need for POS tagging

POS Tag Sets: Before we discuss the different approaches to automatic POS tagging, we need to work with a standard set of tags that is we need to define an inventory of POS labels for the word classes. A number of probable syntactically and semantically important distinctions can be associated with the basic POS tags leading to very large tag sets. A very coarse tag set consists the POS tags we discussed in the previous section, but this tag set is not sufficient to describe language. Other tag sets include the Brown corpus which uses 87 tags. The Penn Treebank POS tag set consisting of 45 tags is a simplified version of the Brown tag set and is currently the de facto standard used for English. There is also a very large tag set the Prague Dependency Treebank (Czech) with 4452 tags. In this chapter we will discuss in detail the Penn Treebank tag set (Figure 10.4) and its use in POS tagging. The use of this tag set is shown for 2 example sentences (Figure 10.5). Brown Corpus, WSJ, and Switchboard are some corpora tagged with POS.

Noun			Adjective			Others		
NN	singular or mass	boy, snow	**JJ**	base form	big	**FW**	foreign word	
NNS	plural	boys	**JJR**	comparative	bigger	**LS**	list item marker	1, 2, One
NNP	singular proper noun	TCS	**JJS**	superlative	biggest	**PDT**	pre-determiner	all
NNPS	plural proper noun	Indians	**Adverb**			**POS**	possessive ending	's
Verb			**RB**	base form	fast	**PRP**	personal pronoun	1, you, she
VB	base form	play	**RBR**	comparative	faster	**PRPS**	possessive pronoun	your, one's
VBD	past tense	played	**RBS**	superlative	fastest	**RP**	particle	up,off
VBG	gerund / present participle	playing	**Prepositions**			**SYM**	symbol	+, *, &
			IN	sub-conj	of, in, by	**UH**	interjection	oh, oops
VBN	past participle	played	**TO**	to	To	**WDT**	wh-determiner	which, that
VBP	non-3sg present	play	**Others**			**WP**	wh-pronoun	what, who
VBZ	3sg-present	plays	**CC**	Conjunction	and, or	**WPS**	possessive wh-	whose
MD	modal verb	can	**DT**	determiner	a, the	**WRB**	wh-adverb	how where
			CD	cardinal number	one, two	9 others - Dollar and pound signs, quotes, parenthesis, punctuation marks		
			EX	existential there	there			

Figure 10.4: Penn Treebank POS Tag Set

The/DT passionate/JJ commentators/NNS discussed/VBD the/DT match/NN

There/EX are/VBP girls/NNS dancing/VBG there/RB

Figure 10.5: Use of Penn Treebank POS Tag Set

Ambiguity in POS Tagging: A word is considered ambiguous if it can be associated with more than one POS. Common POS ambiguities in English include Noun-Verb – play, Adjective-Verb- singing, Noun-Adjective – normal. Most word types occur with only one tag, but however a large fraction of word tokens in a corpus are ambiguous. One of the simplest ways to tag a word is to pick the most frequent tag which surprisingly gives an accuracy of 90%. Another method is to examine the local context namely the preceding and succeeding words and/or tags. Some sentences where the same word needs to be tagged differently.

Example 10.1: "play" can be a noun or a verb
We watched the **play/NN** in the theatre.
We **play/VBP** football every Saturday.

Example 10.2 – "around" can be a preposition, particle, or adverb

I went to the theatre **around/IN** the corner.

I never got **around/RP** to calling you.

The new car I told you about costs **around/RB** Rs.30 Lakhs.

A very common example that showcases ambiguity is shown in Figure 10.6. Here many words have multiple lexical tags and depending on context the correct POS tag needs to be chosen. Here for the word "like" two different tags are chosen based on context.

Time	moves	like	a	river
NN	NN	VBP	**DT**	**NN**
	VBZ	VB	**LS**	
		JJ	SYS	
		IN	FW	
			NNP	

Life	flows	like	a	stream
NN	NN	VBP	**DT**	**NN**
	VBZ	VB	**LS**	
		JJ	SYS	
		IN	FW	
			NNP	

Figure 10.6: Ambiguity in POS Tagging

Creating a POS Tagger: One of the best rule-based tagger is the inductive method based Brill's POS tagger for English language that learns a set of rules automatically based on a given corpus and then tags words following these rules. Here we will be discussing machine learning based POS taggers. Generally, to handle disambiguation POS taggers rely on learned models. In case of a language which has a tagged corpus that corpus is used for tagging a new corpus. In case of new languages, a defined tag set is needed and then a corpus is annotated with this tag set. In either case, for POS tagging, a learning method (for example HMM) is chosen, then the model is trained with the training corpus and then the model is evaluated with a disjoint test corpus (Figure10.7). The two types of information are useful for POS tagging are relations between words and tags and relations between tags and tags. Evaluation is carried out by measuring tagging accuracy that is percentage of tokens tagged correctly. Accuracy of most current English POS taggers (with Penn Treebank tag set) using HMM is 96-97% while that of the baseline that is using the most frequent tags is about 92%. However, accuracy of POS tagging for English in other domains as well for other languages may be significantly lower.

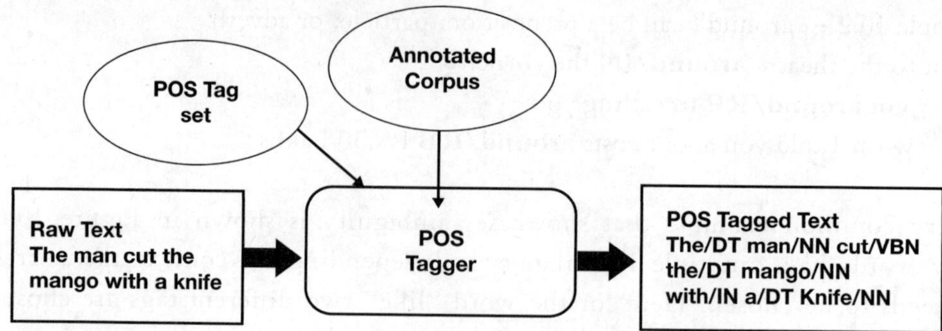

Figure 10.7: POS Tagger

10.3 Sequence Labelling and POS Tagging

As you may recall, POS tagging is essentially a sequence labelling problem where for a given input sequence of word tokens $w_1, w_2 \ldots w_n$, we need the output sequence of POS tags $t_1, t_2 \ldots t_n$ one per word (Figure 10.8). This concept of mapping of a sequence of words to sequence of labels is also applicable to other NLP tasks such as Named Entity recognition, text chunking and shallow parsing, word alignment of parallel, text etc. Viewing sequence labeling from the classification perspective, each word needs to be classified in a class space C (of tags). This classification approach can be independent (each word is treated independently) or dependent (each word is dependent on other words). Integration of contextual information about tags of words and joint assignment of tags in the word sequence is not considered in the classification approach.

Word	w_1	w_2	w_3	w_4	w_5	w_6	w_7	w_8
	The	man	cut	the	mango	with	a	knife
POS Tags	t_1	t_2	t_3	t_4	t_5	t_6	t_7	t_8
	DET	N	V	DET	N	PREP	DET	N

Figure 10.8: POS Tagging as Sequence Labelling

Statistical POS Tagging: The task of predicting the sequence of labels given the sequence of word (Figure 10.8) can be statistically stated as finding the most likely sequence of tags $t = (t_1, t_2 \ldots t_n)$ for the given sequence of words $w = w_1, w_2 \ldots w_n$ as given by Equation 10.1

$$t^* = argmax_t \, P(t|w)$$

(10.1)

Let us now discuss the difference between probabilistic classification and probabilistic sequence labelling.

- **Traditional Classification:** The probabilistic approach to classification can be defined by the equation (Equation 10.2)

$$y = argmax_y \, P(y|x) \tag{10.2}$$

where x is the input data and y is a single label and is an independent output and the dependency is only within y and x (Figure 10.9 (a)). This classification can be used to classification the sequence as a whole.

- **Sequence Labelling:** The probabilistic approach to sequence labelling is defined as discussed before by the equation (Equation 10.1)

$t^* = argmax_t \, P(t|w)$ where w is the input word sequence vector and t is vector or matrix of tags and is a structured output. Moreover, there is dependency between both the tag and word (t,w) and between tags (t_i, t_j) (Figure 10.9 (b)). Sequence labelling can be applied to any problem that requires tagging of components in a sequence but here we are discussing the case of POS tagging.

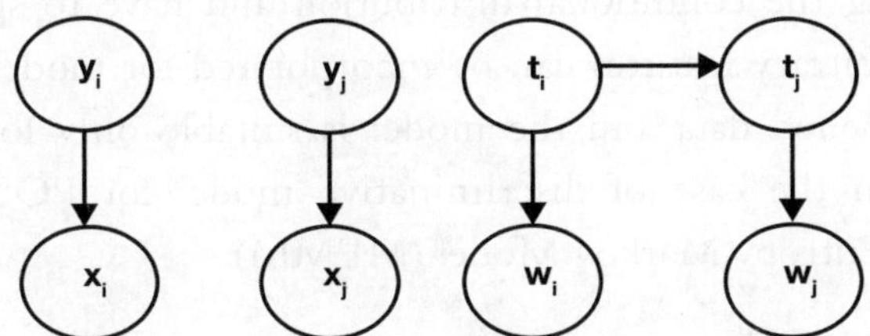

Figure 10.9: Classification and Sequence Labelling

10.4 Modelling Approaches to Sequence Labelling

There are basically two modelling perspectives when we discuss probabilistic sequence labelling approaches namely generative models and discriminative models.

Generative Models: When we apply Bayes rule to the POS sequence labelling problem (Equation 10.1), $t^* = argmax_t \, P(t|w)$, we get (Equation 10.3) which gives rise to the generative model.

$$argmax_t \, P(t|w) = argmax_t \, \frac{P(t|w)}{P(w)}$$

$$= argmax_t \, P(t,w)$$

$$= argmax_t \, P(t)P(w|t) \tag{10.3}$$

Finding the sequence of tags t that gives maximum probability for the given the sequence of words is the task to be carried out. Using Bayes theorem, we essentially model the joint probability of tags and words p(t,w), which we decompose as the prior probability of the tag p(t) and the likelihood probability of the word given the tag p(w|t). We essentially model the joint probability of tags and words. Models based on joint distributions of labels and observed data are called generative models. Here a stochastic process first generates the POS tags and then generates the words in the sequence based on these POS tags. Generative models provide a full probabilistic specification for all the random variables; however the dependence assumption has to be specified for prior probability p(t) and the likelihood probability tag p(w|t). These models are flexible and can even be used for unsupervised learning. In the case of generative model for POS tagging we will be discussing Hidden Markov Model (HMM).

Discriminative Models: These models directly model the conditional probability of labels given the words that we model what we are actually interested in (Equation 10.3).

$$t^* = argmax_t\, P\left(t|w\right) = argmax_t\, f\left(t|w\right) \tag{10.3}$$

Here we are specifying the conditional distribution and have to specify only the target variable. Moreover, arbitrary features can be incorporated for modelling $p(t|w)$. However, there is a need for labelled data and the model is suitable only for supervised or semi-supervised learning. In the case of discriminative model for POS tagging we will be discussing Maximum Entropy Markov Model (MEMM).

10.5 Hidden Markov Model (HMM) for POS Tagging

Before we discuss Hidden Markov Model (HMM) for POS tagging let us first discuss the concept of Markov random processes and simple Markov models.

10.5.1 Markov Models

Markov process (named after Andrei Andreyevich Markov (1856 –1922)) is a simple stochastic process in which the distribution of an immediate future state depends only on the current state and not on how it arrived in the present state. A Markov random process is a random sequence having the Markov property. For observable state sequences (state is known from data), this leads to a Markov chain model. A finite Markov model is called discrete if it has:

- N distinct states, which begins at some initial state(s) ($t = 1$). Then at each step ($t = 1, 2,…$), according to transition probabilities associated with current state, the system moves from current to next state which can also be in some cases same state according to transition probabilities associated with current state.

The Markov model is thus associated with two properties:

- **Markov Property:** Only state of the system at time t determines the state of the system at time $t+1$ (Figure 10.10 (a)).
- **Stationary Assumption:** In general, a process is called stationary if transition probabilities are independent of t (Figure 10.10 (b))

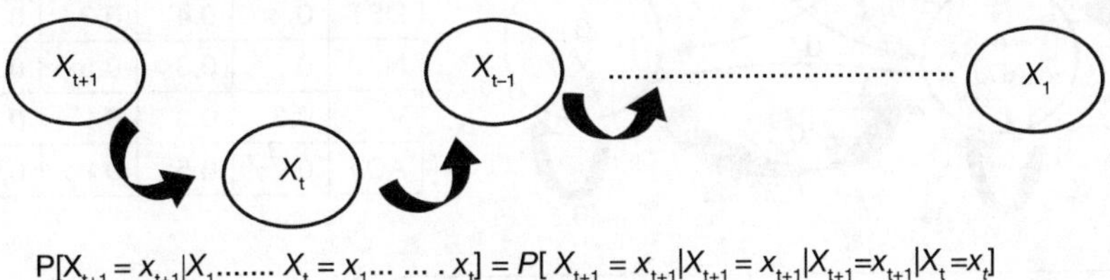

Figure 10.10 (a)

Stationary Assumption
for all t, $P[X_{t+1} = x_j|X_t = x_i] = p_{ij}$
The above equation indicates that the system is in **state i**, the probability of the next move to **state j** in the system is p_{ij}, it docs not depend on the value of **t**

Figure 10.10 (b)

Figure 10.10: Property and Assumption of Markov Models

Formally the Markov model can be specified as given in Table 10.1

Table 10.1: Components of Markov Model

$Q = q_1, q_2, \ldots\ldots q_N$	A set of states
$A = a_{11}, a_{12}, \ldots\ldots a_{nn}$	A transition probability matrix A, each a_{ij} representing the probability of moving from state i to state j $\sum_{j=1}^{n} a_{ij} = 1 \forall i$
$\pi = \pi_1, \pi_2, \ldots\ldots \pi_N$	An initial probability distribution over states π_i is the probability that the Markov chain will start in state i. Some states j may have $\pi_j = 0$ indicating that they cannot be initial states. $\sum_{j=1}^{n} \pi_i = 1$

The example shown in Figure 10.11 shows the use Markov chain in POS tagging where the path with the highest probability is considered the probable tagging. Here we assume that initial state probabilities (π) and the state probabilities (A) are assumed to be available.

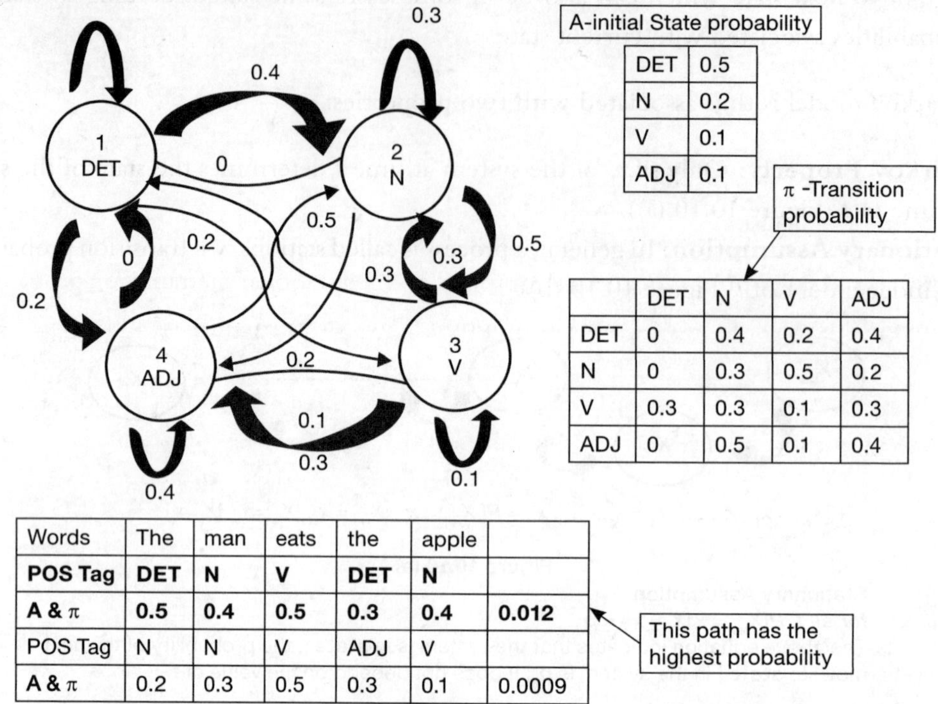

A-initial State probability	
DET	0.5
N	0.2
V	0.1
ADJ	0.1

	DET	N	V	ADJ
DET	0	0.4	0.2	0.4
N	0	0.3	0.5	0.2
V	0.3	0.3	0.1	0.3
ADJ	0	0.5	0.1	0.4

Words	The	man	eats	the	apple	
POS Tag	**DET**	**N**	**V**	**DET**	**N**	
A & π	**0.5**	**0.4**	**0.5**	**0.3**	**0.4**	**0.012**
POS Tag	N	N	V	ADJ	V	
A & π	0.2	0.3	0.5	0.3	0.1	0.0009

Figure 10.11: Example of POS Tagging using Markov Model

10.5.2 Hidden Markov Models – The Basics

A Hidden Markov Model (HMM) is an extension of a Markov model where the input symbols and the states are different. In essence the current state is not known. The probability for a sequence of observable events can be computed by the Markov model. However, the hidden states or the states that are not directly observable are the states of interest in many contexts. In the case of POS tagging, we do not observe the POS tags in a text, what we observe are the words and from this word sequence we must infer the tag sequence.

As discussed before the generative model can be described using the following equation (Equation 10.4)

$$argmax_t \, P(t|w) = argmax_t \, P(t)P(w|t) \text{ (this is a joint probability distribution)} \quad (10.4)$$

Two assumptions are associated with the two components of the joint probability. The assumptions are:

- **Markov Assumption:** The first components of the joint probability can be defined by the equation (Equation 10.5)

$$P(t) = P(t_1, t_2, t_3, \ldots, t_n) = P(t_1)P(t_2|t_1)P(t_3|t_2, t_1)\ldots P(t_n|t_1, \ldots, t_{n-1}) \quad (10.5)$$

Here the e state transition is defined based only on the previous and current state. The state of the system at time $t+1$ depends only on the state of the system at time t (Figure 10.10 (a)). This is as shown in Equation 10.6

$$P(t) = P(t_1, t_2, t_3, .., t_n) = P(t_1) P(t_2|t_1) P(t_3|t_2)..P(t_n|t_{n-1}) = \prod_{i=1}^{n} P(t_i|t_i - 1) \quad (10.6)$$

We can also define n-gram model over POS tags in which case it is called higher order HMM.

- **Stationary Assumption:** In general, a process is called stationary if transition probabilities are independent of the state t. This assumption is similar to Markov models.

  A new assumption associated with output is given below:

- **Output–independent Assumption:** This assumption states that all observation frames are dependent on the state that emitted them, and not on any other observations. This assumption is to do with the second term of the joint probability of Equation 10.3. In the case of POS tagging, we assume that the words emitted depends only on their tag (Equation 10.7).

$$P(w|t) = P(w_1|t_1) P(w_2|t_2)..P(w_n|t_n) = \prod_{i=1}^{n} P(w_i|t_i) \quad (10.7)$$

The Hidden Markov Model is formally specified as given in Table 10.2. Now, we have two model parameters n and m, and there are three probability measures A, B, π. Figure 10.12 shows the HMM formalism.

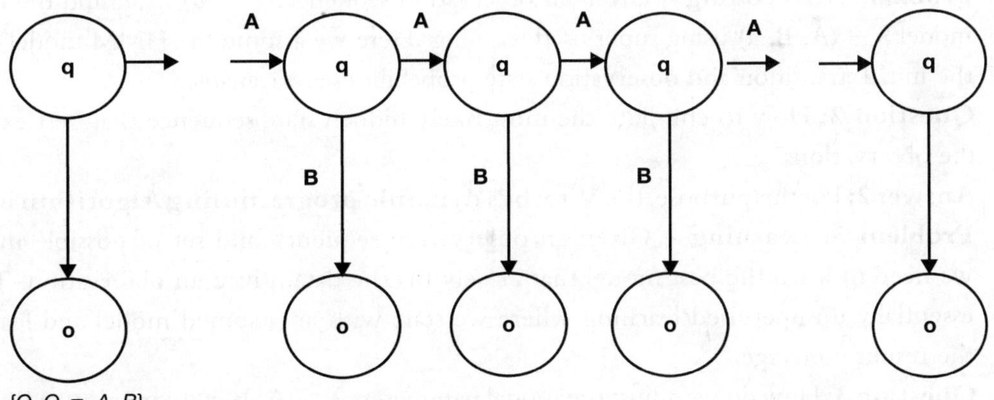

Figure 10.12: HMM Formalism

Building the Observation Sequence: Given this formalism, the observation sequence can be built as follows, assuming T is the number of observations.

- Set t = 1.
- Choose an initial state q_t according to the initial distribution.
- Choose o_t according to the symbol probability distribution.
- Transit to a new state q_{t+1} according to the state transition probability distribution.
- Set t = t + 1, return to step 3 while t< = T.

10.5.3 The Three Problems associated with HMM

There are three problems associated with HMM namely:

- **Problem 1: Evaluation** – Compute the probability of a given observation sequence. $O = o_1, ..., o_T$ given the HMM model $\lambda = (A, B, \pi)$ using supervised learning. Here we assume the HMM model that is the initial, transition and observation state probabilities are available.

  Question 1: How do we compute the probability of this observation word sequence O given the model?

  Answer 1: For this purpose, the Forward – Backward dynamic programming algorithm – the **Baum Welch algorithm** is used.

- **Problem 2: Decoding** – Given an observation sequence, $O = o_1, ..., o_T$ and the HMM model $\lambda = (A, B, \pi)$ using supervised learning. Here we assume the HMM model that is the initial, transition and observation state probabilities are available.

  Question 2: How to compute the most likely hidden state sequence that best explains the observations?

  Answer 2: For this purpose, the **Viterbi's dynamic programming Algorithm** is used.

- **Problem 3: Learning** – Given an observation sequence and set of possible models, we need to learn the best model that closely fits the data, given an observation. This is essentially unsupervised learning where we start with an assumed model and learn till the results converge.

  Question 3: How do we adjust the model parameters $\lambda = (A, B, \pi)$ to maximize $P(O | \lambda)$?

  Answer 3: For this purpose, the **Expectation Maximization (EM) heuristic** is used.

10.5.3.1 Problem 1: Evaluation - Baum Welch Algorithm

Let us discuss the Markov assumptions which states that probability of the occurrence of word w_i at time t depends only on occurrence of word w_{i-1} at time t-1. This assumption approximates the probability of the sequence of words as (Equation 10.8):

$$P\left(w_1, w_2, w_3, .., w_n\right) \approx \prod_{i=2}^{n} P\left(w_i \mid w_{i-1}\right) \tag{10.8}$$

A common way of representing the Hidden Markov Model is the Trellis Diagram shown in Figure 10.13. In this diagram we have the starting state s_0 which influences the states s_{11}, s_{12}, $s_{1,3}$, $s_{1,4}$ with observation at time t_1 being o_1 and so on until finally we end up with the states $s_{T,1}$, $s_{T,2}$, $s_{T,3}$, $s_{T,4}$ at time t_T with observation O_T.

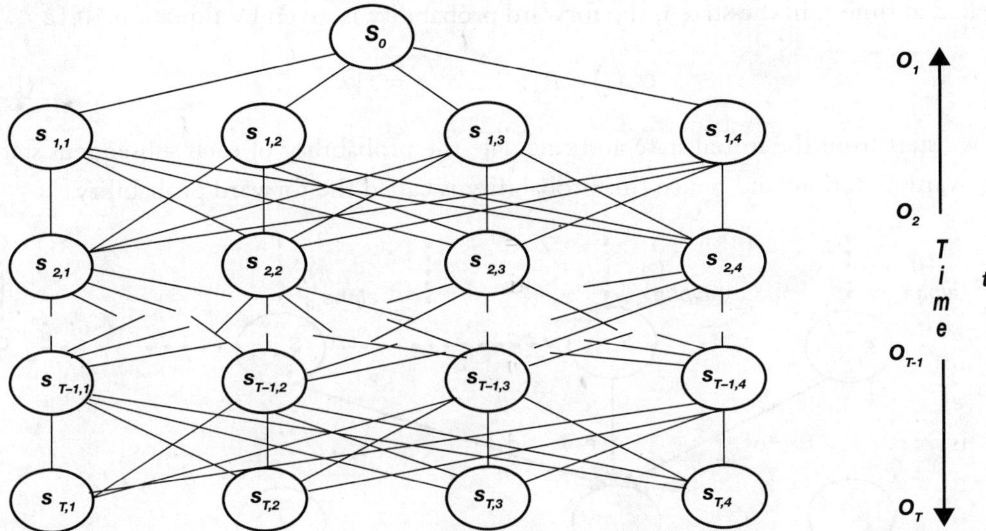

Figure 10.13: Trellis Diagram

During evaluation, given the observation sequence $O = o_1, \ldots, o_T$ and an HMM model, the probability of the observation O given the model needs to be computed. In other words, the probability of a given sequence of observations has to be computed. This likelihood of a sequence can be determined by either the forward procedure or the backward procedure. We will discuss the Forward algorithm which is essentially a dynamic programming algorithm. The backward algorithm can be similarly explained. The Forward algorithm can be used with two options, one the "Any Path" method where the likelihood is measured using any sequence of states of length T, and the second option the "Best Path" method where we choose an HMM by the probability generated using the best possible sequence of states. Finding the probability that a given HMM model was used to generate a specific sequence of symbols O is termed as the Evaluation problem.

Here, the model starts at state q1 with initial probability π_{q1}, followed by the transition probabilities $a_{q1,q2}$, $\ldots\ldots\ldots\ldots a_{qT-1,qT}$.

$$P(Q|\lambda) = \pi_{q_1} \cdot \prod_{t=1}^{T-1} a_{q_t,q_{t+1}} = \pi_{q_1} \cdot a_{q_t,q_2} \cdot a_{q_t,q_2} \cdots a_{q_{T-1},q_T} \qquad (10.9)$$

$$P(O|Q,\lambda) = \prod_{t=1}^{T} P(o_t|q_t,\lambda) = b_{q_t,o_1} \cdot b_{q_2,o_2} \cdots b_{q_T,o_T} \qquad (10.10)$$

$$P(O|\lambda) = \sum_{all\ Q} P(O|Q,\lambda) \cdot P(Q|\lambda) \qquad (10.11)$$

Forward Probabilities: Given a HMM λ, the partial observation $o_1 \ldots o_t$ has been generated at time t, in the state i, the forward probability is given by Equation 10.12.

$$\alpha_t(i) = P(o_1 \ldots .o_t, q_t = s_i|\lambda) \qquad (10.12)$$

Here we start from the initial state and calculate the probability of each subsequent state in the forward direction, and hence this probability is called the forward probability.

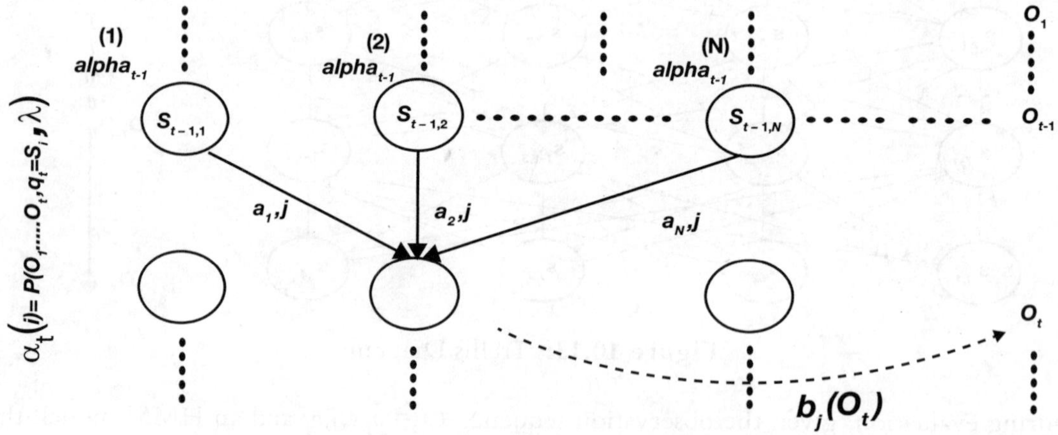

Figure 10.14: Forward Probability

The forward probability at a time slice t of a state j is the sum of each the N forward probabilities i at time slice $t-1$ multiplied by the transition probability of each state i at time slice $t-1$ to the state j under consideration slice t at t time (Figure 10.14). This sum is then multiplied by the emission probability of observing o_t at state j (Equation 10.13).

$$\alpha_t(j) = \sum_{i=1}^{N} \alpha_{t-1}(i)\, a_{ij}\, b_j(o_t) \qquad (10.13)$$

Forward Recursion: As we have already discussed, forward probability (Equation 10.14)

$$\alpha_t(i) = P(o_1 \ldots .o_t, q_t = s_i|\lambda) \qquad (10.14)$$

is calculated using forward recursion. The initialization is as follows (Equation 10.15):

$$\alpha_1(i) = \pi_i b_i(o_1) \tag{10.15}$$

Here, the initial forward probability of state i at time slice 1 is the product of the initial probability of state i and the probability of emitting the observation o_1 at state i at time slice 1. The forward recursion is determined as follows (Equation 10.16):

$$\alpha_{t+1}(j) = \left[\sum_{i=1}^{N} \alpha_t(i) a_{ij}\right] b_j(o_{t+1}) \tag{10.16}$$

Here, the forward probability at time slice $t+1$ is determined by taking into account the forward probabilities of all states at time slot t, the transition probabilities from state i to state j (the state whose forward probability is to be determined) and the emission probability of the observation at time slice $t+1$ at state j, the forward probability at time slice $t+1$ is determined.

Finally, we have the termination as follows (Equation 10.17):

$$P(Q|\lambda) = \sum_{i=1}^{N} P(o_1\ldots.o_t, q_t = s_i|\lambda) = \sum_{i=1}^{N} \alpha_T(i) \tag{10.17}$$

For the brute force approach of solving problem 1, the time taken is of the order of $2T*N^T$ computations where T is the number of time slices in the sequence and N is the number of states in the HMM. However, the time complexity of the forward algorithm described here is of the order of N^2T computations.

Backward Probabilities: Considering the backward direction starting from the last state and traveling to the initial state, similar to the forward probability the backward probability given an HMM can be determined. Given the state at time t is i, and the HMM model λ the generation of the partial observation $o_{t+1} \ldots o_T$ is given by the equation (Equation 10.18).

$$\beta_t(i) = P(o_{t+1}\ldots.o_T|q_t = s_i, \lambda) \tag{10.18}$$

Here since we start from the final state and calculate the probability of each previous state in the backward direction, the probability is called the backward probability. The backward probability at a time slice t of a state j is the sum of each the N forward probabilities i at time slice t+1 multiplied by the transition probability of each state j at time slice t+1 to the state i under consideration at t time that is slice t.

10.5.3.2 Problem 2: Decoding – Viterbi Algorithm

Given the observation sequence $O = o_1, \ldots, o_T$ and a HMM model, the state sequence that explains the observations in the best manner has to be determined. In other words, the most probable sequence of states, given a sequence of observations are required to be calculated. For this decoding we describe Viterbi's dynamic programming algorithm. As we discussed, for the solving the Evaluation problem was the efficient determination of the sum of all paths through an HMM. For solving the decoding problem, the best path that is the path with the highest probability needs to be determined. Given a set of symbols O, the HMM model λ, the most likely sequence of hidden states $Q=q_1...q_T$, (the state sequence with maximum probability) that led to the given sequence of observations $o_1,o_2,...,o_T$) needs to be determined (Equation 10.19):

$$Q = \arg\max_{Q'} P(Q'|O,\lambda) \tag{10.19}$$

When we want to find the most probable state sequence we use the assumption that if we know the identity of Q_i, then the most probable sequence on $i+1,...,n$ does not depend on observations before time i. For this purpose, we use the Viterbi algorithm.

Viterbi Algorithm: Similar to computing the forward probabilities, when instead of summing probabilities over transitions from previous states, the maximum probability at each and every time slice is considered then this is called the Viterbi algorithm. In the case of Viterbi algorithm, we have Equation 10.20) as follows:

$$\delta_t(j) = \left[\max_{1 \leq i \leq N} \delta_{t-1}(i) a_{ij}\right] b_j(o_t) \tag{10.20}$$

As we can see, instead of considering the summation of forward probabilities of all the preceding states, in the case of Viterbi recursion, we consider only the transition from the state where the product of the state probability and the transition is the maximum. Here, the forward probability and backward probability can be combined (Equation 10.21).

$$P(O|\mu) = \sum_{i=1}^{N} \alpha_i(t)\beta_i(t) \tag{10.21}$$

The initialization of the Viterbi algorithm at time slice 1 and state I is as given blow (Equation 10.22).

$$\delta_1(i) = \pi_i b_j(o_1), \; 1 \leq i \leq N \tag{10.22}$$

Then at each recursive step, we find the maximum probability from one of the N states as shown by the induction (Equation 10.23 and Equation 10.24).

$$\delta_t(j) = \left[\max_{1 \leq i \leq N} \delta_{t-1}(i) a_{ij}\right] b_j(o_t) \tag{10.23}$$

$$\delta_j(t) = \max_{x_1 \ldots x_{t-1}} P\left(x_1 \ldots x_{t-1}, o_1 \ldots o_{t-1}, x_t = j, o_t \right) \tag{10.24}$$

The state sequence which maximizes the probability of seeing the observations to time t–1, landing in state j, and seeing the observation at time t. Then, we find the argument maximum to find the termination condition (Equation 10.25, Equation10.26 and Equation 10.27).

$$\psi_t(j) = \left[\arg\max_{1 \leq i \leq N} \delta_{t-1}(i) a_{ij} \right], 2 \leq t \leq T, 1 \leq j \leq N \tag{10.25}$$

$$\delta_j(t+1) = \max_i \delta_i(t) a_{ij} b_{jo_{t+1}} \tag{10.26}$$

$$\psi_j(t+1) = \arg\max_i \delta_i(t) a_{ij} b_{jo_{t+1}} \tag{10.27}$$

In this way, the best sequence of hidden states that gave rise to the given set of observations is as given below (Equation 10.28 and Equation 10.29):

$$p^* = \max_{1 \leq i \leq N} \delta_T(i) \tag{10.28}$$

$$q_T^{\,*} = \arg\max_{1 \leq i \leq N} \delta_T(i) \tag{10.29}$$

The final sequence of states is computed by working backwards as given as below (Equation 10.30):

$$q_t^{\,*} = \psi_{t+1}\left(q_{t+1}^{\,*} \right), \quad t = T-1, \ldots, 1 \tag{10.30}$$

10.5.3.3 Problem 3: Learning – Expectation Maximization Algorithm

In this section, we will discuss the hardest problem associated with HMM– the learning problem. Given an observation sequence O = (O$_1$ O$_2$ ... O$_L$), and a class of models, we want to determine the specific model that "best" explains the observations. We want to use the sequence of observations in order to "train" an HMM and learn the optimal underlying model parameters that is essentially we are learning the transition and observation probabilities, assuming that hidden states are observable during the learning process. Up to now, we have assumed that we know the underlying model. Using annotated training data to train these model parameters is difficult and/or expensive and moreover often the training data is unlike the current data. In this scenario, the parameters need to be maximized with respect to the current data, i.e., a HMM model λ', has to be determined (Equation 10.31):

$$\lambda' = \arg\max_{\lambda} P\left(O \mid \lambda \right) \tag{10.31}$$

Parameter Estimation: We first make an initial guess for the transition probabilities $\{a_{ij}\}$ and observation or emission probabilities $\{b_{km}\}$. We need to then compute the probability that one hidden state follows another given the guessed values of $\{a_{ij}\}$ and $\{b_{km}\}$ and sequence of observations which are computed using forward-backward algorithm. This is the E step of the Expectation Maximization algorithm. Now using these computed probabilities, we make an improved guess for the transition and observation probabilities $\{a_{ij}\}$ and $\{b_{km}\}$. This is the M step of the Expectation Maximization algorithm. We then repeat this process until convergence. This algorithm converges to correct values for $\{a_{ij}\}$ and $\{b_{km}\}$ assuming that the initial guess was close enough. We just assume a model and given the model and observation sequence; we update the model parameters to better fit the observations.

Disadvantages of HMM: HMM models do not use rich feature information which is required to discriminate the tags especially when the tagging is complex or tagging data is sparse. Another issue is the inability to tag unknown words although some word-based features such as suffixes can be useful for such tagging.

10.6 Feature Functions and Sequence Labelling

Before we discuss MEMM and CRF for POS tagging, let us discuss feature functions used for sequence labelling in general.

Feature Functions for Sequence labelling: Standard features include:

- **Unary Features:** These features capture relationship between input x and a single label or tag in the output sequence y that is between x_i and y_i.

  POS Tagging

  The man ate the apple

  DET N V DET N

  Here the relationship is between word and POS tag —example "the" and "DET"

  Named Entity Recognition (NER)

  Ram went to Delhi

  NAME PLACE

  Here the relationship is between word and NER tag —example "Ram" and "NAME"

- **Markov Features:** These features capture relationships between adjacent labels or tags in the output sequence y that is between y_{i+1} or y_{i-1}.

  POS Tagging

  The man ate the apple

  DET N V DET N

The above two features could also be defined based on a corpus as the number of times word w has been tagged as t, number of times tag t_i is followed by tag t_{i+1}, etc. When using both the above feature types, the size of the feature vector is constant with respect to the input length. However, there is a need for richer features which are discriminative. These features include:

- **Word-based Features:** These features include word capitalization and prefixes (un-,dis, im-) and suffixes (-ly, -ed, -ness) of words.
- **Linear Context Features:** These features indicate specific direction of the context as well as longer linear contexts such as the words to the right of the current tag.

While Unary and Markov features have been handled by HMM models, linear context features need discriminative sequence models such as MEMM and CRF that can incorporate such sentence level features.

Now the question arises as to how these features can be used to tag the input x. These features can be binary such as $f_{\text{first-letter-in-capitals}}(\text{Chennai}) = 1$, $f_{\text{first-letter-in-capitals}}(\text{water}) = 0$ or integer (or real valued) such as $f_{\text{no-of-vowels}}(\text{Chennai}) = 3$. The feature functions used depends on the specific task and the training data used.

We need to understand how to express these functions as probabilities. First a real–valued weight w is associated with each feature function that explains class or tag type c. Using this concept, we can define a real–valued score for predicting class or tag for the input c (Equation 10.32), which is exponentiated to avoid negative values (Equation 10.33).

$$score(x,c) = \sum_i w_{ic} f_i(x) \tag{10.32}$$

$$score(x,c) = \exp\left(\sum_i w_{ic} f_i(x)\right) \tag{10.33}$$

Then in order to get a probability distribution over all classes or tag types c, the scores are renormalized (Equation 10.34)

$$P(c|x) = score(x,c) / \sum_j score(x,c_j)$$

$$= \exp\left(\sum_i w_{ic} f_i(x)\right) / \sum_j \exp\left(\sum_i w_{ij} f_i(x)\right) \tag{10.34}$$

Models of the form given in Equation 3.33 are called log linear models. Examples of such log linear models include Maximum Entropy Markov Model (MEMM) and Conditional Random Fields (CRF).

10.7 Maximum Entropy Markov Model (MEMM) for POS Tagging

MEMMS are discriminative models of the tags **t** given the observed input sequence **w** (Equation 10.35) as shown in Figure 10.15.

$$P(T\mid W) = \prod_i P(t_i\mid w_i, t_{i-1})$$

(10.35)

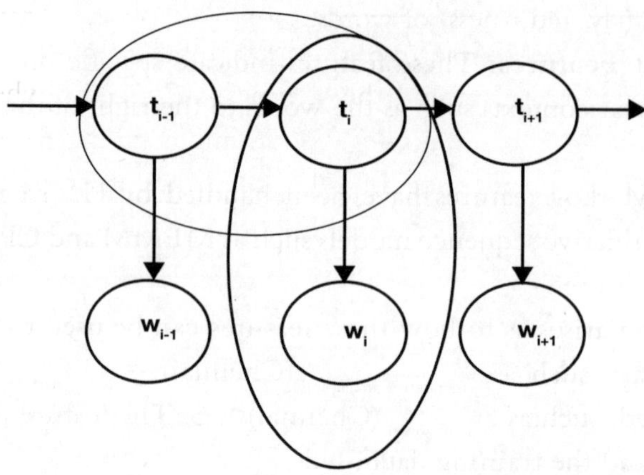

Figure 10.15: MEMM for POS Tagging

In MEMMS, the Model distribution $P(T\mid W)$ with a set of features $\{f_1, f_2, \cdots, f_j\}$ is defined on T and W. The features are collected from the training data but nothing about distribution $P(T\mid W)$ is assumed other than the collected information. Now the entropy is maximized as a criterion. Assuming bigram MEMM, we need to find the posterior probability of the tag sequence T given the word sequence O. We get Equation 10.36 as follows:

$$P(T\mid O) = \arg\max_t \prod_i P(t_i\mid o_i, t_{i-1})$$

(10.36)

Using the Unary and Markov features and weights we get Equation 10.37 as follows:

$$P(t_i = t\mid o_i, t_{i-1}) = \frac{exp\left(w \cdot f\left(t_i = t, o_i, t_{i-1}\right)\right)}{\sum_{t'\eth T} exp\left(w \cdot f\left(t_i = t', o_i, t_{i-1}\right)\right)}$$

(10.37)

In MEMM decoding, given the observation sequence $O = o_1,\ldots,o_T$ and the MEMM model we want to find the tag sequence that best explains the observations. In other words, we need to compute the most probable sequence of tags, given a sequence of words. For this decoding we use Viterbi's dynamic programming algorithm that was used in HMM Model. Equation 10.38 gives the associated equation to find the best sequence of tags ending in s_j using the backward algorithm.

$$M[i,j] = \max_k M[i-1,k]P\left(s_j\mid o_i, s_k\right), 1 \le k \le K \ 1 \le i \le n \qquad (10.38)$$

Here M represents the trellis, k the number of states and n the number of time steps. For learning the weights of the features of the model, the Gradient Descend algorithm is used.

Disadvantages of MEMM: The main disadvantage of MEMM is the complexity of the maximum entropy algorithm and the slowness of training when the dataset is large. Moreover, the maximum entropy model is a sub model and the entropy is optimized on these sub models and not on the global model. MEMMs are also associated with the label bias problem as the conditional models are based on per state normalization.

10.8 Condition Random Field Model (CRF) for POS Tagging

One of the solutions to the sub model optimization problem associated with MEMMs is to optimize the parameters in a global model simultaneously as it is carried out. Here CRF models can be specified as follows (Equation 10.39):

$$P\left(t_1 \ldots . t_n \mid w_1 \ldots . w_n\right) \qquad (10.39)$$

The important aspect of CRF is that there is no Markov assumption. The entire sequence of states or Tags T and observations or words W are mapped to a global feature vector by normalizing over entire sequences (Figure 10.16).

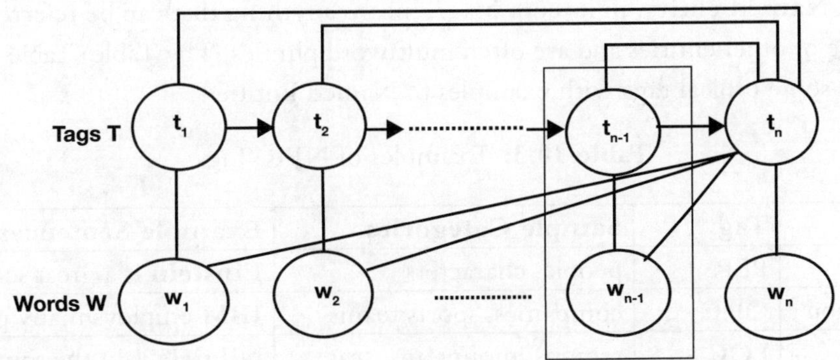

Figure 10.16: CRF Model for Sequence Tagging

P(T|W) can be specified in a similar manner to MEMM but with global features (Equation 10.40).

$$P(T|W) = \frac{exp(\lambda \cdot f(T,W))}{\sum_{S'} exp(\lambda \cdot f(T',W))} = \frac{exp(\lambda \cdot f(T,W))}{Z(W)} \tag{10.40}$$

Here each F_k in f is a global feature function. F_k can be computed as a combination of features using a linear chain CRF (Equation 10.41) and each local feature depends on previous and current tags.

$$F_k = \sum_{i=1}^{n} f_k(s_{i-1}, s_i, O, i) \tag{10.41}$$

Differences between MEMM and CRF: Both the models are based on maximum entropy principle and incorporate rich feature information where feature design is flexible. CRF models are computationally more complex. While MEMM models predict P(T|W) using the Markov assumption while CRF does not. MEMM uses local features while CRF uses global features resulting in a global optimized model.

10.9 Deep Learning for Sequence Labelling – Named Entity Recognition (NER)

Most of the sequence labelling techniques discussed in this chapter considered POS tagging as the example. Let us now discuss another NLP task Named Entity Recognition (NER) formulated as a sequence labelling problem and discuss the use of deep learning techniques for the task. **Named entity**, in its core usage, means anything that can be referred to with a proper name or other entities and are often multiword phrases. The Table (Table 10.3) given below gives some typical tags with examples of Named Entities.

Table 10.3: Examples of NER Tags

Type	Tag	Sample Categories	Example Sentences
People	PER	people, characters	**Einstein** is a great scientist
Organization	ORG	companies, sports teams	**IBM** employs many people
Location	LOC	regions, mountains, seas	**Nilgiris** is in the south
Geo–political entity	GPE	countries, states, cities	**India** is rich In cultural heritage

Type	Tag	Sample Categories	Example Sentences
Facility	FAC	bridges, buildings, airports	**Napier Bridge** is very crowded
Vehicles	VEH	Planes, trains, automobiles	**Rajadhani** is a popular train
Dates	DATE	Absolute or relative dates or periods	**15th December 2020** is an important day for me
Money	MONEY	Monetary values, including unit	**Rs. 1000** is too high for this dress
Time	TIME	Times smaller than a day	I met him at **8.00 PM**

Named Entity Recognition (NER): The task of named entity recognition (NER) is finding spans of text that constitute single named entity and to tag the type of the entity basically a structured prediction problem. Some of the applications of NER include sentiment analysis – finding the sentiment towards a particular person or organization, question answering – answering questions about an entity and information extraction – extracting facts and relations about entities. NER is associated with two issues namely segmentation (finding the correct spans of text that make up a named entity) and type ambiguity (Washington could be tagged as PER or GPE). An example (Example 10.3) for an NE tagged piece of text is given below:

Example 10.3

The rise in petrol prices was announced by [$_{ORG}$ **Indian Oil**] spoke person [$_{PER}$ **Ram Kumar**] effective from [$_{TIME}$ **Monday**] [$_{TIME}$ **9.00 AM**], with an increase of [$_{MONEY}$ **Rs.5**] per litre. This announcement caused a great rush at petrol stations in [$_{LOC}$ **Chennai**], [$_{LOC}$ **Mumbai**] and [$_{LOC}$ **Delhi**].

BIO Tagging: Now we need to convert the structured prediction problem into a sequence labelling problem with one label per word. For this purpose, we use BIO (Beginning, Inside, Outside) tags. Here B– prefix before a tag is a token that *begins* a span, **I**– prefix before a tag are tokens inside a span and O are tokens outside of any span. Example 10.3 is now shown with one tag per word (Example 10.4).

Example 10.4

[$_{O}$]The [$_{O}$]rise [$_{O}$]in [$_{O}$]petrol [$_{O}$]prices [$_{O}$]was [$_{O}$]announced [$_{O}$]by [$_{B\text{-}ORG}$ **Indian** $_{I\text{-}ORG}$ **Oil**] [$_{O}$] spoke [$_{O}$]person [$_{B\text{-}PER}$ **Ram** $_{I\text{-}PER}$ **Kumar**] [$_{O}$]effective [$_{O}$]from [$_{B\text{-}TIME}$ **Monday**] [$_{B\text{-}TIME}$ **9.00** $_{I\text{-}TIME}$ **AM**], with an increase of [$_{MONEY}$ **Rs.5**] per litre. This announcement caused a great rush at petrol stations in [$_{B\text{-}LOC}$ **Chennai**], [$_{B\text{-}LOC}$ **Mumbai**] and [$_{B\text{-}LOC}$ **Delhi**].

Neural Sequence Tagger: Using a human-labeled training set of text annotated with tags, supervised machine learning algorithms such as Hidden Markov Models, Conditional Random Fields (CRF)/ Maximum Entropy Markov Models (MEMM), Neural sequence models (RNNs or Transformers) and bi–LSTM models have been designed. In this section, we will discuss the use of Neural sequence tagger. A powerful mechanism is to make predictions based on both the past and the future. Therefore, we have two LSTMS, one running up-to-down and the other running down-to-up (Figure 10.17). First, the words are embedded using both Character and GloVe embedding. This concatenated representation is given to both the down-to-up and the up-to-down LSTMS, the outputs of which are concatenated and given to the CRF layer to obtain the BIO tags.

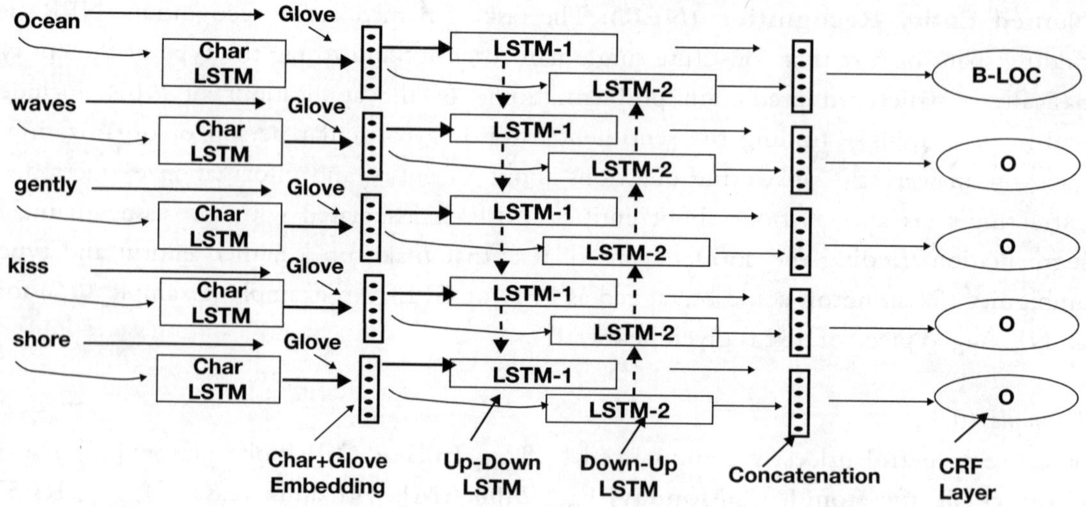

Figure 10.17: LSTM architecture for NER

Summary

- Outlined the basics of Parts-of-Speech.
- Explained the process of and need for of Parts-of-Speech (POS) tagging.
- Described the ambiguity in POS tagging.
- Outlined the concepts of sequential labelling and POS tagging.
- Described the modelling approaches to sequential labelling.
- Discussed in detail Hidden Markov Model (HMM) for POS tagging.
- Outlined the feature functions associated with sequence labelling.
- Explained Maximum Entropy Markov Model (MEMM) for POS tagging.
- Described the details of Condition Random Field Model (CRF) for POS tagging.
- Outlined briefly the use of deep learning for sequential labelling using Named Entity Recognition as an example.

Exercises

Suggested Activities

1. Using either a language or software of your choice and available tools implement the use of HMM models for POS tagging and NER.

2. **Case Study – Part-of-Speech Tagging:** Using Penn Treebank dataset (https://www. kaggle.com/datasets/aliakay8/penn-treebank-dataset), assign part-of-speech tags. Train Hidden Markov Models (HMMs) on labelled POS tagging datasets using appropriate features. Evaluate model performance using metrics like accuracy, precision, recall, and F1-score

Self-Assessment: Multiple Choice Questions

Give answers with justification for correct and wrong choices:

1. Parts-of-Speech are not called as
   i. Lexical categories
   ii. Morphological classes
   iii. Syntactic classes

2. Each POS category occurs
   i. in same contexts but has the different syntactic functions
   ii. in same contexts and has the same syntactic functions
   iii. in different contexts but has the same syntactic functions

3. can, may and should are examples of
   i. auxiliary verbs
   ii. verbs
   iii. adverbs

4. Closed class categories are composed of a small, fixed set of grammatical function words for a given language and include
   i. Pronouns, Prepositions, Pronouns
   ii. Pronouns, Nouns, Adjectives
   iii. Conjunctions, Determiners, Verbs

5. One of the most popular POS tag set having 45 tags is:
   i. Brown Treebank POS tag set
   ii. WSJ Treebank POS tag set
   iii. Penn Treebank POS tag set

6. "He can **duck** and escape" Here "duck" is an example of
   i.   MD – modal verb
   ii. VB –base form verb
   iii. NN- singular noun

7. Given an input of word tokens w_1, w_2 .... w_n, we need the output of POS tags t_1, t_2 .... t_n one per word. This approach is called
   i.   Sequence labelling
   ii. Classification
   iii. Clustering

8. argmax p(t) p(w|t) where t is the tag and w word defines t
   i.   Discriminative modelling
   ii. Generative modelling
   iii. Deep learning

9. A simple stochastic model in which the distribution of future states depends only on the present state and not on how it arrived in the present state is a
   i.   Markov Model
   ii. Hidden Markov Model
   iii. Maximum Entropy Markov Model

10. A process where transition probabilities are independent of time slice is said to have
    i.   Markov property
    ii. Entropy property
    iii. Stationary assumption

11. An extension of a Markov model in which the input symbols are not the same as the states is called
    i.   Condition Random Field Model
    ii. Hidden Markov Model
    iii. Maximum Entropy Markov Model

12. In the case of POS tagging we assume that the words emitted depends only on their tag – this assumption is called as
    i.   Output–independent assumption
    ii. Input–independent assumption
    iii. Stationary assumption

13. Computing the probability of observation word sequence given the HMM model is done using
    i.   Markov algorithm
    ii. Viterbi algorithm
    iii. Baum Welch algorithm

14. Viterbi algorithm is a

    i. Dynamic and unsupervised algorithm

    ii. Static and unsupervised algorithm

    iii. Dynamic and supervised algorithm

15. For the learning of HMM model the following algorithm is used

    i. Naïve Bayes algorithm

    ii. EM algorithm

    iii. SVM algorithm

16. Word–based Features are

    i. include word capitalization, prefixes and suffixes

    ii. indicate specific direction of the context

    iii. capture relationships between adjacent labels or tags

17. Discriminative model of the tags **t** given the observed input sequence **w** is called

    i. HMM

    ii. CRF

    iii. MEMM

18. One of the solutions to the sub model optimization problem associated with MEMMs is to

    i. optimize the parameters in a local model simultaneously as it is carried out

    ii. capture relationships between adjacent labels or tags

    iii. optimize the parameters in a global model simultaneously as it is carried out

19. __________ models predict P(T|W) using the Markov assumption.

    i. MEMM and CRF

    ii. HMM and MEMM

    iii. HMM and CRF

20. bi–LSTM model

    i. words are embedded using both Character and GloVe embedding

    ii. words are not embedded

    iii. words are embedded using linear context features

Self-Assessment: Match the Columns

No		Match	
1	POS categories	**A**	given an observation sequence, $O = o_1,...,o_T$ and the HMM model $\lambda = (A, B, \pi)$ using supervised learning
2	Input to the POS tagging task	**B**	is a sequence of word tokens w and output is a sequence of POS tags t, one per word

No		Match	
3	Prague Dependency Treebank	C	converting the structured prediction problem into a sequence labelling problem with one label per word
4	Discriminative Models	D	associated with the label bias problem as the conditional models are based on per state normalization.
5	Markov Process	E	are defined distributionally by the morphological and syntactic contexts that they appear in
6	Decoding problem	F	directly model the conditional probability of labels given the words
7	Evaluation problem	G	optimize the parameters in a global model simultaneously as it is carried out
8	MEMM	H	very large tag set with 4452 tags
9	CRF	I	is a simple stochastic process in which the distribution of future states depends only on the present state and not on how it arrived in the present state
10	BIO tagging	J	given the observation sequence $O = o_1, \ldots, o_T$ and an HMM model, computing the probability of O given the model

Short Questions

1. How do we define POS tags and why is POS tagging important?
2. Given the following examples –POS tag them using Penn Treebank tag set
    i. The girl sang and danced.
    ii. The boy run in the park in the morning.
    iii. If I study well, I can pass.
    iv. The clever boy quickly caught the fraudster.
3. Discuss ambiguity in POS tagging. Illustrate with three examples showing different types.
4. Give and explain the block diagram of a POS tagger.
5. Describe in detail how POS tagging can be described as a sequence labelling problem.
6. Discuss generative and discriminative approaches to sequence labelling.
7. Describe in detail the Markov model.

8. Explain the basics of HMM.

9. Discuss the three problems associated with HMM in the context of POS tagging.

10. Outline the Baum Welch algorithm used in HMM in detail.

11. Describe the Viterbi algorithm used in HMM in detail.

12. Given an observation sequence $O = (O_1\ O_2\ \ldots\ O_L)$, and a class of models, we want to determine the specific model that "best" explains the observations – explain how this learning is carried out using EM algorithm.

13. Outline some of the disadvantages of HMM.

14. Describe the feature functions used for sequence labelling.

15. Outline the use of MEMM for Named Entity Recognition and outline some of their disadvantages.

16. Outline the use of MEMM for Named Entity Recognition.

17. Compare and contrast MEMM and CRF models for POS tagging.

18. Explain the use of deep learning for sequence labelling using POS tagging as an example.

CHAPTER 11

Syntactic Processing

11.1 Syntax and Parsing

Syntax can be considered as patterns that describe the formation of phrases and sentences from words. The term "syntax" is derived from the Greek language and means "arrangement". In essence syntax refers to the way words are arranged together and the relationship between them. More formally grammar associated with syntax defines the rules, principles and processes that govern structures of sentences of a language. Though syntax of different languages can be very different, but every language is associated with systematic structural principles described by syntax. Syntax in general is important because it gives the linguistic typology and, in most languages, gives the relative position of subjects (S), objects (O) and verbs (V) of a language.

Example 11.1

Consider sentence in English "I caught the ball" (SVO).

From the NLP perspective, syntax is useful for applications such as grammar checkers, question answering, information extraction and machine translation.

Grammar Rules of English: In order to understand parsing, the breaking up of a sentence into its grammatical components we need to understand grammar rules. The general abbreviations used and a sample of English grammar rules is given in Figure 11.1.

Abbreviations					
S - sentence, NP - Noun Phrase, VP - Verb Phrase, ADJ - Adjective, ADV - Adverb, Prep - Preposition, PP - Prepositional Phrase, WH-N P - wh-question noun Phrase, AUX - Auxiliary Verb, PosPro - Posessive Pronoun					
No	**Rule**	**Example**		**Rule**	**Example**
Sentence			**Verb phrase**		
R1	S → NP VP	The man eats	R11	VP → Verb	enjoy
R2	S → VP	Show me the photo	R12	VP → Verb NP	enjoy a good meal

R3	S → Aux NP VP	Will you show me the photo?	R13	VP → VP PP	enjoy a good meal in the night
R4	S → Wh-NP VP	Which is the capital of India?	R14	VP → Verb PP	enjoy on Friday
Noun phrase			R15	VP → Verb NP PP	think I need a new stove
R5	NP → Noun/Pronoun	man, I	R16	VP → Verb VP	want to cook today
R6	NPR → DET Noun	the man	**Coordination**		
R7	NP → DET ADJ Noun	the big man	R17	NP → NP and NP	the cups and the saucers
R8	NP → PosPro Noun	my book	R18	NP → Noun and Noun	cups and saucers
R9	NP → NP PP	the man in the market	R19	VP → VP and VP	I sang and danced
Prepositional phrase			R20	ADJ → ADJ and ADJ	big and bold
R10	PP → Prep NP	in the evening	R21	S → S and S	The boy came and the girl danced

Figure 11.1: Sample Grammar of English

Example 11.2

Let us consider an example sentence "The man eats a good meal". We use the grammar rules given in Figure 11.1 and some terminals given below:

Verb → eats,   DET → the,   Noun → man,   Noun DET → a,   Noun → meal,   ADJ → good

S the sentence is composed of NP and VP (R1). The first NP is composed of DET and Noun (R6) – word DET "the" and word Noun "man". Now the VP is composed of Verb and NP (R12) – word Verb "eats". Now the NP of rule 7 is composed of DET, ADJ and Noun– where word DET "a", word ADJ is "good" and word for Noun is "meal". Here the symbols corresponding directly to words are called terminals and other symbols are non-terminals. In this context verbs are sometimes subcategorized as transitive and intransitive.

Parsing: Parsing is considered as the process of obtaining the syntactic representation of a sentence using a defined set of grammar rules. The main two different types of syntactic representations are the constituent or phrase-structure tree and the dependency tree. Due to syntactic ambiguity, there can be more than one syntactic representation for a single sentence.

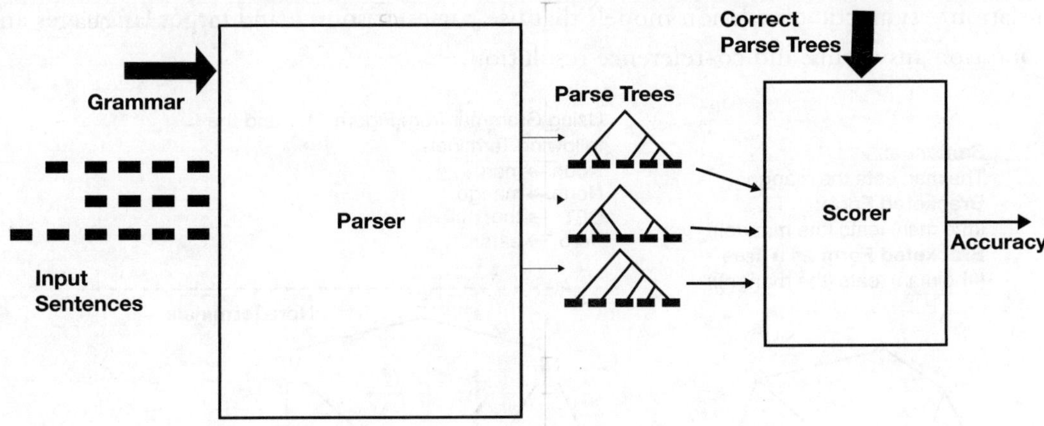

Figure 11.2: Parsing Method

Parsing is thus defined as a method to obtain the parse trees associated with sentences and calculate the score associated with each tree and hence calculate accuracy of the parser (Figure 11.2).

11.2 Constituent Parsing and Context-Free Grammar (CFG)

A sentence structure can be represented as a collection of nested constituents. Constituent is a group of neighbouring words that are in some way closer to each other than to other words in the sentence and behave as single units. These units show up in the same distributed environment, and can appear in different places. Constituents larger than a word are called phrases and phrases in turn can contain other phrases. Each phrase could be replaced by another of the same type of constituent. Phrase structure or constituent grammar concentrate on constituency relation. Sentences can have hierarchical structures. Basically, a sentence is made up of two parts – subject which is typically a noun phrase (NP) and predicate which is typically a verb phrase (VP). NPs and VPs in turn are made up of other components. A constituent parse can be represented with bracketing to represent hierarchical structures. Bracketing, components, and constituent tree are shown in Figure 11.3. Here again, we will consider the grammar shown in Figure 11.1. In the constituent tree, the non–terminals correspond to phrases, S (sentence), NP (noun phrase), VP (verb phrase) and so on. Nodes which are pre-terminals just above the actual words correspond to POS tags and the terminals correspond to the words in the sentence. There are many applications of constituent parses such as language modelling – predicting the next word based on syntactic structure, machine translation – syntactic translation models that use parses of source and target languages and for question answering and co-reference resolution.

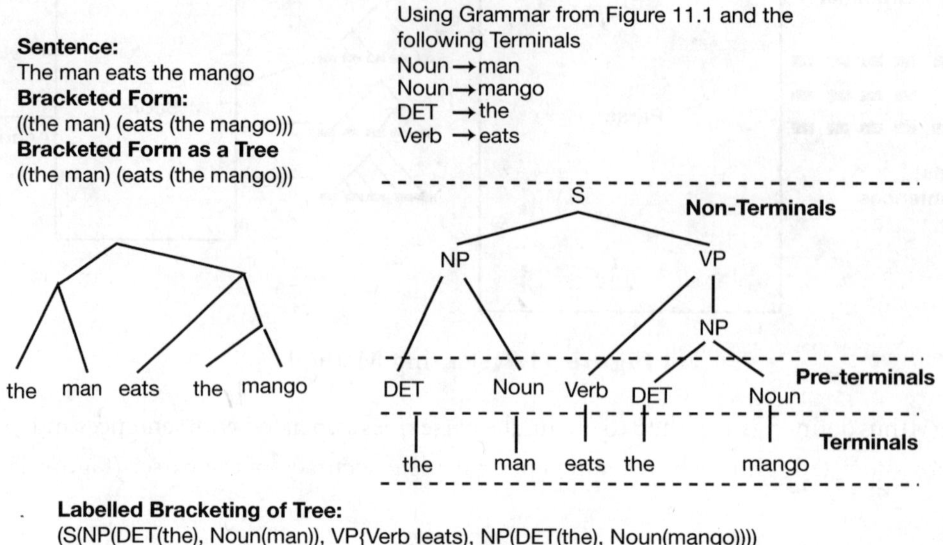

Figure 11.3: Constituent Representation

Context-free grammars (CFG): CFG defines in a formal way how symbols in a language combine to form valid sentences. In other words, the grammar defines what meaningful constituents are and how they are formed from other constituents and in this way describes the valid structure of a language. In terms of NLP, the context free grammar is a tuple $<N, \Sigma, R, S>$ as described in Table 11.1.

Symbol	Description	Examples
N	Finite set of non-terminal symbols	Phrasal Categories - NP, VP, S POS (Pre-terminals) – Noun, Verb, DET
Σ	Finite alphabet of terminal symbols	The, man, mango, eat (the words)
R	Set of production rules (rewrite rules) of the form $A \to \beta, \beta \in (\Sigma, N)$	$S \to NP\ VP$ Noun $\to$ man
S	Start symbol	

Table 11.1: Symbols of Context-free Grammar

CFG essentially has rewrite rules (productions) to rewrite non-terminals as terminals or other non-terminals (refer to grammar given in Figure 11.1). This grammar is called context-free because a rule to rewrite a non-terminal does not depend on the context of that non-terminal that is the left-hand side of the rule is only a single non-terminal without any context defined. It is possible to obtain infinite strings given a finite set of productions. This is because CFGs capture recursion using recursive rules where the same non-terminal can appear on both sides of a production rule – for example "NP → NP PP". The sequence of rewrites corresponds to bracketing thus resulting in hierarchical tree structure. Given a CFG, a derivation shows the sequence of productions used to generate a string of words for example the sentence "The man eats a good meal with ice-cream" and this is visualized as parse tree (Figure 11.4). In the NLP context, given a sentence, finding its constituent parse is a well-known task and mostly based on Penn Treebank which is a large corpus of annotated parse trees. Treebanks of parsed sentences exist for many genres of English as well as for many other languages.

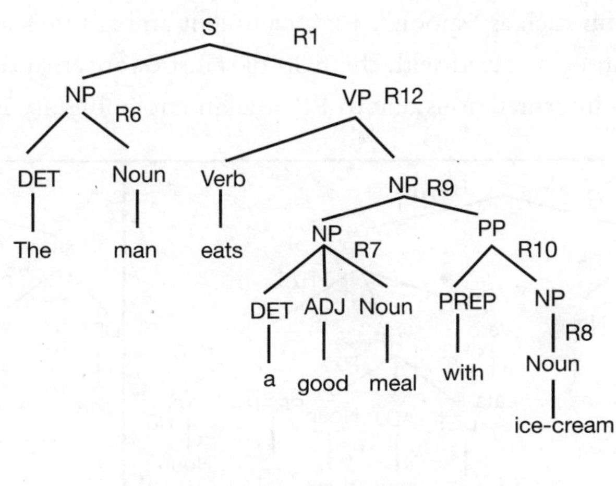

Figure 11.4: Derivations and Parse Tree with CFG

11.3 Syntactic Ambiguity

There are many types of ambiguities associated with syntactics. The main types are Prepositional Phrase (PP) attachment ambiguity and Coordination ambiguity.

PP Attachment Ambiguity: Prepositional Phrase (PP) attachment ambiguity occurs when the prepositional phrase can be associated with different constituents such as NP or VP using different rules.

Example 11.3

Consider the sentence "The man eats a good meal with ice-cream". We use the grammar rules given in Figure 11.1 and add some more terminals to Example 11.2

$$Prep \rightarrow with, \qquad Noun \rightarrow ice\text{-}cream$$

We will get the following two parse trees as given in Figure 11.3. Figure 11.5 shows the example of two parse trees obtained by applying different rules (rules applied are as shown in Figure 11.1). We see that at node VP two rules can be applied R15 or R12 resulting in parse trees as shown in Figure 11.5(a) and Figure 11.5(b) respectively. Here the second parse tree is the correct one since ice-cream here is an accompaniment of the meal and not an instrument of eating such as "spoon". PP attachment ambiguity is associated with English like languages and can be resolved with the help of statistics or semantics. Another example (Example 11.4) with 5 interpretations due to PP attachment ambiguity is given below:

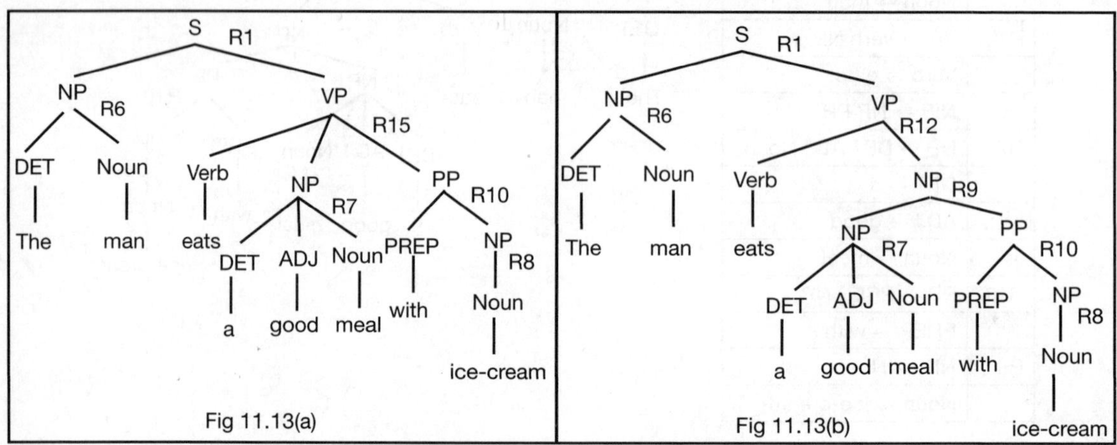

Figure 11.5: Ambiguity in Parsing

Example 11.4

I cooked the chicken ((in the pot on the table) in the kitchen)
I cooked the chicken (in the pot (on the table in the kitchen)
I cooked ((the chicken in the pot) (on the table) in the kitchen

I cooked (the chicken (in the pot on the table)) in the kitchen

I (cooked the chicken in the pot) (on the table in the kitchen) – correct interpretation

   Coordination Ambiguity: Coordination ambiguity can occur because NP and VP constituents cannot enforce subject-verb agreement (Example 11.5). Another coordination ambiguity often occurs when modifiers are used (Example 11.6) where interpretation depends on actual situation.

Example 11.5

Bears (eat (leaves and barks)) – correct interpretation

Bears ((eat leaves) and barks)– no subject –verb agreement

Example 11.6

young (boys and girls)

(young boys) and girls

11.4 Probabilistic CFG

Due to the ambiguities described and many other types of ambiguities, we are likely to get many parses for a sentence based on CFG tuple $<N, \Sigma, R, S>$. In order to tackle these ambiguities, we need to score the derivations to indicate their plausibility. Probabilistic CFG (PCFG) adds a top-down production probability per rule and hence each rule R in the tuple (Equation 11.1)

$$A \rightarrow \beta \; p \; where \; p = P(\beta \mid A) \tag{11.1}$$

When probabilities are assigned to rewrite rules, the probabilities corresponding to each left-hand side non-terminal must sum to one. In other words, PCFG assigns probabilities to the sequence of rewrite operations or derivatives that eventually terminate in terminals. To calculate the probability of a parse tree for a given sentence S, the parse tree T for the sentence S where the derivative is comprised of n rules taken from set of rules R of the form $A \rightarrow \beta$ is given in Equation 11.2

$$P(T,S) = \prod_{i=1}^{n} P(\beta \mid A) \tag{11.2}$$

We can estimate $P(\beta \mid A)$ using maximum likelihood estimates or equivalently using frequency of occurrence as given below (Equation 11.3)

$$\sum_{\beta} P(\beta|A) = \frac{C(A \to \beta)}{C(A)} \qquad 11.3$$

During inference, for the input sentence S, define $T(S)$ to be the set of trees whose leaves reading from left to right, match the words in S (Equation 11.4).

$$t*(s) = \operatorname*{argmax}_{t \acute{o} T(S)} p(t) \qquad 11.4$$

PCFG learnt from Penn Treebank using Maximum Likelihood Estimate resulted in F1 score of 71%. State-of-the-art parsers have a F1 score of about 92%. PCFGs give partial solution to syntactic ambiguity. The weaknesses of PCFGs include lack of sensitivity to structural frequencies and lexical information.

11.5 CKY Parsing Algorithm

Fundamentally parsing is search through a space of all possible parses. Here parsing can be bottom–up where one starts from words of the sentence and then construct the full tree or parsing can be top-down where one starts from the start symbol and proceed to expand to get the sentence. CKY (Cocke-Kasami-Younger) algorithm is an efficient bottom–up parsing algorithm. The algorithm is very important in the NLP context, be used for both recognition and parsing problems and works for both CFG and PCFG.

Chomsky Normal Form (CNF): The basic CKY algorithm supports only rules that are in Chomsky Normal Form. In CNF form, the rules can be only of two types:

- $NT \to w$ – this is the pre-terminal rule (example Noun $\to$ man) – the only type of unary rule allowed that is generation of words given POS tags.
- $NT \to NT_1\ NT_2$ these non-terminal rules can only be binary in nature ($S \to NP\ VP$) and there can be no rules that mix non-terminals and terminals.

It is possible to convert any CFG to an equivalent CNF form that defines the same language although the parse trees look different. For this to be carried out we need to get rid of any unary rules with non-terminal on left-hand side, any rule that mixes terminals and non-terminals on left-hand side by appropriately writing the grammar and convert any n-ary rules to binary rules. This can be carried out as shown in Figure 11.6 (a). The corresponding trees are shown in Figure 11.6 (b).

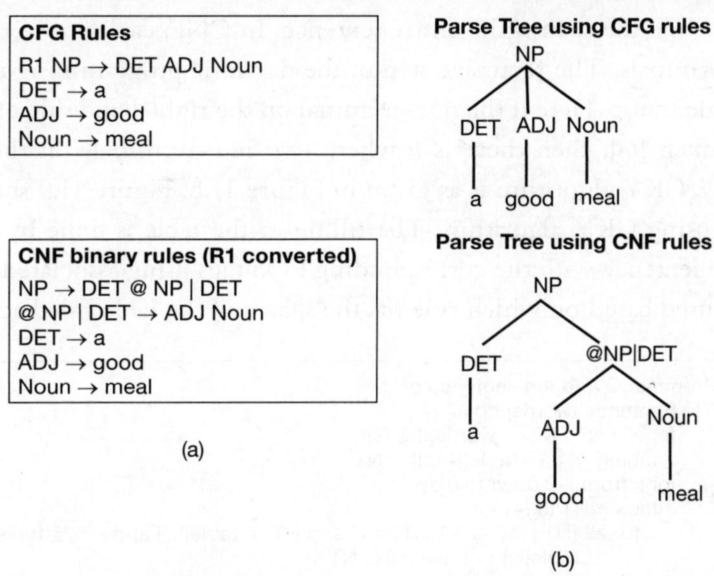

Figure 11.6: Rules and Parse Trees of CFG and CNF

CKY – Parsing: We are given the grammar $<N, \Sigma, R, S>$ where the rules R are in CNF and a sentence as a sequence of words $w = (w_1, w_2, \ldots \ldots w_n)$. The goal of the CKY algorithm is to produce a parse tree for w. We refer to substring of w as span (i, j) to refer to words between i and j. Let us understand how rules and these spans work (Figure 11.7).

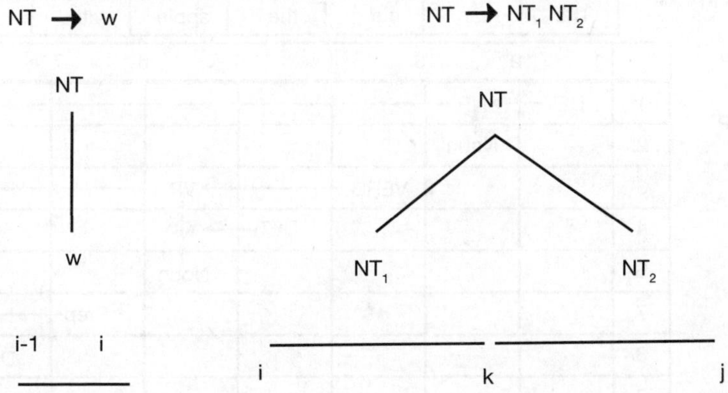

Figure 11.7: Span of CKY Algorithm

As with most dynamic programming approaches, we go to the appropriate table entry to find the correct answer. The dynamic programming approach fills the tables of partial solutions to the sub-problems until they contain all the solutions to the entire problem that is the root of the parse tree is S and the span is the entire sentence. In CNF, each non-terminal generates only two non-terminals. The recursive step of the dynamic programming needs to select a split point and rule to use. Here if the non-terminal on the right-hand side of the production rule spans the token $[i,j]$, then there is k where two non-terminals on the left-hand side span $i=k$, and $k–j$. CKY algorithm is as given in Figure 11.8. Figure 11.9 shows an example sentence parsed using CKY algorithm. The filling of the table is done by first associating each word in the sentence with the corresponding POS tags using associated rules. Then the binary rules are used based on which rule fits the span and the table filled accordingly.

```
Given Grammar G and the sentence of
for j = 1 to Sentence (words) do
        for all { NT I NT → words[j] ∈ G}
          table[j–1, j] ← table[j–1, j] ∪ NT
        for i=from j–2 downto 0 do
          for k = i+1 to j–1 do
            for all {NT | NT → NT₁NT₂ ∈ G and NT₁ ∈ table[i,k] and NT₂ ∈ table[i,k]}
              table[i,j] ← table [i,j] ∪ NT
```

Figure 11.8: CKY Algorithm

CNF Grammar

S	→	NP VP
NP	→	DET Noun
NP	→	NP PP
VP	→	Verb NP
VP	→	VP PP
PP	→	Prep NP
DET	→	the
DET	→	a
Noun	→	man
Noun	→	apple
Noun	→	Knife
Verb	→	cut
Prep	→	with

	The	man	cut	the	apple	with	a	knife
i	1	2	3	4	5	6	7	8	9
1	DET	NP							S
2		Noun							
3			VERB		VP				VP
4				DET	NP				
6					Noun				
7						Prep			PP
8							DET	NP	
9									Noun

Figure 11.9: CKY Table–An Example

CKY-PCFG: As we have already discussed, PCFG gives us a mechanism for assigning probabilities to different parses of the same sentence and we are concerned with finding the best parse tree that is the parse tree with the highest probability, The CKY-PCFG algorithm calculates the maximum probability parse by storing the probability of each phrase within each cell of the CKY table as we fill it. Each cell of the table for the span [i,j] and label NT with the maximum over splits and rules as given in Equation 11.5:

$$table\left(i, j, NT\right) = P\left(NT \rightarrow NT_1 NT_2\right) * table\left(i, k, NT_1\right) * table\left(k, j, NT_2\right) \qquad 11.5$$

11.6 Earley's Parsing

Earley's parsing is a dynamic programming top-down parsing approach. In this parsing, one should be a start state S in the final column of the table that spans from 0 to $n+1$ and is the parsing should be complete that is $S - \alpha \cdot [0, n+1]$. Here the table is swept from 0 to $n+1$ and new predicted states are created by the rules in the grammar, new incomplete states and new complete states are created by advancing existing states as new constituents are discovered. Earley's parsing solves the left-recursion problem without having to alter the grammar or artificially limiting the search. However, it is ensured that a state that is already in the chart is never placed again, and the states are copied before advancing them.

0 The	1 man	2 cut	3 the	4 apple	5 with	6 a	7 knife	8
0 Root . S	0 Det. the	1 N man	2 V cut	3 Det the	4N apple.	5 P with.	6 Det a	7 knife
0 S.NP VP	0 NP.Det N	0 NP Det N	2 VP V.NP	3 NP.DET N	3 NP DET N	5 PP P.NP	6 NP Det.N	6 NP Det N
0 NP.Det N	1N.man	0 S NP.VP	3 NP.Det N	4N.man	3 NP NP PP	2 PP P.NP	7N.man	5 PP P NP.
0 NP.NP PP	1N.apple	0 NP NP.PP	3 NP.NP PP	4N.apple	0 S NP.VP	6 NP.Det N	7N.apple	2 PP P NP.
0 Det. the	1N.knife	2 VP.V NP	3 Det. the	4N.knife	0NP NP. PP	6 NP.NP PP	7N.knife	6 NP NP.PP
0 Det. a		2 VP.VP PP	3 Det. a		5 PP.P NP	6 Det.the		8 PP.P NP
		2 PP.P NP			5 VP.V NP	6 Det.a		3 NP NP PP.
		2V . cut			5 VP.VP PP			2 VP V NP.
		2 P.with			5P. with			2 VP VP.PP
					5V.cut			0 NP NP PP.
								0 S NP VP.
								8 P.with

Grammar
ROOT → S, S → NP VP, NP → Det N, NP → NPPP
VP → V NP, VP → VP PP, PP → P NP, Det → the, Det → a,
N → man, N → apple, N → Knife, V → cut, P → with

A-Predict
B-Scan
C-Complete

Figure 11.10: Steps of Early's Algorithm

Earley's Parsing Algorithm: The basic steps of the Earley algorithm are that all the states possible are predicted upfront and then a word is read and new predictions added and this is continued till we reach the end of the sentence and if we have reached $N+1$ and the parse is completed we have succeeded. The three basic steps of Earley's algorithm are as given below (Equations 11.6-11.8):

Scan *(a, j)*

$$\langle A \rightarrow \alpha \cdot a \, \beta, \, i, \, j \rangle \vdash \langle A \rightarrow \alpha \, a \cdot B, \, i, \, j+1 \rangle \qquad 11.6$$

Scan is used when in the next step we see a terminal in the rule and the terminal matches the word we are currently at. An example is shown as B in Figure 11.10

Predict *(j)*

$$\langle A \rightarrow \alpha.X\beta, \, i, \, j \rangle \text{ and } X \rightarrow \delta \vdash \langle X \rightarrow .\delta, \, j, \, j \rangle \qquad 11.7$$

Predict is used when in the next step we see a non-terminal in the rule, and here we predict or add all rules associated with that non-terminal and also iteratively add all rules associated with all other non-terminals resulting from that prediction. An example is shown as A in Figure 11.10.

Complete *(k)*

$$\langle A \rightarrow \alpha.X \, \beta, \, i, \, j \rangle \text{ and } X \rightarrow \delta., \, j, \, k > \vdash \langle A \rightarrow \alpha X.\beta, \, i, \, k \rangle \qquad 11.8$$

Complete is used when on scanning we can complete the span from i-k because of the appropriate rules present from i-j and j-k. An example is shown as C in Figure 11.10. The steps of the Earley's algorithm using an example is shown in Figure 11.10.

11.7 Dependency Parsing

Another way to view the syntax of a sentence highlights relations between, for example subject and object is the dependency grammar. Dependency is a syntactic, semantic or any other relation between a pair of tokens. Dependency grammar has bilexical dependencies between two words where one is called the head and the other word is the dependent. Here nodes are the words generally associated with POS tags while the directed arcs encode syntactic dependencies and the labels of the arcs indicate the type of relation between the nodes. There are labels like "nsubj" and "dobj" on the arcs. Sometimes semantic information can be derived from the dependencies, for example dependency relation "nsubj" is often the agent of the action while "dobj" (direct object) are often patients. Verbs are normally heads while their subjects and objects are dependents. Dependency syntax is not associated with non-terminals (as in CFG), here words are directly linked to each other. Heads in the dependency syntax determine the syntactic category of the relation and is obligatory. The form of the dependent depends on the head (agreement between nouns and verbs for example). An example of a dependency representation is given in Figure 11.11.

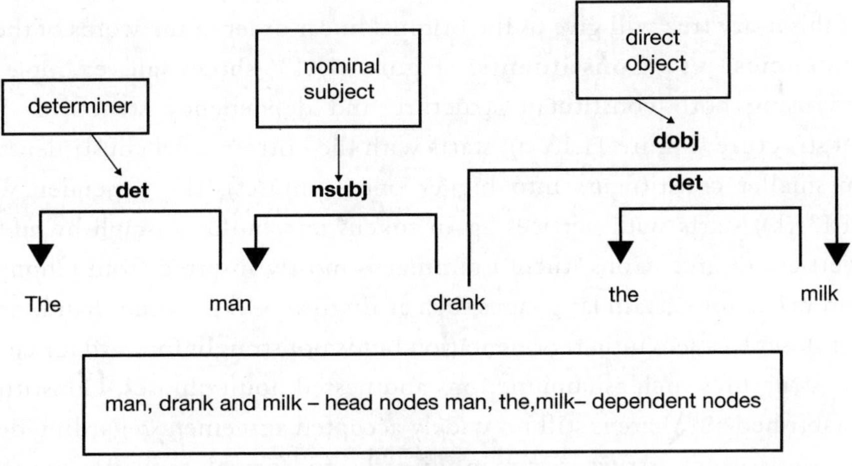

Figure 11.11: Dependency Representation

A dependency structure is a directed graph $G = (V, A)$ consisting of a set of vertices V and arcs A between them. In the dependency tree, single root vertex with no incoming arcs and every vertex has exactly one incoming arc except root and there is a unique path from the root to each vertex in V. Unlike phrase-structure trees, dependency trees are not tied to the linear order of the words in a sentence. Adding a constraint derived from the linear order of words in a sentence allows for more efficient parsing algorithms. Dependency relations belong to the structural order of a sentence, not the linear order. This is different from a phrase-structure tree, where the syntax is constrained by the linear order of the sentence (a different linear order yields a different parse tree).

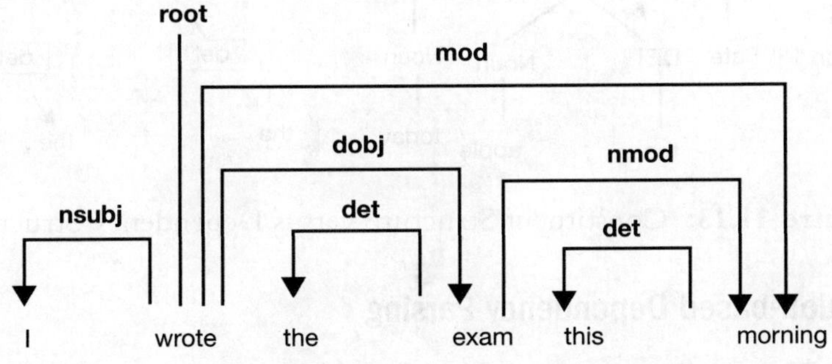

Figure 11.12: Example showing Projectivity

Projectivity: An arc between a head and dependent is projective if there is a path from the head to every word between the head and dependent (shown in example in Figure 11.12). A projective dependency tree has no crossing arc when all vertices are lined up in linear order and arcs are drawn above. If we have a projective dependency tree, then the inorder traversal of this n–ary tree will give us the original linear order of the words of the sentence.

Dependencies vs Constituents: Figure 11.13 shows an example sentence represented using both constituent structure and dependency structure. While the constituent structure (Figure 11.13 (a)) starts with the bottom level constituents or tokens and group smaller constituents into bigger ones (phrases), the dependency structure (Figure 11.13 (b)) starts with vertices again tokens and builds a graph by adding edges between vertices or arcs. Constituent grammar is mostly inspired from Chomsky and is mostly appropriate for certain languages such as English. On the other hand, dependency grammar is closer to a semantic representation but is not straight forward for certain types of syntactic structures such as conjunctions and nested noun phrases. Constituency tests are well established but there is still no widely accepted agreement regarding dependency relations. Constituency structures map directly to formal semantic representations than dependency. Grammatical relations are easily identified in a dependency parse. Dependency parses of semantically similar sentences across languages are similar. Both constituent and dependency structures are used in NLP, however dependency parsing provides useful information for many NLP tasks such as information extraction, machine translation, question answering, sentiment analysis, etc. Moreover, dependency parsing is faster and more language independent.

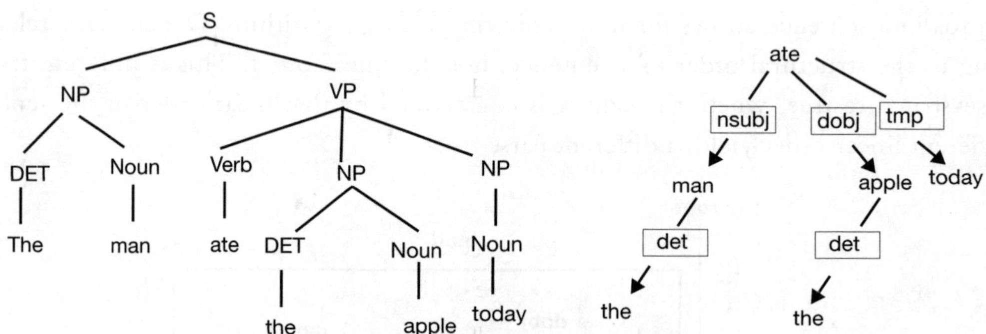

Figure 11.13: Constituent Structure versus Dependency Structure

11.7.1 Transition-based Dependency Parsing

Here transition refers to the operation of searching for a dependency relation between each pair of tokens. The projective version has worst case time complexity of $O(n)$ for parsing.

Here we will discuss the top-down, bottom-up shift-reduce projective parsing approach designed by Nivre. It consists of three components, the stack S, the buffer list of input prefixed with token "root" stack I and the set of arcs A.

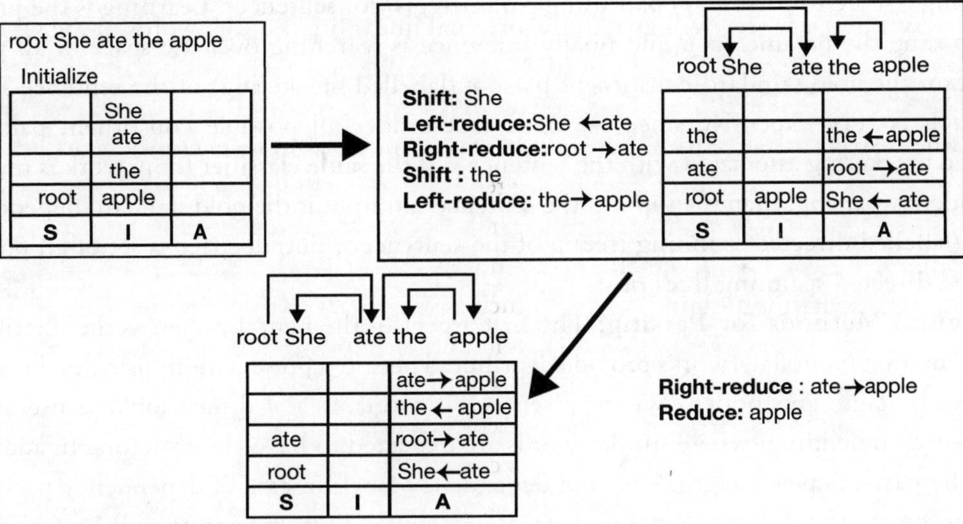

Fig 11.14: Example Showing Steps of Dependency Parsing Algorithm

The following are the operations of the algorithm:

1. **Initialize** as <root, W (words of the sentence), ϕ > - Initialize the stack S with root, the input with words of the sentence and A as empty.
2. **Left-reduce** – Here left rule is formed as $\text{Top}S \leftarrow \text{Top}I$ which is added to stack A and $\text{Top}S$ is removed from the stack S.
3. **Right-reduce** – Here right rule is formed as $\text{Top}S \rightarrow \text{Top}I$ which is added to stack A and $\text{Top}I$ is shifted to S.
4. **Shift** – Here word at top of I is shifted to top of stack S.
5. **Terminate** – The parsing is completed when all the words in input buffer I are completed, S contains only root and head verb, and A contains all the dependency arcs.

Let us consider the sentence: "She ate the apple". The various stages of the problem after the various rules are applied and the output obtained are shown in Figure 11.14.

11.8 Machine Learning and Neural Network Approaches to Parsing

Classification Framework for Parsing: One of the simplest methods for constituent parsing is the use of the machine learning based classification framework. This can be expressed as follows (Equation 11.9).

$$Classify\left(x,\theta\right)=\underset{\gamma}{\operatorname{argmax}}\ score\left(s,p,\theta\right) \qquad\qquad 11.9$$

where s is a sentence, p is the constituent parse, θ are the parameters. Modelling involves assigning a score to parse (s, p) pair using parameters θ for sentences. Learning is the process of choosing the parameters θ and finally inference is searching over the space of all parses to obtain the gold standard constituent parse p (labelled bracketing) of the sentence s This approach is very expensive since we need to consider all possible constituent parses or labelled bracketing associated with the sentence s. If the same classifier framework is used for dependency parsing, then the input is the sentence s, output is the gold standard dependency parse (labelled directed spanning tree) p of the sentence s, output space is set of all possible labelled directed spanning trees of s.

Neural Methods for Parsing: The first aspect of the neural parsers is the distributed representation Neural networks provide distributed phrase representations using embeddings for words, tags, and nodes. We represent each word as a d–dimensional dense vector (i.e., word embedding) where similar words are expected to have close vectors. In addition, both the part–of–speech tags (POS) and dependency labels in case of dependency parser are also represented as d–dimensional vectors. Word embeddings for constituent linear parsing can be trained with SkipGram model using large text corpus. Word embeddings can also be conditioned on dependency context where each dependency is converted to a tuple. The smaller discrete sets also exhibit many semantic similarities for example.

Example: NNS (plural noun) should be close to NN (singular noun) and nummod (numerical modifier) should be close to amod (adjective modifier).

In addition, these neural parsers need less independence assumptions. Moreover, neural methods enable the leveraging of pre–trained embeddings for learning the scoring functions. Neural networks can use multiple layers to learn much more complex nonlinear decision boundaries between parses.

The self-attentive decoder has been used for constituency parsing. Here the attention encoder generates a space of representations of each token in the sentence. Then a scoring function score (i,j,k) is learnt for each span from token i to token j with label k. Then the CKY algorithm is used for decoding to find the best tree in the space.

Of the many deep models available for dependency parsing, we will first discuss greedy, transition–based neural dependency parsers. This model is based on dense feature representations. Here we use the transition dependency method already described in section 11.7.1. The aim of the model is to predict a transition sequence from some initial configuration c to a terminal configuration, in which the dependency parse tree is encoded. The model being greedy, the attempt is to correctly predict based on the features of the current configuration $c = (S,I,A)$, one of the transitions either Shift, Left-reduce or Right-reduce at a time, Here S is the stack, I is the input buffer and A is the set of dependency arcs. A feed-forward neural network multi-class classifier can be used for dependency parsing. A set of tokens are extracted based on the stack / buffer positions. A concatenation of the vector representation of word, POS tag and dependency label is the neural representation of a configuration. A softmax classifier assigns classes $p \in C$ based on inputs $s \in \mathbb{R}"$ via the probability (Figure 11.15)

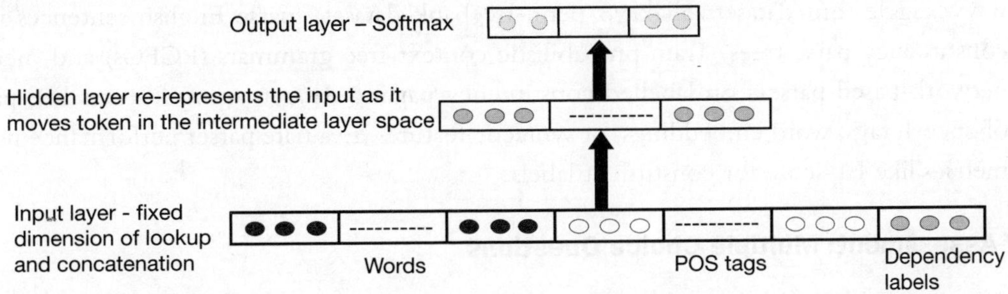

Figure 11.15: Neural Dependency Parser

Summary

- Outlined the basics of syntax and parsing and discussed some simple grammar rules of English.
- Explained context-free grammars and process of constituent parsing.
- Described the different types of ambiguity associated with constituent parsing.
- Outlined the concepts of probabilistic CFG.
- Described Chomsky normal form and the CKY parsing algorithm.
- Discussed in Earley's parsing algorithm in detail.
- Explained the concepts of dependency parsing.
- Outlined the process of transition-based dependency parsing in detail.
- Described machine learning and neural network approaches to parsing.

Exercises

Suggested Activities

1. Using either a language or software of your choice and available tools implement the use of neural models for constituent and dependency parsing.

2. **Case Study – Constituency Parsing for English:** Using Penn Treebank dataset (https://www.kaggle.com/datasets/aliakay8/penn-treebank-dataset), parse English sentences into constituency parse trees. Train probabilistic context-free grammars (PCFGs) and neural network-based parsers on labelled constituency parsing datasets using features like part-of-speech tags, word embeddings, or syntactic features. Evaluate parser performance using metrics like F1-score for constituent labels.

Self-Assessment: Multiple Choice Questions

Give answers with justification for correct and wrong choices:

1. Syntax can be described as the way
    i. words are arranged together and the relationship between them.
    ii. words are arranged
    iii. context of words

2. "syntax" is derived from the Greek language means
    i. grammar
    ii. meaning
    iii. arrangement

3. Relative position of subjects, objects and verbs of a language is given by
    i. sentence
    ii. syntax
    iii. semantics

4. Parsing is considered as
    i. Process of obtaining the syntactic representation of a sentence using a defined set of grammar rules
    ii. Use of grammar rules
    iii. Process of obtaining the syntactic representation of a sentence using a defined set of semantic rules

5. Context free grammar is a tuple $<N, \Sigma, R, S>$ described as
    i. <Non-terminals, Terminals, Semantic rules, Start symbol>
    ii. <Non-terminals, Terminals, Production rules, End symbol>
    iii. <Non-terminals, Terminals, Production rules, Start symbol>

6. CFG essentially has productions
    i.   to rewrite terminals as non-terminals or other terminals
    ii. to rewrite non-terminals as terminals or other non-terminals
    iii. to rewrite non-terminals as terminals

7. When a particular prepositional phrase can be associated with different constituents such as NP or VP using different rules, then it is
    i.   PP attachment ambiguity
    ii. NP attachment ambiguity
    iii. Multiple PP ambiguity

8. PCFG assigns probabilities to
    i.   the sequence of parse trees
    ii. the sequence of non-terminals
    iii. the sequence of rewrite operations

9. Weaknesses of PCFGs include
    i.   lack of sensitivity to structural frequencies and lexical information
    ii. lack of sensitivity to semantic frequencies and lexical information
    iii. lack of sensitivity to grammar rules and semantic information

10. CKY algorithm is
    i.   an efficient top-down parsing algorithm
    ii. an efficient bottom-up parsing algorithm
    iii. an efficient hybrid top-down and bottom-up parsing algorithm

11. The rules of CNF can be only of two types
    i.   The only type of unary rule allowed is the non-terminal rule and other non-terminal rules can be tertiary
    ii. The only type of unary rule allowed is the pre-terminal rule and other non-terminal rules can be tertiary
    iii. The only type of unary rule allowed is the pre-terminal rule and non-terminal rules can only be binary

12. In the case of dynamic programming approach of CNF parsing fills the tables
    i.   of partial solutions to the sub-problems until they contain all the solutions to the entire problem
    ii. of rules used to solve the sub-problems until they contain all the solutions to the entire problem
    iii. of rules used to solve the sub-problems until the complete sentence is completed

13. Earley's algorithm is
    i.   an efficient top-down parsing algorithm
    ii. an efficient bottom-up parsing algorithm
    iii. an efficient hybrid top-down and bottom-up parsing algorithm

14. Earley's parsing
    i. solves the left-recursion problem by altering the grammar and artificially limiting the search.
    ii. solves the left-recursion problem without having to alter the grammar or artificially limiting the search.
    iii. solves the right-recursion problem without having to alter the grammar or artificially limiting the search.
15. The predict rule of Earley's algorithm is used
    i. when in the next step we see a non-terminal in the rule
    ii. when in the next step we see a terminal in the rule
    iii. when on scanning we can complete the span
16. Dependency grammar indicated specific direction of the context
    i. bisyntactic dependencies between two words
    ii. bilexical dependencies between two nouns
    iii. bilexical dependencies between two words
17. Dependency syntax is associated
    i. with non-terminals
    ii. with words
    iii. with POS tags
18. In dependency parsing, if there is a path from the head to every word between the head and the dependent, then the property is called
    i. associativity
    ii. projectivity
    iii. dependency
19. Transition-based dependency parsing by Nivre is a
    i. top-down, bottom-up shift-reduce projective parsing approach
    ii. top-down, bottom-up shift-reduce non-projective parsing approach
    iii. top-down shift-reduce projective parsing approach
20. Neural networks provide distributed phrase representations
    i. using embeddings for parse trees
    ii. using embeddings only for words
    iii. using embeddings for words, tags, and nodes

Self-Assessment: Match the Columns

No		Match	
1	Grammar associated with syntax	A	enable the leveraging of pre-trained embeddings for learning the scoring functions
2	Two types of syntactic representations are	B	Chomsky Normal Form
3	CFG essentially has	C	occurs because NP and VP constituents cannot enforce subject-verb agreement
4	CFGs capture recursion using	D	is a large corpus of annotated parse trees
5	Penn Treebank	E	ensures that a state already in the chart is never placed again
6	Coordination ambiguity	F	defines the rules, principles and processes that govern structures of sentences of a language
7	Probabilistic CFG	G	adds a top-down production probability per rule
8	CKY algorithm	H	the constituent tree and the dependency tree
9	Earley's Algorithm	I	rules where the same non-terminal can appear on both sides of a production rule
10	Neural methods for parsing	J	productions to rewrite non-terminals as terminals or other non-terminals

Short Questions

1. What is syntax and why is it important?
2. Given the following examples —use the grammar given in Figure 11.1 and the necessary terminals in order to give the parse and the labelled bracketing.
    i. The girl sang a beautiful song.
    ii. The boy ran in the park in the morning.
    iii. I think I need a new car.
    iv. The clever boy quickly solved the puzzle.
3. How does CFG defined?
4. Discuss the various syntactic ambiguities giving appropriate examples.
5. What is Probabilistic CFG and why do we need it?
6. Outline the two types of rules allowed in Chomsky Normal Form.

7. Discuss the CKY algorithm in detail.
8. Give the CKY table for the sentence "the beautiful girl sang in the park", listing the required grammar rules.
9. Give the steps of the Earley algorithm for the sentence "the beautiful girl sang in the park", listing the required grammar rules.
10. What is dependency parsing?
11. Outline the differences between constituent and dependency parsing.
12. Discuss transition-based dependency parsing with an example.
13. Give a brief note on the use of classification framework for parsing.
14. What are the advantages of using deep learning for parsing?

Semantic Processing

12.1 Basics of Semantics

Semantics is what we humans do every time by converting data into comprehensible units, relating concepts to instances in the world, applying, revising and sharing the models. From the linguistic viewpoint, semantics is the study of meaning in the form of language use and its evolution over time. From the logical viewpoint, semantics is the study of relationships between words and what they represent. Semantics involve generalization where concepts are organized by type, aggregation where complex concepts are aggregated into simpler ones and common properties could be relationships which connect properties or attributes associating properties with a concept. Other than these aspects, semantics deal with contextual meaning, inferred relationships, causality and granularity. One of the linking notion of semantics are the rich formal models – Ontologies. Ontology was defined by Struder in 1998 as the formal explicit specification of a shared conceptualization. This definition entails that the ontology is formally defined and hence machine readable, the concepts, properties, functions and axioms are explicitly defined, the definitions should capture consensual knowledge accepted by the community and is actually an abstract model of some phenomena in the world. Placing the concepts associated with words in the ontological structure is one way of understanding semantics. There are two approaches to semantics, the intentional approach where the word or sentence is associated with its intrinsic properties (lexical semantics) and the extrinsic approaches where the word or predicate is defined in terms of things in the world, not its intrinsic properties. In this chapter we will be discussing the extrinsic approach.

12.2 Representing Meaning

Representing the meaning of natural language is an important component of language understanding. The main challenge in representing meaning is that a lot of information is left implicit assuming the information needed is already known. Symbolic representation of language conveys the meaning of the sentence and also represents a part of the world associated with the sentence. The meaning representation model of natural language can have the following desirable qualities: verifiability – able to answer a query from the knowledge base, eliminate ambiguity present, cope with vagueness, canonical form – should be able to handle many ways of expressing the same meaning, inference – reason and draw conclusions based on the knowledge base and expressiveness – represent all the meanings required. Examples of sentences showing these issues are given in Table 12.1.

Verifiability	Do college students go to movie houses?
Eliminate ambiguity	College students love visiting actors
Cope with vagueness	Shopping near house is easy
Canonical form	Trends has women clothes Women clothes are available at trends Trends sells women clothes
Inference	Who will bat well today?

Table 12.1: Desirable Qualities of Meaning Representation

A meaning representation model should be able to represent entities which represent individuals (India, Kerala, Ram), concepts which represents general category of individuals (countries, states, people), attributes or properties of entities or concepts (red, beautiful, good) and relations between entities or concepts (like (Ram, Krishnan) and predicates which represent a verb structure. In addition, there should be a knowledge base containing the above for querying.

First-Order Logic (FOL): First order logic also called as first-order predicate calculus (FOPC) is a traditional approach to map ambiguous natural language text to an unambiguous logical form. While propositional logic allows the representation to be as either true or false, FOL is an extension of propositional logic where its predicates assert a relationship among entities. It provides a richer language to mathematically represent natural language statements. However, it requires more complex mechanisms to check for logical consequences. Some of the advantages of first order logic models are that they are flexible, well-understood and widely used. First Order Logic consists of terms, predicates, logical connectives and quantifiers. Terms include constants (Ram), functions such as Food(Indian), and variables. Predicates are used to refer to sets and relations such as Serves (Runs, Indian), etc. Here, predicates can be associated with syntactic categories where nouns and adjectives correspond to one-place predicates such as Country(x) is true if x is a member of a set of countries, Red(x) is true if x is a member of the set of things that are red and verbs can correspond to one-place (Study(Ram) – Ram studied), two-place (Hit(Ram, ball)- Ram hit the ball) or three-place (Give(Ram, Mary, book) – Ram gave Mary the book) predicates. Logical connectives include and ($\land$), or ($\lor$), not ($\neg$) and implies ($\rightarrow$). Quantifiers specified for variables are an important component of FOL. There two types of quantifiers – the existential quantifier $\exists$- which refers to an anonymous object from the domain *(example $\exists x,y$ Movie(x) $\land$ Person(y) $\land$ $\neg$Seen(x,y))* and the universal quantifier - $\forall$ - which refers to all entities in the domain *(example $\forall x$ Movie(x), Superhit(x) $\Rightarrow$ Hero(x, Vijay))*. Inferencing is another important aspect of representation. The knowledge base can be extended by adding new facts or can be used to verify some predicate. Inference can be carried by forwarding chaining using modus ponens to fire applicable implication rules such as given P and $P\Rightarrow Q$, we can prove Q. FOL is associated with standard inference methods that can determine when one statement entails or implies another. Questions can be answered by determining the potential responses that are entailed by given NL statements and background knowledge that are encoded in FOL.

Lambda Notation: Lamda $-\lambda$ -notation is an extension to FOL and provides a way of writing anonymous functions with no function header or function name but only defines the key aspect-the **behavior** of the function.

$\lambda x.$(expression mentioning x) – *Example $\lambda x.$Plays(x, Cricket)*

A more interesting *example - $\lambda x.\lambda y.$Likes(x,y)*

Lambda reduction is also allowed where the Lambda expression can substitute for a variable.

Example – $\lambda x.$Plays(x, Cricket))(Ram) becomes Plays(Ram,Cricket)

Combinatory Categorial Grammar (CCG): CCG is a formalism that bridges syntax and semantics. Syntactic categories are for example S, NP and \ (slash). If we have S\NP, it means if we combine syntactic categories on the left-hand side with the verb and so on (Figure 12.1). Parallel derivations of the syntactic parse and lambda calculus expression are carried out and we obtain a parallel instance of function application on the semantics side.

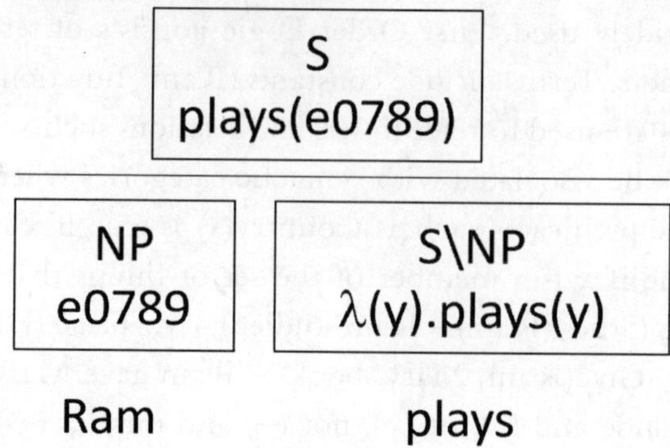

Figure 12.1: Categorical Grammar Output

12.3 Semantic Processing

The process of understanding natural language text by extracting relationships, context, sentiments, etc., is called as semantic analysis. The information obtained from natural language text can range from extracting pre-specified details to obtaining detailed semantic information (Figure 12.2). On the other hand, utilizing semantic aspects, semantic technologies encompass the of process of creating, discovering, processing, managing and reasoning to accomplish business, personal and societal purposes. In essence, semantic processing provides representations that allow the reasoning about entities and their relation with the world, answer

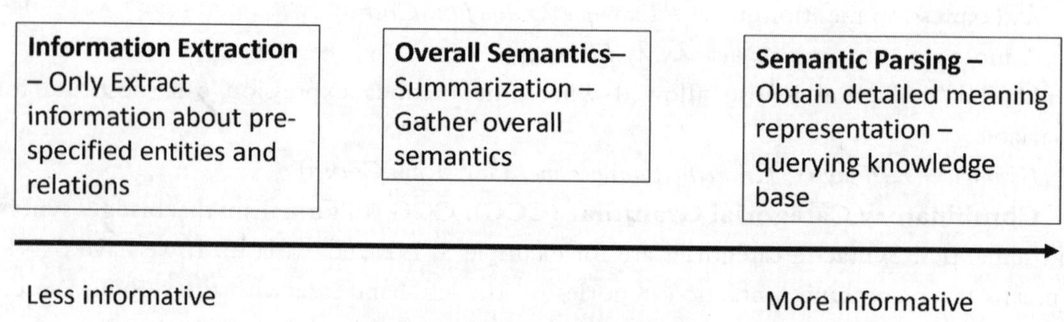

Figure 12.2: Levels of Information from Language

questions based on the content and perform reasoning and inference based on the content. Semantic processing is challenging because multiple linguistic expressions (sentences) can have the same meaning and requires to have the same semantic representation and in addition, single linguistic expression can have multiple meanings and requires ambiguity resolution so different meanings result in different semantic representations. Moreover, language is associated with complex interactions where the presence of different words can change the meaning of others. In addition, due to the above characteristics it is necessary to deal with large input space to learn and large output space to learn from. The general flow of semantic processing is shown in Figure 12.3. Here, we obtain a formal representation from the language which is stored in a knowledge base from which it can be queried and inferenced.

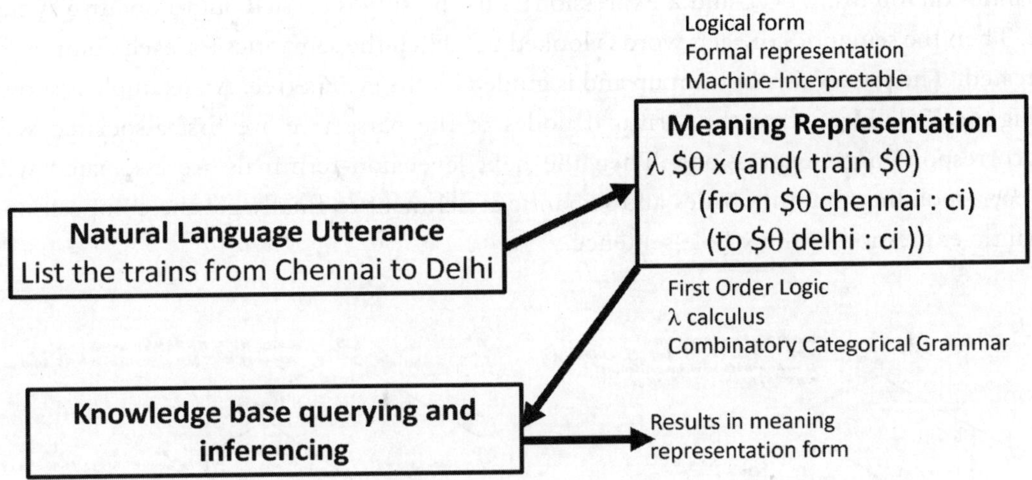

Figure 12.3: From Language to Inferencing

Semantic Processing can be tackled in three ways – a limited shallow information extraction approach where concepts are extracted without understanding the complete text, the principled theoretically motivated compositional semantic approach and finally the midway semantic role labelling approach. In this chapter, we will be discussing the last two approaches. On comparing semantic parsing and machine translation, both involve translating from one semantic representation into another and involve use of complex structures related in complex ways. Moreover, some of the techniques are needed by both such as co-occurrence analysis and sentence alignment. However, whereas in semantic parsing the target representation needs to be machine readable while in machine translation, the target representation needs to be human-readable following rules of natural language.

12.4 Compositional Semantics

Compositional analysis approach creates a logical representation that accounts for all the entities and relations present in a sentence. Compositionality involves discovering the meaning of a sentence from the meanings of parts and the manner of their combination. Usually in syntax- oriented languages that uses the syntax-oriented approach to compositional analysis, the parse tree and the sentence are fed to the semantic unit that is the semantic grouping and relations are derived from the parse tree. We can start with the parse tree and build semantics on top using FOL and λ expressions. First parsing is carried out to obtain a syntax tree. Then the semantics of each word is looked up. Then the semantics for each component is created. The process is a bottom up and is guided by the syntax tree. An example is shown in Figure 12.4. Here, first the terminal nodes of the parse tree are first associated with the corresponding λ expressions. Then the next level non-terminals are associated with the corresponding grammar rules and semantic attachment to finally get the compositional semantic expression of the whole sentence.

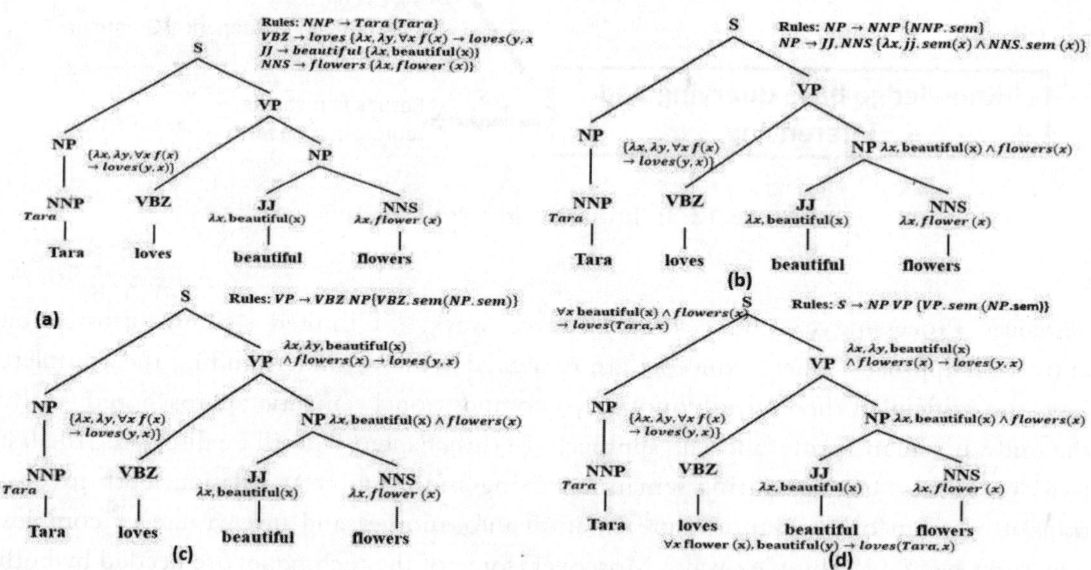

Figure 12.4: Compositional Semantics

12.5 Neural Semantic Parsing

Conversion of a natural language sentence into a machine-readable logical lambda representation can be carried out using neural networks. We need to learn a model which maps natural language input $I = x1 \cdots x|l|$ to a logical form representation of its meaning $O = y1 \cdots y|m|$. The input

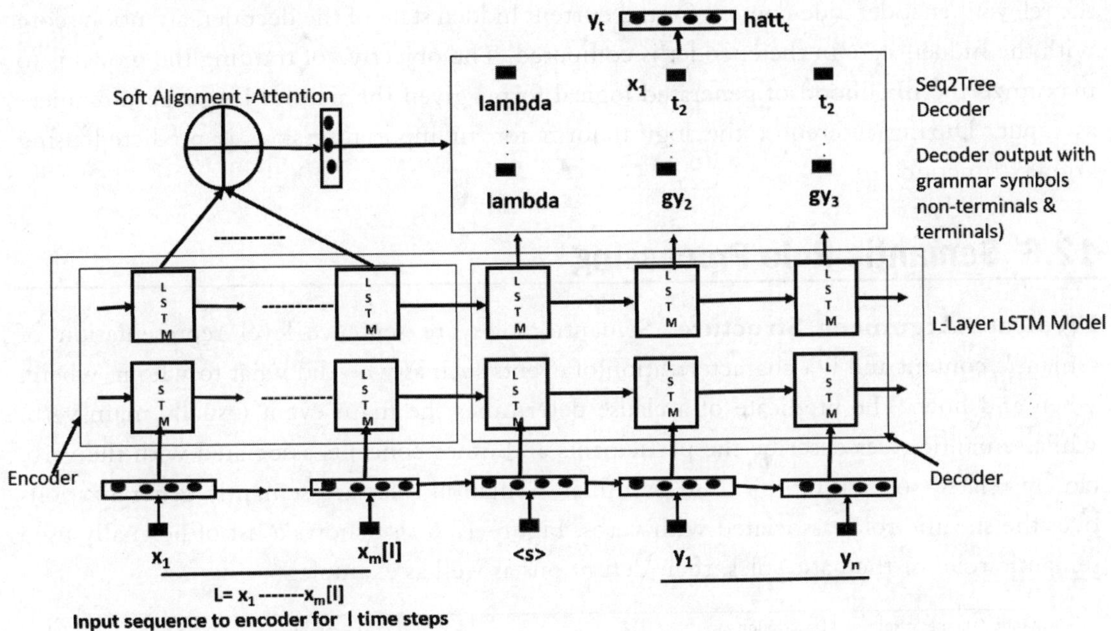

Figure 12.5: Neural Semantic Parser

I and output O are considered as sequences. The encoder and decoder are two different 2-layer recurrent neural networks with long short-term memory (LSTM) units which recursively process tokens one by one. The first $|l|$ time step is carried out by the encoder, and the subsequent $|m|$ time steps are carried out by the decoder.

The neural sequence parser with attention mechanism is shown in Figure 12.5 The tokens of the input sequence $x_1, \cdots x|l|$ are encoded into l vectors. However, the traditional encoder–decoder based Seq2Seq model ignores the hierarchical structure of logical forms. In other words, it fails to utilize bracket pairs to generate well-formed output. Therefore, the Seq2Tree decoder is designed as a hierarchical tree decoder in order to capture the compositional nature of meaning representations. The decoder generates logical forms in a top-down manner and the hierarchical tree structure is tackled using "nonterminal" tokens to indicate subtrees. Here the tree is obtained by replacing tokens between pairs of brackets with non-terminals. After encoding input q, the hierarchical tree decoder uses the decoder to generate tokens at depth 1 of the subtree corresponding to parts of logical form. This process terminates when no more non-terminals are generated and the logical form consists only of terminals. In this manner, the Seq2Tree model hierarchically generates the tree structure. In the decoder the current hidden state does not only depend on its previous time step but also a non-terminal parent-feeding connection where the hidden vector of the parent nonterminal is concatenated with the inputs and fed into LSTM. In order to find the relevant encoder-side context for the current hidden state of the decoder, attention score with the hidden state in the encoder is computed. The objective of training the model is to maximize the likelihood of generated logical forms given the natural language utterances as input. During inference, the logical form for an input utterance is predicted using argmax function.

12.6 Semantic Role Processing

Predicate–Argument Structure: Semantic roles are sentence-level representation of semantic content and is a characterization of events such as who did what to whom, where, when and how. The predicate of a clause determines the main event (usually main verb) while semantic roles describe the participants and other concepts associated with the verb, closely related to t Fillmore's Case grammar. Semantic roles are semantic generalizations over the specific roles associated with verbs. Figure 12.6 also shows a list of normally used semantic roles or thematic roles, their definitions as well as examples.

Semantic /Thematic Role	Description	Example
Agent	The volitional causer of an event	**The man** ate the mango.
Patient	An essential participant that undergoes change as a result of the event	**The man** ate **the mango.**
Experiencer	The experiencer of an event	**The girl** was hungry.
Force	The non-volitional causer of an event	**The tsunami** destroyed the ship.
Theme	The participant directly affected by an event	The girl kept **the toy** on the shelf.
Result	The end product of an event	The king built **the temple**
Content	The proposition or content of a propositional event	I enquired **"Did you see my mother?"**
Instrument	An instrument used in an event	The boy cut the apple with **a knife**
Beneficiary	The beneficiary of an event	I sang the song for **my friend.**
Source	The origin of the object of a transfer event	I travelled from **Chennai.**
Goal / Destination	The destination of the object of a transfer event	I went to **Delhi.**
Completion	A goal of a temporal process	I will study until **morning**
Duration	A resource of a temporal process	I cleaned the car for **4 hours**
Recipient	An animate goal of an act	I sent the cake to **Ram**
Location	The place at or in which an event takes place.	The purse was under **the bed**
Manner	Indicates how the event is being carried out	She sang the song **beautifully**

Figure 12.6: List of Semantic Roles with Examples

While grammatical relations such as subject, object, etc., are morpho-syntactic, thematic roles convey conceptual aspects. These roles help to generalize different surface realizations of predicate arguments. Semantic roles do not always correspond directly to grammatical relations (Figure 12.7 (a)). In other words, a semantic role is the underlying relationship between the main verb in a clause and other components of the clause.

Sentence	Grammatical Relation	Semantic Role
Ram broke the window with the bat	Ram = Subject	Ram=Agent
The bat broke the window	The bat= Subject	The bat = Instrument
The window broke	The window= Subject	The window = patient

(a)

The boy	broke	the toy	with	the hammer
Agent		*Theme*		*Instrument*
The hammer	broke	the toy		
Instrument		*Theme*		
The toy	broke			
Theme				
The toy	was broken	by	the boy	
Theme			*Agent*	

(b)

Figure 12.7: Grammatical Structures and Semantic Roles

The argument structure of a verb is the lexical information about the arguments of a predicate and their semantic and syntactic properties. Argument structure can be viewed as an intermediate structure between and syntactic-function structure and semantic-role structure. Argument structure indicates the argument positions of the lexical head of the predicate, in a syntactic structure. Semantic roles are useful because they help generalize and give the same semantic roles to arguments irrespective of different surface realizations (Figure 12.7 (b)). The number and type of arguments that the argument structure takes differs from verb to verb. In the English language some verbs are intransitive, transitive, and some di-transitive. Intransitive verbs take only a subject (example "she sleeps"), while transitive verbs take both a subject and an object (example "I hit the ball"), and ditransitive verbs take a subject, an object, and an indirect object (example "I gave Ram the book"). However, this type of classification of verbs is not valid for many languages.

Selectional Restrictions: Selectional restrictions are constraints that the verb imposes on the concepts that are allowed to fill the semantic roles of its arguments. For example, for the verb "eat", the constituent filling the semantic role of Theme should be "edible" In other words, "edible" is the selectional restriction of the semantic role Theme of verb "eat". Some typical examples of selectional restrictions include agents and beneficiaries should be animate, instruments should be tools, patients of "eat" should be edible and sources and destinations of "go" should be places. One way of representing these selectional restrictions is by incorporating this restriction as a predicate of FOL, however this approach is computationally expensive. Another approach is to state selectional restrictions in terms of synsets of WordNet. Taxonomic abstraction hierarchies or ontologies (e.g., hypernym links in WordNet as explained in preceding chapters) can be used to determine if such constraints are met. Many syntactic ambiguities like can be resolved using selectional restrictions.

12.6.1 Semantic Role Labelling Task

Semantic role labelling is the task of automatically identifying and labeling the thematic roles to the arguments of each verb in a sentence. Given a sentence and the parse of the sentence, consider each verb in the sentence and for each constituent associated with the verb we need to decide if that constituent is an argument of the verb and if it is, labelling the constituent with the appropriate semantic role. In some cases, syntactic cues can help in semantic role labelling although it provides only a preference. Semantic role is sometimes indicated by a particular syntactic position examples include grammatical relation agent indicates subject, direct object indicates patient, object of a particular preposition (object of "with" – instrument, object of "for" – beneficiary, object of "from" source, object of "to" goal). However, often the association of the object of a particular preposition to a particular semantic role is also influenced by selectional restrictions of the verb and the object.

However, acquiring all the selectional restrictions and taxonomic knowledge required for semantic role labelling is a difficult task. Moreover, effectively applying knowledge in an integrated fashion to simultaneously determine correct parse trees, word senses, and semantic roles is hard.

Semantic Role Labelling Pipeline: The general semantic role labelling pipeline consists of two steps – identification of words that are predicates and then identification and labelling of all the arguments for each predicate. If the sentence sequence has n predicates than the sequence needs to be processed n times. The argument identification could use rules based on full syntax trees, could use a binary classifier indicating if the sequence is an argument or not or could be a combination of both methods. After identification of arguments its labelling can be carried out using a classifier such as SVM or logistic regression where most of the features used is syntax based and we obtain a label distribution for each argument. Argmax over different roles determines the actual role, however there is no guarantee that the labelling is well formed. Therefore, statistical or empirical methods that can automatically acquire and apply the knowledge needed for effective and efficient semantic role labelling is required. Semantic role labelling can be treated as a sequence labeling problem where for each verb we can try to label the constituents of the verb with appropriate semantic roles. We can apply standard sequence labeling methods such as token classification or HMMs. As already discussed, parse trees can help identify semantic roles through exploiting syntactic clues. Given a syntactic parse of the sentence, for each predicate (verb), each node in the parse tree is labelled as either not-a-role or one of the possible semantic roles. We will discuss the machine learning approach of parse node classification for semantic role labelling in the next section.

12.6.2 Parse Node Classification for Semantic Role Labelling

Here we consider semantic role labelling as a parse-tree classification problem where any machine learning algorithm can be used but however, choosing the right set of features for the classifier is the important aspect. The common features used here are the *phrase type* that is the syntactic label of the candidate role filler (e.g., NP), *parse tree path* that is the path in the parse tree between the predicate and the candidate role filler, *position* that is whether the candidate role filler precedes or follows the predicate (verb) in the sentence, *voice* that is whether the predicate is in an active or passive voice, and the *head word* of the candidate role filler. Let us discuss the parse tree path further and then we will discuss an example highlighting these features (Figure 12.8). Parse node classification also has some disadvantages. Not all the useful features have been utilized. Some method can be used to enforce additional constraints (for example transitivity of verbs) and then, the most likely assignment of roles can be based on probability.

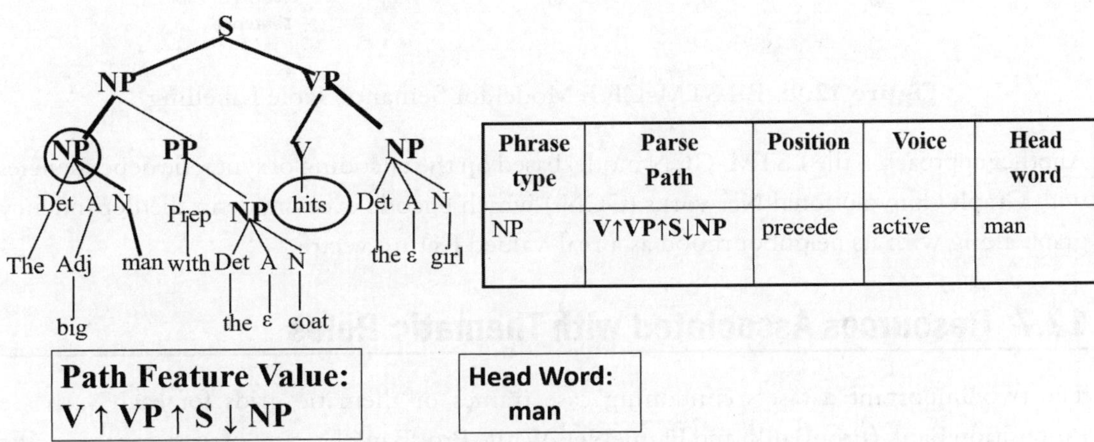

Phrase type	Parse Path	Position	Voice	Head word
NP	V↑VP↑S↓NP	precede	active	man

Figure 12.8: Features for Parse Node Classification

12.6.3 Neural Approaches to Semantic Role Labelling

The earliest neural approach to semantic role labelling considered it as a sequence labelling problem where argument identification and role labelling were carried out simultaneously. The BIO scheme (discussed in preceding chapter) was used for argument labelling. Here word encoding was carried out, sentence embedding was performed using LSTM and decoding resulted in the argument labelling. The approach did not use any syntax information and therefore did not need the costly process of encoding treebank syntax. Another similar BIO scheme based end-to-end learning approach to semantic role labelling was based on RNNs. Again the model did not use syntax information and here the sentence encoding was carried out using BiLSTM. Conditional Random Fields (CRF) layer was used for label prediction by focussing on sentence level information (Figure 12.9).

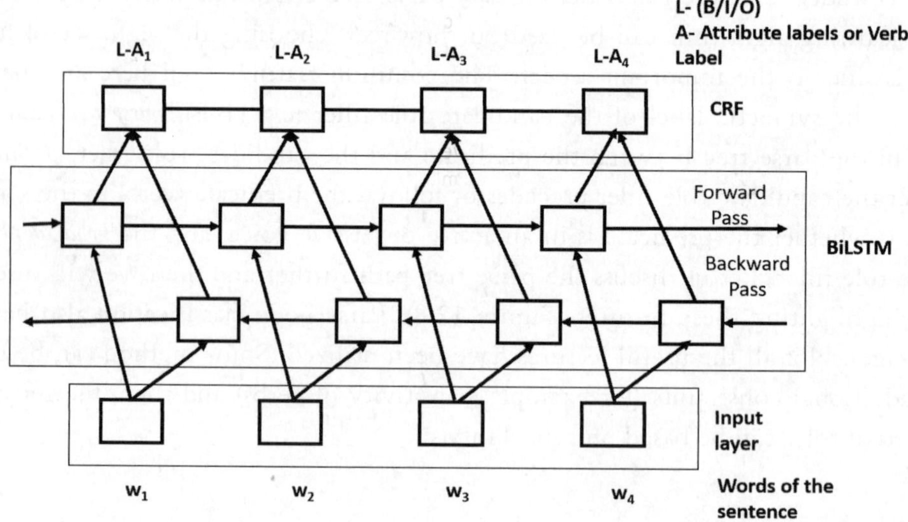

Figure 12.9: BiLSTM–CRF Model for Semantic Role Labelling

Another approach is the LSTM-GCN model based on the encoding of syntactic dependencies with Graph Convolutional Networks (GCNs) which encode every node in the dependency graph along with its neighbourhood as a real-valued feature vector.

12.7 Resources Associated with Thematic Roles

The two important datasets containing case frames or thematic grids for each verb are Proposition Bank (PropBank) and FrameNet. While PropBank has a set of verb-sense specific "frames" with informal English glosses describing the roles having many domain-specific variants, FrameNet is based on frame specific thematic roles or frame semantics and has a large number of frame-specific labels. Both these datasets have been described in Chapter 5. For each semantic predicate, identify the constituents in the tree that are arguments to that predicate. Let us re-look at an example using PropBank where the semantic roles are defined. In PropBank semantic roles are of two types – core semantic roles and modifier semantic roles (Figure 12.10 (a)). We see that "give" is a di- transitive verb and has three main roles and the other roles common to most verbs explaining the when, where, etc (Figure 12.10 (b)).

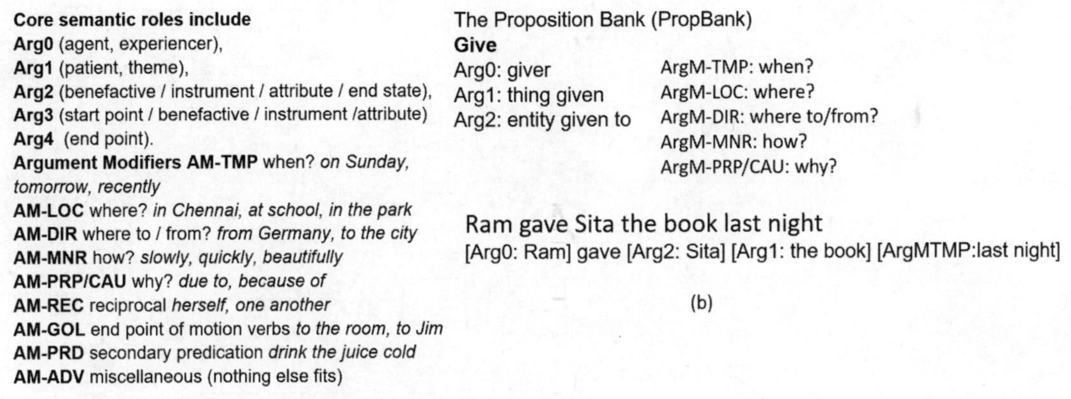

Figure 12.10: PropBank with an Example

Summary

- Outlined the basics of semantics.
- Defined meaning representation and explained its desirable qualities.
- Explained with examples the different components of First Order Logic representation and how it can be extended using Lambda notation.
- Briefly discussed combinatory categorical grammar.
- Outlined the concepts of semantic processing.
- Explained the various approaches to semantic processing.
- Outlined the neural approach to semantic parsing.
- Outlined the list of semantic roles with illustrative examples and described resources associated with it.

- Explained predicate argument structure, selectional restrictions and their connections to semantic role processing.
- Outlined briefly the semantic role labelling task and pipeline.
- Explained the parse node classification approach to semantic role labelling.
- Outlined neural approaches to semantic role labelling.

Exercises

Suggested Activities

1. Using either a language or software of your choice and available tools implement the use of deep learning for obtaining logic forms and semantic role labels from natural language text.

2. **Case Study – Semantic Role Labeling (SRL):** Using CoNLL-2005 https://paperswithcode.com/ or FrameNet dataset, identify and classify the predicate-argument structure in a sentence. Train models to label semantic roles for each argument of a predicate using techniques using Transformer-based model.

Self-Assessment: Multiple Choice Questions

Give answers with justification for correct and wrong choices:

1. Semantics involves
   - **i.** Generalization
   - **ii.** Dispersion
   - **iii.** Instantiation
2. One of the linking notion of semantics are the rich formal models called
   - **i.** Lexicon
   - **ii.** Dictionary
   - **iii.** Ontology
3. The formal explicit specification of a shared conceptualization is called
   - **i.** Semantics
   - **ii.** Ontology
   - **iii.** Meaning
4. Extrinsic approach to semantics is defined in terms of
   - **i.** Syntax
   - **ii.** Lexical meaning
   - **iii.** Things in the world
5. Desirable qualities of a meaning representation include
   - **i.** Verifiability, canonical form, unambiguity
   - **ii.** Verifiability, vagueness, unambiguity
   - **iii.** Verifiability, canonical form, ambiguity

6. Logic consists of
    i.   terms, predicates, connectives and quantifiers
    ii. terms, predicates, logical connectives and quantifiers
    iii. terms, logical connectives and quantifiers

7. Reference to an anonymous object from the domain is expressed by
    i.   Logical Quantifier
    ii. Universal Quantifier
    iii. Existential Quantifier

8. A way of writing anonymous functions by only defining the behavior is
    i.   Lambda Notation
    ii. Predicate Notation
    iii. Logical Notation

9. Discovering the meaning of a sentence from the meanings of parts and the manner of their grouping is called
    i.   First Order Logic
    ii. Compositionality
    iii. Propositional Logic

10. The capturing of the compositional and hierarchical nature of meaning representations is carried out by
    i.   Attention Mechanism
    ii. Seq2Tree Decoder Model
    iii. Seq2Seq Decoder Model

11. Semantic roles are
    i.   semantic initiations over the general roles associated with verbs
    ii. semantic generalizations over the specific roles associated with nouns
    iii. semantic generalizations over the specific roles associated with verbs

12. "The girl" in "The girl was hungry" is an example of
    i.   Experiencer role
    ii. Agent role
    iii. Patient role

13. ________ help to generalize different surface realizations of predicate arguments.
    i.   Grammatical relations
    ii. Semantic roles
    iii. Lexical relations

14. In the sentence "The window broke", the grammatical relation and semantic role associted with "The window" are

    i. Subject and Agent

    ii. Object and Instrument

    iii. Subject and Patient

15. Constraints that the verb imposes on the concepts allowed to fill the semantic roles of its arguments is called

    i. Selectional restrictions

    ii. Logical constraints

    iii. Semantic constraints

16. Semantic role labelling can be considered as a

    i. Semantic node classification problem

    ii. Parse-tree classification problem

    iii. Parse-tree completion problem

    iv. capture relationships between adjacent labels or tags

17. BiLSTM- CRF is an approach used for

    i. Semantic role labelling

    ii. Identifying predicates

    iii. Logical form processing

Self-Assessment: Match the Columns

No		Match	
1.	Ontology	A	deal with contextual meaning, inferred relationships, causality and granularity
2.	Compositionality	B	should be able to handle many ways of expressing the same meaning
3.	Sematic roles	C	formal explicit specification of a shared conceptualization
4.	First Order Logic	D	choosing the right set of features is the important aspect
5.	Lambda notation	E	involves discovering the meaning of a sentence from the meanings of parts and the manner of their combination
6.	Canonical form	F	constraints that the verb imposes on the concepts that are allowed to fill the semantic roles of its arguments

7.	Completion	G	provides a way of writing anonymous functions with no function header or function name but only defines the key aspect–the behavior of the function
8.	Selectional restrictions	H	Description of semantic role- A goal of a temporal process
No		**Match**	
9.	Parse node classification	I	semantic generalizations over the specific roles associated with verbs.
10.	Semantics	J	an extension of propositional logic where its predicates assert a relationship among entities

Short Questions

1. How do we define semantics and what are the two basic approaches to semantics?
2. Explain the desirable qualities a meaning representation should have.
3. Discuss in detail the various components of FOL representation with illustrative examples.
4. Outline the different aspects of semantic processing.
5. Given the example "The girl ate the apple', explain the process of obtaining compositional semantic expression with suitable diagrams. Assume and show the grammar used.
6. Explain a neural semantic parser in detail.
7. Give three examples that show that grammatical relations and semantic roles can be different.
8. Given the following sentences:
   i. The man ate the apple with a fork in the park in the evening.
   ii. The boy bought his friend a book.
   iii. I love singing for my friend.
   iv. I like to travel from Chennai to Puducherry by road.
   v. The floods damaged the garden badly.
   vi. Mark the arguments and identify their semantic roles.
9. Outline the pipeline for semantic role labelling and explain why semantic role labelling is difficult.
10. Discuss the process of parse node classification for semantic role labelling in detail.
11. Describe the BiLSTM-CRF model used for semantic role labelling.
12. What are the resources based on semantic roles? Discuss one such resource with an example.

Discourse, Dialogue and ChatGPT

CHAPTER 13

13.1 Basics of Discourse

Discourse conveys the coherent structure of language which is above the level of words, clauses or sentences. Discourse is a linguistic unit and is a group of collocated and coherent sentences that is these multiple sentences have meaningful connections between them. Discourse can be classified based on number of participants as either monologue or dialogue (conversation), or based on mode of interaction as in text or speech. In this chapter, we will be dealing with text only. Discourse analysis comprehends and generates language based on the context. Computational discourse analysis (CDA) is a branch of linguistics that uses computational methods to study how language is used in different contexts and for different purposes. In general discourse, segmentation is the separation of a documents into a linear sequence of subtopics. There are multiple kinds of linguistic context associated with discourse such as **discourse context** (where an utterance sits in relation to a document, conversation, speech, etc.) **physical context, and social context** such as the person speaking, the audience and the objective of the discourse. One important component of cohesion in discourse analysis is discourse segmentation where given a raw text, the document is separated into a linear sequence of subtopics or units. Relations between words in two units (sentences, paragraphs) hold them together. A discourse is composed of three main parts, the first and most important being the social context, the next being the important details and third and least important being other general information.

NLP is used to discover the linguistic structure of a group of sentences which in turn can support many applications such as text summarization, information extraction, question answering, etc. Discourse Processing identification of the structure of topic, coherence, co-reference and in some cases conversation structures. Discourse mechanisms deal with longer-range analysis based on the coherence of thought rather than word or sentence based semantic analysis. Discourse is associated with two aspects namely cohesion and coherence.

13.2 Cohesion and Coherence

Cohesion and coherence are concepts used in discourse analysis to describe the properties of a text that helps in readability and effective idea communication.

13.2.1 Cohesion

Cohesion is the grammatical and lexical relationship between different elements of a text that enables the structural elements of the text to behave as a whole. Cohesion is conveyed by formal linguistic elements such as repetition and reference and the semantic relationships between sentences and within sentences determined by lexical and grammatical relationships. The main three types of features used for discourse cohesion and coherence are lexical overlap or lexical chains, coherence chains and cue words or discourse markers. Lexical chains are sequences of words or lexical units that are semantically related, independent of the grammar structure of the text. These lexical units may be connected through different semantic relationships, such as synonymy, antonymy, hyponymy or meronymy. Coherence chain on the other hand link the sentence–to–sentence topic sequence of the whole document. Discourse markers are words or phrases that link phases or sentences and help in connecting, managing and organizing the text, without changing its general meaning. Discourse markers are used in many ways such as to mark the beginning of a new part of the conversation (example -so), a change in focus (example – well), shift in focus (example – anyway), response (example-right).

Discourse segmentation can be carried out using supervised machine learning where the labelled instances have place markers between sentences, paragraphs or clauses which are marked as yes or no depending on whether the place markers are discourse boundaries or not. The features that can be used for this learning task include discourse markers or cue words, word overlaps, number of coreference chains that cross boundaries, etc.

13.2.2 Coherence

Coherence is a very general principle of interpretation of the text in context where mainly semantic relationships deal with text as a whole. Thus, coherence makes the concepts and ideas conveyed by the text make sense to the reader and writer of the text and makes the text conceptually behave as a whole. Coherence relations are meaningful relationships between the sentences in discourse. These coherence relations reveal the structure of the discourse. Some of examples of the relations associated with coherence are as follows:

Here we assume that S_0 and S_1 are two sentences that come one after another.

- **Explanation:** In this type of relation, we infer that a state or an event conveyed by S_1 causes the state or event conveyed by S_0.

  Example: I went to the restaurant **because** I was hungry.

- **Occasion**: A change of state can be inferred from the information conveyed by S_0 and whose final state can be inferred from S_1, or vice versa.

  Example: Ram went home to get dressed. Then he went to his friend's party.

- **Parallel**: Here we infer a set of facts conveyed by S_0 and another similar set of facts conveyed by S_1.

  Example: Ram wanted a ball and Geetha wanted a doll.

13.2.2.1 Rhetoric Structure Theory (RST)

Rhetorical structure theory is a descriptive theory where the notion of nuclei and satellites is the foundation, a hierarchical structure to define discourse and the coherent relations that link the minimal units of text called spans are also called as rhetorical relations in the Rhetoric Structure theory or RST. RST addresses text organization by means of these relations and offers an explanation of the coherence of texts by postulating a hierarchical, connected structure of texts. Rhetorical relations hold between arguments called a **nucleus** and a **satellite**. Some relations (for example, List) have multiple nuclei but no satellite. Spans that are more central to the purpose of the text is called nuclei while satellites are secondary for the purpose. Spans are joined into discourse relations and in turn Spans that are already in a discourse relation may enter into new relations resulting in a hierarchical or recursive structure.

Relations: Every relation consists of four components **constraints** on the nuclei, constraints on the satellites, constraints on the combination of nuclei and satellites and effects that in essence describe the goals and beliefs of the reader and writer and the effect of the utterance on the reader. We will define some of the rhetorical relations in this section. Rhetorical relations can broadly be classified as subject matter relations, multi-nuclear relations and presentational relations. Here we give only few examples of relations in each class.

Subject Matter Relations

Subject matter are informational relations where the effect is to make the reader recognize the relation in question.

Circumstance: Nucleus (N) is the span expressing the events or ideas associated with the interpretative context while interpretive context of situation or time is the satellite (S).

Example: While I was working in the factory (S), I saw the girl (N).

Condition: Action or situation (N) that results only on occurrence of the condition (S).

Example: You will get first rank (N) only if you study well (S).

Elaboration: S presents additional detail about the situation or some element of subject matter which is presented in N.

Example: Cricket players are popular (N). I like Dhoni (S).

Multi-Nuclear Relations

RST relations having spans with equal importance are known as multi- nuclear relations.

List: An item (N_1) and another item (N_2).

Example: I like to play cricket (N_1). I adore Sachin Tendulkar. (N_2).

Sequence: An item (N_1) and the next item (N_2).

Example: I fried the onions (N_1), added the vegetables (N_2) and then poured the water (N_3).

Contrast: One alternative (N_1) and another alternative (N_2).

Example: I like to play cricket (N_1) but he likes to play football. (N_2).

Joint: Two unconstrained text spans (N_1 & N_2).

Example: The oranges were sour (N_1) and they were costly (N_2).

Presentational Relations

Presentational relations are intended by way of satellites to increase some perspective of the reader, such as the desire to act or the degree of positive regard for, belief in, or acceptance of the nucleus.

Background: Text (N) whose understanding is facilitated by another text (S).

Example: I wrote all the answers correctly and in time (S). I got first rank (N).

Justify: (N) A text and (S) information supporting the writer's right to express the text.

Example: I don't like maths (N). It is very difficult (S).

Enablement: An action (N) and information to aid in performing the action (S).

Example: Take the form from the table (S) and fill it (N).

Motivation: An action (N) and information to increase the desire to perform the action (S).

Example: Eat healthy food (N). Healthy food helps you to reduce weight (S).

Schemas: Schemas are abstract patterns that define the structure of text. These schemas defined in terms of relations specify the way in which the spans of text co-occur. Five types of schemas are defined as given in Figure 13.1.

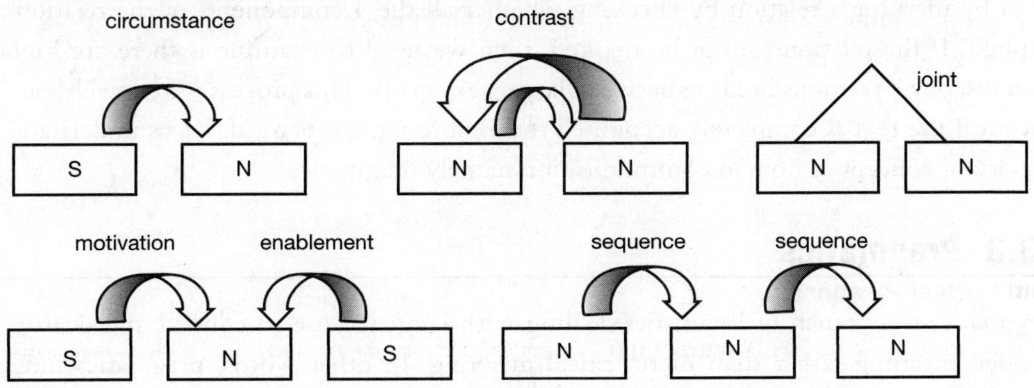

Figure 13.1 Examples of the Five Types of Schemas

RST Tree: In the RST framework, a text's discourse structure is represented as a tree with four types of components namely the leaves that correspond to minimal discourse units, the internal nodes of the tree that correspond to contiguous text spans where each node is characterized by its nucleus (the essential unit of information) and this node is also characterized by a rhetorical relation between two or more non–overlapping, adjacent text spans.

Discourse Treebank: The Rhetorical Structure Theory (RST) Discourse Treebank consists of 385 Wall Street Journal articles taken from the Penn Treebank and annotated with discourse structure associated with the RST framework. However, the Penn Discourse Tree Bank (PDTB) v 2.0 is a theory independent annotation of corpus of 2304 articles from Wall Street Journal with text spans of connectives and their arguments and features encoding the semantic classification of connectives, and attribution of connectives and their arguments.

13.2.3 Automatic Coherence Assignment

When given a sequence of sentences or clauses, coherenace assignment involves coherence relation assignment between two components of the sequence and discourse parsing which is the extraction of the discourse tree or graph to represent the entire dicourse. One simple existing approach to automatic coherance assignment is the identification of cue phases in the text, segmentation of text into discourse segments based on cue phrases and then relation based classification of the segments. In the case of RST analysis, the text is first segmented into units which may be Elementary Discourse Unit (EDU) such as clauses/ sentences or Complex Discourse Unit (CDU) such as paragraph/document. Each unit and its neighbours are examined to determine and mark the discourse relation holding between them by marking a relation by checking whether all the 4 components of the relation are satisfied. If the relation cannot be marked, then we need to examine is there are higher-level discourse relations holding between larger text spans. This process is iteratively carried out until the text is completely accounted for. Before we go forward, let us understand an important concept of human communication namely pragmatics.

13.3 Pragmatics

Pragmatics is a branch of linguistics dealing with language use in context and deals with implied meaning rather than mere lexical meaning. In other words, pragmatics indicate how humans make sense when they communicate and explores how the context in which something is uttered influences its meaning. In this scenario, context can be divided into four types:

- **Social context:** This context indicates social identities, relationships, and setting.
- **Physical context:** This context indicates the location, the surrounding and actions.
- **Linguistic context:** This context indicates conversation history, discourse context.
- **Other forms of context** indicate shared knowledge, etc.

13.4 Dialogue Systems

Dialogue Systems or Conversational Agents are designed to carry on a conversation with a human user. Basically, there are two types – **Task-based Dialogue Systems** that are designed to help human user to accomplish a particular task such as booking a ticket and **Chatbots** that are designed a casual conversation with the human user. In discourse, the speaker communicates to a passive audience, in order to enable them to construct a similar model of the state of affairs without receiving any feedback from the audience. On the other hand, in dialogue, both the speaker and the listener are present and active participants. Each participant has their own mental model of the state of affairs and the communication succeeds if there is grounding in dialogues where both parties are able to understand the mental models of each other.

Properties of Human Conversation: Conversation between humans is an intricate and complex joint activity. Let us understand how humans converse with each other. Consider some of the phenomena that occur in the conversation between a human travel agent and a human client.

Speech Acts: A key insight into conversation was given by Austin (1962) and later on modified by Searle (1969) where each utterance in a dialogue is a kind of action being performed by the speaker. These actions are commonly called as speech acts or dialogue acts. In other words, a speech act is any utterance that serves a function in communication. While the locutionary act is the actual act of uttering, the illocutionary act refers to the type of speech act that is being performed, this is, the function that the speaker intends to fulfil. The perlocutionary part, on the other hand, is the *effect* that an utterance could have on the hearer or addressee. The classification of speech acts by Searle is given in Table 13.1.

Searle's Speech Act Classification (1979)			
Speech Act	**Illocutionary Point**	**Examples**	**Example Sentences**
Assertives	To commit the speaker to something being the case (truth value)	Assertions, statements, claims, hypothesis	I am happy about the job
Directives	Attempts by the speaker to get the hearer to do something	Commands, requests, invitations	I advise you to work hard.
Commissives	Commit the speaker to some future course of action	Promises, pledges, vows	I promise you that I will finish the job.
Expressives	Express a psychological state	Congratulations, apologies, condolences	I am sorry about the result.
Declarations	These speech acts, they create new states of affairs by representing them as being the case.	Baptisms, marrying, hiring/firing, terminating a contract	I married her yesterday.

Table 13.1: Classification of Speech Acts

Grounding occurs if there exists a set of **mutually agreed beliefs** among the participants in a dialogue. Here both the participants provide feedback to each other. The two participants of a dialogue contribute to the conversation by establishing and adding to the common ground. When two participants P and Q are taking part in a dialogue there is a need for Q to provide evidence to P that Q has understood what was conveyed by P. This can be indicated by Q by continuing to listen to P, by Q continuing with a relevant next contribution (example – so what now?), an acknowledgement by Q, a demonstration that Q has understood by paraphrasing or repeating what P has conveyed.

Turns: A dialogue is a sequence of turns each a single contribution from one speaker to the dialogue.

Side-sequences or Sub-dialogues and Dialogue Structure: Conversations have structure. Consider, for example, the local structure between conversational speech acts. There are adjacency pairs associated with dialogue where examples include Questions set up an expectation of an Answer, Proposals are often followed by Acceptance (or Rejection). However, sometimes the two components of the adjacency pair may be separated by a side sequence or sub-dialogue.

Pre-sequences: In some cases, questions often have pre-sequences, where a user starts with a question about the capabilities before making an actual request.

Initiative: Initiative indicates who has control over the dialogue. Sometimes a conversation is completely controlled by one participant. However, in normal human–human dialogue, it is common to have **mixed initiative** where the focus shifts back and forth between the participants. While mixed initiative is common in actual human–human conversations, it to achieve this for an automated dialogue system.

Inference and Implicature: Inference is also important in dialogue understanding. Here the speaker expects the hearer to draw certain inferences, that is understand more information than is actually conveyed by the words uttered. This is indicated by Grice theory of conversational implicature. Grice proposed that what enables hearers to draw these inferences is that conversation is guided by a set of maxims, general heuristics that play a guiding role in the interpretation of conversational utterances. One such relevance maxim is the maxim of relevance which says that speakers attempt to be relevant, they don't just utter random speech acts. These subtle characteristics of human conversations (speech acts, grounding, turns, dialogue structure, initiative, and implicature) are among the reasons it is difficult to build dialogue systems that can carry on natural conversations with humans.

13.5 Task Based Dialogue Systems

Task oriented dialogue systems are capable of performing a **task-driven dialogue** with a human user. Such tasks include making travel or hotel reservations, telephone call routing, customer support systems, scheduling a meeting, tutoring systems, etc. Task-oriented dialogue acts can be related to negotiation such as suggestion (I recommend this flight), offer (I will pack it for you), acceptance (Sure. I will book the room) and rejection (No. I cannot book that room). Normally, these systems are speech to speech systems and consist of the following modules – takes input from ASR (speech recognizer) and NLU components, maintains some sort of internal state, interfaces with task manager and passes output to natural language generation or text-to-speech modules. The simplest type of task-based dialogue system was the Air Travel Information Service (ATIS) where given an utterance, a reply is predicted using a simple slot-filling solutions. If the purpose of the dialog is to complete a specific **task** (e.g., book a plane ticket), that task can often be represented as a **frame** with a number of **slots** to fill. A **frame** is set of **slots**, each to be filled with information of a given **type** and associated with a **question** to the user (Table 13.2). Here, a very restricted knowledge structure representing possible user intentions for the given task is assumed to be available. The slots indicate what questions to ask, and task would only be completed if all necessary slots are filled. Here, some slots are mandatory while others are optional.

Airline Reservation System (Slot-Filler)		
Slot	**Semantic Type**	**Question**
Origin	city	What city are you leaving from?
Destination	city	Where are you going?
Departure Date	date	What day would you like to leave?
Departure Time	time	What time would you like to leave?
Airline	airways	Which airline would you prefer?

Table 13.2: Slot-filler Scheme

The semantic type indicates the semantic type of the answer. During the task, the human user may give some information about the task. This information is used to fill the slots and for those mandatory slots that are left unfilled, the system asks relevant questions resulting in a mixed-initiative dialogue. Depending on the complexity of the task, multiple frames can be triggered and filled with appropriate task-oriented dialogue. The dialogue manager of the task-based dialogue system can be rule-based where it acts based on keywords where the dialogue is a path through a tree or finite state graph structure given in the form of rules. This manager can be statistical where the transition rules are learnt from a corpus of similar task dialogues.

13.6 Chatbots

The simplest types of dialogue systems are conversational agents or chatbots. These chatbots can carry on extended unstructured conversations with humans thereby mimicking the characteristics of human–human conversations. While taking part in a conversation Grice specified four maxims that are to be followed:

- **Maxims of Quantity:** Make your contribution to the conversation as informative as necessary.
- **Maxims of Quality:** Do not say what you believe to be false.
- **Maxim of Relation:** Be relevant.
- **Maxims of Manner:** Avoid obscurity of expression. Avoid ambiguity. Be brief. Be Orderly

Rule-based Chatbots: It is interesting to note the very first NLP system is the chatbot system ELIZA. ELIZA was developed in 1966 at the MIT Artificial Intelligent Laboratory by Joseph Weizenbaum. It is pattern–action rule-based system and simulates conversations based on hand-craft scripts that mimic a Rogerian psychotherapist. When a patient chats with ELIZA, the input text is analyzed looking for the presence of a keyword, and then the rule associated with the keyword generates responses. While ELIZA is able to carry on a conversation, however its ability to communicate and scope of its knowledge are limited. A sample of a conversation with ELIZA is given in Figure 13.2.

```
ELIZA : Hello, I am ELIZA.
You    : I am angry.
ELIZA : Why are you angry?
You    : I am angry that I did not win.
ELIZA : Why did you not win?
You    : I do not know
ELIZA : Did you enjoy not knowing?
You    : Are you angry?
ELIZA : We are taking about you
You    : ...........
```

Figure 13.2 A Sample Script from ELIZA

Another well-known chatbot developed by Colby in 1975 is PARRY which also simulates how a human would behave in a text-based conversation using a simple pattern-matching algorithm similar to ELIZA but was incorporated with a personality and a better controlling structure and moreover was able to pass the Turing Test. ALICE created in 2005 was the first online chatbot and pattern matched with 41,000 templates to generate responses.

Corpus-based Retrieval based Chatbots: Another method of building chatbots is by mining a huge amount of human–human conversations. For this purpose, datasets have been created by crowd sourcing, often instructing them to use personas and the knowledge provided. Datasets are also gathered from large pseudo-conversations happening on Twitter and other social media platforms. Another common practice is to extract possible responses from knowledge sources such as Wikipedia. Moreover, the turns that humans take when carrying on conversations can also be used for training. Many corpus-based chatbots produce responses to a user's turn in context by retrieval methods where information is retrieved based on some corpus that is appropriate given the dialogue context. Corpus-based chatbot algorithms thus draw on that focus on single responses not considering overall long-term conversational goals. The retrieval system assumes that the user's turn gives rise to a query q, and the task is to retrieve with a response r from the available corpus C. Here, we score the various potential responses obtained from the corpus C based on the context q and the tf–idf similarity between r and q.

13.7 ChatGPT

We will now discuss a widespread chatbot used today. OpenAI released ChatGPT a free to use application of NLP in November 2022. A large variety of domains has utilized ChatGPT and has become one of the game changers in the use of NLP both for the common man and for many businesses. Basically, ChatGPT utilizes natural language processing to create humanlike conversational dialogue that can respond to questions and compose various written content, including articles, social media posts, essays, code and emails.

13.7.1 ChatGPT and ChatGPT Plus

The free to use ChatGPT is currently based on the GPT model GPT-3.5. GPT models are based on transformer-based architecture, which handle sequential text data and uses a stack of transformer encoder layers to analyse and comprehend text in a highly parallelized manner (discussed earlier in Chapter 9). Pre-training involves training a sizable quantity of textual data to pre-train the language model to generally comprehend the underlying patterns, syntax, and contextual relationships in the text. The model is refined on downstream tasks after pre-training, allowing it to perform well in a variety of NLP applications, including text generation, translation, sentiment analysis, and more. The GPT model carries out two kinds of prediction tasks namely next-token prediction where the model when given a sequence of words is able to forecast the next word and masked-word prediction where again given a sequence of words is able to predict a "masked" word in the sequence. The GPT-3.5 version of the model has over 175 billion parameters. The GPT-3.5 has the same transformer design as its forerunners, but it has a much bigger model size with over 175 billion parameters and can absorb more complex linguistic subtleties and produce replies that are more logical and contextually accurate because of the larger model size and moreover the model allows lesser toxic content.

The current version of the GPT that is ChatGPT Plus used GPT-4 which is incorporated into a subscription-based version of ChatGPT. GPT-4 is a multimodal model which accepts and interprets both image and text inputs including different styles of text to generate text outputs up to 25,000 words at a time in any style in multiple language. It displays almost human-level performance on various professional and academic oriented tasks since it can be a direct instruction. ChatGPT Plus is based on the GPT-4 model and has plugins for maths, science, language, media and business. ChatGPT Plus can be integrated with web browser and has a code interpreter that can run and display Python Programs.

13.7.2 Concepts of ChatGPT

The key components of ChatGPT are the hidden or latent space, foundation or pre-trained models, prompts, generative architectures and fine tuning.

Latent space is a lower-dimensional compressed representation of data that captures its essential features. The first step in pre-processing for language models like GPT-4 involves breaking text into smaller chunks or tokens which can be character, word or longer span and building a statistical distribution model created from its very large training set. This vector embedding based representation of text converts variable-length text into fixed-size vectors in high-dimensional space which captures semantic meaning and relationships and enables mathematical similarity calculation. In essence, the latent space of this model captures the underlying structure and deviations in the original high-dimensional data space in which similar data points are closer together in space which enables the capture of important features of the data. This makes the representation useful for learning data features and for finding simpler representations of data for analysis. Moreover, new data points that are similar to data points in the training data can be generated because the representation learns to plot data points from the latent space back to the original space. The smooth interpolation between data points enables creative exploration of the capabilities of the generative model which is possible because the gradual change in the generated data is obtained from small changes in the latent coordinates and the facility to perform meaningful manipulations over data. Moreover, the model learns to differentiate the several causes of differences such as style and content and adapt these factors between different samples.

Foundation or Pre-trained Models: The foundation model or Large Language Models (LLMs) used by ChatGPT such as GPT-3.5 or GPT4 is trained on a large amount of data.

Knowledge is gathered in the form of a vast volume of text from information publicly available on the internet, licensed from third parties, and provided by human trainers and represented as vector embeddings in the latent space. LLMs use massive corpora and uses natural language processing to understand and generate humanlike text-based content in response. It achieves contextual understanding and has memory units in their architectures. The function next word prediction is used to store and retrieve relevant information which enables production of coherent and contextually accurate responses. This foundation model is a task independent model that learns general characteristics of natural language and is adaptable or fine tunable for the creation of specialized models and generation of multiple applications.

Generative Pre-trained Transformer (GPT): Generative architectures are the building blocks that enable generative modeling. GPT is a transformer–based model which is an encoder-decoder architecture, can automatically transform one type of input into another type of output for NLP tasks (discussed in Chapter 8). Attention mechanism of GPT enables the capturing of dependencies between different parts of the input text. Applications include Generating coherent and contextually relevant text, text completion, question answering, translation, summarization.

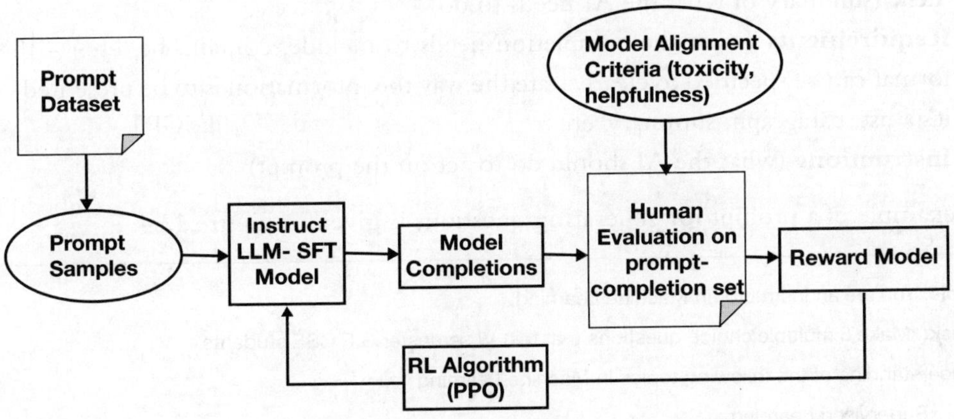

Figure 13.3 Architecture of ChatGPT

Fine–Tuning: As discussed, the foundation model is GPT-3.5 or GPT-4 adaptable or fine tunable to the creation of specialized models and generation of multiple applications. Fine tuning is performed with Reinforcement Learning with Human Feedback (RLHF) that aligns ChatGPT to human preferences. By utilizing small amounts of feedback from a human evaluator it is possible to guide the understanding of the goal and the appropriate reward function. Let us discuss the flow of the RLHF in detail (Figure 13.3). Initially, an instructive LLM with acceptable performance for some tasks is chosen to carry out supervised fine-tuning. The pre-trained language model is fine-tuned on a relatively small amount of demonstration data curated by labelers, to learn a supervised policy (the SFT model) that generates outputs from a selected list of prompts. This represents the baseline model. Then labelers are asked to score a relatively large number of the SFT model outputs completions based on alignment criteria like helpful, honesty and harmlessness. This way a new dataset consisting of comparison data is created mimicking human preferences. A new model is trained on this dataset called reward model. The reward model is used to further fine-tune and improve the SFT model. The outcome of this step is the so-called Proximal Policy Optimization model.

Prompt: Prompts are the defining component of ChatGPT Plus and is essential for obtaining accurate and relevant outputs from AI models. Some general guidelines for prompting for useful completions include the need for prompts to be in natural language, to be clear, avoiding ambiguity and using precise and specific keywords or phrases that provide relevant context or background information to help the model. Relevant samples can be included to show the type of output needed. It is important to neutrally frame the prompts to avoid unintentional bias. One good structure to be used for most prompts consists of the following four components:

- **Role** (act as…)
- **Task** (summary of what the AI needs to do)
- **Requirements** (what the completion needs to include, contain, be, etc.) – the desired format can be specified to clearly state the way the information is to be presented– whether it's a list, paragraph, summary, etc.
- **Instructions** (what the AI should do to act on the prompt)

An example of a prompt for generating questions is given in Figure 13.4.

Role: You are an Instructor in Machine Learning.

Task: Make 3 multiple choice questions that test VI semester B.E CSE students understanding of the following topics in Machine Learning

- Supervised Learning
- Overfitting
- Clustering

Requirements: For each question, provide the correct answer and then write feedback to students about the correct and incorrect options.

Instructions: Link the topics together in your feedback to help students connect ideas together.

In your feedback, provide questions that encourage students to explore these ideas more themselves, instead of giving them the answer directly.

* Please note that component names are not part of the prompt.

Figure 13.4 Example of a Prompt for Question Generation

13.7.3 Architecture of ChatGPT

The ChatGPT architecture is as shown in Figure 13.5. Here knowledge is gathered in the form of a vast volume of text from information publicly available on the internet, licensed from third parties, and provided by human trainers. The text is represented as vector embeddings, a distributed representation of text which is in numerical form that enables the capturing the semantic meaning and relationships and also enable mathematical similarity calculation. The attention mechanism permits the capture of dependencies between different parts of the input text and generates contextually relevant responses by allowing focusing on specific words or tokens in the input sequence while generating the output. The Foundation model used by ChatGPT such as GPT-3.5 or GPT4 is trained on a large amount of data and is adaptable or fine tunable to the creation of specialized models and generation of multiple applications. Fine tuning is performed with Reinforcement Learning with Human Feedback (RLHF) that aligns ChatGPT to human preferences. by utilizing small amounts of feedback from a human evaluator to guide the understanding of the goal and the appropriate reward function.

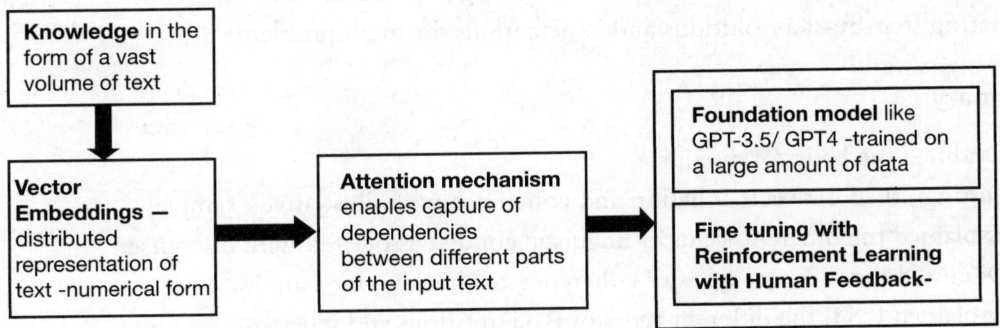

Figure 13.5 Architecture of ChatGPT

13.7.4 Advantages and Disadvantages of ChatGPT

One of the major advantages of ChatGPT is that it has been trained on a wide variety, lots of genre and various languages. The training of large language models with huge volume of data gives it the advantage of understanding of the context of the input it receives. One of the disadvantages of ChatGPT include that it can be biased if the data provided to it is not representative of the real world. ChatGPT has another disadvantage that some of the responses generated may not be logical or reasonable. Another major disadvantage is that it lacks the ability to infer and hence cannot solve complex problems or answer complex questions.

13.7.5 Applications of ChatGPT

ChatGPT has gained popularity and widespread adoption making it the fastest-growing consumer application in history. This is because ChatGPT goes beyond mere repetition by incorporating a deeper understanding of the input, generating unique responses that align with the flow of the conversation rather than pattern-based output. ChatGPT's learning from massive amounts of data, innovative approach and creativity make it suitable for a vast array of real-world applications. ChatGPT applications include supporting developers to write simple code snippets. Quality of custom enterprise software can be improved through fraud detection. ChatGPT can export ideas across a variety of topics but however the quality and relevance of ideas depend strongly on the way the context or constraints the prompt. ChatGPT can be used to helps users turn seemingly worthless raw unstructured data coming from multiple sources and extract patterns, trends, and relevant information, improving customer experience based on their behaviour. When provided topic, tone, styles, length, etc. ChatGPT is capable of content writing. ChatGPT is capable of generating a concise summary of the key information and main points from a long piece of text. ChatGPT can provide personalized and interactive studying experiences for maths learners capable of generating step-by-step solutions and explanations for math problems.

Summary

- Outlined the basics of discourse.
- Distinguished between cohesion and coherence with illustrative examples.
- Explained the different kinds of linguistic context associated with discourse.
- Discussed the different types of coherence relations with examples.
- Explained RST, the different types of RST relations and schemas.
- Outlined the process of automatic coherence assignment.
- Outlined the difference between Task-based Dialogue Systems and Chatbots.
- Outlined some of the properties of human conversation.
- Explained Searle's classification of speech acts.
- Described Task-based Dialogue Systems.
- Discussed the four maxims of Grice.
- Explained in detail the architecture of ChatGPT.

Exercises

Suggested Activities

1. Using ChatGPT, create a question bank according to Bloom's Taxonomy for a subject of your choice.

2. Develop a virtual research assistant for computer science research using ChatGPT. Include at least 4 capabilities you think a researcher will need.

3. **Case Study 1 – Educational Chatbot for Tutoring and Assistance:** Using Educational dialog datasets https://paperswithcode.com/, build a chatbot that can assist students with learning tasks, providing explanations, answering questions, and maintaining coherent discourse over multiple interactions. Train a discourse-aware chatbot using a combination of domain-specific knowledge and conversational AI techniques. Utilize datasets containing dialogues between students and tutors, annotated with discourse structure and educational content.

4. **Case Study 2 – Therapeutic Chatbot for Mental Health Support:** Using counseling chat logs (https://www.kaggle.com/datasets/thedevastator/synthetic-therapy-conversations-dataset), develop a chatbot capable of providing empathetic and supportive responses to users experiencing mental health challenges, maintaining a coherent and supportive discourse throughout the interaction. Train a discourse-aware chatbot using techniques from psychology, counseling, and natural language processing. Utilize datasets containing dialogues between therapists and clients, annotated with discourse strategies, empathetic responses, and therapeutic techniques.

Self-Assessment: Multiple Choice Questions

Give answers with justification for correct and wrong choices:

1. A group of collocated and coherent sentences is called
    i. Semantics
    ii. Syntax
    iii. Discourse
2. Discourse context indicates
    i. where an utterance sits in relation to a document, conversation, or speech
    ii. where an utterance is made in a physical environment
    iii. the person speaking, the audience and the objective of the discourse.
3. Cohesion is
    i. a very general principle of interpretation of the text in context where mainly semantic relationships deal with text as a whole

    ii. the grammatical and lexical relationship between different elements of a text that enables to behave as a whole

    iii. the pragmatics between different elements of a text that enables to behave as a whole

4. Coherence is considered as

    i. a very general principle of interpretation of the text in context where mainly semantic relationships deal with text as a whole

    ii. the grammatical and lexical relationship between different elements of a text that enables to behave as a whole

    iii. the pragmatics between different elements of a text that enables to behave as a whole

5. The relation where we infer a set of facts conveyed by one sentence and another similar set of facts conveyed by the succeeding sentence is the

    i. Explanation Relation

    ii. Parallel Relation

    iii. Justification Relation

6. Rhetorical relations hold between arguments called

    i. a nucleus and a satellite

    ii. a topic and sub–topic

    iii. discourse and context

7. Circumstance is an example of

    i. Subject matter relation

    ii. Multi–nuclear relation

    iii. Presentation relation

8. A branch of linguistics dealing with language use in context and deals with implied meaning is called

    i. Discourse

    ii. Cohesion

    iii. Pragmatics

9. Chatbots are designed to

    i. to help human user to accomplish a particular task

    ii. to have a casual conversation with the human user

    iii. to have a formal conversation with the human user

10. A single contribution from one speaker to the dialogue is called

    i. turn

    ii. grounding

    iii. initiative

11. Task oriented dialogue systems generally uses

    i. Lexical rules

    ii. Grammar rules

   iii. Slot-filler Scheme

12. The first chatbot designed was

    i. PARIS

    ii. ELIZA

   iii. ALICE

13. The ChatGPT is based on

    i. Generative Pre-Trained Transformers

    ii. General Pre-Trained Transformers

   iii. Generative Pre-Trained Text

14. ChatGPT uses reinforcement learning with human feedback for

    i. Pre-training

    ii. Fine-tuning

   iii. Interfacing

Self-Assessment: Match the Columns

No		Match	
1.	Discourse	**A**	mimic a Rogerian psychotherapist.
2.	Social context	**B**	A type of presentational relation.
3.	Pragmatics	**C**	interpretation of the text in context where semantic relations deal with text as a whole.
4.	Cohesion	**D**	transformer-based model.
5.	Coherence	**E**	descriptive theory where the notion of nuclei and satellites is the foundation.
6.	Background	**F**	refers to the type of speech act and the function that the speaker intends to fulfil.
7.	Rhetorical structure theory	**G**	linguistic unit which is a group of collocated and coherent sentences.
8.	Illocutionary act	**H**	conveyed between sentences and within sentences by lexical and grammatical relationships.
9.	ELIZA	**I**	the person speaking, the audience and the objective of the discourse.
10.	ChatGPT	**J**	deals with implied meaning rather than mere lexical meaning.

Short Questions

1. Outline the basic concepts of discourse.
2. Distinguish between cohesion and coherence with illustrative examples.
3. Explain the different kinds of linguistic context associated with discourse.
4. Discuss any five types of coherence relations with examples.
5. What is RST? Discuss.
6. Discuss the three types of RST relations with two examples of each.
7. Explain five types of RST schemas.
8. Outline the process of automatic coherence assignment.
9. Distinguish between Task-based Dialogue Systems and Chatbots.
10. Outline some of the properties of human conversation.
11. Explain Searle's classification of speech acts.
12. Write a short note on Task-based Dialogue Systems.
13. Discuss the four maxims of Grice.
14. Explain in detail the architecture of ChatGPT.
15. Outline the fine-tuning mechanism used by ChatGPT.
16. Give some examples of prompt that can be used for academic research.

Applications of NLP

CHAPTER 14

14.1 Introduction

In this chapter, we discuss some important applications of NLP such as machine translation, information extraction, question answering, summarization, sentiment analysis, and an example of domain-specific NLP – biomedical NLP. We discuss the task, different methods used for the task, and in most cases the evaluation strategies. We discuss machine learning and neural-based approaches to most tasks. We also touch upon the role of NLP for generative AI tasks and vice versa. It is to be noted that this set of applications is not exhaustive and more sophisticated applications as well as methodologies are continuously evolving.

14.2 Machine Translation

The first application we will discuss is machine translation which is also one of the initial NLP applications attempted. Machine Translation (MT) or automated translation is a process of translating text from one language (source language) to another (target language) without human involvement. Today, machine translation goes beyond simple word-to-word translation to communicate the full meaning of the original language text in the target language by analyzing all components of the text and understanding how the words interact with one another. Challenges associated with MT include the requirement for common sense understanding and the interpretation of idioms, the occurrence of typological differences and alignment issues between source and target languages, and the absence of large text data pairs, especially for low-resource languages.

History of MT: The timeline of machine translation is shown in Figure 14.1. The first infamous demonstration of automatic MT was the translation of selected 60 sentences from Russian to English by Georgetown University partnering with IBM in 1954 but the tool was not general enough for everyday use. It was in 1962 that the Association for Machine Translation and Computer Linguistics (now the Association for Computer Linguistics) was formed in the US. In 1966, the Automatic Language Processing Advisory Committee (ALPAC) published a report claiming that MT was too expensive to justify further research and funds. However, SYSTRAN, founded in 1968, utilized Rule-based MT (RBMT) for Russian–English translation. Rules-based machine translation used grammar and language rules, developed by language experts, and dictionaries, customized to a specific topic or industry. RBMT was time-consuming to create, the rules needed to be manually fed for each language and often generated inaccurate outputs for ambiguous or idiomatic text.

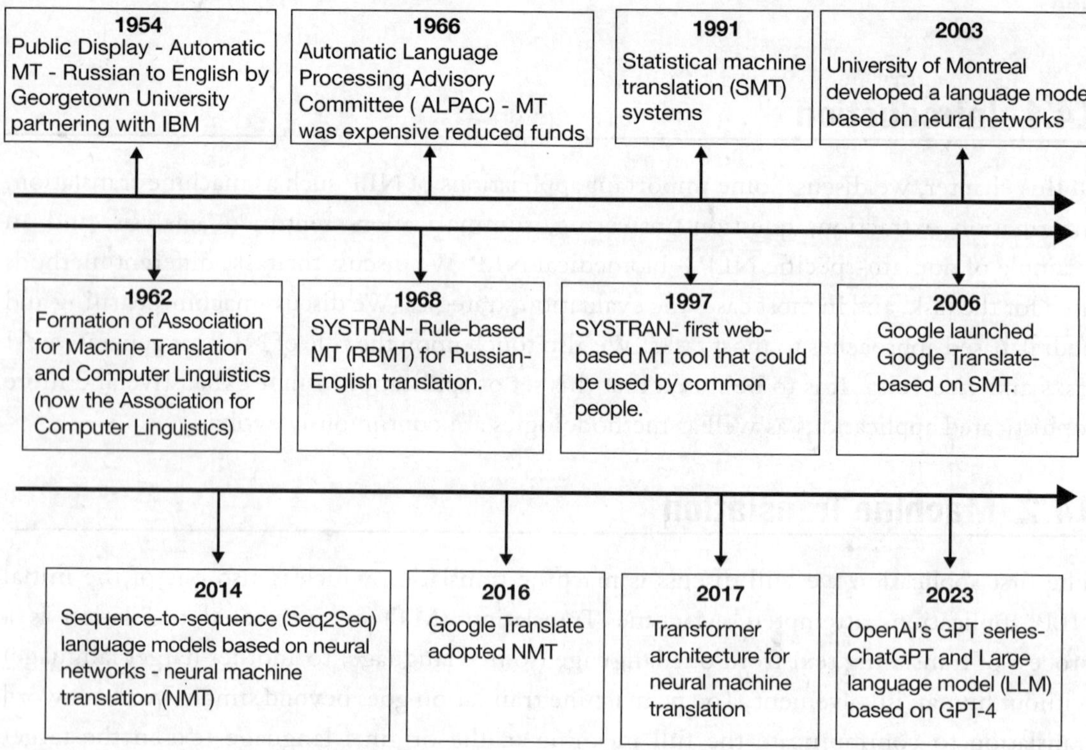

Figure 14.1 History of Machine Translation

IBM developed the first statistical machine translation (SMT) systems in 1991. SMT systems do not rely on linguistic rules and words but utilize a bilingual corpus of text to identify patterns in the languages that could be converted into statistical data. These models performed significantly better than RBMT and quickly became very popular. In 1997, SYSTRAN launched the first web-based MT tool that could be used by common people. In 2006, Google launched Google Translate, which was based on SMT.

In 2003, researchers at the University of Montreal developed a neural network-based language model. In 2014, neural machine translation (NMT) came into existence as an exciting alternative to SMT primarily due to development of the sequence-to-sequence (Seq2Seq) language models based on neural networks. NMT teaches itself how to translate by using large neural networks with larger corpora and are more reliable when translating long strings of text with complex sentence structures. Google Translate adopted NMT in 2016. However, NMT is time-consuming, requires heavy computational resources, and may still not work for domains that it has not been trained for. 2017 saw the introduction of transformer architecture which improved neural machine translation. In 2020s, OpenAI's GPT series, including tools like ChatGPT and Large language model (LLM) based on GPT-4 (2023) built feature language models with large-scale neural networks and advanced features. These systems also had translational capabilities but still need to be specifically designed for translation. SMT and NMT will be discussed below.

14.2.1 Statistical Machine Translation (SMT)

Statistical machine translation (SMT) basically learns a probabilistic model using a large amount of parallel data. The first SMT model was developed by IBM based on the concept of noisy channel. In order to find the best translation from source language S to target language T, the translation is modelled as (Equation 14.1).

$$T^* = \text{argmax}_T P(T|S) \tag{14.1}$$

The modelling is simplified using Bayes approach (the noisy channel approach) as follows (Equation 14.2)

$$T^* = \text{argmax}_T P(T|S)$$

$$= \text{argmax}_T P(S|T)P(T) \tag{14.2}$$

Where $P(S|T)$ is the translation model and $P(T)$ represents the language model.

The simple translation model $P(S|T)$ is a noisy channel since it attempts to capture the faithfulness of the translation using a parallel corpus. The language model $P(T)$ captures the fluency of the translation and is trained on a large monolingual target language corpus. The translation model goes from target to source language only through word alignments (Equation 14.3) designed for word–based translation.

$$P(S|T) = \sum_a P(S,a|T) \tag{14.3}$$

Assuming that the length of the target sentence $T = t_1, t_2, \ldots\ldots t_n$ where n is its length. The IBM translation models assumes that the model generates the length, alignment and words of the source language along with the probabilities. In case of IBM model 1, the probabilities are as follows:

Length probability $P(m|n)$ is defined as the probability of generating a source sentence of length m given that the target sentence is of length n.

Alignment probability $P(a|m, n)$ assumes that all alignments have equal probability that is for each position a_1, a_2,...... a_m any one of the target positions $n+1$ is picked up uniformly at random.

Translation probability is the probability of translating into the source language given position and target language.

Later on, this simple model (Model 1) was modified to tackle word alignments and later phrase alignments. This progression in complexity resulted in the development of 5 models.

In **Model 1,** these are the only parameters we have to learn and is thus a simple lexical translation.

In **Model 2,** alignment distortion parameters are introduced which allows alignment to be conditional on sentence lengths.

Model 3 introduces an extra fertility model where fertility is modeled using probability distribution that is the probability indicates the possible number of target words that each source word can generate.

Model 4 added relative alignment model where each word is dependent on the previously aligned word and on the word classes of the surrounding words.

Model 5 fixed deficiency problem where the alignment model is enhanced with more training parameters in order to overcome the model deficiency.

Model 6 combined a HMM trained alignment model in a log linear way with Model 4.

14.2.2 Evaluation of Machine Translation

A translation is directly evaluated based on adequacy that is the goodness of the translated text in terms of preserving the content of the source text and fluency that is the goodness of a well-formed target language text. Human evaluator can also rank translated sentences relative to each other. Automatic evaluation compares the performance of the machine translation system and a professional human translation and helps in improving the success of evaluation. For this purpose, a numeric translation closeness metric is needed. A few of the popular automatic evaluation metrics used are given below:

14.2.2.1 BLEU (Bilingual Evaluation Understudy)

BLEU is the most popular MT evaluation metric. It requires only reference translations for evaluation, especially for comparing two translation systems. BLEU, a precision-based score, computes a similarity score between the machine created translation and one of the human written translations. This precision–oriented metric measures the amount of the system output that is right. It does measure the extent to which the reference translation is fully reproduced in the output of the translation system.

BLEU uses n-gram precision usually 1, 2, 3, or 4 grams. Given the predicted (through machine translation) and target sentences (human generated), the 1-gram, 2-grams, 3-grams and 4-grams precision scores is computed. Next, these precision scores (typically for N-4) with uniform weights for each n-gram precision weighted with $w_n = N/4$ are combined as follows (Equation 14.4):

$$\text{Geometric Average Precision}(N) = \exp\left(\sum_{n=1}^{N} w_n \log p_n\right)$$

$$= \prod_{n=1}^{N} p_n^{w_n} \tag{14.4}$$

$$= (p_1)^{\frac{1}{4}} \cdot (p_2)^{\frac{1}{4}} \cdot (p_3)^{\frac{1}{4}} \cdot (p_4)^{\frac{1}{4}}$$

The computation of Brevity Penalty is the next step (Equation 14.5) where the very short sentences are penalized by Brevity Penalty. Assuming that c is the projected length of the predicted sentence and r is the target length of the target sentence.

$$\text{Brevity Penalty} = \begin{cases} 1, & if\ c > r \\ e^{(1-r/c)}, & if\ c \leq r \end{cases} \tag{14.5}$$

if the predicted sentence is much longer than the target, the maximum value of Brevity Penalty is limited to 1. The Brevity Penalty is multiplied with the Geometric Average of the Precision Scores to obtain the final Bleu Score (Equation 14.6).

$$\text{Bleu}(N) = \text{Brevity Penalty} . \text{Geometric Average Precision Scores}(N) \tag{14.6}$$

The main disadvantages of the BLEU measure that brevity penalty is not a good measure of recall and the higher order n-grams used may not indicate grammatical correctness of a sentence.

In addition, BLEU scores show best results when evaluated on large test corpora so that scores are averaged over many sentences. The BLEU scores of individual sentences are not very reliable. Translation quality especially the semantic quality cannot be detected by BLEU metric due to inability to detect synonym matching and perceive multiple proper word orders.

14.2.2.2 METEOR (Metric for Evaluation of Translation with Explicit Ordering)

METEOR addresses some of the weaknesses of BLEU metric by using the concept of having a good unigram matching strategy. A recall–oriented measure, METEOR uses harmonic mean where it combines both precision and recall (Equation 14.7).

$$F_{mean} = \frac{P.R}{\alpha P + (1 - \alpha) R} \tag{14.7}$$

METEOR defines precision P as number of matches divided by the number of words in the translation, while recall R is defined as the number of matches divided by the number of words in the reference translation and parameter α controlling the relative weight for precision and recall. Normally METEOR associates a large bias towards recall where recall is weighted 9 times more than precision (Equation 14.8).

$$F_{mean} = \frac{10 P.R}{9P + R} \tag{14.8}$$

In addition to the F_{mean}, a fragmentation penalty which biases the score against translation that have many short sequences of consecutive matches, called chunks us used by METEOR. Fragmentation is calculated as the number of chunks divided by the number of unigram matches. The fragmentation is calculated as shown in Equation (14.9), with default parameters of $\beta = 3.0$ and $\gamma = 0.5$. The value of γ determines the maximum penalty ($0 \leq \gamma \leq 1$). The value of β determines the functional relation between fragmentation and the penalty.

$$Pen = \gamma . frag^{\beta} \tag{14.9}$$

Finally, the METEOR score for the alignment between the translation and reference strings is calculated as (Equation 14.10):

$$Score = (1 - Pen) . F_{mean} \tag{14.10}$$

METEOR compares only unigrams, single words, for matching but does so using several stages of word matching for alignment between the system output and the reference translations. The three stages used are exact matching where strings which are identical in the reference and the translation are aligned, stem matching where stemming is carried out so that words with the same morphological root are aligned and synonymy matching where words which are WordNet synonyms are aligned. In each of these stages, words that were not matched in previous stages are considered for matching.

METEOR does not penalize longer answers but however incorporates a level of linguistic knowledge in the form of its stem and synonym matching allowing it to identify similarity between the translated output and the reference translation. The main disadvantage of Another disadvantage of METEOR is that it does not incorporate knowledge from multiple reference translations into its score.

14.2.3 Neural Machine Translation (NMT)

Neural machine translation (NMT) carries out machine translation using an end-to-end neural network model. These models use massive parallel datasets of source and translated pairs of sentences to train a model capable of translating between any two languages. The most common NMT model is the Encoder Decoder architecture called a sequence-to sequence (seq2seq) model composed of two recurrent neural networks (RNNs) used in tandem to create the translation model. RNN is a network that operates on a sequence and uses its own output as input for subsequent steps. The encoder is for language understanding of the source language where it reads an input sequence and outputs vectors, while the decoder is for language understanding and generation of the target language which reads encoder outputs as input to produce an output sequence. Figure 14.2 shows the model which reads the input sentence $s_1 s_2 s_3$ and produces $t_1 t_2 t_3 t_4$ as the output. The model stops after outputting the </s> the end of sentence token.

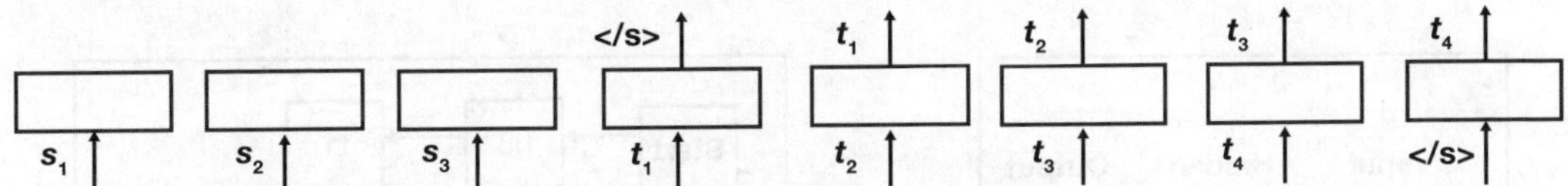

Figure 14.2 Input–Output of LSTM Model for Neural Machine Translation

Given the source language sentence s and a target language sentence t, NMT uses seq2seq models to calculate the conditional language model. It is an extended language model where we concatenate the source and target text and the decoder predicts the next word of the target sentence t. This conditional language model calculates the probability of the next word of target sentence given the source sentences. NMT directly calculates $P(T|S)$ given below (Equation 14.11)

$$P(t|s) = P(t_1|s)P(t_2|t_1,s)P(t_3|t_1,t_2,s) \cdots P(t_T|t_1,\ldots,t_{T-1},s) \tag{14.11}$$

Let us discuss the encoder-decoder architecture in detail. Figure 14.3 shows the encoder-decoder model of NMT where the encoder processes the sentence of the source text (Tamil) to produce its embedding which is given as input to the decoder.

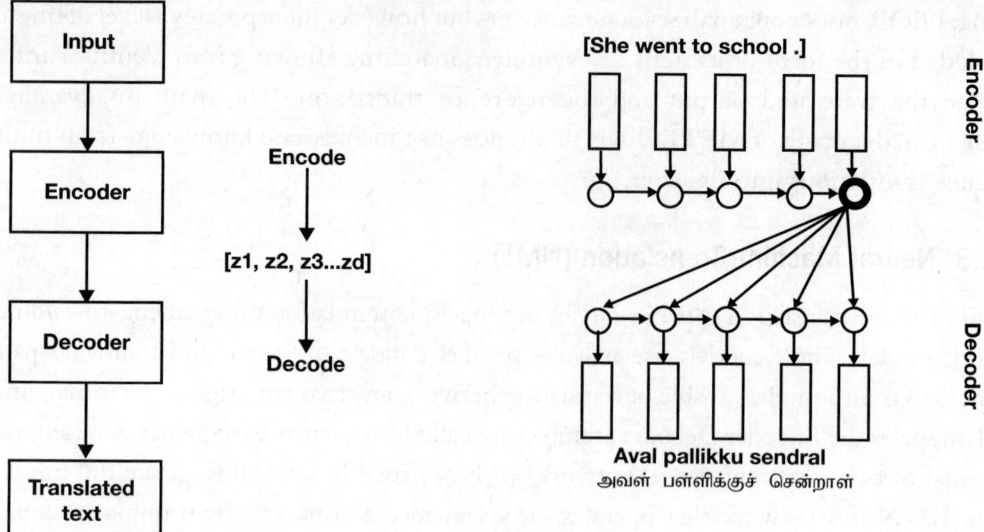

Figure 14.3 General Encoder–Decoder Model for Neural Machine Translation

This model has the power to map sequences of different lengths since the input sequence and output sequence are not correlated. Figure 14.4 shows the detailed RNN based encoder-decoder model used for machine translation.

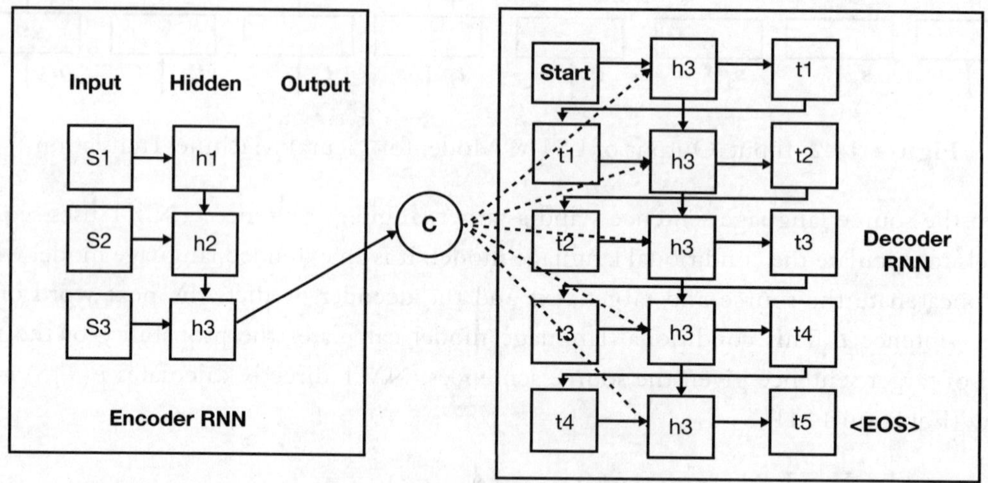

Figure 14.4 RNN-based Encoder-Decoder Model for Machine Translation

The encoder consists of a stack of RNN units where each RNN accepts a single token of the source sequence, processes information about that token and propagates it forward. At each time-step, the corresponding word of the input sentence is fed separately into the encoder which is used to update a hidden vector of the encoder. The hidden states are computed by applying appropriate weights to the previous hidden state and current input (Equation 14.12) where the hidden state at time t, h_t is a function of weighted output of layer at t-1, h_{t-1}, and the input at time t, x_t

$$h_t = f\left(W^{(hh)}h_{t-1} + W^{(hx)}x_t\right) \tag{14.12}$$

The final hidden state produced by the encoder encapsulates the information of all input words of the source sentence and enables the decoder to make predictions about the target sequence. A decoder thus interprets the context vector obtained from the encoder. The hidden state acts as the initial hidden state of the decoder where the output of the final cell of the encoder is input to the first cell of the decoder network. Using these initial states, the decoder starts generating the output sequence, where outputs of the previous time-step is taken into consideration for future predictions. The decoder also consists of a stack of RNN units where each RNN accepts a hidden state from the previous unit and produces an output as well as its own hidden state. The hidden state at a time t is calculated based on the previous hidden state as given below (Equation 14.13) where the hidden state at time t, h_t is a function of weighted output of layer at t-1, h_{t-1}. The output y_t at time step t is computed where softmax is used to obtain a probability vector as given below (Equation 14.14)

$$h_t = f\left(W^{(hh)}h_{t-1}\right) \tag{14.13}$$

$$y_t = softmax\left(W^S h_t\right) \tag{14.14}$$

The main drawback of the above encoder-decoder model is its inability to extract strong contextual relations from long semantic sentences or the context or relations within its substrings which is specifically important in the case of machine translation. Encoder–decoder model with attention has already been discussed in Chapter 9. Rather than just encoding the input sequence into a single fixed context vector, the attention-based model creates the context vector that is selectively filtered specifically for each output time step and hence train the decoder model with full sequences and the filtered words to obtain predictions.

In the case of machine translation, attention helps to both aligning and translating a long piece of sequence source text. Attention enables alignment by identifying which parts of the input sequence are relevant to each word in the output and helps in translation by using the relevant information to select the appropriate output.

Another recurrent network used for machine translation is LSTM. One of the main advantages of LSTM when compared to RNN is its ability to learn long-term dependencies and capture complex patterns from the sequential data. Additionally, LSTM cells can avoid the vanishing or exploding gradient problem, allowing them to learn from longer sequences and hence can be used to translate a long sentence from one language to another without forgetting or distorting the meaning.

14.3 Information Extraction

Information extraction (IE) can be defined as the task of filling pre-defined slots from segments of the given text by selecting and understanding the limited relevant parts of the text. The objective of IE is to make the information useful by structuring the information in a semantically precise manner that allows inference algorithms to process the information. Generally, IE systems extract information that is clear and factual and answering a question such as *"Who did what to whom when?"* ignoring parts of the text not required to gather the above information (Figure 14.5).

Example	Air India appointed Dr.Ramesh as the new CEO on 5th January.
Slot	**Filler**
Who	Air India
What	Appointed as the new CEO
Whom	Dr.Ramesh
When	5th January

Figure 14.5 Example of Slot–Filler

This task of transforming unstructured information in a text into a structured database can be applied to different genres of text such as newspaper articles, web pages, scientific articles, classified ads, medical notes, etc. IE can consist of the following main subtasks namely Named Entity Recognition (NER), entity linking and relation extraction.

14.3.1 Named Entity Recognition

Named entity recognition is the task of identifying spans of text that correspond to typed entities and classifying these named entities typically as Person, Organization, Location, Time, etc. (a list already given in Table 10.3). In the example shown in Figure 14.5, Air-India is Organization name, Dr Ramesh is a Person and 5th Jan is Time. In the 1990s, IE was funded by DARPA (Defence Advanced Research Projects Agency) which conducted an annual competition which focused on extracting information about terrorist activities, industrial joint ventures and company management changes from newspaper articles. Initially a rule-based system with hand-written regular expressions was used for NER.

One **machine learning approach to NER** is formulating the task as a classification problem where Naïve Bayes or Maximum Entropy models were used to classify substrings of the text as "*to be extracted*" or not. Another approach to NER was the machine learning based sequence model. BIO Tagging is used to convert the structured prediction problem into a sequence labelling problem with one label per word as described in Chapter 10. The machine learning model was trained with a set of representative training documents where each token was labelled with its entity class or other (O). Then features were designed appropriate to the text and NER classes. Features include the words themselves, previous or next word to indicate context, POS tags of the above words and the context associated with the NER label which can be the previous or next label. Then a sequence classifier such as HMMs or MEMMS can be used to predict the labels from the data. The NER sequence model can also be tackled using neural based approaches as discussed in Chapter 10.

14.3.2 Entity Linking

Entity Linking is the task of disambiguating named entities to match with their corresponding entities in a knowledge base (e.g., Wikidata, DBpedia, or YAGO), by identifying the correct referent for a mention in context. Entity linking can be formulated as a learning to rank problem where given a mention x, some set of candidate entities y(x) for that mention, and context c, the highest scoring entity y' from that set is selected as given by Equation 14.15 where Ψ is the scoring function described over the mention x, candidate y, and context c. The parameters of the scoring function are learnt by minimizing the ranking loss.

$$\hat{y} = \underset{y \in Y(\lambda)}{\mathrm{argmax}}\ \psi(y, x, c) \tag{14.15}$$

14.3.3 Relation Extraction

Relation Extraction recognizes a set of ordered tuples over elements of a domain that is identifying if the set of named entities are instances of a relation, typically from a small set of predefined relations. One of the earlier set of predefined relations were defined by ACE (Automatic Content Extraction) community which included relations like **Role** relates a person to an organization or a geopolitical entity whose subtypes were member, owner, affiliate, client, citizen, **Part** generalized containment subtypes such as subsidiary, physical part-of, set membership, **At** was permanent and transient locations subtypes such as located, based-in, residence and **Social** were relations among persons with subtypes such as parent, sibling, spouse, grandparent, associate. The initial approach to relation extraction was a **rule-based approach** where handwritten rules were used to identify lexico-syntactic patterns called Hearst patterns which were used for high-precision relation extraction especially hypernym–hyponym pairs that is–a relations. For example, *"Fruits such as apple are good for health"* can use the pattern *"X, such as Y (and/or Z)"* implying that X is a hypernym of Y. The rule–based approaches have high precision but low recall and moreover hand–written rules used by this approach are hard to maintain.

The use of **machine learning is another approach** to relation extraction. Relation extraction utilizing supervised learning is formulated as a $n+1$ classifier problem for n relations (with one extra class to indicate no relation exists) that identifies the relation between a pair of entities that appear in the same sentence. The features that are generally used for this problem are word based features such as bag of words for each entity, bag of words and bigrams between entities, NER based features such as NER types of both entities of the pair, distance between both entities (#words, #NERs,...) and the syntactic path between the entities including presence of particular constructions, chunk based-phrase paths and constituent-tree paths. Labelled data for the relations under consideration taken from a representative corpus is utilized to train the classifier and then used to find all pairs of named entities to decide if 2 entities are related and then the actual type of relation is determined. This two-step process results in faster training by eliminating invalid pairs. Any of the classifiers such as Maximum Entropy, Naïve Bayes or SVM can be used for the classification. The main disadvantage of the supervised approach is the need for labelled training data and the limited number of types of relationships considered.

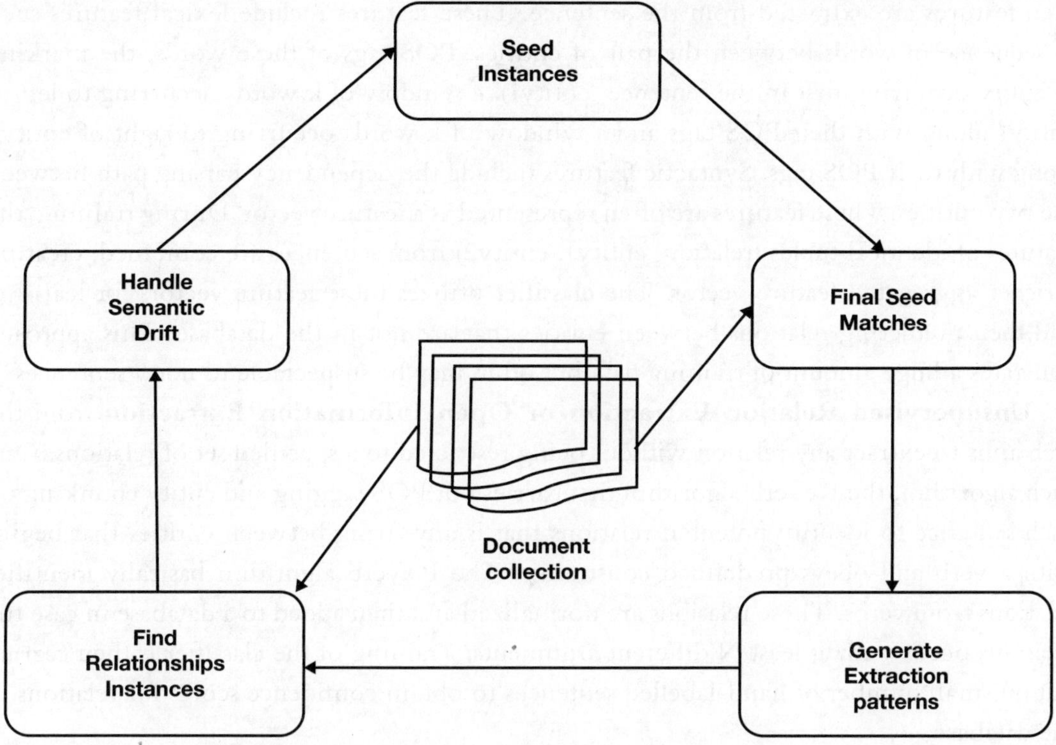

Figure 14.6 Semi-supervised Relation Extraction

Semi-supervised relation extraction is another approach used for relation extraction where some seed instances are given and the occurrence contexts of these sentences are determined. Based on these contexts, seed patterns are generated which are then used to obtain new instances of the relations by scanning sentences from the unlabelled document corpus. The newly obtained instances are used to obtain additional seed patterns associated with the relations. This process is repeated until a given stop criteria is met. This approach takes advantage of easily available unlabelled data but however requires that we have seeds for each relation. Moreover, the process is sensitive to the original set of seeds and may lead to semantic drift which needs to be handled (Figure 14.6).

Distant supervision for relation extraction uses a large online database of structured semantic data such as FreeBase to obtain a huge number of seed tuples associated with a set of relations and entity pairs that participate in the relations. Initially all entities in the sentences are identified using entity taggers and in case a sentence has two entities that form a relation then features are extracted from the sentence. These features include lexical features such as sequence of words between the pair of entities, POS tags of these words, the marking of entity occurring first in the sentence (entity1), a window of k words occurring to left of entity1 along with their POS tags and a window of k words occurring to right of entity2 along with their POS tags. Syntactic features include the dependency parsing path between the two entities. These features are often represented as a feature vector. During training, the features of identical tuples (relation, entity1, entity2) from sentences are combined, creating a richer aggregated feature vector. The classifier utilizes these feature vectors for learning and then predicting relations between entities that are not in the database. This approach generates a huge amount of training data but often may be suspectable to noisy sentences.

Unsupervised Relation Extraction or Open Information Extraction from the web aims to extract any relation without being restricted to a specified set of relations. One such algorithm, the ReVerb algorithm first carries out POS tagging and entity chunking on each sentence to identify potential relations that is any string between entities that begins with a verb and obeys predefined constraints. The ReVerb algorithm basically identifies relations from verbs. These relations are normalized and then added to a database in case the relations occur with at least N different arguments. Training of the classifier is then carried out on small number of hand-labelled sentences to obtain confidence scores for relations in the database.

Finally, we will discuss the **neural approach to relation extraction**. The initial work on relation extraction using deep learning was based on a supervised learning paradigm with a hand–labelled training corpus. The model considers the relation extraction task as a multi-class classification problem, where the model assigns a relation class to a sentence containing the mentioned entity pair. The end–to–end neural network architecture has three main building blocks namely an input layer, a convolution layer, and a classic neural network layer. The input layer implements a lookup table to transform input sentences into word vectors using lexical features and a synonym dictionary. The convolution layer is implemented using a sequential kernel, which maps word vectors from the input layer to a new vector space. The output of convolution layer is fed to the neural network with softmax to compute classification probability. One problem with this approach is that we have no indication on which entity pair we are classifying. To tackle this issue, two positional embeddings are incorporated for each of the two entities under consideration indicating the distance of each word to the two entities (Figure 14.7). Another issue is the handling of multiple instances in the case of distance supervision where labels are assigned to a set of sentences, each containing the pair of entities but however not all of which will express the relation between them. An attention mechanism is used to capture which sentences in the input is to be considered.

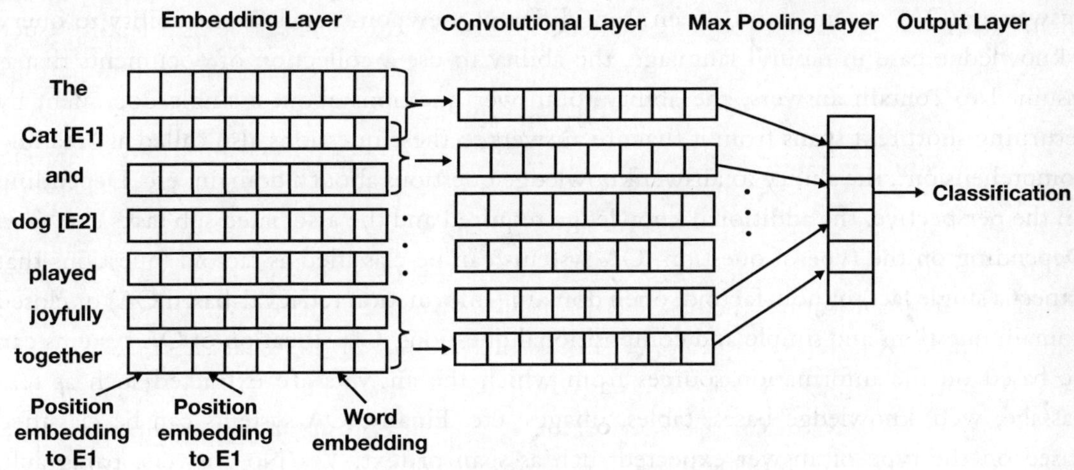

Figure 14.7 Neural Approach to Relation Extraction

Neural OpenIE is an encoder–decoder based framework, which treats relation extraction task as sequence-to-sequence generation problem, where input is a sequence of tokens and output is a sequence of tokens with delimiters indicating entities and relation boundaries. In this architecture, there are 3-layers of LSTM network in both the encoder and decoder. The encoder receives text sequence of varying length as input and converts it into a hidden representation. The decoder takes the encoder's output and attention information as input and passes it to the LSTM network followed by softmax to generate the final output sequence. The model uses a copying mechanism to reduce the number of unknown words in the output sequence.

14.4 Question Answering

The goal of question answering is to build systems that automatically answer questions posed by humans in a natural language from a large collection of documents. The most famous example of question answering systems was IBM Watson system which defeated two of greatest champions of Jeopardy in 2011.

14.4.1 Introduction

The applications of question answering are many and include search engines, dialogue systems, and is considered as a testbed for evaluating the understanding of human language by the computer. The taxonomy of question answering systems can be based on perspective of usage, question type, type of information sources and answer type (Figure 14.8). Question answering (QA) systems can be seen from different viewpoints such as the ability to query a knowledge base in natural language, the ability to use a collection of documents that is assumed to contain answers, the ability to answer questions about a single document by returning short text spans from it that are answers to these questions also called as "reading comprehension", the ability to answer knowledge questions about a domain, etc. Depending on the perspective, the additional knowledge required and the associated sub tasks can vary. Depending on the type of question, QA systems can be classified as factoid (questions that expect a single fact) or non-factoid, open domain (Information retrieval–based QA) or closed domain questions and simple and compositional questions. Classification of QA systems can be based on the information sources from which the answers are extracted such as text passage, web, knowledge bases, tables, images, etc. Finally, QA systems can be classified based on the type of answer expected such as span of text, Yes/No answers, paragraph, database entry, list, opinion, summary, etc.

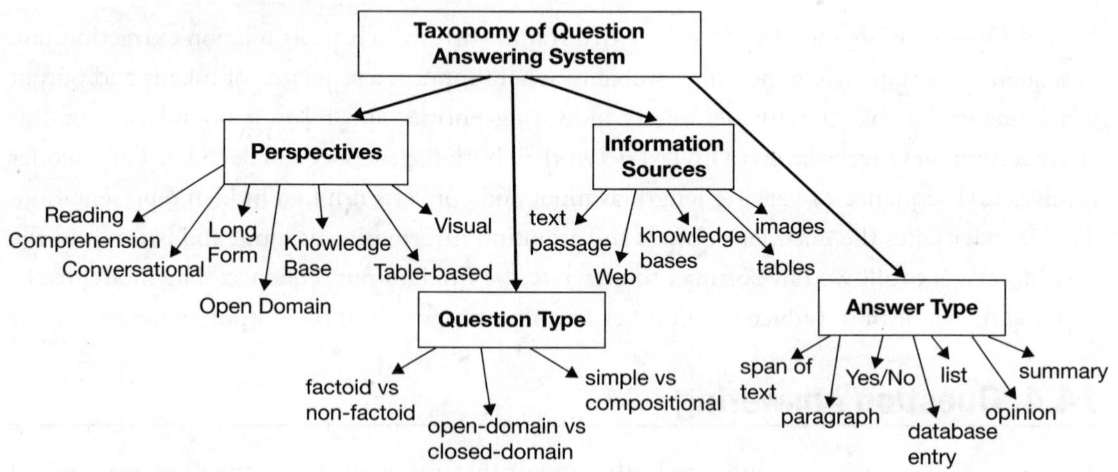

Figure 14.8 Taxonomy of Question Answering Systems

14.4.2 Information Retrieval-based Question Answering

One of the popular used QA systems is the information retrieval-based factoid QA which essentially consists of three steps namely question processing, document and passage retrieval and answer extraction (Figure 14.9).

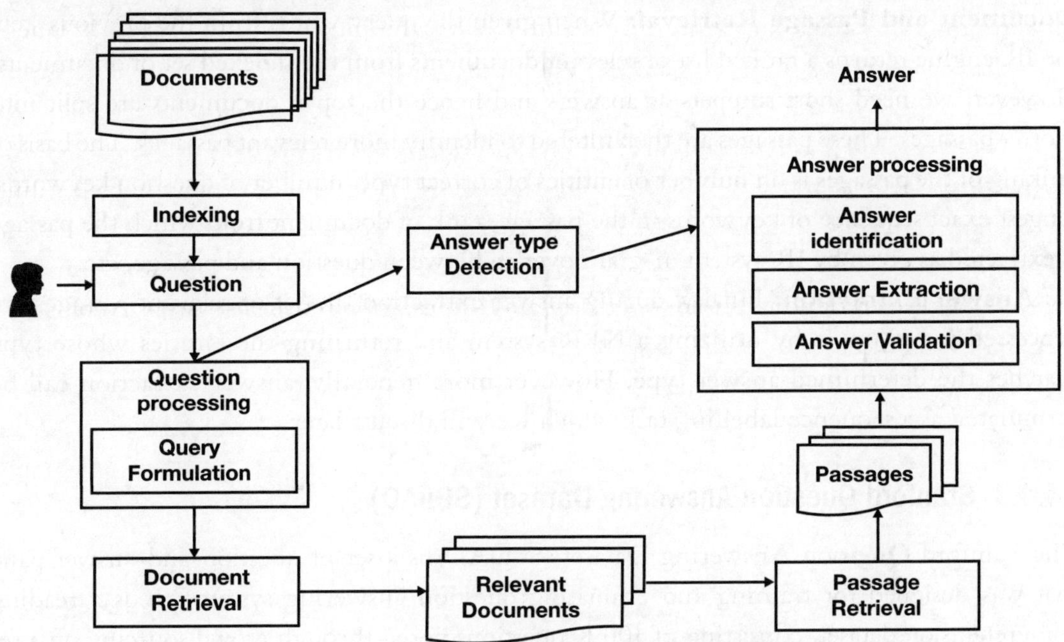

Figure 14.9 Information Retrieval-based Question Answering

Question Processing: The task of question processing is query formulation or the extraction of query words that is the keywords that have to forwarded to the retrieval system to match with the potentially relevant documents. In addition, answer type detection that is the detection of the expected entity type of the answer is also carried out. The answers to many common factoid questions fall into a small number of categories which in simple cases can be identified by the type of question word alone (examples include who – person, where –location, where – location, when- time). However, in many cases the question word along with noun or verb associated with it determines the entity type (example which country – country). Answer type detection system can be trained using supervised learning where features used include words or word embeddings, POS for each word, question headword, etc.

In some cases, focus that is the string of words in the question that the answer is likely to replace is detected as shown in the example given below:

Example: Which Indian city is the largest?

Query words: "Indian city is the largest."

Answer type: City

Focus: Which city

Document and Passage Retrieval: When given the query words from the previous step, the IR engine returns a ranked list of relevant documents from the indexed set of documents. However, we need short snippets as answers and hence the top *n* documents are split into shorter passages. These passages are then filtered to identify more relevant passages. The basis of ranking of the passages is on number of entities of correct type, number of question keywords, longest exact sequence of keywords in the passage, rank of document from which the passage is extracted as given by IR system, n-gram overlap between question and passage, etc.

Answer Extraction: Finally, during answer extraction the set of relevant passages are processed for example by utilizing a NER system and returning the entities whose type matches the determined answer type. However more generally, answer extraction can be formulated as a sequence labelling task which we will discuss later.

14.4.3 Stanford Question Answering Dataset (SQuAD)

The **S**tanford **Qu**estion **A**nswering **D**ataset (SQuAD) is a set of question-and-answer pairs that was designed for training and evaluating question answering systems. It is a reading comprehension dataset, consisting of 100 K questions posed through crowd sourcing on a set of Wikipedia articles, where the answer to every question is a segment of text, or *span*, from the corresponding reading passage usually 100~150 words. In SQuAD2.0, 50K unanswerable questions were added, since for good performance of the models it is necessary to know when to abstain from answering a question. This large-scale supervised dataset became an important component for training effective neural models for reading comprehension. SQuAD still remains the most popular reading comprehension dataset; it is "almost solved" today and the state-of-the-art models developed using this dataset exceeds estimated human performance.

14.4.4 Machine Learning Approach to Reading Comprehension

As already discussed, reading comprehension is an important testbed for evaluating how well computer systems understand human language and many other NLP tasks such as information extraction and semantic role labelling can be reduced to a reading comprehension problem. Conventional feature-based approaches are generally used for the SQuAD reading comprehension task where features used for building the feature vector include word or bigram features, parse tree matches, dependency labels, length, and part-of-speech tags. First a list of candidate answers is generated for which feature vectors are constructed and a machine learning model such as multi-class logistic regression model is used.

14.4.5 Neural Models for Question Answering System

The general architecture of neural based reading comprehension QA systems is shown in Figure 14.10. The initial step is the construction of embeddings of the context (the passage of text) and the question. One-hot or Word2Vec combined with other linguistic features such as part-of-speech, named entity, and question category, are used to represent semantic and syntactic information. Contextualized word representations pre-trained by a large corpus is currently being used to encode contextual information. These embeddings are then given to the feature extraction module which uses deep learning models like recurrent neural networks (RNNs) and convolution neural networks (CNNs) to mine contextual features from context and question embeddings. These features are used by the context-question mapping module to obtain the correlation between the context and the question which plays a significant role in predicting the answer. To determine the context that is more important for answering the question, either unidirectional or bidirectional attention mechanism is used to emphasize parts of the context relevant to the query. Often in order to mimic the rereading process a multi-hop mapping process is used. The answer prediction module outputs the final answer based on information accumulated from previous modules. Based on the form of answer outputs required, the output of this module is a word or entity from the original context, or in the case of span extraction, subsequence of the given context.

BiLSTM-based reading comprehension: The overall block diagram of biLSTM model is shown in Figure 14.11. The question as well as the passage are encoded using word/char, respectively. Passage-to-question and question-to-passage attention mechanisms are used to emphasize the appropriate context. The question LSTM computes a single question vector q. The modelling layer is another biLSTM layer where the LSTM predicts start and end positions of the answer span. These positions are based on two learned classifiers that depend on the word embeddings of each passage pi and on the question vector q. The question vector q is a weighted average of the biLSTM-based embeddings of the question words where the question word weights bj are given by the normalized, exponentiated dot product of each word embedding with a single, learned, relevance weight vector w. For the passage vector, each token is input as an embedding (e.g., GloVe), concatenated with its POS tag or Named entity recognition label, a 0/1 flag indicating whether it occurs in the question, and a token-specific attention-based embedding of the question.

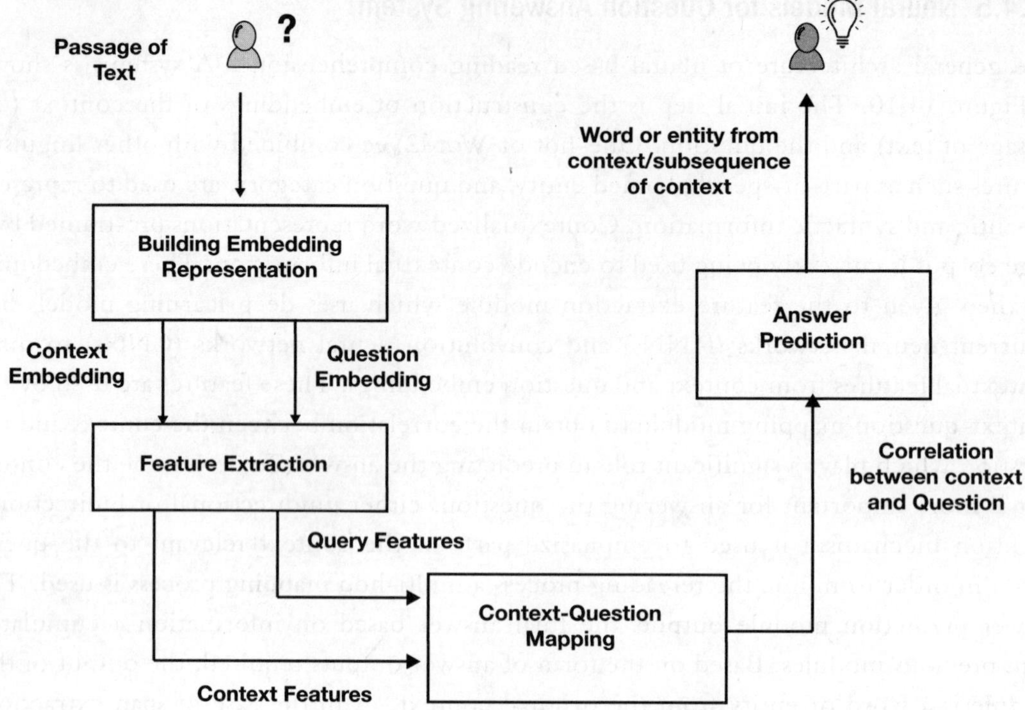

Figure 14.10 Neural–based Reading Comprehension QA Systems

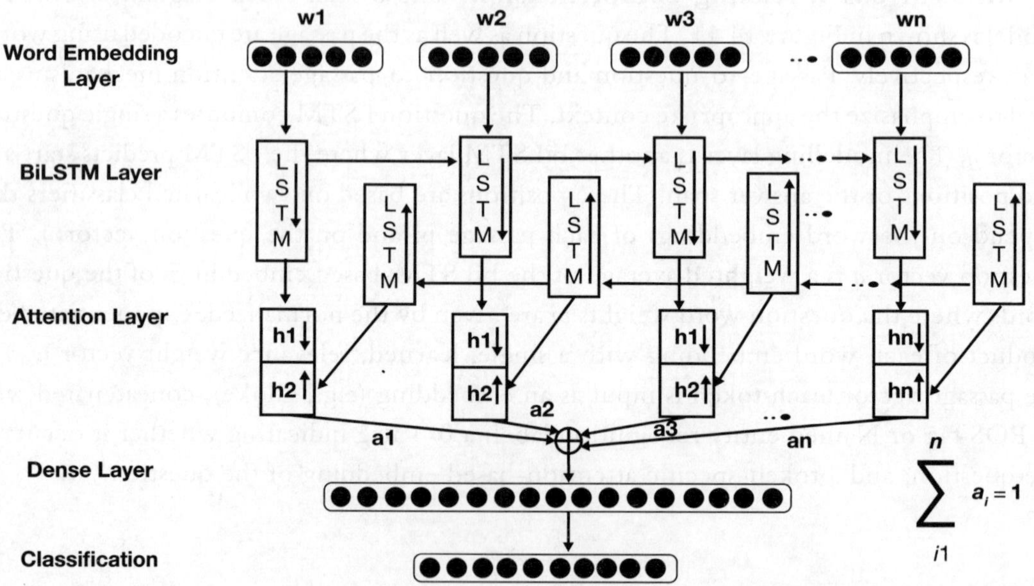

Figure 14.11 BiLSTM-based Model for Reading Comprehension

BERT for Reading Comprehension: As we have already discussed, BERT is a deep bidirectional Transformer encoder pre-trained on large amounts of text with two training objectives namely Masked language model (MLM) and Next sentence prediction (NSP). In the case of reading comprehension, the question acts as one segment, passage as the other segment of the BERT model and the answer is the prediction of two endpoints in the second segment indicating the answer span.

14.4.6 Evaluation of Question Answering System

One method of evaluation of QA systems is using exact match (EM) score which indicates an exact match between the prediction and the ground truth given in an evaluation dataset such as SQuAD. Another metric is the F1 score which rewards partial matches between the prediction and the ground truth answers. For development and testing sets, 3 gold answers are collected, because there could be multiple plausible answers. The predicted answer to *each* gold answer is considered and the average of all the examples for both EM and F1 are taken into account.

Another measure used for question answering is the mean reciprocal rank (MRR) metric which is used to evaluate systems that return a ranked list of items (here: answer spans). Here rank(ques) is defined as the highest rank of any correct answer for a question Q, and rRank(ques) = 1/rank(ques) when at least one correct answer is returned, and rRank(ques) = 0 when no correct answer is returned. The reciprocal rank of a query response is the multiplicative inverse of the rank of the first correct answer: 1 for first place, $\frac{1}{2}$ for second place, $\frac{1}{3}$ for third place and so on. In general, the mean reciprocal rank is the average of the reciprocal ranks of results for a sample of pool of Q queries (Equation 14.16)

$$MRR = \frac{1}{|Q|} \sum_{i=1}^{|Q|} \frac{1}{rank_i} \tag{14.16}$$

where rank $rank_i$ refers to the rank position of the *first* relevant document for the *i*-th query.

14.5 Summarization

The objective of summarization is to take a text and produce an abridged version that contains information that is important and relevant to a user. There are many applications of summarization such as providing outlines or abstracts of any document or article, summarizing email threads or the action items from a meeting and simplifying and compressing sentences. Summarization can be categorized depending on whether input is a single document or multiple documents, whether the output is required to be extractive, abstractive or compressive, or whether the focus of the task in generic or query focussed. In single document summarization, the objective is to obtain an abstract, outline or headline while in multi-document summarization, given a group of documents, the task is to create a gist of the content for example from a series of news stories on the same event or from a set of web pages about a particular topic. In extractive summarization, selected segments of the original text are extracted to form the summary while in abstractive summarization, new text is generated using NLP techniques.

14.5.1 Process of Summarization

Extractive summarization basically involves content selection. The approach is to choose sentences that contain salient or informative words. One approach to defining salient words is by using *tf–idf* approach where each word w_i in the document j is weighted by *tf–idf* (Equation 14.17) where tf_{ij} is the term frequency that is the number of times word or term t appears in document j and idf_i is inverse document frequency.

$$weight\left(w_i\right) = tf_{ij} \times idf_i \tag{14.17}$$

Another method is to choose a smaller set of salient words using mutual information or log-likelihood ratio.

The supervised machine learning method generally utilizes a labelled training set of good summaries for each document. The sentences of the document and the sentences in the corresponding summary are aligned. From these alignments, features such as position and length of the sentences, word informativeness, cue phrases and cohesion indicators are extracted and used to train a binary classifier to classify whether the sentence from the document should be in the summary or not. However, it is difficult to get labelled data and the performance is comparable to the methods discussed earlier.

14.5.2 Neural Approaches to Summarization

One neural approach to abstractive summarization based on attention-based seq2seq encoder-decoder models. The feature rich encoder has embeddings each for POS. NER and discretised *tf* and *idf* values, all concatenated together and inputted to the encoder. Then we have the generator/pointer model. During the generator mode, the softmax layer is used to produce a word while during the pointer network mode, the word from one of the source document positions is copied. During pointer mode, the embedding from the source is used as input for the next time-step. The hierarchical attention weights of the encoder at the word level are re-scaled by the corresponding sentence-level attention weights.

14.5.3 Evaluation of Summarization

An important intrinsic metric used to evaluate summaries is the Recall Oriented Understudy for Gisting Evaluation (ROUGE) which is founded on BLEU already discussed previously. Here given a document D and an automatic summary S, N humans are requested to give a set of reference summaries of the document D. Then ROUGE is defined as the percentage of bigrams from the reference summaries that appear in S (Equation 14.18).

$$ROUGE-2 = \frac{\sum_{s\in\{RefSummaries\}}\sum_{bigrams\ i\in S}\min\left(count\left(i,X\right),count\left(i,S\right)\right)}{\sum_{s\in\{RefSummaries\}}\sum_{bigrams\ i\in S}count\left(i,S\right)} \tag{14.8}$$

14.6 Sentiment Analysis

Sentiment analysis is also known as subjectivity analysis, opinion extraction, opinion mining and sentiment mining. Sentiment analysis is described as the identification of the emotional tone behind a body of text. In essence, sentiment analysis is the computational study of opinions, sentiments, evaluations, attitudes, appraisal, affects, views, emotions, subjectivity, etc., expressed in reviews, blogs, discussions, news, comments, feedback, etc. Sentiment analysis is associated with holder or source of the attitude, the target or aspect of the attitude and type of attitude which can be from a set of types such as like, love, value, desire, etc. or more commonly a simple weighted polarity such as positive, negative or neutral with associated strength. Therefore, the sentiment analysis task can be simple – is the attitude positive or negative, more complex as ranking the attitude of the text on a scale from 1 to 5 or advanced where we need to also detect the target, source and complex attitude types.

14.6.1 Approaches to Sentiment Analysis

An algorithm for simple sentiment analysis where we need to find only whether a document expresses positive or negative sentiment, is to consider it as a text classification task where sentiment words such as great, excellent, bad, worse are important features. The movie review dataset was used for this task. Using unigrams as features, SVM was used for the classification. One major issue that had to be tackled was the handling of negation. Normally counts of lexicon categories, counts of all words and bigrams have also been used as features for classification. However, this method only worked well if the training and testing set were similar.

Aspect-based sentiment analysis is only easy if the entity whose sentiment is to be analysed is known such as different aspects of movies in movie reviews. However, for blogs, discussions, etc., both the entities and aspects are unknown and moreover there are many comparisons with other entities. Extracting aspects of entities is important and frequent nouns and noun phrases, opinion and target relations, proximity or syntactic dependency may be used by standard IE techniques.

14.6.2 Sentiment Lexicon

Sentiment lexicons are lists of words and expressions used to express people's subjective sentiments or opinions. These list of words or phrases are also called polar words – where positive – beautiful, wonderful, good, excellent, etc., while negative–bad, poor, terrible, etc. Many of these words may be both context and application domain dependent. Methods to compile such lists such as dictionary-based methods typically use WordNet synsets and hierarchies to acquire opinion words. SentiWordNet is a lexical resource for opinion mining. It assigns to each synset of WordNet three sentiment scores: positivity, negativity, objectivity. Corpus-based methods use a double propagation use dependency between opinion words and the items the data they modify in the corpus to obtain the lexicon but however require a large corpus to get good coverage.

14.7 Generative AI and NLP Applications

Generative AI or GenAI, short for Generative Artificial Intelligence, are designed to generate new, original data that resembles human-created data from various types of data, including images, videos, music, and most prominently, text. Generative AI models capture complex patterns and relationships within the vast amounts of existing data and use this knowledge to create new, previously unseen content. These models are recurrent neural networks (RNNs) and transformers. Applications of Generative AI include various types of data, including images, videos, music, and most prominently, text.

The reliability of generative AI based **virtual chatbots** used by professionals including doctors depend on qualitative training data. NLP can help "understand" and cleanse datasets to train GenAI chatbots. Later, chatbots can share automated prompts with NLP systems to analyze, translate, categorize, and publish them online for universal reach. GenAI and NLP can help in capturing region-specific cultural and language traditions and hence reduce time spent on localizing content in various languages for purposes of **translation** of books and news. NLP technologies can help **accelerated database preprocessing** for GenAI by replacing poor-quality user inputs with better alternatives in order to update empty and inconsistent database records. Generative AI models along with NLP assist in **content creation** by generating engaging articles, product descriptions, and creative writing pieces. The application of GenAI for NLP applications is evolving and in all likelihood the future holds the development of hitherto unknown innovative NLP applications.

14.8 Biomedical NLP

A variety of biomedical text data is readily available including medical literature (MEDLINE, PubMed, PMC), electronic health records (EHRs), clinical notes, research articles, patents, social media, and other healthcare-related documents. NLP techniques can be used on biomedical data to extract valuable information including relationships, disease characteristics, tumour classifications, and treatment recommendations, summarize and organize knowledge, identify patterns and trends and assist in clinical decision support, outcome prediction, and patient care improvements, compare treatment strategies, assess trial results and various healthcare applications. summarize, and organize knowledge.

Information Extraction (IE) from biomedical documents or from EHRs can help in identifying medical entities, relationships, medical conditions, and supporting clinical decision-making. As discussed in the previous sections IE involves named entity recognition, entity linking and relationship extraction but in this case from a corpus of biomedical documents such as PubMed. In biomedical named entity recognition, the task is to identify and classify entities such as diseases, drugs, genes, proteins, procedures, anatomy and other biomedical terms within text. In the case of biomedical named entity recognition, the entities are specifically correlated with concepts from the Unified Medical Language System (UMLS) Meta thesaurus. In the UMLS Meta thesaurus, all the different names or synonyms are clustered into a single concept and associated with a Concept Unique Identifier. In addition, UMLS has a semantic network that categorizes the concepts into 135 semantic types (broad categories) and 54 semantic relationships (between types). The method for discovering mentions of particular semantic types is to find the spans of text that constitute the entity mention and then classify the entities according to their semantic type and associate it with the UMLS taxonomy. Using UMLS the named entities are normalized for example *RA, Rheumatoid Arthritis and atrophic arthritis* will be assigned the same ontology code *(C0003873)*. Some of the UMLS relations of interest include locations of a biomedical entity such as *LocationOf (anatomical site, disease/disorder), LocationOf(anatomical site, sign/symptom),* or degree of relation such as *DegreeOf(modifier, disease/disorder).*

Relation learning takes as input a pair of entities and outputs either a relation or no relation label. During training all pairs of entity pairs are assigned a gold relation label and given to a classifier such as SVM and then the new pair of entities is given to the model to assign the label. The features used include words of the mentions, context words, distance between the words of the pair, entity types and entity context, POS tags of entities and POS tags between entities, dependency features, distance to common ancestor in the dependency tree, dependency path features, governing or dependent word, head word of phrases between entities, phrase head context, entity similarity, etc. Relations that can be extracted from biomedical literature include gene-disease associations, protein-disease associations, protein interactions, gene cluster identification, etc. IE can also be used to extract entities and associated timeline of activities in the EHR which can be used for personalized treatment decisions. **Text summarization** is often needed to generate concise and informative summaries of research articles and clinical notes to facilitate effective information retrieval. **Sentiment Analysis** of biomedical text helps in analysing patient reviews, assessing sentiment in clinical notes, and understanding public perceptions of healthcare topics.

NLP in drug discovery normally requires extracting and connecting the entities extracted from different documents, data sources and ontologies to form knowledge graphs (Figure 14.12). The entities extracted from the documents are linked to the associated ontologies for example – gene to gene ontology (GO), disease to disease ontology (DO) and phenotype to human phenotype ontology (HPO) These are in turn linked to the genes associated with drugs obtained from data sources of drugs such as Drug Bank, PharmGKB, etc., and human proteins from PPI data source. This knowledge graph can used for inferencing new drugs for diseases. NLP is also used to discover sentiments from medical blogs mainly of two medical sentiment aspects, status of health condition and outcome of treatment. Medical blogs can also be analysed for pharmacovigilance mining. Many medicines have side effects and these can be therapeutic or adverse. The bad effects called adverse side effects (ADRs) cause a large number of emergencies. Pharmacovigilance is defined as the detection, assessment and understanding of ADRs. One way of obtaining information about ADRs is through appropriate text and sentiment mining of medical blogs.

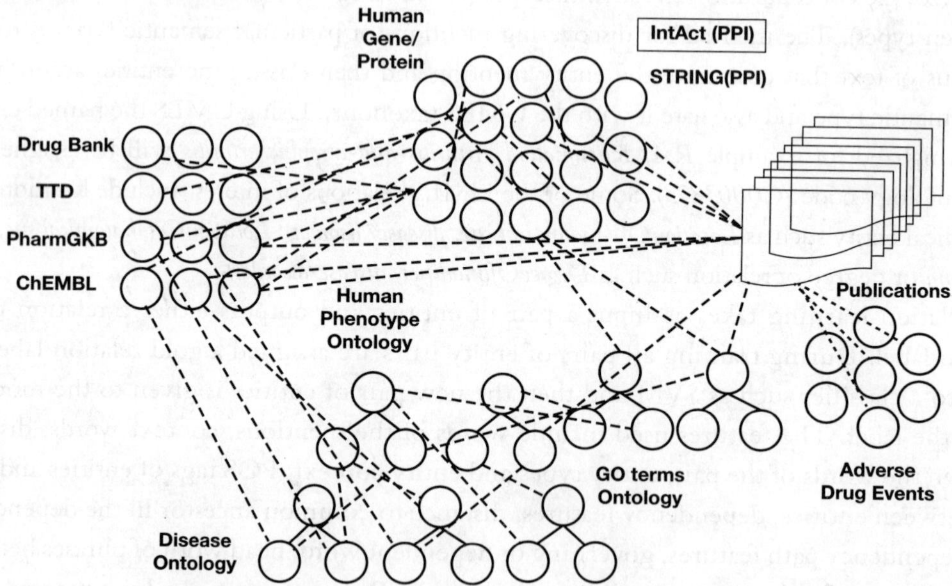

Figure 14.12 Knowledge Graph for Drug Discovery

BioBERT: As already discussed biomedical text mining is evolving as an important task. The use of general purpose pre-trained models is not as effective for biomedical text due to the different word distributions between general domain corpora and biomedical corpora. A pre-trained language model BERT adapted for biomedical corpora, BioBERT (Bidirectional Encoder Representations from Transformers for Biomedical Text Mining), is the first developed domain-specific language representation model and was pre-trained on large-scale biomedical corpora. BioBERT is first initialized with weights obtained from BERT. Then, biomedical domain corpora specifically PubMed abstracts and PMC full-text text articles were utilized to pre-train BioBERT. Finally, fine-tuning and evaluation of BioBERT was carried out on three popular biomedical text mining tasks (NER, Relation extraction and QA).

Summary

- Introduced machine translation, its history and methodologies used for machine translation including the neural approach.
- Explained the evaluation of machine translation.
- Discussed different aspects of information extraction including perspectives and methodologies.
- Explained different perspectives and approaches to question answering.
- Outlined the different aspects of summarization.
- Explained the concept and approaches to sentiment analysis.
- Discussed in detail various perspectives of biomedical NLP.

Exercises

Suggested Activities

1. Fill the following table for applications of encoder decoder neural network approaches.

Problem	Encoder Input	Attention	Decoder Input	Decoder output
Machine translation				
Question Answering				
Information Extraction				
Summarization				
Relation Extraction				

2. Implement a biomedical knowledge graph construction using data sources and pre-trained models of your choice.

3. **Case Study 1 – Text Summarization:** Using CNN/Daily Mail dataset (https://huggingface.co/datasets/cnn_dailymail), generate concise summaries of long documents. Train models for extractive and abstractive summarization using sequence-to-sequence models and transformer-based models. Utilize datasets containing articles and corresponding summaries. Evaluate summarization quality using metrics like ROUGE scores.

4. **Case Study 2 – Question Answering:** Using SQuAD dataset (Stanford Question Answering Dataset – https://huggingface.co/datasets/rajpurkar/squad), generate answers to questions based on a given context passage. Fine-tune pre-trained transformer model BERT on QA datasets. Use techniques span prediction and sequence classification to extract answers from the context passage. Evaluate model performance using metrics like Exact Match and F1-score.

Self-Assessment: Multiple Choice Questions

Give answers with justification for correct and wrong choices:

1. The first automatic MT was the translation of selected sentences d
   i. from Russian to English
   ii. from French to English
   iii. from Russian to French

2. One of the first companies that worked on machine translation was
    i. Google
    ii. Amazon
    iii. SYSTRAN
3. The three probabilities used by the IBM model of translation are we use
    i. Length probability, Alignment probability and Language Probability
    ii. Length probability, Translation Probability and Language Probability
    iii. Length probability, Alignment probability and Translation Probability
4. __________ a precision–based score, computes a similarity score between the machine created translation and one of the human written translations.
    i. METEOR
    ii. BLEU
    iii. ROUGE
5. __________ a recall–oriented metric is the relative frequencies of word sequences.
    i. METEOR
    ii. BLEU
    iii. ROUGE
6. In the case of neural machine translation, __________ helps both aligning and translating a long piece of sequence source text.
    i. Alignment probability
    ii. Attention
    iii. Embedding
7. The task of identifying spans of text that correspond to typed entities and classifying them is called
    i. Relation Classification
    ii. Information Extraction
    iii. Named Entity Recognition
8. A rule-based approach to relation extraction used lexico-syntactic patterns called
    i. Schank patterns
    ii. Hearst patterns
    iii. Lex patterns
9. Distant supervision for relation extraction uses a large online database of structured semantic data such as
    i. Freebase
    ii. SQuAD
    iii. GO

10. The system which defeated two of greatest champions of Jeopardy in 2011 is
    i. Alexa
    ii. QA
    iii. Watson
11. SQuAD is the
    i. set of question-and-answer pairs
    ii. set of documents with summaries pairs
    iii. set of sentences with sentiment polarity labels
12. MRR metric is the
    i. Mean Ranking Rate metric
    ii. Mean Reciprocal Rank metric
    iii. Maximum Ranking Ratio metric
13. An important intrinsic metric used to evaluate summaries is the
    i. BLEU metric
    ii. METEOR metric
    iii. ROUGUE metric
14. The detection, assessment and understanding of ADRs is called
    i. Sensitivity Analysis
    ii. Pharmacovigilance
    iii. Reaction Analysis
15. The first domain-specific language representation model pre-trained on large-scale biomedical corpora
    i. BioBERT
    ii. MedBERT
    iii. BioEncoder

Self-Assessment: Match the Columns

No		Match	
1	The first automatic MT	A	ability to learn long-term dependencies and capture complex patterns from the sequential data.
2	IBM developed	B	different names or synonyms, are clustered into a single concept and associated with a Concept Unique Identifier.
3	Language Probability	C	Georgetown University partnering with IBM in 1954.

No		Match	
4	BLEU metric	D	task of disambiguating named entities to match with their corresponding entities in a knowledge base.
5	Advantage of LSTM for MT	E	defined as the percentage of bigrams from the reference summaries that appear in system generated summary.
6	Entity Linking	F	the first statistical machine translation (SMT) systems in 1991.
7	ReVerb	G	Query words, Answer type and Focus.
8	Question Processing	H	probability of translating into the source language given position and target language.
9	ROUGE	I	precision–oriented metric measures how much of the system translated output is correct.
10	UMLS	J	algorithm for unsupervised relation extraction from the web aims to extract any relation without being restricted to a predefined set of relations.

Short Questions

1. Give a brief note on the history of machine translation.
2. Discuss in detail IBM's statistical approach to machine translation.
3. Outline the different metrics used for evaluating machine translation.
4. Explain the neural approach to machine translation.
5. Discuss in detail the machine learning approaches to the three tasks of information extraction.
6. Explain the taxonomy of question answering systems.
7. Discuss in detail information retrieval-based factoid QA system.
8. Outline BiLSTM-based reading comprehension system.
9. Explain the neural approaches used for summarization.
10. Give a brief note on sentiment analysis.
11. Explain the use of NLP techniques in drug discovery.

Ethical Aspects of NLP

CHAPTER 15

15.1 Introduction – Ethical Aspects of NLP

Many of the ethical concerns associated with building machine learning and deep learning systems are also applicable to building NLP applications. There is a general idea that language is all about words and what they mean but it actually is about people and how they use words to convey what they mean. The data we work with, the natural language text is produced by real people. The NLP community makes extensive use of resources available created by people on the internet and as applications based on NLP are becoming pervasive among the general public, ethical issues are required to be addressed. The decisions that are made about data, methods and tools have impact on people and the societies they live in. Ethics is associated with NLP in many ways such as issues between the people who produce data and the general population, the biases inherent in the data, and the effect on real–world applications and its consequences, who benefits and who are at a disadvantage.

The main ethical concerns are about bias, privacy, misinformation, and the difficulty to understand how these systems make decisions. These concerns (Figure 15.1) are given below:

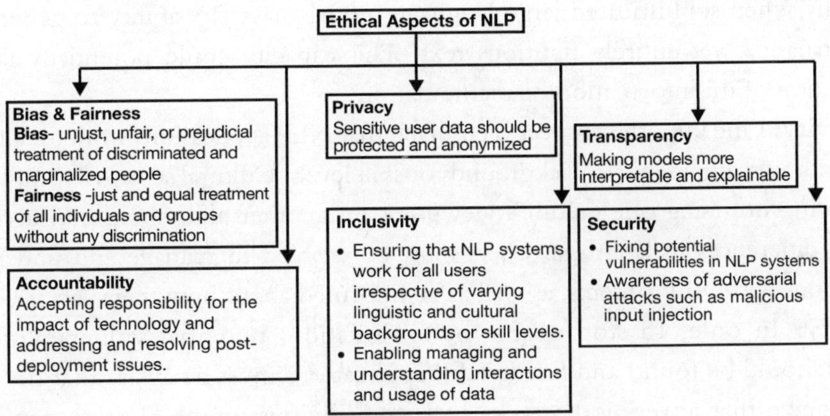

Figure 15.1 Ethical Aspects of NLP

- **Bias and Fairness:** Bias is defined as the unjust, unfair, or prejudicial treatment of discriminated and marginalized people by NLP systems. The bias in text data often stems from predispositions that influences dialogues, views, and understanding of information. One type of bias is data bias where NLP models trained on skewed datasets have the potential to reinforce and magnify preexisting societal biases. NLP models learn from the data they are trained on, meaning that if the training data contains biases, the model likely will reflect these biases as well. To guarantee equitable representation, training data must be carefully selected. In addition, NLP models themselves may exhibit model bias. Bias should be minimized in both the deployment and training stages of the NLP system. **Fairness** in NLP is concerned with the just and equal treatment of all individuals and groups without any discrimination. In other words, an NLP model should not amplify or perpetuate existing biases, stereotypes, or assumptions about certain groups.

- **Privacy:** NLP frequently handles substantial volumes of textual data, some of which may contain sensitive information such as confidential business documents or private communications that can be exploited for nefarious purposes. Sensitive user data should be protected and anonymized with the appropriate safeguards in place. Before gathering and using user-generated text data, informed and clear consent must be obtained.

- **Transparency:** Due to the black-box nature of some advanced NLP models, understanding their decision-making processes can be difficult. Transparency necessitates efforts to make models more interpretable and explainable, especially in the case of sensitive or critical applications.

- **Accountability:** Developers and organizations that use NLP must accept responsibility for the impact of their technology. This includes addressing and resolving post-deployment issues. Moreover, it is critical to understand and follow the legal frameworks governing data protection and privacy. The misuse of NLP technologies poses a significant risk especially when sophisticated large language models have the ability to generate realistic and persuasive, yet entirely fictitious text. This capacity could potentially facilitate the propagation of misinformation or manipulation.

- **Inclusivity:** One important aspect is ensuring that NLP applications work for all users, even those with varying linguistic backgrounds or skill levels. Cultural sensitivity must be ensured by avoiding imposing one culture's viewpoint on another and taking into account subtle cultural differences in language. Users must be enabled to manage and understand their interactions with NLP systems, as well as be informed about how their data is being used.

- **Security:** In order to stop misuse or exploitation, potential vulnerabilities in NLP systems should be found and fixed. NLP applications must be aware that there is a need to recognize that adversarial attacks such as malicious input injection can be used to manipulate NLP models.

In this chapter, we discuss one of the important ethical concerns associated with NLP systems namely bias and fairness.

15.2 Bias

Bias in NLP models refers to the presence of unfair or prejudiced treatment towards certain groups or individuals based on characteristics such as race, gender, religion, or ethnicity in the algorithms, models, or data used in NLP systems.

15.2.1 Types of Bias

The many forms of bias (Figure 15.2) are as follows:

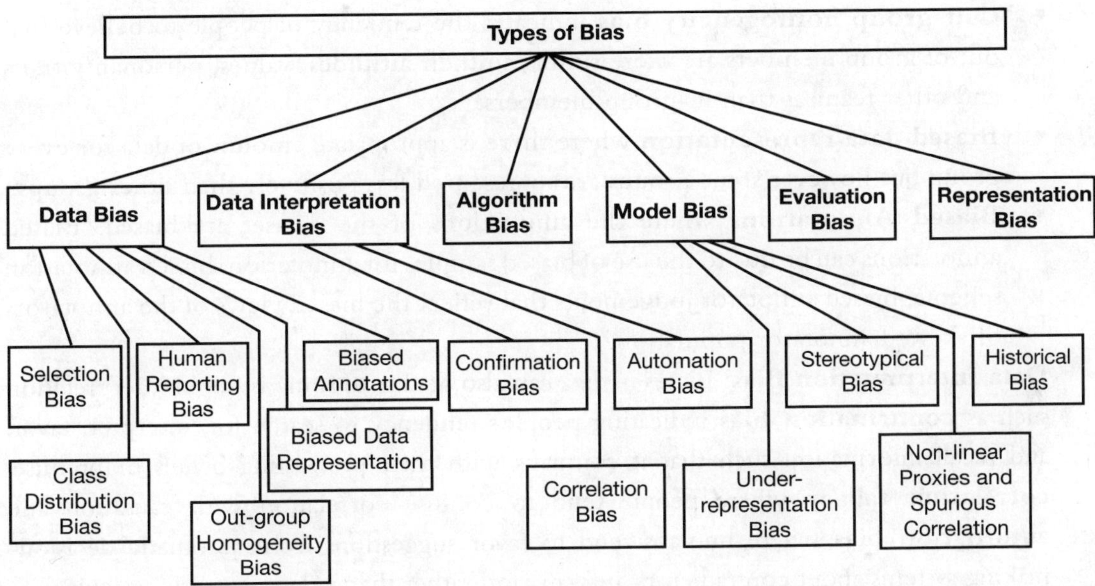

Figure 15.2 Types of Bias in NLP

- **Data Bias:** NLP models trained on data from the internet can learn and perpetuate gender, racial, or socio–economic biases present in the training data, leading to discriminatory outcomes during classification and predive analysis. Bias in data can be due to a variety of reasons as given below:
  - **Selection bias** where selection does not represent a random sample but favours certain groups. Examples include when men are over–represented in web-based news articles and twitter conversations leading to gender bias. If the training data contains stereotypes, prejudices, or cultural biases, NLP models may learn and

perpetuate these biases. For example, if a sentiment analysis model is trained on social media data, it may learn biases associated with certain groups or topics.

- **Imbalanced class distributions and noise** in the training data can lead to biased model predictions. For instance, if a sentiment analysis dataset contains more positive reviews than negative ones, the model may struggle to accurately predict negative reviews. Biased distribution can be due to historical, representation, or sampling bias in data where some populations are underrepresented or omitted from data. Moreover, if the training data contains errors, inconsistencies or misleading information, the model's performance may be negatively impacted, leading to biased outcomes.

- **Human reporting bias** occurs when the frequency with which people write about actions, outcomes, or properties does not reflect the actual real-world frequencies or the actual degree to which an attribute is typical of a group of entities.

- **Out-group homogeneity bias** indicates the tendency of people to believe that out of group members are more similar in their attitudes, values, personality traits and other features than in-group members.

- **Biased data representation** where there is appropriate amount of data for every group but however some groups are represented less positively than other groups.

- **Biased Annotations** where the annotations of the dataset are biased. Biased annotations can be due to the use of biased samples for annotation, biased annotation scheme, biased annotator judgements that reflect the biased views of the annotators or skewed annotator population.

- **Data Interpretation Bias:** Biases in data can also be due to some issues in interpretation such as **confirmation bias** indicating people's tendency to search for, interpret, favor, and recall information such that it confirms with their preexisting beliefs or premise, **correlation fallacy** where people tend to confuse correlation with causation and **automation bias** where humans tend to favor suggestions from automatic decision-making systems about contradictory information rather than non-automatic systems.

- **Algorithmic Bias:** The design and implementation of NLP algorithms can also introduce bias. Certain algorithms may inherently favour certain groups or perspectives over others, leading to biased outcomes.

- **Model Bias:** Bias in NLP models refers to the presence of unfair or prejudiced treatment towards certain groups or individuals based on characteristics such as race, gender, religion, or ethnicity. These biases can emerge during the training and fine-tuning phases of a model, as the training data often reflects the biases present in the data sources. NLP models learn to predict and generate text based on patterns they observe in their training data. If the training data is biased, the models will inevitably encode and amplify these biases in their outputs. There are different types of biases that can manifest in NLP models, such as stereotypical bias, underrepresentation bias and historical bias. **Stereotypical bias** involves reinforcing stereotypes about certain groups, leading to unfair generalizations and skewed representations in the output of the model. **Underrepresentation bias** arises when certain groups are underrepresented in the training data both in terms of features and samples and hence is likely to perform poorly when processing text related to those groups since model performance inherently favors groups with rich features and a large, diverse sample set. **Historical bias** occurs when NLP models learn from historical texts that contain biases from the past, and these outdated and harmful views tend to get propagated.

Models can sometimes learn complex, **non-linear proxies and spurious correlations** between features and annotations that often reflect social biases and are difficult to detect and eliminate. For example, a model could easily predict the gender of subjects because women were photographed overwhelmingly frequently in the kitchen and the model correlated the existence of a kitchen in the image as a proxy for female gender.

- **Evaluation Bias:** The metrics used to evaluate NLP systems may not adequately account for biases, leading to an incomplete assessment of their performance. If evaluation metrics do not consider fairness, models may appear to perform well overall while still exhibiting biased behaviour.

- **Representation Bias:** NLP models may struggle to accurately represent or understand certain demographics, dialects, or languages, leading to disparities in performance across different groups.

15.2.2 Bias in Language Models

Language models are used in critical decision-making systems which impact people, their unfair encoding and amplification of biases can pose serious harm for already-marginalized communities. Harms include representational harms where systems reinforce the subordination of some groups as well as allocational harms where system allocates or withholds a certain opportunity or resource. Therefore, the mitigation of biases and ensuring fairness even for simple NLP tasks such as named entity recognition is important since these types of NLP tasks form core building blocks for more complex downstream applications like text summarization, identity verification, etc.

15.3 Fairness Metrics for Evaluating Bias

One simple way of evaluating algorithmic bias is disaggregating the data by creating for each subgroup a subgroup −prediction pair and comparing them across sub-groups- Example: (women, profession identification) and (man, professional identification). Often confusion matrix (Figure 15.3) is used to find fairness and inclusion similar to the methods used for text classification as discussed in chapter 3 but however here we carry out the classification across subgroups. Some of the fairness metrics used for NLP models is described below:

Confusion matrix - Fairness and Inclusion		
NLP Model Predictions		
Positive	**Negative**	
Exists and Predicted True Positive (TP)	Exists and Not Predicted False Negative (FN)	Recall = TP / (TP+FN) False Negative Rate
Not Exist — Predicted False Positive (FP)	Not Exist — Not Predicted True Negative (TN)	False Positivity Rate Specificity
Precision = TP/TP+FP False Discovery Rate	Negative Predictive Value False Omission Rate	
Equal Opportunity Fairness Criterion - Recall is equal across sub-groups **Predictive Parity Fairness Criterion** - Precision is equal across sub-groups		

Figure 15.3 Confusion Matrix for Fairness and Inclusion

Demographic Parity is a fairness metric which is defined as the proportion of each segment of a specific class (e.g., gender) should receive positive outcome at equal rates. A positive outcome is the preferred decision, such as "getting admission", "getting a loan" or "being shown the ad". As mentioned earlier, the difference should be ideally zero, but lower values are acceptable. In other words, the goal of demographic parity is to ensure that the predictions of the NLP models are independent of membership in a sensitive group. For example, in the context of a resume screening model, equal selection would mean that the proportion of applicants selected for a job interview should be equal across gender groups.

Equalized Odds fairness metric ensures that a NLP model performs equally well for different groups. It is stricter than demographic parity because it requires that the predictions of NLP model should be independent of sensitive group membership and have the same false positive rates and true positive rates. This metric prevents the generation of more false positive predictions for one group versus others. Equalized odds do not create the selection issue discussed in the demographic parity section above.

Equal Opportunity fairness measure is a less strict version of equalized odds measure that only considers conditional expectations with respect to positive labels that is requiring equal outcomes only within the subset of records belonging to the positive class. In the hiring example, equal opportunity requires that the individuals in one group who are qualified to be hired are just as likely to be chosen as individuals in another group who are qualified to be hired. However, by not considering whether false positive rates are equivalent across groups, equal opportunity does not capture the costs of misclassification disparities.

Prediction Parity fairness metric concerns prediction and is defined as the prediction being equal across all subgroups.

15.4 Detecting Bias

Detecting bias in NLP models is a crucial step towards achieving fairness and equity in their applications. Bias detection in NLP refers to the identification and mitigation of biases present in text data or NLP models. Bias can manifest in various forms, including gender bias, racial bias, ideological bias, and more. Detecting and addressing biases is crucial to ensure fairness, reduce discrimination, and promote ethical NLP applications. Some the following methods and techniques are used for bias detection:

- **Corpus analysis** is used to identify patterns of bias. Potential biased language or associations are identified by examining word frequencies, co–occurrence statistics, and sentiment analysis. Manual annotation or crowdsourcing can also be used to label examples of biased content for analysis.

- **Lexicon–based approaches** develop lexicons or word lists that capture biased language. by including terms associated with different biases, such as gender stereotypes or racial slurs. By comparing the text against these lexicons, biased language usage can be flagged.

- **Machine learning approaches** are used to detect bias in text. Classifiers are trained to distinguish between biased and unbiased text, or to predict the presence of specific biases. Supervised learning methods can be used with annotated datasets, while unsupervised approaches, such as topic modeling, can identify latent biases.

- **Contextual analysis** is used to determine the context in which bias occurs to understand its impact. Biases can manifest through framing, emphasis, or omission of certain information. Understanding the context can help identify subtle biases that may not be apparent through simple lexical analysis.

- **Bias auditing** is one technique where the model's outputs are manually examined for signs of bias. Human reviewers assess the system's behavior to identify instances where it may produce biased content.

- **Bias metrics or fairness metrics** are used to quantify bias in NLP models. These metrics measure the extent to which a model exhibits bias and identify potential disparities by analyzing its predictions across different demographic groups. These metrics can assess disparate impact, unfairness in predictions across demographic groups, and other dimensions of bias.

- **User feedback** can be used to identify and address biases in NLP applications. Soliciting feedback from affected communities and involving stakeholders can provide valuable insights into biases that might have been overlooked.

Bias detection in NLP is an active research area, and various tools, libraries, and resources are available to aid in bias analysis and mitigation. It is essential to approach bias detection with caution, ensuring diverse and representative datasets, and continuously improving detection methods to reduce biases and promote fairness in NLP systems.

15.5 Approaches to Mitigate Bias

Once biases are detected, techniques can be applied to mitigate their impact. This can involve retraining models on more balanced or unbiased datasets, introducing fairness constraints during model training, or developing post-processing methods to adjust model outputs and reduce bias. Addressing bias in NLP is crucial to ensure that NLP systems are fair, equitable, and representative.

15.5.1 Practical Steps for Detection and Mitigation of Biases in NLP

- Developing a datasheet for each dataset and documenting such properties as motivation, composition, collection process and recommended uses of the dataset.
- Hiring a socially and ethnically diverse set of AI and ethical experts who can help anticipate and mitigate any biases before they impact the public, and look for ways to improve representation for groups who are typically under-represented.
- Initiating an auditing process to regularly monitor for new and existing biases that might emerge from the NLP algorithms.
- Establishing standards for NLP training data and the sharing of word embeddings and large language models, in order to help increase transparency and accountability around their use in NLP applications.
- Regularly evaluating the security of NLP datasets to ensure that language is not a target of a social media influence campaign that could skew the outcome.

15.5.2 Approaches to Data Bias Mitigation

- **Debiasing the datasets involves** diversifying the dataset and is currently the method most widely accepted. For instance, if a dataset constantly surrounds the word "nurse" with female pronouns, it can be debiased by include data for male nurses. Data preprocessing for mitigating bias includes techniques such as re-sampling underrepresented groups, re-weighting training data, and removing biased examples from the training data.

- **Fairness constraints** are introduced during model training, ensuring that the model's predictions do not disproportionately favor or harm any specific group.
- **Adversarial training** involves training a separate model to identify and mitigate bias in the main NLP model. This adversarial model seeks to reduce the impact of biased attributes in the output. We will discuss technique more in detail in a succeeding section.
- **De-biasing post-processing** can be used to identify and mitigate bias in its output after the model has been trained. This can involve re-ranking or rephrasing results to reduce bias.

15.5.3 Approaches to Model Bias Mitigation

Addressing bias in NLP models is crucial for ensuring fairness and accuracy in various applications. Some approaches include:

- **Diverse and Representative Training Data:** To counteract bias from training data, curating diverse and representative datasets is essential. This ensures that the model learns from various perspectives and does not favor one group.
- **Bias-Aware Labeling:** When labeling data, consider implementing bias-aware guidelines for annotators. This helps minimize labeling bias and ensures that the labeled sentiments are more accurate and fairer. Annotators should be instructed to focus on the sentiment expressed in the text, not personal beliefs, avoid labeling based on the author's identity, gender, or other attributes and in case the sentiment is ambiguous, label it as such rather than guessing.

15.5.4 Adversarial Learning for Mitigating Bias

Introduction: Another data-driven method for mitigating bias is "adversarial learning." This technique trains two models, namely the "discriminator" and the "generator," in opposition to each other. The discriminator model focuses on identifying bias within the NLP model, while the generator model aims to generate unbiased data. These models engage in an iterative process, continuously improving their abilities. As the discriminator becomes more adept at identifying bias, the generator becomes increasingly proficient at creating unbiased data. This iterative process plays a vital role in refining and optimizing the performance of the model. The success of the approach was evaluated across various NLP tasks, including sentiment analysis, natural language inference, and question answering. The approach is able to uncover subtle forms of bias that might otherwise go unnoticed by manual inspection or statistical analysis. One significant limitation of the above method is the computational expense associated with training the discriminator and generator models.

Architecture of Adversarial Learning for Mitigating Bias: The main objective of adversarial learning for mitigating bias is to train the NLP model to be robust against biased input and reduce its susceptibility to making biased predictions. The architecture of adversarial learning for mitigating bias consists of the following components:

Main Model: The main model **M** is the primary NLP model trained for a particular NLP task using a combination of unbiased and perturbed (biased) samples and optimizing it for both the primary NLP task and robustness against bias.

Adversarial Learning Module: This module is responsible for aiding the main model to be robust and consists of two main components:

- **Generator (G):** This model is responsible for creating perturbed or biased samples or associations in order to enhance robustness.
- **Discriminator (D):** This model is responsible for distinguishing between original (unbiased) and perturbed (biased) samples and thus detecting biases.

The architecture makes use of training data which is the raw text corpora used for training the main NLP model.

Flow diagram of Adversarial Learning for Mitigating Bias: The flow diagram (Figure 15.4) is described below. The initialization step is where all the models the main model (M), generator (G), and discriminator (D) are initialized with random weights. The training objective involves optimizing the main model for its primary task while ensuring robustness against biased input. The discriminator assists in achieving this objective by providing feedback on the samples. The adversarial learning module iterates between generating perturbed examples (G), training the discriminator (D), and training the main model (M). The training consists of three steps. In the first step, the generator (G) is used to generate perturbed (biased) samples from the unbiased samples of the training data. For this purpose, the generator uses techniques such as synonym replacement, style transfer, or other text transformation methods. During the second step, the discriminator (D) is trained and optimized to correctly classify the samples (unbiased or perturbed) using the adversarial loss (L_{ADV}). This model is optimized to correctly classify the input as unbiased or perturbed (biased). Finally in the third step the main model (M) is trained using a blend of unbiased or perturbed (biased) samples. This model optimized using a combination of the main model task loss (L_M) and the adversarial loss (L_{ADV}) to ensure robustness against biased input. The adversarial learning process continues for multiple iterations to enhance the overall robustness of the main model against bias until convergence or a predetermined number of epochs is completed.

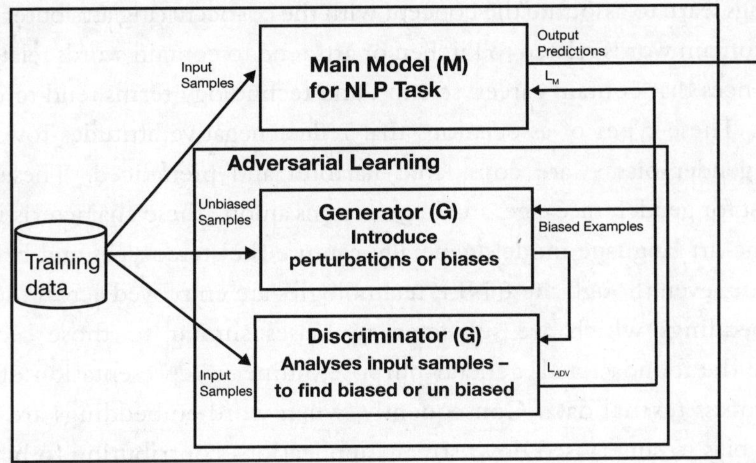

Figure 15.4 Flow diagram of Adversarial Learning for Mitigating Bias

Hyperparameters such as learning rates, regularization terms, and adversarial strength are tuned to achieve a balance between performance and bias mitigation. The performance of the main model is evaluated regularly on unbiased test sets to ensure that bias mitigation efforts do not compromise task performance. A diverse and representative dataset should be used for training, ensuring that biases in the data are explicitly addressed during adversarial training.

15.6 Mitigation of Bias for Deep Learning

In this section, we will discuss bias in word embedding, large language models and generative artificial intelligence (GenAI).

15.6.1 Introduction – Word Embedding

Word embedding models automatically discover hidden patterns in word co-occurrence statistics of language corpora in addition to grammatical and semantic information. They assign a high-dimensional vector to each word in a given language in such a manner that the semantic relations or similarity between the words are indicated by the closeness of the vectors.

15.6.2 Bias and Word Embedding Models

Word embedding vectors which are numerical depictions of text data are exposed to more than just semantic information because we look for hidden patterns and use them to build embeddings. When words representing concepts appear frequently with certain attributes, word embeddings learn to associate the concept with the co-occurring attributes. For example, sentences that contain words related to kitchen or arts tend to contain words related to women. However, sentences that contain career, science, and technology terms tend to contain words related to men. These types of associations that reflect negative attitudes toward one social group – here gender bias – are considered harmful and prejudiced. These stereotypical associations exist for gender, race, age, and intersections among these characteristics. Moreover, most state-of-the-art language models generally capture the stereotypes and biases present in American culture, even though these NLP technologies are employed across the world.

Word embeddings which are subjected to biases similar to those seen in human culture provide the foundational, general-purpose, numeric representation of language for machines to process textual data. Consequently, when word embeddings are used in NLP, they propagate bias to supervised downstream applications contributing to biased decisions that reflect the statistical pattern of the data. These downstream applications perform tasks such as information retrieval, text generation, machine translation, text summarization, and web search. These biases also affect consequential inferences about individuals such as job interviews, university admissions, essay scores, content moderation, and many more decision-making processes. Consequently, propagation of social group bias in downstream NLP applications would not only perpetuate existing biases but potentially exaggerate harmful biases in society that will affect future generations.

15.6.3 Bias Measurement Methods – Word Embedding

Here, we will discuss two bias measurement methods used in the context of word embedding, namely Word Embedding Association Test (WEAT) and neighborhood bias metric. The Word Embedding Association Test (WEAT) is a way to examine the associations in word embeddings between concepts. The WEAT test measures the degree to which a model associates sets of target words with sets of attribute words. The association between two given words is defined as the cosine similarity between the embedding vectors for the words. Neighborhood bias metric for gender bias quantifies bias as the percentage of male socially biased words among the k nearest socially biased male- and female-neighboring words in the embedding space, where words are projected onto a gender subspace. This metric is based on the idea that bias can be observed with the clustering of socially marked gendered words. For example, even after debiasing, the word "nurse" might not be close to gender-definitional feminine words in the embedding space but might still be close to other socially-biased female words such as "receptionist," "caregiver," and "teacher."

15.6.4 De-Biasing Word Embedding

By altering the actual vector-representations of words, de-biasing can be achieved to a certain extent. These methods involve re-weighting or altering word vectors to make them less biased. A technique that removed the gender direction from word embedding can be done by taking gendered pairs such as ("he", "she") and transforming the vector space such that each word not in a gendered pair is equally close to both words in each gendered pair within the vector space.

Another method, the Hard Debias algorithm reduces gender bias by transforming the embedding space into unbiased one by eliminating stereotypical information (such the association between "receptionist" and "female") while preserving pertinent gender information (like the association between "queen" and "female"). The Double-Hard Debias algorithm improves the Hard Debias algorithm by eliminating the influence of frequency since word frequency can distort the gender direction. The key idea is to project word embeddings into an intermediate frequency free subspace before applying Hard Debias.

Adversarial Debiasing for word embedding introduces an additional layer to an existing training process as explained in a previous section. Word embedding representation from the original network is given to an adversary, which is tasked with predicting some protected characteristic. The loss gradients generated by this adversary are used to shape the training of the network, such that the network is unable to learn information that would aid the adversary in predicting the protected characteristic. This forces the network to attempt to find a new optima for the loss function which does not utilize the protected characteristic, thus learning a fairer embedding that does not rely upon this characteristic.

Complete data de-biasing of word embedding is not a feasible solution to the bias problems caused in downstream applications since debiasing word embeddings removes essential context about the world. In addition to the undesirable bias, word embeddings capture essential signals about language, culture, the world, and statistical facts. For example, gender debiasing of word embeddings would negatively affect how accurately occupational gender statistics are reflected in these models, which is necessary information for some NLP operations. Moreover, debiasing to remove all known social group associations would lead to word embeddings that cannot accurately represent the world, perceive language, or perform downstream applications. Instead of blindly debiasing word embeddings, raising awareness of these issues and achieving fairness during decision-making in downstream applications would be a more informed strategy.

15.7 Bias in Large Language Models and Generative AI

As we have already discussed, large language models have a general pre-trained model which is then fine-tuned for specific tasks. A single debiased model hosted on a centralized hub would enable developers to effortlessly build fair applications. With task-specific debiasing methods which cannot transfer fairness to other tasks on the other hand, developers will have to apply debiasing methods themselves – a step that most likely not all developers have the time, skill, and literacy for. Only fairness transfers enable the application of LLMs to different tasks with fair results, thus utilizing their true power. Adversarial debiasing method can be used to mitigate bias in transformer-based LLMs. For example, effective and relatively computationally efficient debiasing method can be applied to pre-trained transformers on the language generation task *autocompletion* enabling fairness improvements to the downstream task *text classification* without further adjustments at a performance cost.

Generative AI enables machines to create human-like content and this aspect results in a challenge – bias in AI-generated NLP outputs. AI-generated content perpetuates biases that can lead to real harm. In healthcare, biased data might result in recommendation of treatments that favor one group over another, resulting in unequal medical care. In the criminal justice system, biased algorithms based on biased data could lead to unfair sentencing. In the workplace, biased NLP could perpetuate discrimination in hiring decisions or promotions. These are real-world consequences of biased NLP that need to be handled. Mitigating bias in these systems ensures fairness and equity. Adversarial training already discussed previously where one neural generates content, while the other evaluates it for bias, helps the generative model become skilled at avoiding biased outputs. Similarly, data augmentation and resampling techniques using diverse training data that introduces a variety of perspectives and backgrounds into the training dataset helps NLP models to understand different demographics and thus learn to generate fairer and more representative content.

15.8 Case Studies

IBM Project Debater

IBM's Project Debater, is an AI system designed for debating hard to ensure the maintenance of neutrality and avoidance of bias while arguing complex topics. In order to tackle this requirement, IBM took a multi-pronged approach. They incorporated diverse training data, ensuring various perspectives were considered. Additionally, they implemented real-time monitoring algorithms to detect and rectify potential bias during debates. As a result of these initiatives Project Debater demonstrated remarkable prowess in conducting balanced debates, alleviating concerns about bias and showcasing the potential of bias mitigation techniques in real-world applications.

Google's BERT Model

Google's BERT, a prominent language model, encountered issues related to gender bias in search results and recommendations. Google initiated a comprehensive effort to address this bias. They retrained BERT using gender-neutral language and balanced training examples. Furthermore, they fine-tuned the model's ranking algorithms to prevent the reinforcement of stereotypes. Google's actions led to more inclusive search results and recommendations that were less likely to perpetuate gender biases.

15.9 Challenges and Future Directions

There are still many challenges and some possible future directions associated with mitigating bias in NLP. These include

- **Complex and Evolving Nature of Bias:** Bias in NLP is a complex issue, and new forms of bias can emerge as NLP models and applications evolve. Keeping pace with these complexities and adapting mitigation strategies is a challenge. There is a need to develop sophisticated bias detection and mitigation techniques using federated and self-supervised learning techniques.
- **Data Limitations:** Bias often stems from biased training data. Methods to collect and curate diverse, representative, and unbiased datasets is a complex task. Moreover, there are no established standards for evaluating the quality of datasets used in training NLP models applied in a societal context. Promoting inclusivity in NLP teams and across the development process to reduce biases is important.
- **Ethical Dilemmas:** Addressing bias is an ethical issue. Deciding the definition of fairness and striking the right balance between various interests remains a moral challenge. Hence developing and implementing comprehensive ethical frameworks and guidelines to ensure fairness, transparency, and accountability is the need of the hour.
- **Regulatory Landscape:** Currently, no regulation exists to audit NLP systems that pose potential threats to equity, justice, and democracy. The evolving regulatory environment adds complexity and navigating privacy laws, ethical guidelines, and standards is challenging for organizations developing NLP applications. Collaboration between governments, organizations, and experts to establish clear regulatory standards for bias mitigation is required.

- **Awareness and Education:** A diverse set of expert humans-in-the-loop can collaborate with NLP systems to expose and handle AI biases according to standards and ethical principles. Training a new type of diverse workforce that specializes in NLP, machine learning and ethics to effectively prevent the harmful side effects of NLP technologies would lessen the harmful side-effects. Ensuring that developers, users, and policymakers know the implications of bias in NLP is another challenge.

In conclusion, there is an urgent need for regulatory mechanisms, a diverse AI ethics workforce, and technical approaches to prevent NLP technologies from accelerating its harmful side-effects.

Summary

- Introduced the ethical aspects associated with NLP.
- Explained in detail the various types of bias.
- Discussed the various fairness measures for evaluating bias.
- Outlined the various methods of detecting bias.
- Discussed the various approaches to mitigating bias including data bias and model bias.
- Explained the adversarial learning approach of mitigating bias.
- Outlined the mitigation of bias in deep learning.
- Discussed the bias from the perspective of large language models and generative AI
- Briefly discussed two case studies involving mitigating of bias.
- Outlined the challenges and future directions associated with mitigating bias.

Exercises

Suggested Activities

1. Fill the following table with applications that can be affect a subgroup because of bias in each domain. Give examples not discussed in text.

Type of Data Bias	Domain of Application
Gender	Employment
Gender	Healthcare
Gender	Marketinge
Community	Employment
Community	Social Welfare

2. Implement an adversarial learning bias mitigation that handles demographic parity and equal opportunities that handles a hiring scenario.

3. **Case Study – Bias in Language Models:** Using social media text investigate and mitigate biases present in language models, which can perpetuate stereotypes or discrimination. Analyze datasets for demographic biases or stereotypes. Use adversarial training to reduce biases in language models. Evaluate model fairness and performance across different demographic groups using fairness metrics.

Self-Assessment: Multiple Choice Questions

Give answers with justification for correct and wrong choices:

1. Accountability in the context of ethical issues associated with NLP includes
    i. addressing and resolving post-deployment issues
    ii. making models more interpretable and explainable
    iii. obtaining informed and clear content from the user
2. Out-group Homogeneity bias indicates
    i. not reflecting the real-world frequencies
    ii. representing some groups less positively than other groups
    iii. tendency of people to believe that out of group members are more similar in their features than in-group members

3.   Biased annotations can be due to the use of
    i.   biased samples for annotation, biased annotation scheme and biased annotator judgements
    ii.   biased samples for annotation and biased data representation schemes
    iii.   biased annotation scheme and biased model representation schemes
4.   Fairness metric defined as the proportion of each segment of a specific class receiving positive outcome at equal rates is called as
    i.   Equal Opportunity
    ii.   Demographic Parity
    iii.   Equal Odds
5.   Fairness measure that considers conditional expectations with respect to positive labels requiring equal outcomes within the subset of records belonging to positive class is called as.
    i.   Equal Opportunity
    ii.   Demographic Parity
    iii.   Equal Odds
6.   Biases can manifest through framing, emphasis, or omission of certain information. This type of detection of bias is called
    i.   Bias Auditing
    ii.   De-biasing
    iii.   Context Analysis
7.   Diversifying the dataset is called
    i.   Introducing fairness constraints
    ii.   De-biasing
    iii.   Training a separate model
8.   When annotators are instructed to focus on the sentiment expressed in the text, not personal beliefs and to avoid labeling based on the author's identity, gender, or other attributes, then it is called
    i.   Bias-Aware Labeling
    ii.   Diverse and Representative Training
    iii.   Biased Annotations
9.   Discriminator model of adversarial learning
    i.   focuses on identifying bias within the NLP model
    ii.   focuses on generating unbiased data
    iii.   focuses on removing bias from main NLP model

10. Generator model of adversarial learning
    i. focuses on identifying bias within the NLP model
    ii. focuses on producing unbiased data
    iii. focuses on removing bias from main NLP model
11. The bias measure that measures the degree to which a model associates sets of target words with sets of attribute words is the
    i. Neighborhood Bias
    ii. WOB test
    iii. WEAT test
12. De-Biasing Word Embedding involves
    i. Re-weighting and altering word vectors
    ii. Adding more word vectors for de-biasing
    iii. Removing biased word vectors
13. System that used real-time monitoring algorithms to detect and rectify potential bias during debates is
    i. Google Debator
    ii. IBM Project Debater
    iii. Bert Debator
14. Google retrained BERT using
    i. Sensitivity Analysis
    ii. Gender-neutral language and balanced training examples.
    i. De-biasing examples
15. Deciding the definition of fairness and striking the right balance between various interests remains a moral challenge. This is called
    i. Balancing fairness issue
    ii. Bias issue
    iii. Ethical issue

Self-Assessment: Match the Columns

No		Match	
1.	Ethics associated with NLP	A	Human reviewers assess the system's behavior to identify instances where it may produce biased content
2.	Accountability	B	fairness metric that requires that the predictions of NLP model should be independent of sensitive group membership, and have the same false positive rates and true positive rates.

3.	Inclusivity	C	eliminates the influence of frequency since word frequency can distort the specific bias direction.
4.	Demographic Parity	D	techniques such as re-sampling underrepresented groups, re-weighting training data, and removing biased examples from the training data.
5.	Equalized Odds	E	issues between the people who produce data and the general population and the biases inherent in the data,
6.	Bias Auditing	F	fairness metric which is defined as the proportion of each segment of a specific class (e.g. gender) should receive positive outcome at equal rates.
7.	De-biasing	G	quantifies bias as the percentage of subgroup A's socially biased words among the k nearest socially biased subgroups A and B -neighboring words in the embedding space, where words are projected onto a gender subspace.
8.	Adversarial Learning	H	critical to understand and follow the legal frameworks governing data protection and privacy
9.	Neighborhood bias metric	I	mitigating bias by training the discriminator and the generator, in opposition to each other and hence training the NLP model to be robust against biased input and reduce its susceptibility to making biased predictions –
10.	Double-Hard De-bias algorithm	J	NLP applications work for all users, even those with varying linguistic backgrounds or skill levels

Short Questions

1. Outline the ethical aspects associated with NLP.
2. Discuss in detail the different types of data bias in NLP.
3. Explain what is meant by algorithmic bias, evaluation bias and representation bias in the context of NLP.
4. Outline the different types of data interpretation bias and model bias in the context of NLP.
5. Discuss the various fairness measures for evaluating bias in NLP

6. Outline the various methods of detecting NLP
7. Discuss the practical steps for detection and mitigation of NLP bias.
8. Discuss the various approaches to mitigating bias including data bias and model bias.
9. Outline in detail the adversarial learning approach of mitigating bias using an illustrative diagram.
10. Write a brief note on bias and word embedding models.
11. Discuss bias from the perspective of large language models and generative AI
12. "The effect of bias in generative AI models is dangerous". Comment
13. Outline any two existing systems that take care of bias.
14. Discuss the challenges and future directions of mitigating NLP bias

References

1. Anthony Gillioz, Jacky Casas, Elena Mugellini, Omar Abou Khaled, "Overview of the Transformer-based Models for NLP Tasks", Conference: 2020 Federated Conference on Computer Science and Information Systems, 10.15439/2020F20, 2020

2. Gomez, Lukasz Kaiser, Illia Polosukhin, "Attention Is All You Need", Computation and Language, 2023

3. Bharati A., Sangal R., Chaitanya V, "Natural language Processing: a Paninian perspective", PHI, 2000

4. Bengio Réjean Ducharme Pascal Vincent Christian Jauvin, "A Neural Probabilistic Language Model", Journal of Machine Learning Research, 3, 2003

5. Binggui Zhou, Guanghua Yang, Zheng Shi, and Shaodan Ma, "Natural Language Processing for Smart Healthcare, IEEE REVIEWS IN BIOMEDICAL ENGINEERING, 2022

6. Christopher D. Manning, Hinrich Schütze "Foundations of Statistical Natural Language Processing", 1st Edition, The MIT Press, 1999

7. Daniel Jurafsky, James H. Martin, "Speech and Language Processing: An Introduction to Natural Language Processing, Computational Linguistics and Speech Recognition: United State (Prentice Hall Series in Artificial Intelligence), 2000

8. Daniel Jurafsky, James H. Martin, "Speech and Language Processing," 3rd Online Edition https://web.stanford.edu/~jurafsky/slp3/

9. Deng, "Deep Learning in Natural Language Processing" 1st ed., Springer 2018

10. François Torregrossa, Robin Allesiardo, Vincent Claveau, Nihel Kooli, Guillaume Gravier, "A Survey on Training and Evaluation of Word Embeddings", International Journal of Data Science and Analytics (2021), springer 11:85–103

11. Hobson Lane, Hannes Hapke, Cole Howard, "Natural Language Processing in Action: Understanding, Analyzing, and Generating Text with Python" First Edition. Manning; 2019

12. Jacob Devlin, Ming-Wei Chang, Kenton Lee, Kristina Toutanova, "BERT: Pre-training of Deep Bidirectional Transformers for Language Understanding", Computation and Language, 2019

13. Jacob Eisenstein, "Introduction to Natural Language Processing (Adaptive Computation and Machine Learning series)", Illustrated Edition, The MIT Press 2019

14. James Allen, "Natural Language Understanding" 2ditione, Pearson Education, 1994

15. Jienfeng Gao, "An Introduction to Deep Learning for Natural Language Processing", International Summer School on Deep Learning, 2017Jon Krohn, "Deep Learning for Natural Language Processing", 2nd Edition, Pearson, 2020

16. L. Page, S. Brin, and T. Winograd, "PageRank Citation Ranking: Bringing Order to the Web", https://www.eecs.harvard.edu/~michaelm/CS222/pagerank.pdf

17. Margaret Mitchell, Kai-Wei Chang, Vicente Ordóñez Román, Vinodkumar Prabhakaran, "Bias and Fairness in NLP", EMNLP-IJCNLP Tutorial, 2019

18. Matthew E. Peters, Mark Neumann, Mohit Iyyer, Matt Gardner, Christopher Clark, Kenton Lee, Luke Zettlemoyer, "Deep contextualized word representations", https://doi.org/10.48550/arXiv.1802.05365, 2018

19. Michael Collins, "Tutorial: Machine Learning Methods in Natural Language Processing, January 2003, Lecture Notes in Computer Science, DOI:10.1007/978-3-540-45167-9_47, Conference: Computational Learning Theory and Kernel Machines, 16th Annual Conference on Computational Learning Theory, 2003

20. Philipp Koehn, "Statistical Machine Translation",Cambridge University Press, 2010
21. Raymond S. T. Lee, "Natural Language Processing: A Textbook with Python Implementation" 1st ed.. Springer; 2024
22. R´emi Lebret, Ronan Collobert, "Rehabilitation of Count-based Models for Word Vector Representations", DOI: 10.1007/978-3-319-18111-0_31
23. Ronan Collobert, Jason Weston, Leon Bottou, Michael Karlen, Koray Kavukcuoglu, Pavel Kuksa, "Natural Language Processing (almost) from Scratch", Journal of Machine Learning Research 12 (2011)
24. Scott Wen-tau Yih, Xiaodong He and Jianfeng Gao, Microsoft Research, Redmond, WA, "Deep Learning and Continuous Representations for Natural Language Processing", NAAL_HLT Tutorial, 2015
25. Shafiq, Guisppe, Raymond, Gabriel, "Discourse Analysis and its Applications, ACL-19, Tutorial
26. Siddiqui T., Tiwary U. S, "Natural Language Processing and Information Retrieval", OUP, 2008
27. Studer R, R. Benjamins, and D. Fensel," Knowledge engineering: Principles and methods", Data & Knowledge Engineering, 25(1–2):161–198, 1998
28. Susan McRoy, "Principles of Natural Language Processing", 2021
29. Tomas Mikolov, Ilya Sutskever, Kai Chen, Greg Corrado, Jeffrey Dean, "Distributed Representations of Words and Phrases and their Compositionality", https://doi.org/10.48550/arXiv.1310.4546, 2013
30. Wayne Xin Zhao, Kun Zhou, Junyi Li, Tianyi Tang, Xiaolei Wang, Yupeng Hou, Yingqian Min, Beichen Zhang, Junjie Zhang, Zican Dong, Yifan Du, Chen Yang, Yushuo Chen, Zhipeng Chen, Jinhao Jia iang,Ruiyang Ren, Yifan Li, Xinyu Tang, Zikang Liu, Peiyu Liu, Jian-Yun Nie and Ji-Rong Wen, "A Survey of Large Language Models", >arXiv:2303.18223, 2023
31. Xin Rong, "word2vec Parameter Learning Explained", https://arxiv.org/abs/1411.2738
32. Yoav Goldberg, Graeme Hirst, "Neural Network Methods in Natural Language Processing (Synthesis Lectures on Human Language Technologies)", Morgan & Claypool Publishers, 2017
33. Yoshua Bengio, Réjean Ducharmem, Pascal Vincent , Christian Jauvin, "A Neural Probabilistic Language Model", Journal of Machine Learning Research 3 (2003) 1137–1155
34. Yue Zhang, Zhiyang Teng, "Natural Language Processing: A Machine Learning Perspective", 1st Edition, Cambridge University Press, 2021
35. Zellig S. Harris (1954) Distributional Structure, WORD, 10:2-3, 146-162, DOI: 10.1080/00437956.1954.11659520

Index